THE GREAT ISSUES
OF POLITICS

LESLIE LIPSON
University of California, Berkeley

THE GREAT ISSUES

OF POLITICS

*An Introduction to
Political Science*

New York   *PRENTICE-HALL, INC.*   1954

To

DAVID

PREFACE

Every book should capture and, as far as possible, reproduce the spirit of its subject matter. As interpreted here, politics is the arena of controversy about some permanent issues which must be faced constantly but may be variously solved. The solutions differ in method as they do in substance. Sometimes the method is to use violence, though at a more mature level discussion is employed. Discussion captures the essence of controversy by its appraisal of alternatives, presentation of pros and cons, and review of practice and experiment.

The best way to discover truth, as ancient philosophers observed, is through the interplay of viewpoints and exchange of information which discussion supplies. Books are the next best substitute for direct discussion face-to-face, and this book explores the nature of politics by engaging in a discussion with the reader. Although plenty of factual material is contained in these pages, it is not my primary intention to cram the reader's mind with masses of descriptive data concerning the structure of government and the operations of the state. That method, though leaving the reader with a sense of repletion of a sort, can be harmful to one's intellectual digestive system. Learning facts is not identical with understanding their significance, and of the two the latter is far more important.

To understand politics it is necessary not only to know what has happened and is happening, but, even more, to grasp its meaning. The materials of politics consist of historical events, of opinions about them, and of ideal aspirations for what might be. Such data become significant when marshalled and classified in terms of the basic problems that form the kernel of the political process, for neither the actual nor the ideal makes sense unless it is fitted into a conceptual framework.

My aim in writing this book has been to suggest to those who are concerned about politics a method of analysis which I have found helpful in understanding a complex subject and which I hope will be helpful to others. What is attempted here is to explain the character of politics by a systematic treatment of its fundamental issues, which first are analyzed separately and then are studied in unison. Throughout this work the alternative solutions to the several issues are illustrated by examples chosen from different historical periods, by comparisons of contrasted types of government, and by the arguments between rival philosophies. Each issue, however, is discussed in the manner that seems most appropriate to its elucidation rather than in accordance with a stereotyped, uniform pattern. The organization of some chapters, therefore, is primarily analytical; of others, chronological. In some cases, history predominates over philosophy; elsewhere, it is the reverse.

A survey chart of the great issues of politics is provided at the end of the book.

A number of friends were generous of their time in reading the whole manuscript or sections of it and have given me valuable criticisms. I record here my debt to the late Lloyd H. Fisher and to Pedro Muñoz Amato, Roy C. Macridis, Peter H. Odegard, Frank M. Russell, and Robert A. Scalapino. To William A. Pullin of Prentice-Hall I am grateful for expert editorial guidance. My wife has given me many fruitful suggestions and her constant encouragement. The dedication to the youngest of my family is inadequate recompense for all those occasions when priorities of writing deprived father and son of each other's company.

Leslie Lipson

ACKNOWLEDGMENTS

Quotations from the works of other writers have been reprinted in this book with the consent of the following publishers whose kind permission is herewith acknowledged:

Jonathan Cape, Ltd., of London; Doubleday and Company, Inc., of New York; and the Trustees of the T. E. Lawrence Estate; for the excerpt from *The Seven Pillars of Wisdom* by T. E. Lawrence.

The Clarendon Press of Oxford, England, for the excerpt from W. Hamilton Fyfe's translation of Tacitus' *Germania*.

J. M. Dent and Sons, Ltd., of London, and E. P. Dutton and Company, Inc., of New York, for passages from *The Republic* by Plato, translated by A. D. Lindsay; *Leviathan* by Hobbes; *Second Treatise of Civil Government* by Locke; *Discourse on Political Economy* by Rousseau, translated by G. D. H. Cole; *The Federalist* by Hamilton, Madison, and Jay; *Utilitarianism, Liberty and Representative Government* by Mill; all printed in Everyman's Library.

The Hafner Publishing Company, Inc., of New York, for the excerpt from Montesquieu's *Spirit of the Laws*, translated by Thomas Nugent and introduced by Franz L. Neumann, in the Hafner Library by Classics.

Harcourt, Brace and Company, Inc., of New York, and John Murray, Ltd., of London, for the excerpt from *Religion and the Rise of Capitalism* by R. H. Tawney.

Henry Holt and Company, Inc., of New York, for the excerpt from *American Government* by William Anderson.

Houghton Mifflin Company of Boston, for excerpts from the English translation of *Mein Kampf* by Adolph Hitler.

Alfred A. Knopf, Inc., of New York, for a passage from *Man and His Works* by Melville J. Herskovits and one from *Mutual Aid* by Peter Kropotkin in the English translation.

Longmans, Green and Company, Inc., of New York, for an excerpt from *Illustrated English Social History* by G. M. Trevelyan.

The Macmillan Company of New York, for passages from *Economic Interpretation of the Constitution of the United States* by Charles A.

Beard, *The Web of Government* by Robert M. MacIver, and *The Encyclopedia of the Social Sciences.*

Oxford University Press, Inc., of New York, for excerpts from *The English Constitution* by Walter Bagehot, printed in *World's Classics*, and *The Modern Democratic State* by A. D. Lindsay.

St. Martin's Press, Inc., of New York, and The Macmillan Company, Ltd., of London, for the passage from *The Golden Bough* by James Frazer.

Mrs. George Bambridge; Doubleday and Company, Inc. of New York, the Macmillan Company of Canada, and Methuen and Company, Ltd. of London, for the quotation from *The Seven Seas* by Rudyard Kipling.

CONTENTS

As I was born a citizen of a free State, and a member of the Sovereign, I feel that, however feeble the influence my voice can have on public affairs, the right of voting on them makes it my duty to study them.

ROUSSEAU

But howsoever, an argument from the Practise of men, that have not sifted to the bottom, and with exact reason weighed the causes, and nature of Common-wealths, and suffer daily those miseries, that proceed from the ignorance thereof, is invalid. For though in all places of the world, men should lay the foundation of their houses on the sand, it could not thence be inferred that so it ought to be. The skill of making, and maintaining Common-wealths, consists in certain Rules, as doth Arithmetique and Geometry; not (as Tennis-play) on Practise only: which Rules, neither poor men have the leisure, nor men that have had the leisure, have hitherto had the curiosity, or the method to find out.

HOBBES

In so complicated a science as political economy no one axiom can be laid down as wise and expedient for all times and circumstances and for their contraries.

JEFFERSON

CHAPTER 1

INTRODUCTION TO THE STUDY OF POLITICS

Man and His Environment. Understanding is the beginning of freedom. For to be free is to control our environment; and seldom can we master what we do not understand. This does not mean, however, that everything in the universe which is knowable becomes controllable. We may, for example, be students of astronomy. We may learn about the shape and movement of the earth and observe the sun, stars, and planets. Applying that knowledge, and obeying the limitations that physical forces impose, we can navigate a ship across an ocean or fly an airplane around the globe. But despite all the information we amass concerning heavenly phenomena, they lie entirely beyond human influence. The best, indeed the only, course that we can take in such matters is to adjust to what are necessities and then design our pattern of life accordingly.

This is not true in the relations that unite a man with his fellow men. Social conduct, social organization, and social institutions are primarily the product of human activity, past and present. Being man-made, they are not predetermined for us by any external, and therefore uncontrollable, force. Rather, they are molded through causes that originate in man himself. Hence they contain little, if anything, that is inevitable or unalterable by human will. Poverty, depression, despotism, and war—which are among the worst scourges that afflict humanity—are generally more disastrous than floods, hurricanes, earthquakes, blizzards, or volcanic eruptions; and whereas the latter are not of our making, the former originate largely in ourselves when our own doings turn into our undoing.

The Obstacles to Progress. It would then appear self-evident that what men create can be fully comprehended by men and ultimately controlled. If that be so, what is there to prevent us from being the masters of our social fate? Why are we not more successful in treating the maladies of a disordered world? The obstacles that lie in the path of human betterment are many and major. First is a mass inertia which arises from widespread passivity. There are many who fear the disturbances that accompany the process of innovation and doubt their ability to control its course. Frequently, therefore, they resign themselves to known evils rather than risk the unpredictable chances of change. Second, to a much larger extent than we realize, we are the creatures of habit and captives of the past; and though it is to the past that we also owe the freedoms we enjoy, the sanctity of age has the effect of prolonging many a practice that restricts the opportunity to invent and improve. Our home upbringing, our school education, our civic training, have stamped on each of us an imprint of the surrounding social order, to whose design our adult behavior generally conforms. Moreover, that design has resulted from the slow accumulation of labors which occupied many centuries and deposited their legacy in the institutions, procedures, and ideas that we inherit. We have been shaped into what we are by all our yesterdays, and it is difficult for a single generation to undo or refashion speedily the work of many.

The paralysis of the will that stems from habit or timidity is not the only impediment to progress. Action can also be inhibited by paralysis of the intellect. Most of us, before we act, want to be reasonably sure about what we are doing or whither we intend to move. Not only do we lack agreement about our objectives and the means of realizing them, but we cannot always be sure about our diagnosis of current ills and their causes. We may be dedicated to fine ideals such as democracy, freedom, justice, welfare. But we dispute their definition because each of these grand generalizations means different things to different people, and how it should be applied to any particular circumstances is always arguable. We dislike depressions. We hate wars. We want to prevent these from starting, or, if they do begin, we want to end them. But do we know for certain what their causes are and can we confidently prescribe how they may be avoided? Considering that so much is at stake in the policies that governments choose, how high is the probability that our answers will be correct?

Many of the puzzles that confront us when we face the problems of our social system and seek remedies for them have a common source—the facts that human society is composed of millions of persons and that social processes are the sum-product of numberless individual actions. In order to decipher this confusing network of contacts between people, we study the past; we keep note of contemporary events; we look around at our fellow men and at ourselves placed in their midst. But seeing is not the same as having insight. Sometimes we feel as bewildered as if we gazed, uncomprehending, at an ant heap and saw a swarm whose movements we observe but whose meaning we do not fathom. It is hard to obtain an over-all view of a complex society, to spot the details that are significant and those that are causally connected with others. It is even hard for an individual to be certain of his own relation with the group in which he belongs or to recognize what quota he contributes, in however infinitesimal a degree, to a general social mosaic that all have helped to piece together but none has planned. At a time when the economy undergoes inflation, the majority seek to protect themselves by boosting prices, pressing for higher wages, charging bigger fees. Yet the net effect, if too many behave alike, is that nobody benefits since no one is better off. The same can happen in an armaments race, where governments that distrust one another pursue security severally by methods that yield collective insecurity. Rather than act blindly, we search for a rationale, a principle of cause and effect, a set of laws perhaps, that will make the relationships plain. Failing that, the behavior of a mass of men often repeats in essentials the tragedy of Hamlet. For our doubts bring indecision and lead to postponement and delay.

> And thus the native hue of resolution
> Is sicklied o'er with the pale cast of thought,
> And enterprises of great pith and moment
> With this regard their currents turn awry
> And lose the name of action.

Information and Understanding. The price we pay for ignorance about ourselves and our works is to be placed in servitude to others or to circumstance. Several thousand years ago a revolution occurred in politics when law was first committed to writing, instead of being deposited in the memory of a few and passed on from mouth to mouth. Once written, it could more easily be known and studied; its interpretation disputed; and officials punished for not adhering to the text. How significant was that change is shown by the example of contemporary states where the decisions of government remain shrouded in mystery and ordinary people are in the grip of tyranny. If "the proper study of mankind," therefore, "is man," as Pope said, the primary duty of Man the Citizen is to learn about the state. This is something that each man owes to himself for the simple reason that government touches everybody and consequently all of us have an equal interest in its actions. But an understanding of the state is also our duty to society, because in this strenuous world the isolationist from politics is like a tax-evader dodging his share of public responsibility.

Even in states which make a virtue of publicity and expect their citizens to participate in politics, the difficulties in the path of understanding, and thus controlling, a modern government are truly formidable. Not only are its operations obscured by their vastness and complexity, but the information about it is now so detailed and voluminous as well-nigh to baffle the inquiring intellect. Anybody who wants visual proof of this fact has only to observe the size of the catalogue at the Library of Congress, or visit the ever-expanding collections of public archives, or scan the corridors of records in the filing division of a great department. A single episode like President Truman's dismissal of General MacArthur in 1951 occasioned a congressional inquiry whose hearings and testimony filled over 8,000 pages of print. Year by year the task of digesting these enormous amounts of material—all the statutes and statistics, debates and directives, opinions and orders—becomes increasingly difficult. Our civilization stands neck-deep in paper, and those who would think about its problems run the risk of being crushed by the sheer weight of documentation.

Paradoxically, therefore, the sense of helplessness that overwhelms a citizen when government vests its works in secrecy may be repeated under the opposite conditions. Though public acts are subject to public scrutiny, an individual who contemplates the mass of data awaiting his observation and study is apt to feel dwarfed in the presence of his subject. How is he, for instance, to encompass such a phenomenon as the American political system wherein the federal government alone operated in 1952 on an annual budget approaching eighty billion dollars and employed a civil service of more than two and one-half million persons? How can he grasp all the ramifications of so much money, of so many officials? He is consequently tempted to shrug his shoulders in disgust and, abandoning the search for insight, to lapse into indifference. Or, thinking that reason has failed him and that politics are incapable of rational explanation, he may escape into uncritical worship of a leader or into notions that government is determined, independently of his willing, by some uncontrollable forces—whether he supposes them materialistic or supernatural. The result in either case will be the same: the governed will lie at the mercy of their rulers.

Indeed, many doctrines advanced during the last hundred years have invited this fatalistic attitude. The Marxian concept of economic determinism, for instance, regards the form of government as something that is necessitated by basic productive relationships, in which view politics is considered an epilogue to economics.[1] To like effect are the teachings of many a contemporary psychologist, sociologist, and anthropologist, whose principal concern is to explain how we behave in terms of the influences exerted upon us and to emphasize what the environment does to us rather than what we can do with the environment. Thus, whether they intend it or not, they paint their picture of man as a puppet who struts and grimaces according to the pulls of external necessity. Nor can it be denied that these explanations have some color of plausibility when men are seen in the light of their past ancestry and the present pressures that limit their opportunities to choose. But the net effect of such theorizing, when unqualified, is not so much to set men free as to persuade them to resign themselves to their lot.

A Rational Insight into Politics. Rousseau's political classic, *The Social Contract*, opens with the words: "Man is born free, and everywhere he is in irons." He would have been nearer the truth, however, had he written: "Men are born helpless, but everywhere they have the capacity to become free." Reason, when used correctly, can be the great emancipator of mankind, and understanding depends on the possibility of rational analysis. This does not signify that reason cannot be perverted or corrupted. Far from it. Intellec-

[1] See Chapters 4, p. 85, and 5, pp. 121-2.

tuality of a high order has often been enlisted in the service of mysticism, or propaganda, or a dogmatism that imposes some new thralldom. Witness the cases respectively of Plato, Goebbels, and Marx. Nor does it mean that the operations of politics are now, or could ever become, the product solely of reason. This would, of course, be contrary to the truth. Everything can be found in politics that is contained in man himself: ambition, will, love, passion, and hatred, as well as memory, learning, calculation, and logical thought. But the presence of non-rational factors alongside the rational does not preclude a rational analysis of the whole. Many modern students of social organization, taking their cue from psychoanalysis and certain schools of psychology, have compensated for earlier neglect by an exaggerated cult of the irrational. Yet was not the work of Freud, whether correct or not in all his interpretations, a supreme feat of reason? Is not the aim of psychiatry to heal the mentally sick by supplying them with insight into reality, which involves an intellectual awareness of themselves and of their relation to others? Surely it is no devaluation of reason to have used it to illumine the obscurities of the non-rational and to aid in the restoration of emotional health to the ill-adjusted.

Since the state is constructed entirely of, by, and for human beings, its study is a kind of self-analysis. Complete detachment of view is, therefore, impossible. Because the political scientist is personally involved in his subject-matter, his understanding will be colored to some extent by his own preferences. This is unavoidable, but it is not necessarily a fault. Indeed, as will be shown later, the essence of politics consists in choosing between alternatives, so that every governmental act expresses or implies a value judgment. Thus personal involvement may sometimes contribute to clearer insight. If each of us knows how he responds to war, taxes, elections, the flag, and so on, and is honest with himself in recognizing his own motivations, he has some clues to help gauge the responses of others. Hence, being a participant should not disqualify a person from acting as an interpreter. Even so, to be spectator and critic of a play while one is also in the cast does impose a special problem of orientation. From what angle of vision should the action be viewed, and how are its speed and direction to be estimated? How can we pass judgment or reach a wise decision when we are ourselves immersed in the mid-stream of events?

American Foreign Policy as an Example. Perhaps the best way to illustrate these difficulties is by means of examples. If we refer to one or two of the burning issues of our time, we should be able to discern the implications they contain. Take as an instance that most controversial question of American foreign policy: the choice between isolationism or an active role of international leadership. The basic facts are not in dispute and can be readily stated. The people of the United States, on achieving independence, acquired the power to choose their own form of government and direct its policies at home and abroad. Under the system then in vogue in the world, mankind was divided politically into separate states. Within each state the jurisdiction of its own government was complete and self-contained. The bigger, more powerful states did, it is true, make other people their subjects. But the accepted ideal was to become autonomous or, as it was called, sovereign, and to this ideal the United States expressed its adherence in emancipating itself from colonial rule.

During its first century of nationhood the principal influences exerted upon the United States combined to underscore the virtue of independence, and to equate that term with isolation. The energies of Americans were directed to the initial task of filling a continent and deploying the Constitution from the Atlantic to the Pacific. Preoccupied with internal problems and expanding westward, the country focussed its attention on the New World and turned its back upon the Old. This attitude fitted with the preferences of immigrants, many of whom, leaving poverty and persecution behind them, wished to be rid of Europe. In the economic sphere, isolation was a practicable policy, as long as there were abundant resources still to be exploited in the continental United States and the technology of production did not yet require the importation of basic raw materials. In its military aspects, too, the policy served adequately the needs of people who were sheltered by two oceans, who faced no military rival on the American continent, and who had achieved a reconciliation with Britain. The proof of its adequacy, moreover, lies in the fact that between the War of Independence and World War I, the United States was embroiled in only one major holocaust which threatened its security and survival—and that war was a civil one.

The twentieth century has subjected traditional concepts to the challenge of new situations in all corners of the globe. The relative decline of British power, due to that country's loss of its earlier competitive lead and the growing maturity of its former colonies; the rise of an aggressively militaristic Germany and Japan; the revolution in Russia and the spread of Communist party dictatorships; the interlocking of American and foreign economies in wider union; and finally the advent of the airplane, rocket, and atomic bomb—such developments, by changing the character of the world, have reformulated the conditions of American security and prosperity. The United States participated in World War I because it was not to America's interest to see the eastern Atlantic controlled by an unfriendly, undemocratic power. For even more compelling reasons, the United States could not avoid being drawn into World War II when a combination of hostile forces threatened to dominate the whole of Europe and eastern Asia. At the conclusion of that war, the United States joined the United Nations, the newly-founded international organization which may be described as an association of states for the prevention of World War III. Subsequently, in the face of Soviet expansionism and Communist attempts to secure conversions to a rival way of life, the United States has joined with like-minded nations in a further network of commitments (such as the North Atlantic Treaty Organization) and has assumed therein the responsibilities of economic, military, and political leadership.

Such a summary of how American foreign policy evolved from the Declaration of Independence to recent declarations of interdependence touches upon a wide variety of problems. If we are to say what policy is "right" or "best," we must first ask what are the objectives which a nation pursues in its external relations. Do those objectives remain constant or do they alter? When a nation expands in territory, population, and economic and military might, when means of destruction and speed of communication with other powers are revolutionized, do these changed circumstances explain—and, still more, justify—a shift from avoidance to acceptance of international commitments? What issue is involved here? By what criteria do we decide? By what compass can we steer?

Some other changes, equally momentous, can also be mentioned. In the United States a century ago, individual freedom was restricted by the existence of slavery in one-half of the Union. Nor had equality of political rights for citizens yet been achieved. Women were nowhere permitted to vote. Men in various states could qualify for the suffrage only if their property or income reached a specified amount. From such limitations it is a far remove to the vast electorate which in November, 1952, made its choice between Eisenhower and Stevenson. What human values are involved in this increase of the voting public? What political considerations prompted the extension of the suffrage? How has the change affected other sectors of the governmental system? In view of the fact that the same period that witnessed the spread of equalitarianism has also experienced an enlargement of the functions of government, it is natural to ask whether the two changes are connected, and, if so, which has been responsible for the other. Furthermore, what is at stake in the different attitudes with which men regard the spread of state activity? Some maintain that the least governed are governed best, while others deem it the responsibility of the state to provide for its citizens' welfare. In the early decades of American nationhood the commercial interest, as represented by the Federalist party and by Alexander Hamilton, favored a vigorous extension of federal authority. Of recent decades, the policy of business in general has been opposed to the federal government's expansion. Many of those who called themselves liberals in Jefferson's day were distrustful of government and were suspicious of any powers it wielded. Many of our contemporary liberals, on the other hand, argue for a positive conception of the state which would give it plenty to do and would require much power to do it.

Permanent Problems, Changing Solutions. Changes of this kind, though sometimes they appear mystifying, do not necessarily indicate that the political process is one of random caprice or that politicians are hopelessly opportunistic. There are reasons for such differences of policy and for the shift from one choice to another. Indeed, the very fact that alternatives are possible suggests a method of analyzing the state and understanding its politics. This book is written in the belief that political history and contemporary government exhibit certain patterns that render them meaningful. If once these patterns are made clear, numerous events, which otherwise appear chaotic and confusing, fall into place. The remark has been made by a student of military affairs that weapons and equipment may change, but the principles of strategy remain constant. For example, whether one is fighting with bows and arrows or with jet-driven airplanes and atomic bombs, there are always identical problems of morale, training, discipline, and supplies, of deploying the right amount of strength in the right place at the right time, and so on. The subject of politics can be approached in similar fashion. Because our lives are spent amid such flux and turmoil, what tends nowadays to impress us most is a continuous need to adjust, individually and collectively, to technological invention, social innovation, rapidity of movement, economic instability, alarums of war, and doubting of long-held ethical values. Nobody would deny the importance of this element of change or the need to explain it. But at the same time it is the business of the political scientist to discover, if he can, any factors that are constant.

The analysis offered in this book attempts to fill these two requirements. It supplies an interpretation of politics in terms of certain ever-present fundamentals and it reveals the rhythms of their variations and mutations. There are, to put it briefly, certain basic issues which all governments face and must somehow settle. These issues are permanent. They never disappear. They cannot be evaded. They do allow, however, for alternative solutions, which leave mankind with the possibility of choosing and of moving from one preference to another. Because changes occur in the circumstances within whose context these problems are tackled, the need for change is a factor as constant as the issues themselves. Conditions, techniques, methods, and institutions are highly variable. Political systems resemble one another, or differ, according to their respective methods of solving each basic issue and combining the solutions. In this way it is possible to distinguish intelligibly between the political characteristics of broad historical periods, such as classical antiquity, the middle ages, the nation-state; and of contrasted systems, such as dictatorship or democracy, class rule or equalitarianism, nationalism or international organization.

This approach to the study of politics does not confine the subject under scrutiny to one's own country or one's own century. Indeed, that is its strength, for one cannot understand or analyze without a point of comparison. Just as a man does not fully know his own people until he has delved into the past, so does he lack insight into politics if he limits his comprehension to a single system of government at a particular phase of its history. Human politics forms a seamless web that is woven continuously from past to present and spreads its design from state to state.

Politics Seen as a Unity. Each of the fundamental issues must be observed therefore from the two perspectives of space and time. To do this is to supply a corrective to an undue concentration on the more pressing problems of the moment. Otherwise we tend to forget that what may seem a major problem to us (for example, the relation of the state to the economic order) was not always so, and that controversies over which our ancestors shed blood (for example, the relation of church and state) do not move us to acts of violence today. To understand politics, it is necessary to step, as it were, outside our immediate context in space and time, to see our world as a whole and, in Spinoza's phrase, "under the guise of eternity." For the most part we habitually accept and take for granted the prevailing ideas, the dominant institutions of our environment; and, if on the whole these serve our needs, we judge them to be good. But does this mean that what we are familiar with and approve is right and good only for ourselves, and only here and now? Are our practices and principles equally appropriate for contemporary peoples elsewhere in this troubled world? How does our particular system of government resemble those that have existed in earlier periods of history? Does it exhibit any novel features that are distinctive or even unique? In either case, how do we explain the continuation of the old and the invention of the new?

Meaningful answers to such questions are not possible unless governments are studied by a comparative method. The politics of a particular country may sometimes be understood by comparisons with its own politics in earlier periods; sometimes by comparisons with other peoples, past or present. In this way it becomes feasible to distinguish between what is accidental or transitory and what is fundamental or permanent. In this way, too, the causes of political phenomena may be more accurately divined than would be the case if no such comparisons were attempted. For example, anyone who wishes to know why the United States is a federal union may obtain some clues to the answer by looking at the United States alone. But, since Switzerland, Canada, and Australia are also federal unions, it is likely that a study of the reasons why they too possess this same form of government will lead to valid generalizations about the causes of federalism; and those generalizations will then be more securely founded since they will rest upon a broader base. Hence, throughout this book, the comparative method is widely employed, and the problems of politics are illustrated by examples drawn from any era or continent whose experience is relevant to the issue. We can learn about the nature of government not only by observing modern America, or Britain, or Russia, but also by studying the lessons of the birth of the nation-state, the medieval experiment in church-state dualism, the growth and collapse of the Roman Empire, and the legacy of ancient Athens.

The following chapters seek, therefore, to analyze the factors in politics which are permanent and the alternative solutions which supply the dynamics of change. At the outset it will be necessary to consider politics as a species of group behavior and the state as one type of human association. Chapter 2, therefore, discusses the principles of cooperation and competition, the organization of groups, and the methods by which men and groups combine or conflict. Next come the problems of the emergence of government within the matrix of society, the needs which the state originates to satisfy, and the techniques it employs. That is the topic of Chapter 3. Chapter 4 discusses the study of politics in its relation to other social sciences, and elucidates the great issues that form the hard permanent core of the political process. All of these issues, and the alternative solutions they permit, are then elaborated historically and analytically, throughout Chapters 5 to 14. At the conclusion, in Chapter 15, the dynamics of political change are described in terms of the interplay of each issue upon the rest; a new classification of systems of government is proposed; and the whole analysis is finally applied to the cold wars and burning controversies, domestic and international, that beset this harassed, but stimulating, age.

OF MAN, GROUPS, AND SOCIETY

Why Men Live in Groups. The state is a group of human beings organized in a special way to secure certain results. There are many other groups besides the state in which human beings associate together. While each of these has its distinctive character and problems, all bear a broad resemblance to one another. To understand the state, therefore, it is best to begin with a general discussion of human groups, no matter what their particular type may be. Moreover, since a group derives its significance from the reasons that brought it into existence, the first question to ask is: Why have groups at all?

The Satisfaction of Needs. The fact that mankind everywhere lives in groups must be the product of circumstances that are fundamental to human nature. One universal cause is that each of us has physical and mental requirements that are difficult or impossible for anybody to satisfy alone. From the structure of man as a biological organism many needs arise which are necessities in the strictest sense because to fulfill their demands is an unavoidable condition of survival. The creation of a new life through union of the sexes; training the young from helpless infants into self-reliant adults; the supply of food and clothing by the hunter, herdsman, or crop-grower; the construction of shelter and the assurance of safety during waking hours and sleep; such acts give rise to a network of relationships between persons. Any activity assumes a social character if its completion forces men to depend on one another and consequently to combine together. Out of these basic relationships society is built. Its foundations, there-

fore, are deeply embedded in the necessities without which life itself
could not be sustained.

At the outset of systematic social thought in Europe twenty-three
centuries ago, this truth was stressed by the classic philosophers of
Greece. Plato detected the root-cause of the formation of groups in
"the fact that no one of us is sufficient for himself, but each is in need
of many things." The essentials that he listed are food, shelter, and
clothing. In his view, these are most efficiently provided through a
division of labor where each specializes in the one function for which
he is best fitted by aptitude and training and then exchanges his
own surplus production with that of others. Thus, when social complexities are reduced to their simplest terms, a community "of bare
necessity will consist of four or five men." It is from their mutual
dependence and reciprocal help that a group is born.[1] Plato's illustrious pupil, Aristotle, similarly attributed the birth of groups to man's
necessities, but differed from his master in what he considered fundamental. The origins of society he traced to two relationships in which
human beings need each other to achieve a common purpose. Sexual
union for the continuation of the species is one of these. The second
is "the union of natural ruler and subject that both may be preserved"
—a statement which means that men unite to make security collective,
but involves some additional assumptions to be discussed later.[2]

The needs that impel men to associate are not, however, merely
biological or solely necessities. It is characteristic of man that he
strives for further goals whose gradual attainment has distinguished
him from other gregarious creatures and from his near-relatives
among the primates. As distinct from their necessities, men also seek
many objects and objectives which seem desirable. Such wants are
essential, not for mere living, but for living in a different fashion that
men call good when they approve the results. Thus the social order,
which originated to preserve life, evolves so as to promote a good
life.[3] In the course of this development from necessities to wants men

---

[1] *Republic*, bk. II, sec. 369. See the whole passage from section 369 onwards.
The quotations here and elsewhere are from A. D. Lindsay's translation, published in Everyman's Library (New York: E. P. Dutton & Co., 1935).

[2] See Chapter 5, pp. 97-9, 104. The reference is to *Politics*, bk. I, chap. 2, sec. 2
(1252 a), the translation being Jowett's.

[3] This is a remark of Aristotle's in *Politics*, bk. I, chap. 2, sec. 8 (1252 b). He,
of course, was merely compressing into one sentence the central theme of
Plato's *Republic*.

undergo a profound change psychologically as well as materially. This is signalized above all by the enlargement of their field of choice and by the exercise of critical judgment. It is the earmark of a necessity to be predetermined and inescapable. If men wish to live, for instance, they must have food. Within limits, they may choose what to eat and when; where to find their food, or how. But their goal is fixed without their willing it, since eat they must.

With wants, however, in the broader sense, the area of selection extends both to the means and to the formulation of ends which can be altered, expanded, and arranged in order of priority. The structure that was adequate to provide a rough shelter from wind and rain later evolves into a house with an architectural style. Those who dwell in it develop the institution of the family and by living together infuse into a building the emotional attachments of a home. Food and drink acquire the sophisticated character of dining or diet. Clothing is designed for comfort and fashion. In an advanced modern culture men can take their pick and decide whether they want most to have better orchestras, better automobiles, or better schools and parks. A preoccupation about bare existence belongs to a level of thought and discussion less complex than a concern about a standard of living, for a standard involves comparisons and consequent valuations. The distinction will be readily appreciated by a generation which suddenly found in the experience of total war that its major anxiety had switched from the maintenance of its living standards to the maintenance of life itself. Men whose wants have reached the state of inquiry and reflection about standards of living are making intellectual comparisons and taking ethical choices. When they select their pattern of life from the available alternatives, their preferences are transmuted into terms of good and bad, of right and wrong—in a word, of values.[4] Thus it happens that upon the foundation of vital necessities man, the value-selecting animal, rears this elaborate structure of choices which stamp him as a rational and moral being. In large measure this process of formulating and attaining wants is social in character. "The gains of commonwealths," as Charles E. Merriam has written, "are essentially mass gains." [5] Without associating to-

[4] According to the Book of Genesis it was after Adam and Eve tasted the fruit of the tree of knowledge of good and evil, that they first became specifically human.

[5] *The New Democracy and the New Despotism* (New York, London: McGraw-Hill Book Co., Inc., Whittlesey House, 1939), p. 37.

gether in groups men would never have become, nor could they remain, humanized. So nearly universal is this generalization that the few exceptions which may be cited are of the kind that reinforce the rule. The hermit who would renounce the world and would mortify the flesh to fortify the spirit has generally suffered a blow to his personality by which he is psychologically wounded. He escapes into hatred of humanity or into mystic communion with a superhuman force. Yet the act of a permanent [6] withdrawal, which seems to deny the ties of society, positively acknowledges the power of his fellow men, even while he rejects them, to mold his way of life. The tragic side of his character has been portrayed in Shakespeare's *Timon of Athens*.

Fictitious Views of Man in Isolation. That a human being without any social relationships at all can scarcely be imagined, and that any such creature who did exist would be either subhuman or superhuman, has elsewhere provided a theme for writers of fiction and philosophy. In an oft-cited passage of the *Odyssey*, the Greek epic poet, Homer, described his hero's encounter with the Cyclops, one-eyed giants who "have no government, nor councils, nor courts of justice: but live in caves on mountain tops, each ruling his wives and children and a law unto himself, regardless." Yet even in that case the family formed a social bond; and when he was blinded in his cave by Odysseus, the Cyclops shrieked for the assistance of his neighbors, who rallied to his support.[7] Daniel Defoe, narrating the adventures of Robinson Crusoe, depicted an isolated man who has been a lasting favorite of certain economic theorists. In him they have seen the

---

[6] A temporary withdrawal, on the other hand, has offered in some outstanding cases the leisure and the opportunity for reflection which have been the prelude to intense social activity.

[7] The source is bk. IX of the *Odyssey*, ll. 112-15, on p. 123 in T. E. Lawrence's translation (New York: Oxford University Press, 1932). This passage was cited by Plato (in *Laws*, bk. III, sec. 680) to illustrate an earlier patriarchal society, in which the family was the important group and the male ruled the family. Aristotle, too, quotes it in the *Politics*, bk. I, chap. 2, sec. 1252 b, to repeat the identical point. The Cyclops has provided a stock quotation ever since. Arnold J. Toynbee, writing before the age of atom-bombs when the adjective "atomic" signified a self-sufficient, indivisible unit, refers to him as "the classic picture of an imaginary atomic individual" [D. C. Somervell, ed., *Study of History*, abridgement vols. I-VI (New York: Oxford University Press, 1947), p. 209], which is misleading since the Cyclops, though imaginary, was not, in view of the family relationship, a self-sufficient unit.

archetype of their favorite character, "the Individual," functioning in his purest individualism and rationing his scant resources among conflicting needs. Crusoe, however, did bring to his island the knowledge he had acquired within society, plus some materials salvaged from a shipwreck. And anyhow, as soon as Man Friday appeared, a social relationship began.

Perhaps the grimmest picture of how human beings would behave if there were no bonds to unite them is that drawn by an English philosopher of the mid-seventeenth century. Thomas Hobbes, having sought security in France while civil war between Royalists and Parliamentarians ravaged his native land, proceeded during the 1640's to write his celebrated *Leviathan*. In somber hues he sketched the outline of a pre-social stage wherein, more genuinely than the Homeric Cyclops, man is truly revealed as an "imaginary atomic individual." Hobbesian men are driven by their "naturall passions," of which fear is uppermost, to preserve themselves against attack. Because of their all-pervading suspicions and distrust, they are unable to combine. They search for security in isolation or by getting their blow in first. Thence ensues "a warre of every man against every man. . . . In such condition," he writes, "there is no place for industry; because the fruit thereof is uncertain: and consequently no culture of the Earth, no navigation, nor use of the commodities that may be imported by sea . . . no arts; no letters; no society; and which is worst of all, continuall feare, and danger of violent death; and the life of man, solitary, poore, nasty, brutish, and short." Hobbes concedes that such a state of affairs "was never generally so, over all the world," but he asserts "that there are many places, where they live so now." As evidence he mentions "the savage people in many places of America," who "except the government of small families . . . have no government at all"—an erroneous view of the nature of Indian tribal structure, but one that was widespread in the seventeenth and eighteenth centuries. Hobbes claims to see other analogies in the dissolution of authority through civil war and in the international relations of independent states, though in such cases he confuses the absence or breakdown of the state with the absence or breakdown of society.[8] Doubtless Hobbes has allowed his intellect to be carried

---

[8] For this distinction, see below in Chapter 7, pp. 154-5. The quotations are from the *Leviathan*, Part I, chaps. 13 and 17.

away by his imagination. But he has at least underlined the truth that each requires association with his fellows. The life of man may be justly described as a life lived in groups.

Restraints upon Actions that Harm Others. Another reason why groups are formed lies in the simple fact that people behave in ways which produce consequences for others besides the doer. When an act is done, it is as uncontrollable as a stone that has left the thrower's hand; and its results, direct and indirect, near and remote, are like the widening circle of ripples in a pool. An individual's actions create relationships between persons and thereby become socially relevant.[9] Anybody who is affected by another's action has a concern in the conduct that touches him. Now the effect of one's actions upon others may be beneficial or harmful. It was, for instance, the former possibility that impressed Adam Smith, the Scottish master of laissez faire economics. He suggested that, while pursuing their own self-interest, men may, without knowing or intending it, be "led by an invisible hand" to promote simultaneously the interest of society.[10] How these good effects are produced or whose is the invisible hand, he failed to indicate. In any case, consequences that are generally beneficial create few serious problems since scarcely anybody objects to others for promoting his welfare. It is quite the opposite, however, with acts that prejudice the interests of persons besides the doer. In that event, whoever is harmed seeks protection from conduct which hurts him. Therefore, as Mill concedes and Dewey insists, regulation becomes socially justifiable or necessary. Men organize themselves into groups to control the sort of behavior from whose results they suffer. In this way the desire for self-protection leads to group restraint.

Nor is this all. Social relationships are created not only when some persons act and others are passively affected, but also when people

---

[9] John Stuart Mill, the British exponent of mid-nineteenth century liberalism, draws a distinction between actions that affect only oneself and those that also involve others [*Essay on Liberty*, Everyman's Library (New York: E. P. Dutton & Co.), pp. 72-75, 136-37]. It is very doubtful however, whether such a distinction is tenable. For are there any actions whose effects are confined solely to the self? Mill recognized and raised this difficulty in the *Essay*, but his answer is not to the point. See also the discussion in John Dewey, *The Public and Its Problems* (New York: Henry Holt & Co., 1927), p. 12.

[10] *The Wealth of Nations*, bk. IV, chap. 2. For a discussion of laissez faire, see Chapter 8, pp. 181 ff.

interact upon one another. While independently pursuing their various aims, men clash and collide. Different persons wish to do the same thing or possess the same object. Their ambitions and aspirations bring them into conflict. Each seeks to gain the advantage and outdo his rival, since it is impossible for all to obtain equal satisfaction. Under such circumstances three alternatives are possible. The competitors may be left to battle it out, let come what may. Or people may organize into groups and determine by an established procedure what settlement is due or just to all parties. Third, as an intermediate course, the group may refuse to decide the outcome; but, like a referee in the ring, may prescribe the rules by which the contest shall be conducted. The first of these possibilities is merely Hobbes' "warre of every man against every man" all over again. Its results are so wasteful and mutually destructive that men generally prefer a less disorderly solution. The two latter methods (though one confines itself to the regulation of means and the other embraces the regulation of both means and ends) have in common the fact that each recognizes the desirability of employing group authority to eliminate or lessen the perils of anarchy.

Cooperation Plus Competition. The discussion to this point may now be briefly summarized. Mankind lives in groups, which are formed for one or both of two reasons: to satisfy needs through concerted action and to afford protection against the harmful effects of behavior by others. Thus the basic causes of the organization of groups are cooperation in the quest of common aims and competition in pursuit of divergent ones.

Men must and do cooperate. Men also compete. To say this seems a paradox. Cooperation unites men; competition divides them. Both principles help to explain the formation of groups, yet they mutually contradict. To the extent that men cooperate they cannot compete. Conversely, to the extent that they compete, they can scarcely cooperate. The same persons in the same group cannot simultaneously be competing and cooperating for the same objective. So much is fairly obvious. More paradoxical and more significant, however, is the truth that neither competition nor cooperation can be successful if it exists alone and completely excludes its opposite. Unchecked by the other, each tends towards an extreme position where its very success is suicidal. For example, the practice of competition presupposes that there should be not one monopolist but two or more competitors. If these are truly to compete, they must be matched equally or nearly so. The purpose in competition, however, is to defeat the opponent and, if possible, to drive him out of business. But in that case competition necessarily ceases. Thus, wherever it be unrestrained, competition moves in the direction of monopoly and on attaining its goal destroys the conditions basic to its existence. When competition is really cutthroat, the throat that is finally cut is its own.

Cooperation, though it appears totally different from competition, shares a feature with it. Both principles seek to accomplish the same end: the production of work through the stimulus of an incentive. The methods employed, however, are at variance, for competition relies upon combat and cooperation upon harmony. In order to cooperate men must be organized, and to be organized they must obey rules. Up to a point rules and organization do stimulate incentive because they encourage a systematic pattern of behavior whereby people may work with mutual reliance and dependability. But systems, too, can be self-defeating when they stifle and frustrate the enterprise of those they control. They can be developed to a degree where human energies are no longer fruitfully canalized but wastefully thwarted; where by overattention to methods goals are lost from view; where a desire for order degenerates into a passion for orders. These results can occur in any kind of organization, but their effects are most harmful in certain fields of activity that all too easily are hampered rather than helped by efforts at concerted action. Why is it, for instance, that attempts to direct the themes and styles of creative artists, writers, and musicians are ludicrously inept? Clearly for the reason that the arts originate in an individual's imagination. They spring from the inward experience and sensibilities of the artist with a spontaneity that wilts under control.

Contrasted Views of Human Nature. The truth that men cannot build their lives solely on cooperation or solely on competition, and that attempts to approximate too closely to either extreme prove unworkable in practice, may be further clarified by some contrasted judgments in the fields of ethics, economics, and biology. To consider such extremes is valuable because it illumines the areas between. A temperate zone becomes more meaningful after exploration of the polar and tropical regions between which it lies.

(1) *"Love thy Neighbor as Thyself."* In the realm of ethical theory doctrines abound that emphasize the cooperative side of human relations and prescribe a course of conduct based upon men's need for one another. Witness the injunction of the Gospels to "love thy neighbor as thyself"; or the Golden Rule to "do unto others as you would have others do unto you." In similar vein are these eloquent words of John Donne: "No man is an *iland*, intire of it selfe; every man is a piece of the *continent*, a part of the *maine;* if a clod be washed away by the *sea, Europe* is the lesse, as well as if a *promontorie* were, as well as if a *mannor* of thy *friends* or of thine owne were; any man's *death* diminishes *me*, because I am involved in *Mankinde;* and therefore never send to know for whom the *bell* tolls; it tolls for *thee.*" [11] These and kindred expressions do not describe factually how most people generally feel and behave. They are statements about feeling and behavior as they might be and, in the speaker's view, ought to be. What is perhaps most significant about such doctrines is the continuing gap between the oft-repeated ideals and the persistent realities. To this, without being unduly cynical, anybody may testify who has lived through the first half of the twentieth century. Undoubtedly the reason for the gap is that such precepts overstress human cooperativeness and allow insufficiently for men's capacity to hate and destroy.

(2) *Let Dog Eat Dog.* Opposed to universal benevolence, and equally exaggerated in the contrary direction, are dogmas of universal selfishness. In one passage of *The Prince*, Niccolò Machiavelli thus summarized his view of humanity: "For it may be said of men in general that they are ungrateful, voluble, dissemblers, anxious to avoid danger, and covetous of gain; so long as you benefit them they are entirely yours; they offer you their blood, their goods, their life, and their children, as I have before said, when the necessity is remote; but when it approaches, they revolt." [12] No less self-centered was the characterization offered by Hobbes, who considered that "of the voluntary acts of every man, the object is some *good to himselfe.*" [13] He even goes to the length of arguing that pity "ariseth from the

---

[11] *Devotions*, no. XVII, italics in the original.
[12] It should be noted that elsewhere in *The Prince* and in other works Machiavelli speaks more charitably of his fellow men.
[13] *Op. cit.*, Part I, chap. 14. Italics in the original.

imagination that the like calamity (of another) may befall himselfe," [14] which is as clear a case as may be found of distorting the
facts to save a theory.

In economic thought, and the policies based upon it, occur some
further instances of the same tendency. During the nineteenth century the economic theory most widespread in Britain and the United
States held that the principle of competition not only constituted the
strongest stimulus to work, but also produced the greatest good for
society as a whole and for its members severally. Adam Smith, who
propagated this doctrine, believed the most potent motivation to be
"the natural effort of every individual to better his own condition,
when suffered to exert itself with freedom and security." [15] When
this is harnessed to the principle of the division of labor, which forms
the opening theme of the *Wealth of Nations*, there arises that peculiar link between men, the economic relation, in which each pursues
and satisfies his particular interest and yet simultaneously satisfies the
interest of others. Smith recognized that "man has almost constant
occasion for the help of his brethren." But he goes on to say that it
is in vain for a man to expect that others will help him "from their
benevolence only.... He will be more likely to prevail," runs the
argument, "if he can interest their self-love in his favor, and shew
them that it is for their own advantage to do for him what he requires of them. Whoever offers to another a bargain of any kind,
proposes to do this: Give me that which I want, and you shall have
this which you want." [16] That is selfishness developed to a high degree, but tempered by some qualifications. For Smith concedes that
even self-lovers must cooperate. This he is bound to admit, since,
once the division of labor is chosen as a starting point, it plainly
follows that specialists are mutually dependent.

The contrary problem is the one that has confronted the Russian
Communist Party. Hostile to the principle of competition because
of its association with "bourgeois economics," and dedicated to the

---

[14] *Ibid.*, chap. 6. This definition of pity was refuted by Bishop Butler,
Sermon V, #1, note a, and by Rousseau in the "Discourse on the Origin of
Inequality," in *The Social Contract and Discourses*, G. D. H. Cole, trans.,
Everyman's Library, pp. 196-200.

[15] *Op. cit.*, bk. IV, chap. V.

[16] *Ibid.*, bk. I, chap. 2. For an excellent critique of the nature of economic
exchange see A. D. Lindsay, *The Modern Democratic State* (New York:
Oxford University Press, 1947), pp. 103-105.

attainment of socialism within a classless society, Communist the-
oreticians and policy-makers were disposed to assume that, as soon
as the exploitation of man by man was abolished, there would dawn
a golden age of cooperation for the common good. No longer would
the state be an instrument of class coercion. Freed from their shackles
and imbued with a new sense of oneness, humanity would work for
the good of all. But the course of events under the Communist regime
of the Soviet Union has not conformed to this pattern. Instead of
the Marxian formula, "from each according to his ability, to each
according to his needs," Stalin substituted, "from each according to
his ability, to each according to his work." In a country whose technology was backward, whose productivity was low, and whose independence was threatened by invasion, the demand for output
placed a premium upon "incentives." Hence the organization of the
Udarniki (shock-workers) who were prepared to exceed the norm;
hence the Stakhanovite movement with its speed-up campaign; hence
the differential wage-rates and grants of privileges and distinctions
to exceptional workers. What is more, since theory had to be
changed to suit altered facts, it was eventually discovered that there
is something called "socialist competition" which differs, supposedly,
from capitalist competition.

The State of Nature and the Nature of Society. A final pair of
contrasts should be mentioned. The study of human society was profoundly influenced in the nineteenth century by the spectacular
results of research in the biological sciences. As a consequence, comparisons between the life of human beings and that of other creatures
were treated, not as analogies, but as part of the same order of being.
Thus, from the study of "nature" mankind could derive lessons applicable to their own society. The vital questions then were: What
was the nature of "nature"? What lessons did it teach? As is often
the case, men looked at the same facts, selected different data, and
arrived at opposite conclusions. One line of argument was composed
of variations on the theme of the Greek philosopher, Heraclitus, who
pronounced that "strife is the parent of all things." All the world was
seen as a jungle, and the jungle as a battleground. Nature's law was
to use your claw. It was the lot of the weak to be dominated or exterminated by the strong or the cunning. Such doctrines were applied
by Herbert Spencer to social theory in combination with the other
"natural laws" of Smith's economics. The outcome was simple: let

dog eat dog. Which side did morality then take in the struggle?
Ethics followed nature and condemned the eaten, not the eater.

On this point let Spencer speak for himself:

> Pervading all nature we may see at work a stern discipline, which is
> a little cruel that it may be very kind. That state of universal war-
> fare maintained throughout the lower creation, to the great per-
> plexity of many worthy people, is at bottom the most merciful
> provision which the circumstances admit of. It is much better that
> the ruminant animal, when deprived by age of the vigor which made
> its existence a pleasure, should be killed by some beast of prey, than
> that it should linger out a life made painful by infirmities, and even-
> tually die of starvation. . . . Meanwhile the well-being of existing
> humanity, and the unfolding of it into this ultimate perfection, are
> both secured by that same beneficent, though severe discipline, to
> which the animate creation at large is subject: a discipline which is
> pitiless in the working out of good; a felicity-pursuing law which
> never swerves for the avoidance of partial and temporary suffering.
> The poverty of the incapable, the distresses that come upon the
> impudent, the starvation of the idle, and those shoulderings aside
> of the weak by the strong, which leave so many "in shallows and in
> miseries," are the decrees of a large, far-seeing benevolence. . . .
> Nevertheless, when regarded not separately, but in connection with
> the interests of universal humanity, these harsh fatalities are seen to
> be full of the highest beneficence . . . the same beneficence which
> brings to early graves the children of diseased parents, and singles
> out the low-spirited, the intemperate, and the debilitated as the
> victims of an epidemic.[17]

Ideas like these received an added fillip when Charles Darwin, nine
years after the *Social Statics* had appeared, published his epochal
Origin of Species. If men and monkeys were descended from a common ancestor, whatever conditions promoted the survival of the latter could not fail to be relevant to the former. Darwin, moreover,
offered clues, which Darwinians were not slow to follow, in his
hypotheses of "the struggle for existence" and "the survival of the
fittest." Biological species had evolved by success in combat and by
adaptation to environment. Mankind must, therefore, subdue or be
subdued; destroy or be destroyed.

Opposite inferences, however, were drawn by the Russian anarchist, Prince Peter Kropotkin. While not denying the facts of struggle and competition, he felt that their significance and implications

---

[17] *Social Statics*, part III, chap. 25, 6 (London: John Chapman, 1850), p. 322.

had been greatly overrated. Insufficient attention had been given, in his view, to the facts of cooperation which exists on all rungs of the ladder of evolution, and increases among the more advanced species. From his reading and observations in zoology and anthropology he was led to this conclusion:

"Don't compete!—competition is always injurious to the species, and you have plenty of reasons to avoid it!" That is the tendency of nature, not always realized in full, but always present. That is the watchword which comes to us from the bush, the forest, the river, the ocean. "Therefore combine—practise mutual aid! That is the surest means for giving to each and all the greatest safety, the best guarantee of existence and progress, bodily, intellectual, and moral." That is what nature teaches us; and that is what all those animals which have attained the highest position in their respective classes have done. That is also what man—the most primitive man—has been doing; and that is why man has reached the position upon which we stand now ...[18]

Such varied views reinforce the point that human groupings cannot be attributed to only one of their aspects or explained by a single cause. Society is, therefore, grounded in a paradox. The two principles that chiefly account for the formation of groups are mutually antagonistic. Where one advances, the other by the same measure retreats.[19] Yet they are also complementary, and each has to be mixed with its antithesis to be saved from its own excesses. The oil and vinegar cannot unite; yet they blend. But this is not to say that the two principles have the same value and must be mixed in equal proportions. In fact, the contrary is the case. For of the two, it is cooperation that is the more important. Mankind could exist without competition. It could never exist without cooperation. Even when

---

[18] *Mutual Aid, A Factor of Evolution* (New York: Alfred A. Knopf, Inc., 1925). The quotation is from the concluding paragraph of chap. 2.

[19] The same point underlies Schopenhauer's parable of the porcupines, which Freud cites in *Group Psychology and the Analysis of the Ego*, chap. 6.

"A company of porcupines crowded themselves very close together one cold winter's day so as to profit by one another's warmth and so save themselves from being frozen to death. But soon they felt one another's quills, which induced them to separate again. And now, when the need for warmth brought them nearer together again, the second evil arose once more. So that they were driven backwards and forwards from one trouble to the other, until they had discovered a mean distance at which they could most tolerably exist."

The original can be found in Schopenhauer's *Parerga und Paralipomena* (1851) under the heading of "Parables."

men are acting competitively, they will form into groups where they
cooperate together in order to pursue more effectively their competition against those outside the group. Thus the requirements of
competition do lead men into cooperation. The reverse, however,
does not happen. Men do not find themselves driven into competition
by the need to cooperate. Cooperation is thus the paramount principle; and though humanity must allow for the requisite element of
competition, the social blend should contain a larger amount of the
former and a smaller amount of the latter. To combine the contrasts
and discover the best proportions is the task of group dynamics.

The Common Interest and the Clash of Interests. What effect does
their origin have upon the nature of the groups thus formed? Within
a group what relationships exist between its members? The answers
may be better understood if one more question is put. What is it that
induces men to cooperate and what impels them to compete? Assuredly, people cooperate because they wish to accomplish purposes
that they share in common. They compete, conversely, from an
awareness, and for the fulfillment, of purposes that are distinct. The
genesis of groups, in other words, is to be sought not merely in certain external conditions—in mutual need and the effects of conflict—
but also in the attitudes of people towards these. A group is more
than a state of affairs. It becomes a state of mind. Thus understood,
a group is what results from men's recognition of how they interact
with each other. If so, what forms does this consciousness take?

In seeking to satisfy those needs that call for common action men
have to recognize, discover, or even invent, a bond of union. They
search for likenesses; they merge with the group; they assert their
solidarity. To their separate personalities are added the ties that bind
them. Major consequences now flow from their being associated,
chief among which is that rights and duties become interwoven. A
member of a group seeks an opportunity to act in certain ways. His
desires are claims that he makes upon others of the group; his claims,
when recognized by them, are his rights. The others, correspondingly, expect certain lines of conduct from him. Their expectations,
which he owes in return for the rights accorded him, are his responsibilities. Recognition of rights by the group is linked up with performance of duties towards the group, and among these duties, of
course, is respect for the rights of others. Hence group organization
embodies the principle of reciprocity. He who gives, takes, and he

who takes, gives. The contrary occurs when men consider their purposes distinct and their relationship competitive. They then place the stress on differences, not resemblances; on particularity, not solidarity. Men picture themselves more as separate units than as members of an association. Instead of merging with the group, they strive to emerge from it. The self and its selfish interest loom disproportionately large, while the bonds of union become frayed amid the clash of wills.

Relations between People in a Group. These opposite attitudes are tendencies that exist to some degree in every human group, for in practice, as distinct from principle, each is always qualified and never absolute. For clarity of discussion the two kinds of emphasis—one placed on the individual, the other on the group—can be conveniently distinguished by the terms individualism and groupism. These are concepts that can be applied to the vexed problem of explaining the relation between a group and its membership. Whenever confronted with the difficulty of understanding something complex, such as a society of human beings, the mind seeks to make the problem intelligible by dividing it into parts and observing how they are connected. The question then arises: what is to be regarded as the whole, and what are the parts? Which, in other words, is the unit whose unity has significance? How these queries apply to the study of groups can readily be seen. According to where the emphasis is placed, one may approach the group from the standpoint of the individuals who compose it, or one may approach the individuals from the standpoint of the group to which they belong. In the latter case, human beings can be described as associated in a group. In the former, a group will be said to be made up of its members. Which is the reality that requires explanation? Is it a single human being or a group of them? And, whichever of these is taken to be the unit, how is the other to be understood?

As might be expected, both possibilities have found support. Some argue that the unit is the group and that we individuals are vulgar fractions. Others say that the unit is the single human being. Each view has been defended by analogies that supposedly illustrate the nature of a social group by comparisons with other associations. For those who hold that the group is the unit, a favorite parallel is the biological organism. The members of a social body are then thought to resemble the members of an animal body, wherein all parts are functionally related and none can exist in separation from the rest. On this theory, just as the body has a natural unity, so has a social group. It then becomes a false abstraction to speak of the individual in the sense of a person divorced from relationships with others. An arm lives and moves only as part of an organic whole. Amputated from the body, it dies. An opposite conception results when the individual is taken as the unit. It is then the single human being who is viewed as a natural unity and the group that appears artificial. Society is considered an aggregate, not an organism; a collection, not a collective whole. A group of men are thought to resemble a heap of stones. They are associated, yet separable. A stone may be removed from the heap, and it remains a stone.

The first comment to be made on these contrasts is that their opposition itself needs explaining. If opinions so contrary have been formulated and propagated, each must contain some elements of truth and correspond to certain facts. Plainly there is a sense in which every human being is unique and has a distinct existence, physically and psychically. When the bell tolls for John Jones, John Donne may say that it tolls for me also. But at that moment I can hear it and John Jones cannot—and that is no small difference! Moreover, when a characteristic is attributed to a group, it should not be forgotten that groups as such do not exist, or feel and move, or act and suffer. A group is what its members are. It does only what they do. In speaking about it in the singular, one is generalizing about them in the plural. Yet in another sense a group is an intelligible and describable fact and has a meaning of its own that single human beings do not. John Jones may have died, but the group of which he was a member continues in existence with virtually the same characteristics that it possessed in his lifetime. People are united by an intricate network of connections. They do not merely move in the same direction, like traffic on a one-way street. They react and interact at countless crossroads. Man, the doer, cannot be divorced from the relationships that arise from his cooperation and competition, his needs and deeds. Each such relation is a projection from his personality, and, like a shadow, belongs both to the man who casts it and to the place whereon it falls. Unless the projections are included, their source cannot be properly understood.

But while each viewpoint reposes on the solid ground of fact, it cannot be denied that both have at times taken wing into the thin

air of exaggeration and unrealism. Thus at the higher speculative altitudes theorists have jet-propelled themselves into unsupportable positions. Such errors are always likely to occur in a discussion that
employs the method of reasoning from analogy. The merit of this
method is that it tries to explain something unknown or obscure (a
mysterious X) by comparison with another object (Y) that is well-
known and clear. But the users of analogy tend to forget that the
resemblances they notice hold good only within the limits where
they overlap. The objects compared are plainly not identical (since
to compare identicals would be pointless) but possess besides their
common features other traits that distinguish them.[20] This caution is
necessary for students of human society who, in elucidating their
complex subject, habitually conscript analogies in their service and
work them to death.

(1) *The Organic Theory.* To compare a group with a biological
organism, for example, ceases to make sense when the former is
endowed with all the properties of the latter. A group of persons is
not the same as a single person and the one cannot be described precisely as if it were the other. Yet how frequently does this fallacy
recur! Thus Plato, arguing that the greatest good for a community
is unity, thought this would be attained when all members rejoiced
and sorrowed at the same happenings and what touched one touched
everyone. " 'And is not this,' " runs the Socratic interrogation in the
Republic, " 'that is nearest the condition of a single individual? For
consider, when anyone of us hurts his finger, the whole fellowship
of body and soul which is bound into a single organization, namely,
that of the ruling power within it, feels the hurt, and is all in pain at

[20] A diagram will make this evident. X and Y can be represented by two
long rectangles whose shaded portions contain the points of resemblance and
constitute the analogy. To include the unshaded areas within the comparison
is misleading.

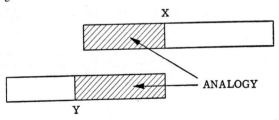

once, whole and hurt part together. And so we say that the man has a pain in his finger. And in regard to any part of the human body whatever, may not the same account be given of the pain felt when a part is hurt, and of the pleasure felt when it is at ease?' 'Yes,' he said. 'And to return to your question, the life of the best governed city comes very near to this condition.' 'Then I fancy that when an individual citizen has any experience, whether good or bad, such a city will most certainly declare that experience its own, and the whole city will share his joy or his sorrow.' " [21] Equally misleading was the judgment of the French-Swiss philosopher, Jean Jacques Rousseau. "The body politic, taken individually," he wrote, "may be considered as an organized, living body, resembling that of men. The sovereign power represents the head; the laws and customs are the brain; . . . the citizens are the body and the members which make the machine live, move and work; and no part of this machine can be damaged without the painful impression being at once conveyed to the brain, if the animal is in a state of health. . . . Nor is it any more credible that the general will should consent that any one member of the state, whoever he might be, should wound or destroy another, than it is that the fingers of a man in his senses should wilfully scratch his eyes out." [22] These notions illustrate the danger of the organic analogy when pressed too far: namely, its tendency to personify the group and then ascribe to it the behavior of a human being.

(2) *The Metaphysics of Descartes.* The contrary doctrine—that the human being is the "true" or "natural" unit and the group an artificial aggregate—has also strayed beyond the area of relevant resemblance into a fairyland of fictions. Of such a kind are many of the assumptions and assertions that pass current under the name of individualism. The fault they share in common is a failure to see the wood for the trees. The individualist has focussed his gaze so closely on the single human being, one and indivisible, that he has difficulty adjusting his vision to scan the human multitude. He sees in segments and finds it hard in consequence to unify his field. He cannot, there-

---

[21] *Republic*, bk. V, sec. 462 (Lindsay's translation).

[22] "Discourse on Political Economy," in *The Social Contract and Discourses*, trans. G. D. H. Cole, Everyman's Library, pp. 252, 264. For a literary presentation of the same doctrine, note the remarks of Menenius Agrippa in Shakespeare's *Coriolanus*, Act I, sc. I.

fore, account satisfactorily for the association of individuals in a group. Just as the organic theory is incapable of explaining the uniqueness and separability of the members of a group, so the rival view flounders in the effort to reunite what its analysis has driven asunder. The impossibility of unscrambling eggs is equalled only by that of putting Humpty-Dumpty together again.

People have nevertheless sought refuge in illustrative analogies, as if these were a talisman to accomplish the impossible. Some excellent examples occur in various philosophies of the seventeenth and eighteenth centuries. Many thinkers of that period started with the sound premise that anything complex should be analyzed into simple parts. Thus in logic and psychology it was argued that all ideas and propositions, however abstruse or abstract, are reducible to what Descartes called "clear and distinct perceptions." Similarly in the study of society it was supposed that the way to understand a group is to break it down into its elements, that is, individuals. But from this premise an inference was drawn that damaged the conclusions. It was assumed that once a whole is divided into parts, everything is present in the latter which is to be found in the former. Or, to say the same in another way, nothing is to be found in the whole which does not appear somewhere in the parts.[23] When this notion is transferred to human society, one arrives at the result that a group has no qualities that cannot be discovered in its members when they are viewed severally. Expressed in mathematical symbols, this would mean that a group can be described as the sum of an addition. Thus, if S stands for Society, and the letters a, b, c, d, etc., represent its individual members, we have the equation: $S = a + b + c + d + \ldots$ An alternative view would be to regard a group as the result, not of addition, but of multiplication. The equation would then read: $S = abcd \ldots$ Seen in this light, a complex whole possesses, by the fact of association, features of its own that are not traceable to its separate parts and that only belong to it when the parts become associated. A watchmaker can take a watch apart and lay all the pieces on a table. But when you look at them, what you see is not a watch;

[23] For examples of this mode of thinking, see Hobbes' *Leviathan* (Everyman's Library), Part I, chap. 5, p. 18; John Locke, *Second Treatise on Civil Government* (Everyman's Library), sec. 135, pp. 184-185; Rousseau, *Social Contract* (Everyman's Library), bk. I, chap. 6, p. 14.

and you cannot tell from the scattered parts what the watch will show you—namely, the time.

(3) *The Social Contract.* Two other false leads of this misguided individualism deserve a mention, since they have exercised so wide an influence. In seeking to explain the mysteries of human association, the individualist theories of the seventeenth and eighteenth centuries utilized two popular parallels. One of these—the fiction of a social contract—may possibly have owed something of its vogue [24] to the contemporary spread of the joint stock company as a convenient instrument for accumulating capital and conducting business on a larger scale. Incorporation of companies produces a relation between human beings which is contractual in character. From this it is a relatively easy step—or slip—to argue that society itself rests on a contractual foundation and then to conjure up the myth of a social contract. The comparison of society with a contract has this much in its favor. A contract does confer on the contracting parties responsibilities and rights which are mutually guaranteed and recognized. Society does the same for its members. A contract involves reciprocity and is the product of a willingness to give and take. So, too, with society. But after that point any resemblances cease to be helpful. The mistake in the analogy is that not all groups are joint stock companies; not all relationships are contractual. Men do not formally enter society in the way they sign a lease or join a partnership. They do not withdraw from society as they would withdraw their money from a bank or quit a job. The bonds that unite a family; the fellowship of scholars and students in a center of learning; the faith that inspires a religious community; the work and the traditions that build a nation—can all this be explained in the language or the spirit of a deed of trust? The richness and complexities of social intercourse cannot be consigned to the four corners of a legal parchment or reduced to the items of an invoice.

(4) *Newtonian Physics.* If the social contract suggested one means of reuniting individuals into groups, another was offered by the physicists. The publication in 1687 of Isaac Newton's *Principia Mathematica* and his formulation of the law of gravity was a great

---

[24] Though differently used to obtain different results, the social contract theory is part of the common stock-in-trade of Hobbes, Locke, and Rousseau, and of lesser writers.

event in intellectual history. Newton's achievement lay in developing a hypothesis that could embrace and explain, as a law of the nature of matter, phenomena so diverse as the fall of an apple from a tree, the ebb and flow of the tide, the rotation of the earth and its revolution around the sun. It then appeared that there could be a system such as the universe, composed of inanimate yet interacting parts, whose union is not organic, but results from the physical properties of matter. If that be so, might not an association of human beings be conceived as an aggregate of atoms or as planets within a solar system? A group could then be explained in terms of attraction and repulsion, of balance and equilibrium, of forces and inertia.

Being novel and ingenious, this idea did not lack support. It was even able to make its imprint on minds as eminent as those of John Locke and Thomas Jefferson. But it could never succeed in being more than a passing fashion or suggestive parallel. As an exposition of the true nature of groups, it was doomed to suffer the fate of all analogies.[25] For the conduct of human beings, though they belong to the world of physical phenomena, does not conform in all particulars to the laws of inanimate matter. Cooperation and competition do not consist only of a series of positive and negative charges. Nor is it true that human actions, even though they have causes, are determined in every case by a compulsive necessity, as the ocean is pulled by the moon. Men are presented with alternative lines of action and are aware of their opportunity to make choices. At least, they think this is the case and believe that their will, though circumscribed by limits, is free within these. Such thinking and beliefs are relevant to their conduct. Human beings are self-conscious, deliberating, reasoning agents; not fully understanding themselves, and therefore not wholly predictable. They do not fall into the orbit of groups, as the moon moves around the earth or as apples fall from trees.

Let us now retrace the course of the argument and see where it has carried us. After observing that men's relationships consist in striving with and against others, and that groups are born both to obtain the results of cooperation and to restrain the effects of competition, we discovered that attempts to build society on the sole basis

[25] See the criticism offered by Woodrow Wilson, *The New Freedom*, chap. 2. Wilson is himself open to criticism, however, for accepting organic theories too readily.

of either groupism or individualism were inadequate. The problem then resolved itself into discussing how these complementary opposites could be combined and what happened within a group when its members were united for some purposes and divided for others. At this point we examined certain interpretations of the nature of groups. Reasoning from analogies appeared to create as many difficulties as it removed. Hence theories about human association which assimilate it to an organic, contractual, or solar system were rejected as either asserting too much or explaining too little. But although such theories are misleading if taken literally or if considered the complete explanation, each of them does offer a clue to the understanding of groups because it serves to highlight some aspect of an obscure subject. These clues can be threaded together if we summarize the principal points in which the various analogies are correct, and those in which they are incorrect.

Thus, a human group resembles an organism in that its members perform various functions and are interdependent. It differs from an organism in that it has no way of thinking, feeling, and acting as one. A group is similar to a contract because those who belong to it give and receive their *quid pro quo*. But it is unlike an ordinary contractual union in that people are not always at liberty to enter or depart as they please and its aims may become multifarious and expansive. A group has in common with the physical universe the fact that both are systems in dynamic motion. But in the physical universe the parts lack the faculty of acting independently and with a purpose.

The Uniqueness of the Human Group. To what conclusion does this summary lead? Presumably to a very simple one—that a group of human beings is something unique, that it forms a class by itself, and that the best way to understand is to see it in its own true colors. The unique quality that all human associations possess can be described as follows: A group is composed of individual members who must become parts of a whole since, unless associated, they are unable to develop themselves. Yet it is the parts, and only these, that possess a consciousness of the self and of the whole, and are thereby capable of contributing to the whole a purpose and an organization. Thus in a paradoxical manner human beings exist separately, but are inseparably united.

The Variety of Groups. That statement, however, does not yet complete the analysis of groups because there are further facts to be observed. One reason why it is difficult to fathom the nature of a group is that we are tempted to regard it as existing by itself and to consider the relations of its members as if these were confined within its borders and did not extend beyond. Such a view is, of course, inaccurate. The truth is that all men belong to many groups. So varied are their relationships that the same human beings, like the pieces in a kaleidoscope, form and reform, combine and recombine, into numerous associations with different patterns. If it is asked why this is so, the reply surely is that groups are no less prolific than the causes of cooperation and the consequences of competition. Groups are many in number because needs are so varied and conflict so frequent.

The best way of describing and classifying groups is by the purpose they seek to fulfill. For example, there are a great many associations created in response to man's material necessities and wants. Such "economic" groups correspond to the innumerable phases of the system of production, distribution, and consumption. A weight has to be lifted that takes the strength of two. A fence between two farms requires repairing and the neighbors do it together. From these instances it seems a far cry to the intricate structures of a modern economy. But just as the symphonies of Beethoven or Tchaikovsky presuppose the simpler harmonics of a bird call or an African tom-tom, so do underlying similarities of principle persist through the evolution of social organization from the rudimentary to the complex. A business firm is an organization of persons engaged in supplying some commodity or service on terms presumably advantageous to themselves and to the recipients. The joint stock company, the legal device of the corporation, a banking or insurance system, a cooperative store, are familiar instruments by which people pool their resources and accomplish on a larger scale results otherwise unattainable. The trade union, once regarded as a criminal conspiracy, has become a recognized part of the established order. Nowadays, after the fashion of the medieval guild, it seeks to promote the security of its members both by providing a standard of skill and by eliminating mutually ruinous undercutting in the competition for jobs.

If a need like the economic which is common to all mankind has produced these economic associations, so other universal or widespread needs have evoked their counterparts. Man is everywhere curious about himself and his environment. He learns and he teaches. He wonders and he ponders. He wishes to know and to understand. As a reasoning animal, whose mind can communicate its thoughts through the faculty of speech, man has a need for education which can be satisfied only by a cooperative endeavor. Our accumulating store of knowledge was transmitted through the generations and is bequeathed to the human race as our common intellectual heritage. To encompass its vast dimensions requires the meeting of many minds in a fellowship of learning. Hence there exists a network of schools, colleges, universities, and adult study groups to provide an organized response to the desire to know. Similarly, but without laboring the point, we may cite other familiar instances where a felt need stimulates association. Belief in a Supreme Being and the wish to worship produced the world's religions and led to the foundation of temples, churches, shrines, synagogues, and mosques. The family group gives companionship to adults, an upbringing to children, and a home. The cultural interests of sufficiently like-minded people find a medium in operas, theaters, art galleries, symphony orchestras, the ballet, and so on; while fondness for recreation and physical exercise yields its crop of sporting and athletic clubs.

The Unity of Society. It is needless to prolong the list, but it is necessary to consider its implications. Human groups, we have seen, are many in number and different in purpose. Some word is wanted which will suitably describe the sum-total of associations. Because of its very generality, the best is the term "society." Thus defined, society comprises the whole gamut of social relationships and organized groups. But that is not all. Besides the fact that society is made up of many groups, there is the no less significant truth that all human beings have numerous memberships. Men are by nature joiners. Each person belongs simultaneously to a collection of groups, no one of which alone embraces all his interests. Not only is society a pluralistic union of groups, but the ways in which every human being is associated are also plural. The numerous groupings into which all men enter bring them sometimes into relations with the same persons, but more usually with different ones. Thus, as a partner in a business firm, *A* may be associated with *B, C, D,* and *E;*

as a university alumnus, with *C, D, L,* and *M;* as a worshipper in a church, with *W, X, Y,* and *Z;* and so on. As the purposes for combination vary, so each finds himself associated with different samples of his fellow-men. Neither in function nor in membership are the groups identical.

These indisputable facts produce most controversial implications. In the first place, the use of the singular term "society" to describe the sum-total of relationships and groups involves a major assumption. One should raise, rather than beg, these fundamental questions: Is society truly a unity? Is there anything that embraces the plurality of groups? If so, what makes it a whole? Does this oneness occur only subjectively in our minds and emotions, or does it also appear externally in an existing structure and organization? A second difficulty arises out of the first. It can be readily seen that the processes of cooperation and competition create relations between men, and that these relations receive an orderly character through the formation of groups. But once the groups have been formed, what is it that regulates the relations between groups themselves? How is the grouping of groups arranged? Human needs and interests cannot be so sliced up as to prevent all chance of contact or overlap. When one speaks of man's economic need, his educational need, his cultural need, and so on, these are not a string of airtight compartments, but the many facets of a personality that functions as a whole. Human beings have needs that interlock. They pursue objectives that conflict. So it is with the resulting groups, as some examples will indicate.

Divided Loyalties of the Individual. Business practices, backed up by economic theory, sanction the lending of capital for interest. But the businessman's religion may frown upon this as the sin of usury. A painter interprets on canvas the world as it appears to him and insists that he pursues his art for its own sake. Yet his critics may charge that he offends the moral, as well as aesthetic, susceptibilities of others and they assert the subordination of art to ethics. A university, dedicated to the discovery and teaching of the truth, admits its students without discriminating as to their race, color, or creed. But the same institution can derive revenues from properties leased only to whites which will fall in value if colored tenants are accepted. Parents wish their children to be educated so that their opportunities may be broadened and improved. But the poverty of the home makes it necessary to increase the family earnings by sending the children into early employment. A man and a woman want to marry. But the church to which one of them belongs forbids the union on the ground that the other party belongs to a different church or has been divorced. A desirable piece of land in a city of expanding population is wanted by an industrial firm to erect a factory which will employ many workers. The same area is sought by educational authorities for a school and playground, by a building contractor for a housing project, by a movie exhibitor for a theater. How are such conflicts resolved? Who arbitrates the merits of the contending claims? On what principles is a decision based?

Such cases are not hypothetical or fictitious. They are actual scenes from the tragicomedy of human life. If they possess drama, it is because any situation of conflict is inherently dramatic. Nor is this conflict one that exists solely between groups. It goes far deeper, since within each human being and inside each group a struggle develops between contrary sentiments, attitudes, habits, and ideas. Each man finds himself belonging to a number of systems that correspond with his respective interests and needs. But these interests overlap, the needs crisscross, the systems clash. As father of a family one has an obligation to his wife and children that may be at variance with his financial circumstances. As the adherent of a religious faith, he may accept dogmas that, as a participant in an educational program, he may be expected to question. As an artist he may seek to portray events truthfully as they appear to him. But in so doing he may run counter to the conventions of the social order by which he is enclosed. Each of these systems—the economic, religious, cultural, family, and the rest—lays claim to the loyalty of its members. Since each system, however, covers only a segment of a man's total needs and interests, the allegiance that each can exact must itself be partial. How then can a person come to a decision when faced with antagonistic demands? Amid so many claims, how is anyone to know which to respect?

The Search for Social Harmony. There are two possible answers to these questions. The competition of loyalties, it is arguable, may be resolved by compromise. Strictly understood, this means that neither of the rival claims is completely satisfied. Instead, an agree-

ment is reached at some position that is intermediate. Each side
succeeds on some points, and concedes on others. But if this is done,
one naturally inquires: Who acts as intermediary? Who brings about
the compromise? On what principles is it based? How are these
determined? Even these queries, however, do not apply to conflicts
which from their nature permit no compromise whatsoever. Take,
for example, the demand of Roman Emperors that they and their
deified predecessors be worshipped as divinities by inhabitants of
their empire. Between this demand and the religious beliefs of their
Christian subjects, no compromise was possible. Or consider the
implications of the most momentous domestic issue that has erupted
in the United States since the achievement of independence: the
institution of slavery. There is no midway point for settlement
between one who upholds the principle that human beings may be
bought, owned, and sold, as the legal property of other human
beings, and one who asserts the contrary principle that they may
not. One view or the other has to be adopted. The twain cannot be
reconciled or harmonized. As the judgment of Solomon indicated,
when two women claimed the same child, the price of compromise
was to kill the baby. The outcome of the slavery question was in
fact left to the arbitrament of war; and arms decided, not which
view was better, but which should, in practice, prevail.

As a second possibility of resolving conflict between groups,
when compromise is impracticable or inadmissible, the loyalty to
one group must bow before the loyalty to another. But how is this
achieved? Who decides which group shall predominate and by what
means it shall triumph? One method is by the use of force, with the
consequent suppression or overpowering of the unsuccessful side.
A second is by the voluntary submission of one side after peaceful
persuasion. A third is by appealing to some larger association which
will choose between opposing claims in the light of a still wider
union. Thus the difficulty of harmonizing cooperation with competition, groupism with individualism, is viewed in broader focus when
it is treated not simply as a matter of relations between persons
within a single group, but as a complex of interrelations between
numerous groups whose members are associated and reassociated in
divers ways. Consequently it is necessary to reframe the question,
raised earlier, of how to describe the relation of the group to the

individual. This can now be more accurately expressed as the problem of organizing a multi-group society out of multi-membered human beings.

An approach to a solution of this problem may be made by referring back to the beginnings of this inquiry. Groups are originally formed to cooperate in the satisfaction of needs and to keep competition within bounds. It now appears, however, that groups themselves may compete with each other and that their conflicting claims upon the loyalty of their members create a special need for orderly settlement of disputes and reconciliation. Hence, competition and cooperation underlie the relations not only of single human beings, but also of their organized groups; and since it is as necessary to resolve the relations of the latter as those of the former, the original problem still remains. Can the principles of social theory and the practices of social organization discover a method of uniting the various groups with their many members and the various members with their many groupings? The search for this union can end only with the discovery of an interest sufficiently broad to absorb all partial, lesser interests and of an association wide enough to embrace the lesser, limited associations. This quest has been the objective of speculation and action for more than twenty-four centuries. It is the "philosopher's stone" of social science.

CHAPTER 3

THE ORIGINS OF THE STATE

The Primary Function of Government. Of the numerous groups that constitute society, the state is the special concern of the student of politics. Like other human associations, however, the state emerges and exists within society. Nobody, therefore, can properly understand the state who views it as a "thing by itself," for any such view would be unrealistic. The tap-roots of government reach down into the same soil that holds and nurtures the family and the church, the corporation, the trade union, and the school. But what is it that stimulates the state to grow in its own particular manner? What are the seeds of the political process? Why is there this institution that we call the state, and where does it originate? These are the questions to which the present chapter attempts an answer. While it is necessary, of course, to distinguish between origins and results, and while we may be more immediately interested to know what the state has grown to be than to analyze how it started, we should not neglect to look at the beginnings since many of the problems of maturity stem from circumstances of infancy that affect subsequent growth.

In the previous chapter groups of various kinds were differentiated according to the need they fulfill and the function they perform. It is because men have an economic need that groups are organized for economic purposes; it is because of educational needs that groups are formed for the purpose of educating; and similarly with other groups. Conversely, one may argue that whenever a group is established, some need must have existed to which it provides the response. Hence, it should be possible to infer the need to which the state responds by studying the functions it undertakes. For the time being, without that precise definition which at this stage would be premature, the need can be described as "political," and the function of satisfying it as "governmental." That is, the state exists to satisfy man's political need by performing the function of government. Thus, in order to understand the state, the character of the political need and of the governmental process must be examined.

Anybody who surveys the vast complex of activities undertaken by the state in different periods and places is bound to wonder why they are conducted by this particular association. He learns that certain functions were assumed by the state long ago, while others are more recent additions. He finds a wide measure of agreement that there are some duties which it is appropriate for the state to undertake and much controversy about the suitability of others. Consequently he begins to ask whether the functions of government can be classified into primary and secondary, original and derivative, essential and optional, accepted and debatable. To answer such questions, the student of politics would find it a help if he could put his finger on any one function and say, "This without dispute is *the* function of the state." Or, approaching the same point from another direction, he should ask, "What is the minimum indispensable function that the state must perform in order to be a state? Is any activity of the state so vital that, were it performed by another association, the latter in effect would be or become the state?"

The Universal Drive for Protection. To these questions the facts of government show an answer. Among the common concerns of all human beings is the desire for security of life and limb. All want to be safe. Everywhere men seek a guarantee that they be protected from physical harm. But though the urge to ward off bodily threats are universal, different means of protection have been employed. It has not been uncommon, for example, for human beings to rely primarily on themselves. On all continents in most historical periods—and almost certainly in the prehistoric—men kept weapons in their homes and carried them on journeys. The first line of defense against attack upon one's person or possessions was also, in a sense, the last. It lay in one's own strong arm, since the help of others, even if mobilized, might arrive too late. But self-reliance was bound under certain circumstances to be inadequate. This was especially so when the likelihood of attack was constant, rather than intermittent; when the techniques available to an aggressor placed the defense at a disadvantage; and when the chief disturbance to one's peace came, not from within the group, but from the organized strength of another group outside. Effective security, therefore, had to be collective security. The protection which men could not obtain by acting singly had to be found by cooperating as a group. But when a need, like this one of protection, remains constant, the method by which the group satisfies it is to develop practices and procedures that have to be continually re-peated. At some stage, by virtue of repetition, these become recog-nized and accepted. They are then endowed with formal organization. In a word, they are institutionalized. What we call an "institution" is simply the outgrowth in systematic form of the repetitive prac-tices with which a group fulfills a common need. The state originates, in short, when a group of persons have institutionalized their own protection.

So far, however, this statement has consisted of assertions rather than proof. What evidence is there to prove that protection is the original function of the state? The answer can be drawn from various sources, including a review of historical data and an analysis of present-day governmental functions. The historical evidence, though fragmentary and circumstantial, is sufficient to justify some highly probable conclusions. Thanks to the research of anthropol-ogists who have classified the various stages in the evolution of man and his cultures, it appears that the earliest period about which anything is known (the Lower Palaeolithic) extended from perhaps 130,000 to 500,000 years back in the past.[1] Unfortunately, surviving archaeological remains and the literary heritage throw few and fitful glimpses on the manner in which men lived and governed themselves more than 5,000 years ago. In most of the world's civil-izations—for example, the Chinese, Indian, Iranian, Egyptian, or European—it is not until the period roughly from 3000 B.C. to 1000 B.C. that enough is known to warrant the use of the term "history" by

[1] See Melville J. Herskovits, *Man and his Works* (New York: Alfred A. Knopf, 1948) pp. 114 et seq., and especially p. 120.

contrast with earlier "pre-history." At the dawn of history, however, the institution of government already existed. Its birth took
place, therefore, in the prehistoric night before the dawn. Hence
any assertion about the origins of the state must repose mainly on
conjecture.

Nevertheless there is testimony to show that an intimate connection has always existed between the organization which a group
adopts for its defense and for its government. When human beings
lived as nomads, hunting or herding their food supply, their mobility necessitated a military or semi-military organization since they
transported with them their families and possessions. The able-bodied
males on their mounts could quickly be transformed into a cavalry;
the carts or wagons of a caravan, into a defensive post. The change
from nomadism to a settled habitat, associated with the shift from
hunting or tending animals to planting crops, altered the tactics of
protection because the objects to be defended—the home and its
source of food—were stationary, and a person who planted a seed
had to remain there until he could collect his crop. Consequently,
though men who became agriculturists preferred living in plains
that were easier to plough and sow and reap, they also required a
defensible frontier on the rim of the plain and a fortress or citadel
in the interior. It was out of this need, and the institutions occasioned by it, that the primary duty of government was founded.

The Evidence of Language and History. On this point language
supplies illuminating evidence, since the origins of our ideas are
to be found in the roots of the words that express them. Many of
our oldest and commonest political expressions originally had the
sense of a limited area, fortified for safety. Thus the Greek *polis*,
ancestor of the term "politics," signified the strong point where
scattered farmers and villagers could gather, where the women and
children would be secure, and where the defense had military advantages.[2] The center of Athenian civic life, and the dominating
feature of its topography, was its "high polis," or Acropolis. The
city of Rome likewise commenced its history as the rallying point
for scattered rural settlements in the Latin plain whose inhabitants
could find protection on the peaks and slopes of the seven hills
beside the River Tiber. One of these hills, the famed Capitoline,

[2] See Ernest Barker's introduction to *The Politics of Aristotle* (New York:
Oxford University Press, 1946) p. lxv.

was crowned, not only by the ancient temple of the Romans'
ranking deity, Jupiter, but also by the *arx*,[3] or citadel. The whole
cluster of buildings atop and between the hills received the name
of *urbs* (whence our adjective "urban") which is derived from the
Sanscrit root, *vardh*, "to make strong." The same may be demonstrated of the institutions bequeathed by the Anglo-Saxons. Our
"town" is the modern descendant of a word that variously reappears
in a group of allied languages. As the Old English *tun*, it signified
an "enclosed place"; as the Celtic *dun*, a fortified place, or camp;
in Old High German, a fence or hedge.[4] The borough, or burgh,
comes from an uncertain source, but may be related to the old
Teutonic *berg-an*, "to shelter." Its primary sense, however, is not
obscure, for in German and Old Norse it chiefly denotes a fortress
or castle.[5]

To the evidence of philology is added the testimony of history.
In many communities, not only has the duty of protecting the
group devolved upon its able-bodied males, but also the privilege and
responsibility of government have often been entrusted to the same
hands that bear or once bore the burden of defense. From numerous
examples that could be cited, a few will illustrate the truth that the
organization of society for government has often been adapted, or
transferred without change, from its organization for war. Under
the Athenian constitution of the seventh century B.C. prior to
Solon's reforms, the citizen body was divided into three classes
with different rights allocated to each. The classes were determined
by property qualifications; but they were also distinguished by their
military functions, as two of the names indicate. In descending order
of rank and wealth, they were the *Hippeis* or cavalrymen; the *Zeu-
gitae*, who could equip themselves for the heavy infantry; and the
Thetes, or laborers.[6] The link between wealth and warfare is
explained by the fact that it cost money to own a horse and pay for

---

[3] *Arx* is an offshoot of the verb *arcere*, "to ward off."

[4] The second syllable of Lon*don* comes from this root.

[5] The original meaning of the term is well expressed in a line of a late
medieval German song which became part of the Lutheran hymnal: *Ein feste
Burg ist unser Gott!* (A strong citadel is our God!)

[6] See E. A. Gardner and M. Cary in *Cambridge Ancient History*, vol. III
(New York: The Macmillan Co., 1923-39), p. 594, where they state, "Though the
property classes were based on wealth, their original purpose certainly was
not fiscal, but rather military, as was the purpose of the Roman *centuriae*."

arms and armor. A parallel to this Athenian example is provided by
Rome, where one of the citizens' assemblies was known as the
Comitia Centuriata. Its organization was intended to reproduce the
"centuries," or "hundreds," which were the basic units in the formation of the Roman army.

As in the Graeco-Roman civilization, so in the Teutonic world
to the north the same carry-over from war to government may be
observed. The Roman historian, Tacitus, who published in the
year 97 A.D. the earliest known literary study of the Germans, thus
describes their tribal organization: "On minor matters their chief
men consult alone: on more important business they all meet. They
provide, however, that all questions, the decision of which lies with
the people, may be previously discussed by the chiefs. . . . Their love
of liberty makes them independent to a fault: They do not assemble
all at once or as though they were under orders: but two or three
days are wasted by their delay in arriving. They take their seats as
they come, all in full armour . . . if the opinion expressed displeases
them, their murmurs reject it: if they approve they clash their
spears."[7] Generalizing from this and similar instances, W. J.
Shephard writes: "The legislative assembly of the modern state
originated in the popular assemblies, the folkmoots of the barbarian
peoples who inundated Roman civilization in the third and succeed-
ing centuries. These tribal bodies included the entire soldiery of the
tribe; in effect, the nation in arms. Their actions were confined to
decisions on matters of supreme importance, such as peace and
war."[8]

Modern experience serves on this point as a confirmation of
ancient history. What happens in the twentieth century to a state
that engages in a major war? When the safety and existence of the
entire community are imperiled, everything is subordinated to the
struggle for survival. The need to organize for defense and attack takes
priority over all other activities. Centers of production are guarded

---

[7] Tacitus, *Germania,* trans. W. Hamilton Fyfe (Oxford: The Clarendon
Press, 1908), sec. 11.

[8] *Encyclopedia of the Social Sciences,* vol. IX (New York: The Macmillan
Co., 1935), p. 356. See also M. J. Herskovits, *op. cit.,* pp. 330-31. A relic of this
practice can still be seen in contemporary Switzerland. Some of the smallest
cantons continue to have as their supreme governing body a mass meeting of
the male citizens, called the *Landsgemeinde,* which the participants attend
equipped with swords.

and expanded. Huge military establishments are thrown together. The whole economy is diverted to the equipment and supply of the armed forces. Abruptly and compulsorily the rhythms and patterns of daily life are changed to a new design. The cells that make up the family group are plucked apart and some are killed. The home itself may suffer destruction. The citizens respond to new stimuli. They dress in uniforms, they drill, they drive toward a goal that is called "victory." And to accomplish this result it is the state that assumes the responsibility. Its functions are promptly enlarged to embrace all aspects of society that have military relevance—which in the total warfare of this century means practically everything. Not only was protection the *raison d'être* of the state in ancient times; but whenever a people are momentarily preoccupied with protecting themselves and destroying an enemy, the state literally "takes over." [9] Furthermore, the state that is defeated, since its defenses are broken, falls under the control of the victors, as happened in the military occupation of Germany, Italy, and Japan, after World War II. In other words, the government of the state that cannot protect itself for the time being ceases in effect to be a government. It is not only from outside, however, that the security of the group can be menaced. Peace may also be threatened from within. The safety of one's persons and security of one's possessions may be disturbed by individuals who are members of the same group. Thus the outlaw or gangster is in the group, but he places himself "out of its law." Furthermore it is possible for conflict between groups—between a corporation and a trade union, for instance—to be carried to lengths where other interests are prejudiced and where the unity of the sociaty to which they both belong may be jeopardized. Government must, therefore, guard against the internal aggressor as well as the external. As this is phrased in the preamble to the Constitution of the United States, while one governmental function is "to provide for the common defense," another is "to ensure domestic tranquility." How does the state meet this need? And what principles are implied in its solution?

The Nucleus of the State. A convenient starting-point would be to examine the account given by Herodotus of an actual historic

[9] For statistical evidence on this point, expressed in budgetary terms, see Chapter 12, pp. 314-5.

event, the consolidation of the ancient kingdom of Media. According to "the Father of History," the Medes were living under anarchical conditions and suffered the perils of insecurity. Their need presented an opportunity that a capable, far-seeing, individual was ready to grasp.

Among the Medes, there was a wise man named Deioces, the son of Phraortes. Deioces coveted absolute power and this was what he did. The Medes, at that time, were living in separate villages and there was much lawlessness throughout the whole land. Being already a person of repute in his own village, and knowing that the just is the enemy of the unjust, he became ever more zealous to practice justice. His fellow-villagers, seeing how he behaved, used to choose him to judge their quarrels. In his ambition for power, he gave them just and straightforward decisions and this conduct brought him great praise from the citizen-body. Consequently when residents of other villages, who formerly had met with unfair judgments, learned that Deioces was the only man whose decisions conformed to justice, they gladly frequented his home so that they too could have him for their judge. Finally they would go to no one else. As more and more litigants kept on appearing when they learned that suits were always settled with fairness, Deioces knew that everything was falling into his lap. Whereupon he announced his unwillingness to hold sessions where he had done so previously, or to continue adjudicating. For, as he put it, it was not profitable to him to settle his neighbors' disputes day after day and neglect his own business. Then when looting and lawlessness broke out among the villages to an extent even greater than before, the Medes assembled and discussed what had taken place, most of the speakers, in my estimate, being friends of Deioces. "Since we cannot live in the country in its present state," they said, "come, let us constitute somebody as our king. Thus the land will be well governed and we shall conduct our affairs without being uprooted by lawlessness." By these arguments they persuaded themselves in favor of a monarchy; and as soon as they began proposing candidates for the kingship, Deioces was the one most proposed and praised by all. So they agreed upon him for their king.[10]

Whether the details that Herodotus relates are entirely accurate or not is a matter on which opinions may differ. The present purpose in quoting the passage is not for the sake of its historical truth, but for the insight which the narrative displays into the fundamentals of the organization of the state. For the argument bores through

[10] Herodotus, *Histories*, bk. I, chaps. 96-98 (my translation).

the many strata of governmental functions until it reaches bedrock. When men conflict with one another in their mutual dealings, they need an orderly process for composing their differences, and a recognized tribunal to give decisions whose binding character they accept. To promote cooperation and to confine competition within limits that are not injurious, society erects protective ramparts. The duties of the mediator, arbitrator, judge, and ruler are like steps on an ascending ladder of government. But the ascent is only possible under two conditions. There must be a widespread understanding that the restraints imposed through law and order are less irksome than the disturbances which erupt in their absence. Furthermore, the tribunal to which disputing parties resort must inspire general confidence on the ground that its procedures are fair and its decisions just. Deioces in the Herodotean story fulfilled these requirements. He was therefore able to found a state and become its king.

More recent history again confirms the observations of the ancients. Whenever human beings are uprooted from their established ways and exposed to the hazards of a new environment, a social bond has to develop anew. Their prime political need is then to organize in common for protection and physical security. The settlement of the United States by European immigrants contains many incidents of this nature. The pioneers who peopled an unmapped and untamed continent were exposed to risks at one another's hands and to the hostility of the Indians whose lands they occupied. Life on the frontier was not far removed from Hobbes' characterization of life in the state of nature—solitary, poor, nasty, and brutish. At times it was also short. A man who rode within sight of another on a backwoods trail did not know whether to trust the stranger, and both had their guns ready for the draw. Wherever something essential was in short supply, such as water in the West, men fought for its control. Ranchers, like medieval barons with retainers, armed their employees to protect boundary stakes and cattle from neighboring rustlers. The conflict between an agriculture based on slaves and one employing free labor brought violence and bloodshed, as in Kansas, and ultimately a civil war. An event like the discovery of gold in California could attract an inrush of adventurers whose aggressive individualism raised the temperature of the economic order to a fever while that of the social order dropped to zero.

In newly settled territories if men came to work and build and stay, rather than to loot and depart, they wanted around them at least that minimum of stability and security without which progress is impossible. Hence they were forced simultaneously to construct a community out of a mosaic of individuals who previously had no connecting ties, and to found a state by establishing law and enforcing order. It was necessary for the state and the community to grow together, since, until and unless political institutions were created, the soft tissue of society was formless and flabby and lacked the skeleton to hold it firmly. A state was born in the West when scattered individuals banded together and established the sheriff's office. The state did not grow up, however, until the sheriff's authority was generally obeyed. Then and only then was a framework of security organized within which other social institutions—economic, religious, educational, and so forth—could proceed about their respective tasks.

Protection, Order, and Justice. What are the implications of this analysis? In the first place, it demonstrates that what began as protection broadened out into something wider. Human beings come to expect more than the physical safety of their own persons. So that they may conduct their ordinary daily dealings with their fellow men, they require a minimum of stability that can only be founded on mutual trust. Furthermore, men also acquire relationships with material goods. Through their labors they accumulate possessions that they regard as property and wish to preserve. Hence the function of safeguarding life and limb is expanded to guarantee a general framework of security that surrounds the relations of men to men and of men to things. The best term to describe the whole system is "order." It is order that is able to grow after protection has been firmly planted, and it is an orderly way of life that government seeks to nurture. This is what the traditional phrases signify that ascribe to government the provision of "law and order" or "peace and good order." In other words, if order is to give peace, it must rest upon law and upon agencies capable of enforcing the law.

Nor is that all. Just as order develops out of protection and is the larger concept that embraces it, so is there a further goal which order strives to realize. A clue to its nature may be discovered in this famous passage by Augustine: "Set justice aside, then, and what are kingdoms but great robberies? because what are robberies but little kingdoms? for in thefts, the hands of the underlings are directed by the commander, the confederacy of them is sworn to-gether, and the pillage is shared by the law amongst them. And if those ragamuffins grow up but to be able enough to keep forts, build habitations, possess cities, and conquer adjoining nations, then their government is no more called thievish, but graced with the eminent name of a kingdom, given and gotten, not because they have left their practices, but because that now they may use them without danger of law." [11] A society may arrive at the stage of an order based on law. It may eliminate anarchy and be systematically organized. But merely to establish order is not enough. Order, viewed ideally, must conform to what men consider just. The kind of order that men prize is one wherein they feel that they are re-ceiving justice. A system that is organized to ensure protection, but where people are not persuaded that they are justly treated, can gain obedience, but not allegiance. Justice consists both in a method and in a certain kind of result. The method is one of fair dealing. The result is to recognize the interests of all individuals and groups and promote a harmony between them. People will feel that they have justice when the community within which they live accords them an equal chance and safeguards their interests in a manner proportionate to the interests of others. As the Herodotean story shows, a government can originate under two conditions. The understanding must be widespread that restraints imposed through order and its law are less irksome than the disturbances that erupt in their absence. Furthermore, the tribunal to which disputants resort must inspire general confidence on the ground that its pro-cedures are fair and its decisions just. Deioces fulfilled these require-ments. He was therefore able to found a state and become its king. But, as Augustine reminds us, if you remove justice, what is there to distinguish between a state and a band of robbers?

The Use and Monopoly of Force. The next question is: By what methods and through what institutions are these results achieved? What happens when a community mobilizes to protect itself, then founds a system of order, and finally establishes justice? Every association of human beings must employ the methods that are

[11] *Concerning the City of God*, XIX, IV, 6. (Trans. John Healey, 1610.)

indispensable, or at least are the best fitted, for performing its special function. Thus, if an institution, such as a school or university, is designed to educate, whatever means are necessary in education are appropriate for that institution to use. The same is true of the state. If the state originates in the need for protecion, to it belong initially any techniques that insure attainment of that objective, and if the state is to progress towards broader goals, the techniques of government must similarly evolve. Granted that protection, order, and justice are ends to which the state successively aspires, what are the means for obtaining each?

Since an institution must possess the means appropriate to its function, it follows that, in order to give protection, the state must have force [12] at its disposal. Protection against attacks from outside cannot be provided unless the group can repel force with force. Likewise, protection against attack from within calls for the establishment of agencies—for example, police, militia, army, courts, and prisons—capable of applying coercion to the disorderly and the lawless. The tribunals that are supposed to settle disputes must be able to enforce their decisions. Otherwise nobody will have assurance that the rules he obeys will be observed by his fellows. It is, therefore, the character of the purpose out of which the state originates, namely to afford protection, that imposes on the state the necessity of employing force. Many of the problems that are peculiar to the state and that distinguish it from other human associations, flow from the simple, but fundamental, fact that the state must use force or it cannot begin to be a state. [13]

Let us consider what some of these problems are. In the first place, because it must employ force, the state inevitably seeks a monopoly of it. This is so, because if there exists within society any concentration of force that the state does not control, it is there that the possibility lurks of offering to the state such resistance as that force permits. Whatever force lies outside the ambit of the

[12] Here and elsewhere, unless the context states otherwise, "force" is used in a literal, not a metaphorical sense. It means physical restraint or coercion, actual or threatened.

[13] This truth is recognized by those anarchists who attack force as such, and argue that to act voluntarily is morally superior to acting under compulsion. Knowing that the state cannot function without possessing its agencies of enforcement, they favor the total abolition of the state in order to accomplish their goal of eliminating coercion of man by man.

state amounts to a proportionate diminution of the power of the state. Hence in order to be unchallenged in performing its protective function, the state seeks to be the sole possessor of coercive techniques. Conversely, whenever force is available for use by associations other than the state, or by persons other than the government, there exist in embryo the potential makings of a substitute state and government. An incident which illustrates this fact is cited by Augustine in the sequel to the passage quoted earlier:

> For elegant and excellent was that pirate's answer to the great Macedonian Alexander, who had taken him: the king asking him how he durst molest the sea so, he replied with a free spirit, "How darest thou molest the whole world? But, because I do it with a little ship only, I am called a thief: thou, doing it with a great navy, art called an emperor." [14]

Alexander could not tolerate the pirate because the state, to maintain itself in existence, must be a monopolist of force whose possession it then attempts to moralize by serving the ideal of the public good. The little gang appears antisocial because it preys upon the larger community and puts its private advantage before the general interest.

History presents innumerable examples of the danger that threatens the state when any force is organized within its midst to break its monopoly. On this point the testimony of the ancient, medieval, and modern worlds is uniform and conclusive. During the sixth century B.C. Peisistratus usurped power in Athens and established a dictatorial regime. To accomplish the *coup d'état* his principal means was to employ a bodyguard assigned to him by his fellow-citizens after he had feigned attacks upon his life.[15] The closing century of the Roman Republic from 133 B.C. to 31 B.C. witnessed a cumulative series of futile efforts by the Senate to control its armies in the field. On the termination of victorious campaigns abroad, successive generals—such as Marius or Sulla, Pompey or Caesar, Anthony or Augustus—were able to bend the government to their will or make themselves masters of the state. There were even periods when the Senate could not keep order in the streets of Rome and lay at the

---

[14] *Concerning the City of God*, XIX, IV, 6. (Trans. John Healey, 1610.)
[15] Aristotle describes this in his *Constitution of Athens*, 14. See also Plato's *Republic*, bk. VIII, secs. 505-506, where the allusion is to Peisistratus and others of his kind.

mercy of the vicissitudes of violence between rival gangs like those of Clodius and Milo. Then when the Republic, which could not rule an Empire, had given way to Emperors who could, the latter, too, were at times made or unmade by the Captains of the Pretorian Guard who garrisoned the capital city, or by army commanders in a distant province. In the Middle Ages when government throughout Western Europe was highly localized in keeping with the feudal system,[16] the Kings of England or France found it difficult or impossible to exercise authority over powerful nobles who were secure in their castles and could place in the field a body of retainers and vassals wearing their livery. If medieval monarchs could not control what the historian, Fortescue, called their "overmighty subjects," it was because the latter had the backing of private armies.

The same in all essentials has been true of the modern state. When would-be dictators rise within the midst of weakly-constituted regimes, they seek to subvert the armed forces and organize militias of their own. In Italy between 1920 and 1922, Mussolini was able to overawe and paralyze the governments in office by mobilizing his Black Shirts and obtaining the passive connivance of the army. Hitler organized thugs to capture the city streets and ended up molesting the whole world. Elsewhere, as in Perón's Argentina, or Franco's Spain, it is by launching a military rebellion that a politically ambitious officer overturns the constituted authorities and installs himself in power. Even the gangs that flourished in various cities of the United States during the prohibition era form an aspect of the same story. When Capone dominated the Chicago underworld in the 1920's and conducted illegal rackets on a vast scale under the eyes of a complaisant mayor and police, was it not in his gunmen that a major portion of the city's authority was located? Nor is it without political significance that what the gangster offers to the victims of his blackmail he calls "protection." The lesson is obvious. The state must either monopolize the force of the community or risk surrender to whoever can muster counterforce for its overthrow. The logic of coercion dictates monopoly.

Officials and the Public. When one speaks, however, of force being monopolized by the state, what exactly is meant? To talk of the state is to employ an abstraction. Acts of government resolve them-

16 See Chapter 11, pp. 272-3.

selves in practice into acts done on behalf of everybody by a limited number. The latter may be variously described as representatives, agents, deputies, officials, or the government. It is characteristic of the state to entrust its use of force to certain known persons who are recognized by the whole community as acting on their behalf. In this sense a distinction can be drawn between public and private, or official and unofficial; and a vastly different social significance may attach to the self-same action according to the persons who perform it and the methods they employ. Thus it is one thing for a mob to track down and lynch a suspect and another for a sheriff to conduct an arrest. It is one thing to carry on a personal vendetta, and another to seek remedies for a wrong through a judicial process. When law reposes in the police rather than in a mob, when defense is secured by a standing army rather than by guerrilla bands, the trained and permanent professional acting under public orders is substituted for the unauthorized acts of private individuals. Save under the extreme necessity of self-defense, the citizen can no longer take the law into his own hands, once it has been entrusted to officials. If he does, his actions lack the character of law and he then becomes an "outlaw."

On the other hand, there are occasions when an emergency arises of dimensions that place it beyond the ordinary resources of official-dom. In those cases, the principle that the official is the agent of the community is reinforced by his invoking the aid of the citizens themselves. Thus under the English Common Law if a policeman blows his whistle when he is attacked or is trying to make an arrest, any able-bodied citizen within earshot must go to his assistance. Similarly, the sheriff in western territories in an earlier day would call out the posse to help him track an outlaw. The theory behind this is that the policeman is the agent of all the citizens. When the latter go to his aid, therefore, they are momentarily doing for themselves what he ordinarily does on their behalf. For similar reasons, under extraordinary conditions that threaten the whole community, reinforcements may be mobilized by doctors fighting a major epidemic, by firemen extinguishing a giant conflagration, or by engineers trying to contain a menacing flood. Finally, in the ultimate case of warfare, the professional army is expanded through universal conscription and all fit persons are enlisted in the service of all.

At this point it would be useful, before the discussion moves on, to summarize the course of the argument thus far. The minimum [17] conditions of a state exist, when a group of persons

(1) are associated, at the very least, for the purpose of protection;

(2) have institutionalized their protection, by repetition of procedures, into a formal system;

(3) have secured for this institution a monopoly of force; and

(4) have recognized officials who act on behalf of the whole group, using force where necessary.

The last-mentioned factor, item (4), suggests the importance of distinguishing between the related, but different, concepts of "state" and "government." Of these two ideas, the state is the broader and inclusive one. The state is a group of human beings organized under the conditions just outlined, and comprising a government as an aspect of that organization. Government consists of those who, as representatives or officials, conduct the functions of the state. It is the part of the state that directs the affairs of the whole. As such, it is a vital part because it is allowed to exercise the coercive force of the whole. This fact provides a basis for differentiating the government from the governed and thus raises a host of questions concerning the relation between the two. Many basic questions of political philosophy and institutions—the nature of authority, the problem of power, the meaning of responsibility, the process of representation—would scarcely have to be considered if it were not for the distinction between a people and their government.

Force and Consent. The government, as was just mentioned, is allowed to exercise the coercive force of the whole. But how does this come about? What is it that permits a few to wield the force of many? The answer can be discovered if one remembers that, though the functions of government begin with protection, they evolve beyond their starting-point. Protection grows into order and order seeks to blossom into justice. Something similar happens with the techniques of government, since a method that is adequate at one stage of development ceases to be so at the next. Force may be sufficient for protection. But to create order, something more is

[17] This statement is not intended as a complete definition. It lists some basic essentials only.

required. This extra something is what is called power. What is power? It is simply force with consent added. How big a volume of consent is debatable. Indeed the quantity may vary, with consequential differences of great importance, as will be seen later. But for the moment it suffices to say that consent plus force equals power.

Let us examine more closely this relation between force and consent. All governments in the world use force, and all are founded on some measure of consent. People want certain results from their government, and they are willing that their officials have the means of bringing those results to fruition. They, therefore, give their consent to the general body of law, which prescribes the order they desire; and, along with the law, they approve coercive enforcement against those who would infringe it.

The nature of this relation between force and the consent that wills it has been so well stated by A. D. Lindsay that his words deserve quotation in full:

> Many people think that the state's use of force gives the lie to the doctrine that government can rest on consent, yet it is also clear that without some sort of consent the government's force would not exist. These puzzles confound more people than should be so confounded. Men have been accustomed so much to think of the law as restraining other people than their respectable selves that they easily think of the state's force as necessary to enable some people to restrain others. . . . But a little consideration will show us that we need and desire the power of the state to restrain ourselves. Consider a simple example from traffic control. We most of us think there ought to be laws regulating traffic, compelling us to light our lamps at a certain time and so on. Such rules have our consent and approval. Yet most of us, if we are honest, know that we are likely to break those laws on occasion and that we are often restrained from breaking them by the sanctions of the law. Most laws are like that. They will work and can be enforced because most people want usually to keep them. The state can have and use organized force because most people usually want common rules and most people want those rules to be universally observed; there must be force because there are rules which have little value unless everyone keeps them, and force is needed to fill up the gap between most people usually and all people always obeying.[18]

[18] *The Modern Democratic State* (New York: Oxford University Press, 1947) vol. I, p. 206.

Power and Authority. Power is an ability to achieve results through concerted action. It is the product of the mobilization of support. It involves a relationship between a group and its agents. The latter may be described as delegates or representatives, in the sense that they obey the group; or as leaders, in the sense that the group obeys them. The building of consent may depend on the capacity of a group to organize itself coherently, formulate its program, and instruct its representatives; or alternatively on the capacity of a leader to attract adherents and win a following.[19] The support elicited will thus be reciprocal. A group supports its agents, while they support the group. Franklin D. Roosevelt held power for more than twelve years because in a critical period he confidently offered programs that gave people new hope. Dwight D. Eisenhower won power because millions of voters thought it "time for a change" and "liked Ike."

But the evolution of governmental techniques does not terminate with power. As order, to be securely stabilized, attempts to gain acceptance as justice, so does power aspire toward a concept yet more advanced. If protection is sustained by force, and order by power, justice requires authority. What does authority mean, and how is it distinguished from power? To understand the contrast, one must introduce a further refinement into the distinction already drawn between the government and the governed. In fact, the governed subdivide into two parts—the supporters of the government and its opponents. This means that the citizens who compose the state are really made up of three groups:

(1) representatives (or leaders) and officials,
(2) those who support them, and
(3) those who dissent.

Power, as was seen earlier, consists of the fusion of (1) with (2). It is able to include that ingredient of force, which makes government ultimately effective, because of the support mobilized in its favor. But the claims of power to hold sway are, by definition, valid only for those who consent. Likewise, the rightness of its

---

[19] A memorable witticism was pronounced during the French Revolution by a politician who saw a mob rush by in the street and dashed out of the house after them, saying, "I am their leader; so I must follow them."

force is justified only in the eyes of those who render it support. Being based upon consent, power is not accepted by those who dissent. The force that power may deploy will be resented, and may be resisted, by those who disagree. Opponents may have to submit to the decisions of power; but submission is different from acquiescence. The imperatives of power may secure compliance; but this is not the same as allegiance.

What demarcates authority from power is that the former is power recognized as rightful. Authority is government that all accept as valid. Its exercise is therefore sanctioned by those who approve the particular act or agent, and is tolerated by those who disapprove. Confronted with power, the citizen has a choice: whether to support or oppose. Confronted with authority, it is his duty to obey. Resistance to power is lawful; resistance to authority, unlawful. Authority is power clothed in the garments of legitimacy.

How this transformation takes place can be illustrated in two episodes, one ancient and one modern. The former of these is the sequel, as Herodotus relates it, to the rise of Deioces to the position of king of the Medes.

> Deioces ordered them to build him a palace worthy of a king and to guard it with spearmen. This the Medes did. They built him a large, strong palace on a site that he picked, and authorized him to select any of the Medes for his bodyguard. Once established in authority, he compelled the Medes to build a single capital city and equip and adorn it, devoting less care henceforth to other towns. In this, too, the Medes obeyed him, and thus he built the great strong fortress called Agbatana with its girdle of walls rising one above the other.... These fortifications Deioces built for himself—especially round his own palace—but the rest of the people he ordered to live outside the walls. When all was completed, Deioces instituted a ceremonial, the first of its kind. Nobody from outside could enter the royal quarters or see the king. All business was transacted by messengers. No one, moreover, could laugh or spit in the king's presence. The reason for surrounding himself with this solemn etiquette was to keep out of sight of his former companions who had been brought up with him, who belonged to equally good families, and who were as brave as he. For, seeing him, they might resent his position and plot against him; but if he were unseen, they might think of him as being of more than common clay. With this protocol arranged and his absolutism established, he was a stern watchdog for justice.... If he learned of anyone waxing insolent, he would send for them and punish them according to their offense.

For he kept his spies and informers up and down the country that he ruled.[20]

Much political science is compressed into this narrative. A number of human beings, suffering from conditions of anarchy, sought to improve their lot. They wished to resolve their disputes by a method that would be fair to the antagonists and by conditions that could be accepted as just. Voluntarily, they turned to one of their members, their need dovetailing with his capacity and ambitions. After repeated experience of him, they found the results they wanted. Continued acceptance of his verdicts created the strongest presumption that they were binding. In order to formalize its new-found security, the group became supporters of Deioces. By these steps the influence he had acquired was converted into power. The latter, once it was recognized and sanctioned, became authority. After this, he was entitled to enforce the law that he expounded. His decisions, compliance with which was formerly optional, were thenceforth compulsory. Resistance or disobedience was visited with coercion.

A comparable modern case—the birth of a state and the erection of the authority to govern it—is described by the man who saw it happening and contributed his share. In the *Seven Pillars of Wisdom*, T. E. Lawrence describes his experience during the first World War when he was attempting in conjunction with Feisal to instigate a revolt of the Arabs against the Turks. A major obstacle was to overcome the ancient tribal jealousies and feuds between the respective Arab chieftains and their followers. So that they would combine and not bicker at cross-purposes, they had to be persuaded to adjust their animosities, merge themselves into a whole larger than the tribe, and accept a superior authority as binding them. This was Feisal's occasion and his challenge. Lawrence thus relates it:

> Except that all its events were happy, this day was not essentially unlike Feisal's every day.... The roads to Wejh swarmed with envoys and volunteers and great sheikhs riding in to swear allegiance.... Feisal swore new adherents solemnly on the Koran between his hands, to wait while he waited, march when he marched, to yield obedience to no Turk, to deal kindly with all who spoke Arabic (whether Bagdadi, Aleppine, Syrian, or pure-blooded) and to put independence above life, family and goods: He also began

[20] Herodotus, *Histories*, bk. I, chaps. 98-100 (my translation).

to confront them at once, in his presence, with their tribal enemies, and to compose their feuds. An account of profit and loss would be struck between the parties, with Feisal modulating and interceding between them, and often paying the balance, or contributing towards it from his own funds, to hurry on the pact. During two years Feisal so laboured daily, putting together and arranging in their natural order the innumerable tiny pieces which made up Arabian society, and combining them into his one design of war against the Turks. There was no blood feud left active in any of the districts through which he had passed, and he was Court of Appeal, ultimate and unchallenged, for western Arabia. He showed himself worthy of this achievement. He never gave a partial decision, nor a decision so impracticably just that it must lead to disorder. No Arab ever impugned his judgments or questioned his wisdom and competence in tribal business. By patiently sifting out right and wrong, by his tact, his wonderful memory, he gained authority over the Nomads from Medina to Damascus and beyond. He was recognised as a force transcending tribe, superseding blood chiefs, greater than jealousies. The Arab movement became, in the best sense, national, since within it, all Arabs were at one, and for it, private interests must be set aside.[21]

There then is a picture of the growth of authority rendered possible because it was founded on consent, with force at its disposal. Feisal met the need of the Arab tribes for a wider system of order, into which he infused his concepts of justice. Thereby his power became authority; and thereby he made history.

The Evolution of Political Ends and Governmental Means. It appears then from this analysis that both the ends of the state and the means of government undergo a progression. Because protection, though necessary, is not enough, human beings construct a system of order; and from order they strive for justice, because the most durable order is the one that men deem just. A similar progression occurs with the techniques that government employs to fulfill these ends. The prerequisite for protection is force. But since the latter alone cannot sustain a system of order, power is generated by the admixture of force and consent. Finally, if order is to culminate in justice, power must be transmuted into authority.

Each stage, therefore, builds upon, and develops beyond, the one preceding. Authority is a shell without a filling if it lacks power,

---

[21] *Seven Pillars of Wisdom* (New York: Garden City Publishing Co., 1938), chap. 30, pp. 175-76.

and power may be flouted with impunity unless it can wield force. Justice enhances, yet depends upon, order without which men could have no confidence in each other or sense of trust; while order itself must be based on the protection that makes them secure. Diagrammatically, these relationships and sequences can be expressed thus: [22]

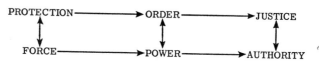

The foregoing account outlines the historical origins of government and sketches an ideal development that some states subsequently realize in practice. Manifestly it does not describe what all states are actually like or what they succeed in becoming. Some states never reach the level of justice. Others advance little beyond protection. In many states the government is unable to convert power into authority. In others again, the blend that produces power consists of more force and less consent. How does this happen and what are the political consequences?

Abuse of Force. The ends of the state—that is, protection, order, justice—are achieved by the means of government—by force, power or authority. It has been said [23] that the end justifies the means. But this is not universally true, because there are some means that no end can justify. The truth is rather to the contrary. Because men do not refrain from passing moral judgments on the methods employed, the means can stultify the end. In the field of statecraft, especially, the implications of this are far-reaching. More perhaps than any institution, the state is peculiarly affected by the nature of the means it has to employ and their abuse may fatally vitiate its ends. The possibility of this occurring arises from two facts already mentioned: the claim of the state to monopolize force, and the choice of representatives and officials to perform the functions of government. The result, when these two facts are combined, is

[22] It should be noted at this point that even justice is not necessarily the final stage of this evolutionary development. Various modern states are striving for a further ideal that lies beyond justice. See Chapters 8, pp. 212-3, and 15, pp. 411-4.

[23] For example, by Machiavelli in *The Prince*.

virtually to place this monopoly in the hands of officialdom. Thus the possibility occurs that the rest of the community may be at the mercy, or under the grip, of their own officials since the latter have means of coercion at their fingertips. Because protection depends on the opposition of force to force, a group which has institutionalized its protection cannot avoid entrusting to officials the means of physical compulsion. In that case what guarantee is there that the force, which is intended to be used for the group, may not be used against it?

Plato expounded this problem in a memorable passage of the *Republic:* [24]

> "Then we are quite clear as to what must be the bodily character-istics of our guardians?"
> "Yes."
> "And as to their mental qualities, we know they must be spirited."
> "Certainly."
> "Then, Glaucon," I said, "with such natures as these, how are they to be prevented from behaving savagely towards one another and the other citizens?"
> "By Zeus," he said, "that will not be easy."
> "Still, we must have them gentle to their fellows and fierce to their enemies. If we can't effect that, they will prevent the enemy from destroying the city by doing it first themselves."

Even more pungently the Roman satirist Juvenal inquired in words that have become proverbial: [25]

"But who will guard the guardians themselves?"

Force, like fire, can be a useful servant of mankind. But it is a dangerous master; and like fire, once it goes out of control, it has vast potentialities for destruction.

The Dangers of Power. Because power consists of force plus consent, the difficulties that attend the use of naked force are still present when the latter is dressed in the raiments of consent to form power. Those in power can abuse the force at their command by seeking to impose their order on the recalcitrant. Furthermore, the means lie at their disposal whenever they are so minded. Hence the existence of force and the construction of power, which are the inescapable products of man's need for protection and order, are

[24] Bk. II, sec. 375, p. 55, trans. A. D. Lindsay (Everyman's Library).
[25] *Sed quis custodiet ipsos custodes? Satires,* No. VI, ll. 347-48.

the root-cause of government's perennial dilemma. Force and power there must be. Otherwise there can be no government; nor can some basic ends of the state be attained. But such means permit restraints upon the opponents of government, which can be extended to the point where freedom is endangered. Power is susceptible to abuse by those who possess it and is then convertible into tyranny. What originates as an instrument of service can culminate in a weapon of enslavement. Hence many of the controversies concerning the organization and functions of the state revolve around the problem of fixing limits within which power may usefully be employed and beyond which it cannot safely be increased.

As applied to power these considerations are more complex than as applied to force. That is because the former includes a quota of consent which is absent, by definition, from the latter. If the state consisted only of an elementary bisection into government and governed, its problems would at least be more clear-cut. In fact, however, all government is an eternal triangle, whose three angles are: (a) those in office, (b) their supporters, and (c) their opponents. Witness the following diagram:

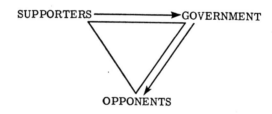

Power flows in the direction that the arrows indicate. It proceeds from the supporters to the government, which exercises it over the opposition. But what makes a vital difference in these relationships is the amount of consent that goes into power, as compared with the volume of dissent. Every government uses force and, initially at least, is supported by some consent. This is true of dictatorships as well as democracies. Lenin, Stalin, Hitler, Mussolini, and their brethren of today, could not have gained power without the support of other persons who accepted their ideas and were content to do their bidding. There is an enormous difference, however, in the respective quantities of force and consent that amalgamate into power, and in the relative importance of each. As a general rule, the broader the area of consent, the less is the need or occasion to employ force. Conversely, wherever the apparatus of force bulks large in the machinery of government and is in constant use, it is reasonable to suppose that the supporters of government are not strong enough to control their opponents by other means. Every police state relies heavily on methods of coercion, because its rulers have not transformed their power into authority and are not backed by enough consent.

Furthermore, the effect on government of the lapse of time must not be forgotten. Power, and even authority, may be constructed upon a foundation of consent that is wide and deep. But as the years pass by, these foundations may crack and crumble. A Deioces may win a kingdom with willing acclaim. Yet he himself in later years, or his successor, may lose support through tyrannical acts. The authority, that was once legitimate and just, may then be perverted into despotism. Temporarily, a ruler or ruling group may continue to wield power with waning consent. In this they may succeed for a while because any organized group is imbued with habits of obedience, is paralyzed by inertia, and is severally inferior to the force mobilized by the ruler.[26] Once rooted, power is not easily shaken. But having consumed its initial capital of consent, it slides into the morass of despotism. Then, when the sustaining conditions of government are removed, when justice vanishes and order has to be imposed, men start inquiring into the purposes that justify acts of government and the insolvency of political pretensions are quickly laid bare. For if the state requires force, or power, or

---

[26] Hence as an English philosopher pointed out in his justification of the ultimate right of a people to rebel, "People are not so easily got out of their old forms as some are apt to suggest. They are hardly to be prevailed with to amend the acknowledged faults in the frame they have been accustomed to.... Great mistakes in the ruling part, many wrong and inconvenient laws, and all the slips of human frailty will be borne by the people without mutiny or murmur. But if a long train of abuses, prevarications, and artifices, all tending the same way, make the design visible to the people, they cannot but feel what they lie under, and see whither they are going, it is not to be wondered that they should then rouse themselves, and endeavour to put the rule into such hands which may secure them the ends for which government was at first erected..." John Locke, *Second Treatise of Civil Government*, secs. 223, 225, pp. 230-31 (Everyman's Library).

authority, to perform a service, it is the continuation of the service and this alone that warrants the continuation of the means.

It is force that thus enables a regime to outlive the consent with which it was formerly endowed. In erecting the force to serve them, men also create a technique for dominating over them. The force, mobilized because of their wish, may later be directed against their wish. This possibility reaches the extreme point when a government has to use force, not for the protection of the governed, but to protect itself against them. In that case the rulers, shielded and guarded in their *Berchtesgadens* and their *Kremlins*, live as if in a constant state of siege. The perils of their position were well understood and are thus described by Plato:

> "It seems to be that in our inquiry on this matter (a good and an evil life) we must get light from the following sources."
>
> "From which?"
>
> "By examining each of those rich individuals in cities who own a great number of slaves; for they have this point of similarity with tyrants, that they are rulers of many. No doubt the tyrant has the best of it in point of numbers?"
>
> "He has."
>
> "You know, I suppose, that they live unconcernedly, and are not afraid of their servants?"
>
> "Well, is there anything for them to fear?"
>
> "Nothing," I said; "but do you see why that is?"
>
> "Yes. The whole city gives assistance to each individual."
>
> "Excellent," I said. "But supposing one of the Gods were to take a man who possesses fifty slaves or even more and were to lift him and his wife and children out of the city and put him down with all his property and his slaves, in a desert place where there would be no free men to come to his assistance, do you not suppose that he would be in the most terrible fright in apprehension lest he and his children and his wife should be killed by their servants?"
>
> "In the worst of frights," he answered.
>
> "Would he not then be compelled to pay court to some of those his slaves, to make them many promises, and to set them free, quite against his desire, and stand revealed as his own servants' toady?"
>
> "He would certainly have to do so or die," he said.[27]

Confusion of Politics with Power. For these reasons—that power, once acquired, may be transformed by abuse—the essence of the

[27] *Republic*, bk. IX, secs. 578-79, p. 278, trans. A. D. Lindsay (Everyman's Library).

state and the nature of the governmental process are often misunderstood. Every student of the state observes that it controls the organized force of the group. Everybody knows, moreover, that those who monopolize force do misuse it at times and with success on some occasions. These are indisputable facts. But clear though they be, they have led to conflicting interpretations. Because force must be wielded by the state if it is to provide protection, and because force, to be effective, must be amassed as a monopoly, many regard this force not merely as the instrument by which the state operates, but as its principal characteristic. Seen from this viewpoint, the state is then differentiated from other associations and defined as a state by virtue of its being the sole rightful monopolist of the force available within society. When so much stress, however, is placed upon the state's exercise of force, this feature is no longer treated as a tool incidental to performing the function of protection. Instead, force is shifted into the central position in the analysis of the state, and the latter is thereupon discussed in terms not of the needs it serves but of the methods it employs. The emphasis is moved from the ends to the means in such a way as to result in a reversal of positions. What once was considered the instrument is now conceived to be the master. Instead of using force to carry out its protective function, the government is pictured as performing that function in order to maintain its capacity to coerce.

The same logic is then extended from the narrow concept of force to the broader one of power. Because government is energized through power, how to accumulate it is described as the central problem of the state. Politics is then considered the arena where the struggle for power is conducted; and power is no longer regarded as the tool through which other results may be accomplished, but as if it were itself the objective to be attained. Under those circumstances, when power is thought of as the be-all and end-all of the state, a complete reversal of means and ends ensues. Arguments that once interpreted the state in terms of the functions it undertakes are twisted into arguments on behalf of the power it must employ. But to do this is to raise some crucial questions about the relation between power and ethics. If the political process is in truth a battle for might, what is its relevance to choices between right and wrong or evaluations of good and bad?

The Ethics of Power. Three views are possible, each of which has at some time or other found an exponent. In the first place, power may be clothed with moral approval and be upheld as good. When the accumulation of power is viewed as the business of the state, it is a simple next step to argue that what conduces to might is right and then to conclude that might is right. Secondly, power may be thought of as unconnected with moral choice and ethical value. The sphere of the state and the processes of politics are deemed amoral or ethically neutral. They have no concern with matters of right and wrong, of good and bad. The latter belong to a different order of inquiry, much as art is often held to exist for art's sake and aesthetics are believed exempt from moral connotations. In this case it makes no sense to pass judgment on the state, except in terms of whether it succeeds in maintaining that power which is its be-all and end-all. The third possibility is that power may be condemned as evil, on the ground that its control of force involves a coercion which is morally reprehensible. If the state, then, is pre-eminently a power-wielding institution that can employ force, condemnation of force leads to condemnation of the state as something immoral. This value judgment is, of course, reinforced by the empirical observation that power is often abused in practice and is employed in ways and for ends that affront a civilized conscience.

The three views lead inevitably to different deductions. The first results in glorification of power and, therefore, of the state that employs it. The second carves out spheres of interest and assigns politics to a separate compartment of life. The third seeks to combat the evils of power either by adopting the extreme position of the anarchist who says that all coercion is morally wrong and that consequently the state must be abolished; or by upholding the less drastic view that the functions of the state had better be confined to a minimum, since, the fewer they are, the less power will be needed. Such divergent conclusions are made possible by the ambiguity contained in the concept of power. Since power combines some force with some consent, people's opinion of power will vary according to whether it is the force or the consent that appears uppermost in the compound. But divergent though they be, the various conclusions share a common origin and derive from the same premises. They spring from a preoccupation with the techniques that the state uses rather than the end which it pursues, and they substitute the former for the latter as the essential criterion of the state.

This false emphasis, with its gratuitous switching of priorities, has given currency to more misconceptions about the processes of government and the place of the state in society than has any other single factor. The same emphasis has also been responsible for a cleavage between different schools of thought concerning the most appropriate manner for political scientists to pursue the study of the state. These alternatives will be discussed in the following chapter, where a new approach will also be introduced.

CHAPTER 4

THE CONTENT AND METHOD OF POLITICAL SCIENCE

The Actual and the Ideal. The controversy over the nature of power has had an important bearing on the problem that forms the topic of this chapter: What is the subject-matter of political science, and which method is most appropriate for elucidating it? This question has been answered in a variety of ways because the approaches of scholars to the subject of politics have differed in no less degree that the practices of politicians. The major points in the debate are these:

(1) Is it the better starting-point to examine states as they are and have been, or to theorize about the state as it might and should be?

(2) What scope is embraced by the study of the state and how large a sector of human activity does this field encompass?

(3) Can our knowledge of politics be made scientific, and, if so, how much of a science can it become?

These queries will be clarified by a review of some contrasted approaches, which can be called respectively after the names of three of their greatest exponents—the Platonic, the Machiavellian, and the Aristotelian.

The Platonic approach discusses the validity and value of political principles in the abstract and expounds the philosophical superiority of one group of ideas over another. On a small scale this is what Plato does in his dialogue, *The Crito*, where his topic is the duty of a citizen to obey the laws even where their application to one's own case appears unjust. On a grand scale, this purpose animates *The Republic*, whose subtitle is *Concerning Justice*, and whose aim is to establish a systematic philosophy of social relationships ordered by government. Plato does not, of course, ignore or neglect to consider the realities of the workaday political world. Far from it. But his analysis and judgments of history are derived deductively from abstract, universal concepts, which are formulated as the ideal canons of a "city founded in heaven." His method is to observe the actual in the context of the ideal, the momentary in the light of the eternal, the particular in the framework of the universal.

The Machiavellian approach, so notably exemplified in *The Prince*, does not exclude reference to ends. On the contrary, *The Prince* is dedicated to a clearly expressed objective: the national unification of Italy. This goal, however, is removed from the plane of discussion. It is stated, or rather taken for granted, instead of being argued. Machiavelli's preoccupation is with the techniques that will lead to the desired goal. His subject matter therefore is the analysis of methods. He supplies this topic with a treatment that is empirical, inductive, and pragmatic. That is to say, he takes for his guide the facts of experience, rather than propositions of abstract reason; he proceeds from the specific to the general, and not the other way round; and he accepts practical success as his criterion of value.

The Aristotelian approach differs from both the Platonic and the Machiavellian. Aristotle is more historically minded than Plato. He pays more respect to the wisdom of experience. He builds much of his argument on the foundations of concrete data, which he organizes and collates as Machiavelli does. But at the same time his inquiries are more philosophical than those of the writer of *The Prince*. He develops a comprehensive theory of politics. For him this is a branch of the study of ethics (that is, of the rules of human conduct), which in turn is an aspect of the whole study of man as a physical, psychological, intellectual, moral, and social being. He is concerned not only with techniques, but also with the choice of ends that he evaluates in terms of the ideals they embody. The essential feature of the Aristotelian approach is precisely in this blend. Aristotle's contribution lay in his effort to fuse the analysis of actual states with a theory of an ideal state.[1] The methodology to which he pointed the way is to combine a survey of states as they are with an evaluation of what the state might be. Aristotle praises the reality in the light of the ideal and submits the ideal to the tests of experience. It is this balance that makes his approach superior to either of the others.

There is an important section of contemporary thinkers who do not share the opinion expressed in the last sentence. These thinkers are pre-eminently Machiavellians in that they make a sharp break between the study of actual states and the abstraction of an ideal state. For them, the former—and this alone—is political science, while the latter is ethical theory or philosophy. The two, in their judgment, may touch each other, but should not mix. They oppose the inclusion of ethical theory in the field of political science because they insist on being "fact-minded" and they do not believe that theories admit of precise, factual definition. Confining themselves to data that are objectively verifiable, they discard the philosophy of the state since the values that it discusses involve the element of subjective preference. That individuals entertain certain values, or prize certain ideals, is a fact that they accept and whose consequences they study. But the nature of those ideals or values is not an article that they desire to debate.

The "Science" of Power. In their zeal to be scientific these thinkers go still further. They consider it necessary for a subject that calls itself a science not merely to avoid speculation in the abstract about controversial ideas but also to fence off an area of human behavior for exact observation. All branches of learning, after all, must concentrate on some portion of human experience in which they proceed to acquire specialized knowledge. Medicine deals with physical health; psychiatry with mental health; aesthetics with

---

[1] The material of Aristotle's *Politics* is mixed. Books IV, V, and VI contain numerous generalizations and examples drawn from the study of 158 Greek states. Books I-III, and VII-IX are primarily devoted to the philosophical examination of ideals. Sir Frederick Pollock calls Aristotle "the founder of political science" because of what he accomplished in Books IV, V, and VI. True, that was an accomplishment. But the greater achievement was the fusion of two methods, not the use of one. "The founder of political science" should be judged by the whole of his work, not by a part of it taken out of context. See Pollock, *History of the Science of Politics*, revised edition (London: Macmillan's, reprinted 1943), chap. 1.

beauty and ugliness; ethics with good and bad, or right and wrong; logic with truth and untruth; economics with wealth; and so on. If these analogies, then, are to be followed, what subject can be marked off for the political scientist? The answer proposed by users of the Machiavellian approach is contained in one word: power. For them the substance of the political process is a struggle to win power, a technique of wielding power, a problem of transferring power. To study power in these various manifestations is the business of the political scientist—provided it is always understood that the ethics of power do not fall within his terms of reference. The political scientist, on this showing, begins with power as a datum. To puzzle out its whys and wherefores is not his concern.[2]

A number of objections to this view may be mentioned. While nobody would deny that power forms an important aspect of the governmental process, it is an error to make power and politics synonymous since that would be equating the part with the whole. Nothing that has to do with the state can be excluded from the subject matter of political science. The human needs, for which satisfaction is sought through the state, the nature of the ideals to which people wish their state to conform—these, as well as the techniques of governing, are appropriate material for the political scientist. And not merely appropriate, but also indispensable. Even power itself cannot be fully understood unless it is interpreted in the context of the circumstances that produce it and the ends it serves. To rivet one's attention to power, ignoring the needs that come before and the results that come after, is to commit the error of shifting one's emphasis from the ends to the means. Viewed in that way the state is seen in distorted focus, like a reflection in a convex or concave mirror. What then appears disproportionately large is the government, the wielders of power, the influential, whose manipulations and stratagems of control are judged only by the test of failure or success.

A great fault of this approach is its tendency to forget that political science has to study the governed quite as much as it studies

[2] Instead of power, Harold D. Lasswell, an eminent member of this school, uses the term "influence." His book, *Politics: Who Gets What, When, How* (New York, London: McGraw-Hill Book Co., Inc., Whittlesey House, 1936) opens with these words: "The study of politics is the study of influence and the influential. . . . The influential are those who get the most of what there is to get."

their government. The state is composed of people as well as politicians; of private individuals as well as officials; of the common man as well as the statesman; of the many as well as the few. Politics is concerned with the well-being of all, and not just with the privileges of influential élites who get most of what there is to get. Indeed, the Machiavellian approach is so far off balance that one may seriously question whether it merits the description of scientific to which it lays claim. Surely a scientific method must include within its frame of reference everything that is relevant to the proper comprehension of the subject. Otherwise, the conclusions that are reached will be partial, misleading, and to that extent false. The study of power, torn out of the context of the total political process, begins as an abstraction and frequently ends as a caricature. Whether the specialists on power recognize it or not, ordinary humanity does submit the pretensions of the powerful to an ethical judgment. The opinions of a wide public concerning the worthiness of power-seekers and power-holders help to determine what power these are allowed to have and keep. A picture of power isolated from ethics does not fully correspond to the facts and is therefore—though it purports to be realistic—patently unrealistic.[3] The study of government must take for its beginning and ending the welfare of the many, and not the power of the few.

But rejecting the view which makes power and politics synonymous still does not settle the basic question: How scientific can our understanding of the state become? The answer is perhaps less obscure than might appear at first glance. Two choices are open to the student of politics. He may fit the subject to the method or the method to the subject. A great many, among whom are the Machiavellians, prefer to do the former. Impressed by the achievements of the experimental method in the physical sciences, and assured that the study of politics can be a science because its title says it is, they try to make their content conform to the method of a science. This they think they do by excluding the philosophy of the state, by observing states only as they are and have been, and by a preoccupa-

---

[3] It should be added that the dedication of political science to the study of power is easily convertible into an authoritarian philosophy of government. Though this does not happen in the thinking of Harold D. Lasswell, it is a manifest characteristic of the works of James D. Burnham. Consult his *Managerial Revolution* (New York: John Day, 1941) and *The Machiavellians* (New York: John Day, 1943), and see also pp. 262-4 below.

tion with power. The result is a literature of books and articles that are rich in information, description, and fact, but are often poor in significance, interpretation, and enlightenment. Many analysts of power are trapped by their own method in the same way as monkeys are sometimes caught by hunters. The latter fasten to a tree a jar with a long thin neck which is barely wide enough to admit a monkey's paw and arm. At the bottom of the jar for bait is a piece of apple of the same size as the opening in the neck. The monkey squeezes his paw down through the neck to grasp the apple, but he cannot pull out his arm unless he lets go the apple. Since he will not release it once he has it in his paw, there he stays—held only by the force of his own foolish desire—until the hunter seizes him. So it is with the power-analysts, who clutch at the bait of science and, having put their fingers around it, remain its prisoners instead of setting themselves free.

Methodology of Political Science. The alternative is to allow the method to be determined by the subject. If political science consists of the systematic study of the goals, institutions, and processes of the state, how can these be understood in their entirety? To achieve such understanding, the political scientist has four tasks to perform: (1) description, (2) analysis, (3) evaluation and (4) theory. Description is the discovery and presentation of pertinent facts with the highest possible degree of accuracy. Analysis involves grouping those facts into patterns that reveal the relationships occurring within the subject-matter. Evaluation means passing judgment and assessing worth in terms of some abstract, ideal standard. Theory is the formulation of that ideal. Let us see how each of these can contribute to our knowledge of government.

Description and Analysis. The raw materials with which the political scientist builds are supplied by the circumstances of political behavior. Some examples are the events and situations described in the following statements: "The United States, which did not join the League of Nations after World War I, became a foundation-member of the United Nations after World War II." "Britain's Labor Government, in office from 1945 to 1951, established public ownership and operation of the Bank of England, all airlines and railroads, the coal and gas industries, the retail distribution of electric power, cable and radio communications with countries overseas, the manufacture of iron and steel, and other undertakings." "The Communist Party, which seized control of the Russian government in the second Revolution of the year 1917, has secured a monopoly of political power in that country." "Asiatic peoples in recent decades have challenged, with success in several instances, their domination by Europeans." So phrased, these assertions contain a record of historical incidents. In themselves, however, they attempt no more than the accurate narration of the facts, and, like any bald chronicle of particular events in time and space, they are as such empty of significance.

What is it that can make them significant? An event begins to acquire meaning when connections are traced between it and other events. Thus the remark about the membership of the United States in the United Nations assumes and implies more than is actually said. The objectives of foreign policy and the methods of attaining them; the relation of national governments to international associations; the obligations and enforceability of agreements between states; the reasons for American membership in the United Nations as contrasted with non-membership in the League; the similarities and differences between the two organizations; these are the considerations that, when understood, can make the original statement meaningful. Likewise, the description of the British nationalization program involves more factors than are stated in the facts: that is, the nature of public ownership and operation of an economic activity, and the implied distinction between public and private ownership; the reasons for such changes, with the arguments used in their favor and against; the selection of the particular undertakings mentioned in the list; the results of the change in each case and the effects on the economy in general; the varying, and perhaps conflicting, calls of service, power, profit, and efficiency. So, too, the comment on the Communist Party in the Soviet Union suggests a wide range of questions. How was Russia governed before 1917? Why did two revolutions take place there in 1917 and what was the character of each? How is the Communist Party organized? How does it maintain its monopoly of power? In what ways has it altered the system of government in Russia, and has it in certain respects revived or perpetuated what it claimed to overthrow?

When one political circumstance is thus related and compared with another, the particulars begin to combine within the framework of the general. It is this work of collecting the separate data of history and classifying them in orderly frames of reference—in short, the art of discovering and discussing what generalizations are relevant and which facts belong where—that constitutes the analytical method.

Evaluation and Theory. But people do not stop with analysis. They also pass judgment on the political process in terms of abstract ideals, many of which have an ethical content. They appraise a program for its "efficiency" or "economy" or "service." They view a policy as contributing to "freedom," to "security," to "the general welfare," or to "private initiative." For example, if a political scientist studies an institution like the American Congress, he will, of course, assemble all pertinent factual data about that body—about its historical growth, its functions, membership, organization, relations with other governmental branches, and so on—and he will organize this information in systematic form. But he will then find a host of additional questions that he is called upon to raise. Are the functions clear-cut and appropriate? Is the workload too heavy? Are the legislative duties, the investigative function, the power of the purse, satisfactorily exercised? Are the members as competent as their responsibilities require? Are they well informed? Do they place special interests before the public good? What is the proper job of Congress? And does it do that job well? Such questions cannot be avoided; and they cannot be answered without reference to certain ideal objectives and criteria. The attempt at answering them is an evaluation.

But what about the values themselves? The political process—not only as discussed in philosophical treatises, but as actually conducted in daily life—abounds with invocations of this, that, or the other, ideal. Men dedicate their governments to life, liberty, and the pursuit of happiness, to equality, to justice, to peace and good order, and similar noble purposes. But how are these defined? How is democracy itself to be interpreted so that we shall know when we have it? What happens, moreover, if one ideal appears to conflict with a second? Life is sometimes sacrificed for liberty. Liberties can be lessened for the sake of equality. The public safety may clash with the rights of the individual. At one stage of their history, a people are embattled for private enterprise; at another, for the general welfare. At one time they prize their freedom from the state; at another, their security through the state. It may be their union that they hold most dear; or states' rights and local independence. The glittering generalities have their place in politics because human beings identify their particular interests with these wide symbols; and then, since men are influenced by their beliefs, the choice of the symbol, the agreement about what it means, and its application in future instances, affect the course of history.

Political Science, Philosophy, and History. Theorizing about values, though a speculative activity, is not independent of reality. The idealizations of philosophy have a habit of becoming the currency of the market-place. Conversely, ideas grow out of experience; and when they are developed into a coherent whole—which is what a philosophy is supposed to be—they serve as a signpost to further experience. Thus Rousseau, repelled by the spectacle of French society and government in the middle of the eighteenth century, wrote a doctrine of protest to which the architects of the French revolution that opened in 1789 appealed for much of their justification. The men who framed the Constitution of the United States adopted many of their principal ideas from the English tradition of constitutionalism and the structure of colonial government. But they further hammered out on the anvil of necessity the new design of a federal union, containing governments of limited jurisdiction, which has provided the model for extensive imitation and further speculation. Political doctrines do not hover in a sealed chamber removed from political actuality. They are an integral part of the living process of government. Consequently, they help us understand the state and render it intelligible to reason. Theory is, in part, a form of mental shorthand, compressing a multitude of connected facts into a few short symbols; and in part it is an aspiration for a future that we should like to see realized.

Politics, as here conceived, is more than merely "the art of the possible," which was Bismarck's definition. It is rather the art of selecting the most worthwhile of whatever policies are possible. In that case the methodology of political science becomes a combination of the two approaches of philosophy and history. The former supplies theoretical abstractions, ethical concepts, and means of evaluation. The latter contributes the description of events as material for analysis. Consequently, the generalizations that the political scientist formulates are of two kinds: those that state what has occurred under given conditions and those that suggest what should occur. He may affirm that "under such and such conditions this behavior has been known to ensue," or that "under such and such conditions this is the proper way to behave." One formula expresses a causal sequence between a condition, a response, and an effect. The other prescribes a rule as a guide to conduct. Summed up in a sentence, the method of political science is an evaluative analysis, uniting description with theory. The same can be said differently in a diagram:

METHODOLOGY OF POLITICAL SCIENCE

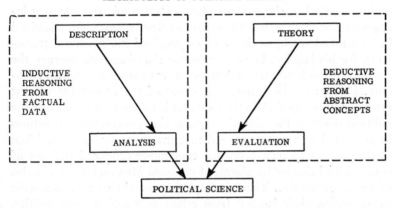

But political science has other links besides those that unite it with history and philosophy. Because its subject of study is an aspect of man's social activity, and because all aspects of society have some connection with one another, political science is related to all the other social sciences. Knowledge that is gained about any phase of human conduct, about the institutions that men build, or the ideas to which they respond in the mass, cannot fail to be of use in similar fields of inquiry. Each social science—history, economics, law, anthropology, ethics, political science, geography, sociology, and social psychology—supplements and fortifies the rest.

From history, as was seen earlier, the political scientist must take his information about the past. The writings of historians form a vast reservoir of material, which he can analyze into meaningful patterns and which can guide him in understanding the present. With its chronological treatment, history offers to the student of politics a sense of growth and development and thus affords insight into the processes of social change. The manner in which each complements the other was expressed by Seeley in this jingle: [4]

> History without political science has no fruit;
> Political science without history has no root.

Political Science and the Other Social Sciences: (1) Economics. The field of economics at one time was not differentiated from that of politics. Many of the political classics—Aristotle's *Politics*, for example, or Locke's *Second Treatise of Civil Government*—discuss topics that nowadays would be considered the province of the economist. Even when the modern phase of economic thought was inaugurated, it was the wealth of nations that Adam Smith examined in his seminal work, so that politics provided the structural framework for his inquiry. Generally during the nineteenth century the subject to which he gave such impetus was known as political economy. Despite the title, however, many of the economists of that century followed a fork in the road that led them to diverge from the political scientist. Pursuing the maxims that governmental functions be restricted to a minimum, and that the economy should hearken to the laws of its own processes, economists produced analyses of competitive behavior by abstract Economic Men under the stimulus of the profit motive. Their findings they sought to make scientific by divorcing their inquiry from ethics as much as from politics, and by employing quantitative data wherever possible. Though this method yielded plenty of ingenious theories and fascinating calculations, it ended with a more fatal divorce—the divorce from the facts of a changing economic system and from social conditions which evoked against Economic Man the revolt of Ethical Man. Latterly, therefore, with the increasing intervention of the state in the economic order, a wiser realism has impelled a *rapprochement* between economic and political studies to the mutual benefit of both.[5] Nowadays such matters as public finance, public ownership, regulation of private firms, industrial relations, employment and unemployment, the distribution of wealth, foreign trade, location of industry, and so forth, require the complementary viewpoints of the two disciplines.

[4] J. R. Seeley, *Introduction to Political Science* (London: The Macmillan Co., 1919), p. 4.
[5] On all this, see Chapter 8, especially pp. 202 ff.

(2) *Law.* No less close and no less ancient is the connection between political science and the study of the law. Because human beings, if they are to have order, must obey some rules, the substance of law and the methods of enunciating and enforcing it are intimately related to politics. It is a political will that lays the foundation of law and determines much of its content. It is the state that provides the structure through which law is formulated and sanctioned. It is government that administers and enforces the law. Every state, no matter what its form of government, develops its own constitutional law. Likewise, every political philosophy embraces or implies a jurisprudence. Seen from a social standpoint, law is a chameleon that takes the color of its environment. In a community of large land-owners the law will not be the same as in an agriculture of peasant farmers. The ownership of property and conditions of labor will be governed by one type of law in a slave-holding society; by another, in a feudal system; and by still other kinds under capitalism or under communism. The constitutional law of a democracy and of a dictatorship lie poles apart.

But while law reflects the social and political context, the picture that it conveys is not identical with the original. The language of law is a command ("do thus-and-so"); or a prohibition ("do not act thus") or a prediction ("if you do thus-and-so, this-and-that will follow"). Law is concerned with classes of persons and classes of situations conceived in general, and often hypothetical, terms. It attaches great importance to orderly procedure; yet, because of its reverence for the precedents of the past, it may continue to adhere to forms that no longer accord with current reality. Likewise, it may establish fictions [6] that are convenient as working formulae, though they do not accurately represent the facts. The student of law holds his mirror up to nature, but often sees therein a refracted image. The political scientist will draw, of course, upon the insights of this neighboring field, since no study of human society can be alien to him. Yet since his approach is both normative, like the lawyer's, and also descriptive, which that of the lawyer is not, he must look at his subject through his own medium in order to correct the distortions of legalism.

---

[6] For example, the fiction that classifies a corporation as a "legal person" and endows it with many of the attributes of an individual; or the principle in British constitutional law that "the King can do no wrong."

(3) *Anthropology*. The dominant trend of modern anthropology, in direct contrast with law, rigidly follows a descriptive and analytical method. The anthropologist of this school observes and compares the cultures of primitive peoples, though he refuses to call them "primitive" because that word expresses a value judgment. Having reacted—and rightly so—against false doctrines of racial and cultural superiority,[7] he then leans so far backward as to shun evaluation altogether. He has imposed upon himself a vow of abstinence from ethics, and plans to keep his science chaste by avoiding contact with the moral philosophers. The material that anthropologists collect, however, is important to the political scientist. The study of human society that the latter conducts is limited to peoples at a fairly advanced stage of development and to the three or four thousand years for which some historical records are available. The merit of anthropological research is that it has increased our knowledge of many societies that lack written records; it has acquainted us with most diverse types of social order and has thus yielded a fruitful field for comparative analysis; it has helped us to understand something of our own remote past by observing "contemporary ancestors"; and it has revealed the origins and significance of many an ancient custom still surviving in our midst.

(4) *Ethics and Social Psychology*. Ethics and social psychology are two complementary fields that have much to offer to the political scientist. Both deal with the relations of man to his fellow men—but with the difference that social psychology concerns itself with behavior and elucidates what men actually do, while ethics is a study of conduct formulating rules for what men ought to do. The links uniting each of these subjects with political science have varied considerably in strength and length. The Platonic and Aristotelian approaches, as was noted earlier, have bound the study of politics close to that of ethics. The Machiavellians, however, including the modern "power school," prefer, like the anthropologist, to sever the link. The objections to their argument have already been stated, and this book adopts the Aristotelian method. To ally politics with ethics, however, implies no exclusion of social psychology. Far from it. Much moral philosophy has been vitiated by its inadequate con-

[7] See Chapter 5, pp. 102-7, 118-9.

sideration of psychological factors, just as many utopian [8] thinkers in politics have lacked the leaven of realism that helps the Aristotelian. While political science must embrace a theory of what the state ought to be, the latter must respect the limits of the possible. Theories about political conduct that are not grounded in an adequate psychology are apt to be defective. This has been well shown in some of the contributions that modern social psychology has made to political science. One half century ago Graham Wallas promoted a ferment with his illuminating little book, *Human Nature in Politics.* Since then the influence of psycho-analysis has been notably represented in the writings of Lasswell.[9] The political scientist of today, therefore, has the opportunity to combine the evaluations of ethics with the analyses of psychology.

(5) *Geography.* Yet another field from which political science can glean much valuable material is geography. This is a discipline that straddles both groups of sciences—the social and the physical— a duality revealed in the definition which calls the subject "the study of the earth as the home of Man." It is to the physical aspect, however, that geographers have generally given more attention. For instance, they have studied tides and ocean currents and climate and rainfall and winds and land forms. All of this is appropriate to the study of the earth. But does it inform us adequately about the home of man? ·

Since all human groupings occupy space on the earth, a geographical factor permeates the social complex. The implications of space are therefore profoundly relevant to our understanding of organized society. The human aspect of geography, complementing and completing the physical approach, has been late in coming into its own, though its influence is at last discernible and strong. Economic geography has been able to throw light on the utilization of

---

[8] In the case of Plato, whose thought was certainly utopian in the *Republic,* it must be recognized that psychology was brought fully into the picture. (See *Republic,* bk. IV, secs. 435-442.) The fault, however, was that Plato used an incorrect psychology.

[9] For example, his *Psychopathology and Politics* (Chicago: University of Chicago Press, 1931), *World Politics and Personal Insecurity* (New York, London: McGraw-Hill Book Co., Inc., Whittlesey House, 1935), *Politics— Who Gets What, When, How* (New York, London: McGraw-Hill Book Co., Inc., 1936).

natural resources, distribution of population, location of cities, direction of trade routes, and like matters. Similarly in the political field the relation of the state to the area over which it extends can be interpreted through the knowledge that geography supplies. The problem of protection, which is the original function of government, involves the strategic strength or weakness of land mass and water, of hill and plain, of river valleys and lines of communication. Not unnaturally, therefore, the label "geopolitics" has been applied to studies that unite the two fields.[10]

(6) *Sociology.* Finally, there is one last discipline, sociology, whose bearing on politics requires a comment. This is a relative newcomer to the family of the social sciences, its name having been popularized in the late nineteenth century by Herbert Spencer. The development of sociology since that time could be called the story of a title in search of a field. Sociology is a subject with a split personality because it came into being in response to two different needs and its exponents have always had two contrasted goals. One need was for a subject that would study those aspects of society that were not covered by other disciplines. As each social science developed its specialization, the economy became the province of one discipline, the state of a second, law of a third, and so on. But it then appeared that there existed gaps and omissions in the form of topics that no field had yet appropriated. The family, religion, the status of women, crime and other anti-social behavior, these and similar problems deserved study because they were essential for rounding out our knowledge of society. Thus conceived, however, sociology would be an amorphous subject, devoid of structure and framework, a science of "leftovers." Hence, to avoid this fate, its more eminent architects developed a unifying concept within whose scope the scattered members of their subject could appear an articulated whole. This is the concept of "culture," by which is meant, in broadest terms, the over-all pattern or design that animates an entire society and supplies it with character and expression.

The step that followed next was not difficult to foresee. It is the curse of specialization that what one gains in depth one loses in breadth. As social sciences have specialized, they have concentrated

---

[10] Like other approaches (for example, the economic) when overdone, geopolitics is liable to abuse. A school of German geopoliticians under the Nazi regime prostituted their subject to justifications of German aggression.

more and more on their prerogatives and "property rights" in their
own sectors. The study of society has, therefore, lost the quality of
a unified view, and knowledge has become excessively departmental-
ized. Some sociologists—and this is greatly to their credit—have
recognized this defect and hoped that through their approach, and
by means of the culture concept, a comprehensive understanding
of society as a whole could be secured. As students of "society" in
its largest sense, they thought to unify the not-so-sociable social
sciences—which would take sociology a long way from being a
science of leftovers!

The Unity of the Social Sciences. But sociologists are not the only
ones who have recognized the need and have volunteered for this
unifying role. Economists of the Marxian persuasion hold the view
that the main outlines of the social order are determined by basic
economic necessities. If that were true, it would, of course, follow
that the subject that studies these latter would take pre-eminence
over other fields. The like claim has been advanced by some psychologists who point out that every social activity is a product of
human motivations, energies, and aspirations, and suggest that society as a whole can best be understood in the light of all-pervasive
psychological factors. Of similar intent are the arguments of various
political scientists, who take their cue from Aristotle's conception
of this field as the "master-science" that has priority over the rest.

It is not at all surprising that attempts at unifying the social sciences have come from so many quarters. Not only does the need
exist, but many disciplines can make out a plausible case for recognition of their own discipline as the co-ordinator. Even though the
sociologists attempt too wide a coverage, it is a helpful hypothesis
to picture the components of society as details of a whole. The economic determinist is guilty of exaggeration; yet it is undeniable that
the social order is interwoven with economic threads. The social
psychologist, by restricting himself to behavior, does not encompass
the entire field of human conduct. Nevertheless, one cannot point
to any area of society to which psychological considerations are
irrelevant. Equally, it must be agreed that society is a larger concept
than the state. But is there any social problem nowadays that is un-
touched by the influence of government? The truth is, in other
words, that society is like a rope all of whose strands are intertwined. Everything social can be studied from a historical aspect, an

economic aspect, and so on, because in their ultimate synthesis all social data are related.

Where, then, does this leave the social sciences? Presumably three possibilities are open. One might argue that all disciplines are free and equal, and that their relations resemble those of independent nation-states under the classical doctrine of sovereignty. But in that case each specialist runs the risk of studying in isolation—more or less splendid; and if society is genuinely a unity, one sacrifices the chance of seeing it whole. A second course is to elevate a single discipline (presumably one's own) into a master-science and trust that somehow one may co-ordinate the other specializations. But to do that is to incur the intellectual danger of a one-track approach to many-sided problems. Thirdly, one may hazard the hope that all the social disciplines, as they mellow with the years, will draw closer together since so many fundamental issues require the collaboration of more than one. Indeed, there are already welcome signs to indicate that a reaction is occurring against excessive specialization and that some day the various fields may enter together under the single tent of "social science." In the meantime what the political scientist can best do is to continue with the analysis and evaluation of his subject, drawing into his service whatever aid he can enlist from allied fields.

Anatomy of the State. Now arises the problem of determining what kind of topics the political scientist should analyze and evaluate. How is he to organize and pattern his subject for clearer comprehension? Of various methods that suggest themselves, the two that merit most serious examination are these:

(1) Concentration upon the state, as an organized system of institutions.

(2) Concentration upon politics, as a dynamic process of deciding fundamental issues.

Let us see what each of these approaches would involve.

The analysis of the state requires an elucidation of the parts that compose it. What this means can be illustrated by a comparison. Anyone who studies a musical composition can analyze it into elements of sound and silence. The pattern these form has five aspects: melody, time, rhythm, volume, and pitch. When the music is played or sung, all five are fused together. The craftsmanship of the composer consists in the kind of emphasis given to each and the manner of harmonizing them. The same, or something like it, can be done for the state, which may be subdivided into its elements in order that the relations between them can be more easily understood. It is useful to conduct an analysis of the state under headings that are common to every type of human association—economic, religious, educational, and the rest. In this way the generic features that all groups share may be compared, while the specific characteristics of each can be differentiated. Thus an analysis of the state should include, and distinguish between, the generic elements and the specific.

What are the components of any group? The first is necessarily the membership, since without this there would be no group. The members are variously named and related according to the nature of the association they form. If it is a church, they are a congregation or are called, in terms of the belief they profess, the faithful. If it is a family, they are parents, children, uncles, cousins—or, all-inclusively, relatives. If a business firm, they are owners, managers, employees. If a state, they are citizens or subjects and rulers or officials. How is membership acquired in the group? Sometimes by the voluntary choice of the person who seeks admission and of the existing members who decide to admit. Thus a person may undergo conversion and then be initiated into a religious faith, or he may apply and be accepted at a school or university. He may obtain appointment to a job in a business firm, be naturalized as a citizen, marry and start a family. Sometimes the act of joining a group is involuntary, as when an infant is born into a family, is baptized into a church, and automatically receives the citizenship of the country of its birth. Similarly, membership in the group may be terminated by voluntary act of the individual or under compulsion from the group. You may sever your link with an organized religion by non-attendance at its devotions, or you may be excommunicated by it. You may quit or graduate from school or college, or be expelled; resign your job or be fired; renounce your allegiance or be deprived of citizenship.

If the members constitute the first element in any group, its functions form the second. For it is to fulfill a purpose by carrying out a certain function that members are associated. How then are the functions of a group to be described? Presumably the chief function of the family is to propagate and live together; of the religious group, to worship; of the firm, to conduct a business; of the state, to protect. Functions such as these cannot be performed without organization, structure, and system. In other words, every organization that maintains its identity and retains its continuity, begets a progeny of institutions. The latter, though variously named, are fundamentally alike in the role they perform. Thus education is institutionalized through schools, colleges, and universities. Religion is organized by means of temples, mosques, synagogues, and churches. Business is carried on by the firm or corporation. The family clusters round the home. Likewise the state expresses itself through government and such specialized agencies as the legislature, law court, administrative department, and civil service.

When an institution is organized, three further elements make their appearance: a body of rules, a governing authority, and revenue. Every association requires a system of rules that define the relations of its members, allot their rights and responsibilities, and prescribe its operating procedures. In a church, this takes the form of canon law and ritual. In the family, the law of marital relations reinforces the moral code of fidelity. A business firm not only has its internal regulations, but also conforms to general trade practices and operates within the framework of laws of contract, property, corporations, and so on. The state is both creator and creature of law and custom. To enforce these rules and give general guidance to the group is the task of its governing authority. This appears under different guises, depending on the nature of the association, as the management, clergy, parents, teachers, or government. Similarly, in every group an essential ingredient is its revenue—if that term is understood to comprise the physical and material resources by which the group accomplishes its purposes. Thus a school or university is maintained by public funds or private fees; a business, by its profits; the state, by taxes and other fees; the family, by its property or income.

Finally, there is one more component without which no association is complete. Every group is both producer and product of the ideas concerning it that exist in the minds of its members. These ideas are an integral part of the life of the group since they embody the hopes and aspirations of its members, expressing their conception of the group's purpose and their understandings about its processes. The ideas that sustain the group are not always explicitly formulated.

TABLE I. THE COMPOSITION OF GROUPS

Elements Common to All Groups	Elements of Religious Groups	Elements of Educational Groups	Elements of Family Groups	Elements of Business Firm *	Elements of the State
1. Members	Congregation The Faithful	Teachers Students	Parents Children	Owners, Managers, Employees	Citizens, Subjects, Officials
a. How they join	Initiation Baptism Conversion	Appointment Admission	Marriage Birth Adoption	Purchase of shares Hiring for Job	Birth Naturalization Residence
b. How they leave	Non-attendance Excommunication	Retirement Resignation Graduation Expulsion	Desertion Death Divorce	Sale of shares Resignation Dismissal	Renunciation Deportation Deprivation of Citizenship
2. Functions †	Worship	Teaching Learning	Cohabitation Propagation	Manufacturing Sales	Protection Justice, Welfare
3. Institutions	Church, Temple, Mosque, Synagogue	School, College, University	The Home	Firm Corporation	The State
4. Rules	Canon Law, Ritual, Mosaic Law, Koran	Regulations Classroom discipline	Marriage Fidelity	Articles of Incorporation Shop rules, etc.	Law Custom
5. Governing Authority	Congregation Clergy	Teachers	Parents	Management Foremen	Government Officials
6. Revenue	Donations Tithes	Grants Fees	Income	Profits	Taxes, Loans, etc.
7. Ideas	Theology Creed	Pedagogy Curriculum	Monogamy Polygamy Polyandry	Property, Private Ownership, Contract, Competition	Political Theory

* The business firm is selected as an example of one type of economic grouping.
† The functions listed in the table are not intended to be complete and exhaustive. Those stated in each case are the central and primary ones not those that are secondary and derivative. All groups tend to acquire additional functions.

89

In certain cases they are inarticulate, and are divined rather than defined. Even if expressed, they may not always be systematized into a coherent philosophy. For example, the kinds of family systems are numerous and various, as are the kinds of political systems. But while political theories are many, theories of the family are relatively fewer. This does not mean, however, that the family group lacks its ideology. Nor, for that matter, can a religion exist without a theological creed for the hereafter and the herenow; a university, without an educational philosophy; or a business firm, without a theory of economic behavior.

The table on page 89 illustrates and summarizes the arguments of the foregoing paragraphs. In the left-hand column are listed the characteristics that groups of all kinds possess in common. In the remaining columns the general is applied to the particular. Thus the state can be seen to contain the same elements as other associations. But in the case of the state these elements differ by name and nature —which is exactly what makes the state a state.

The Physiology of Politics. It would now be possible to describe the state by taking each of these elements in turn, discussing its various features, then piecing the parts together and rebuilding a composite picture of the state as a whole. Useful though such an analysis would be, more is needed if the maximum of meaning is to be extracted from the study of politics. Here the science of medicine offers a guide. In the organization of medical knowledge it is customary to distinguish between anatomy and physiology. The former studies the body by minute dissection into its myriad parts, all of which are identified, described, and labelled. Anatomy tends to devote its main emphasis to the aspect of structure, and the understanding it imparts is about a subject matter considered primarily in static terms. Physiology, however, views the body as a living, articulated whole, moving through a cycle of birth, growth, maturity, decay, and death. Its chief concern is with the process by which the parts function in relation to each other and produce a condition of health or sickness. The emphasis is thus dynamic. Now it is plain that the two approaches, anatomical and physiological, are not completely exclusive. It is impossible for the anatomist to dissect a structure and discuss its parts, unless he also comments on their functions. It is equally impossible for the physiologist to describe a process without mentioning the parts that contribute to it. But what does make a difference is the placing of the emphasis and interest.

Without subscribing to the overworked organic theory of the state (whose excesses were criticized earlier),[11] a political scientist can observe that the analogy with medicine may contribute to an understanding of government. He may therefore choose between structure and process. While he takes both factors into account, which should he regard as more significant than the other? The response to this question can scarcely be in doubt. Both the statics of the state and the dynamics of politics must be considered, but above all else it is a process that the political scientist must study. Although the state is not a biological organism, it is nevertheless changing, active, and mobile. In this spirit its analysis must be conducted. Hence, a survey of the elements of the state should treat them as factors in the vital processes of politics. If so, a way must be found to interpret government physiologically. How can this be done? The answer is that all the elements of the state mentioned above— the members, functions, institutions, rules, governing authority, revenue, and ideas—can be regrouped around a series of basic political issues. To pursue further the parallel between medical and political science, if such elements resemble the state's anatomy, the issues explain its physiology. Thus, it becomes necessary to identify the issues so that politics may be examined in dynamic terms. What issues are these?

The Great Issues. The first concerns the members themselves. Because they are associated within the state, they must stand in some kind of relation to each other. What is that to be? Are all members placed on an equal footing? Or are some superior to the rest? The same question may be differently phrased. Is citizenship exclusive or all-inclusive? If the former, then members of the state are divided into two groups: one having rights of full citizenship, and the other treated less favorably as inferiors or subjects. If citizenship is all-inclusive, however, then everybody enjoys the same basic status without discrimination or limitation. The master principle is a regime of privilege in one case, of equality in the other.

The next issue arises from controversy over the functions that the

[11] See Chapter 2, pp. 28-30.

state performs for its members. Originating in the need for protection, the state has traditionally widened the sphere of its activities. The question is thus inevitably presented, whether there are, or are not, any limits to what the state can effectively, and should rightfully, undertake. On this point schools of philosophy, as well as practices of politics, have been opposed from times ancient to the present. Some have held that no social activity and no group can, or should, be exempt from the jurisdiction of the state. Others maintain that somewhere a boundary line must be set within which the state may freely move, but outside of which it trespasses on alien ground.

Both the third and fourth issues deal with the subject of authority. They are, however, occupied with different aspects of it. One is the problem of determining the origin or source from which authority is derived. This question has become acute because the state, in order to provide services to its citizens, has needed to acquire and exercise power. Since its powers are funnelled into the hands of the government, and since the officials who compose the latter are numerically fewer than the rest of the community, the relation of government to governed becomes a debatable issue. Those who govern, besides claiming authority, seek to justify their use of it; the governed may try to retain the ultimate control over political power. If the distribution of power within the state is conceived in terms of a pyramid,[12] the government can be likened to the apex, and the remainder of the people to the base. Authority can then be imagined either to stem from the base and travel upward to the apex, or to originate in the apex, like the goddess Athene in the ancient myth springing fully armed from the head of Zeus, and flow downwards to the base. Under the first view, the government would be controlled by, and responsible to, the people. Under the second, the people are subjects of those who govern and are duty-bound to obey their commands.

The query about its source, however, is not the only fundamental issue that the existence and establishment of authority evoke. No matter where authority originates—from the base of the pyramid or its apex—another issue concerns the manner in which authority, however derived, is subsequently organized. It is possible, on the one hand, to have power concentrated at a single focal point. Or power

---

[12] As Robert M. MacIver suggests in *The Web of Government* (New York: The Macmillan Co., 1947) chap. 5.

can be subdivided into powers that are dispersed and diffused. These can be parcelled out among separate branches of the government and distributed between different levels. Either the introduction of checks and balances or their removal may be sought, and the machinery of government will vary accordingly.

There remains as the fifth basic political issue the problem of magnitude—with regard both to the area that the state covers and to the population it contains, and the associated problem of relations between separate states. How large or small should be the unit of government? What is the optimum size for a state? Are there limits to its dimensions that the state should not exceed? How are independent states related? These are vexing questions in the cogitations of political theorists and the calculations of statecraft. Since the western world has already experimented with units as diverse as the city-state, nation-state, and empire-state, and continues to strive for new forms of international organization, it is evident that much can be learned from comparing governments of small, middle, large, and mammoth scale, and observing the patterns of interstate politics.

Analysis of the Great Issues. These issues, five in number, can be summarized as follows:

(1) The coverage of citizenship: Is it exclusive or all-inclusive?

(2) The functions of the state: Is the sphere of state activity limited or unlimited?

(3) The source of authority: Does this originate in the people or the government?

(4) The organization of authority: Is power concentrated or dispersed?

(5) The magnitude of the state and its external relations: What unit of government is preferable and operable? What interstate system exists?

Logically, each of the five is distinct from the rest. Each, moreover, can be analyzed alone because each is pivoted around a unique problem. The first issue deals with the reciprocal rights and duties of members of the state; the second, with the scope or ambit of governmental functions; the third, with the birthplace and legitimizing of authority; the fourth, with the mode of organizing power; and the last, with the size of territory and population. The significant feature in all these issues is that they present the opportunity to choose between at least two possibilities. This is in a sense self-evident, because it is the factor of choice that marks the essence of the problem. If there were no room to choose, there could be no issue. The breadth of the choice offered under the various issues can be envisaged in the form of this series of contrasts:

The First Issue is the choice between equality or inequality.

The Second Issue is the choice between a pluralist or monistic state.

The Third Issue is the choice between freedom or dictatorship.

The Fourth Issue is the choice between a dispersion of powers or their unification.

The Fifth Issue is the choice between a multitude of states or a universal state.

Thus described, the choice appears in every case to lie between two alternatives. In actuality, however, as will appear later, there are usually more than two possibilities, because several issues permit solutions at various intermediate stages between the opposite poles. Thus the functions undertaken by government can be more or less limited. Powers can be more or less dispersed. There may be more or less freedom, and so on.

Here, therefore, is a way to make the political process clear and intelligible. The key to its understanding is that five basic issues are involved, and that all five allow a choice. The types of government, and the consequent character of the state, vary with the respective decisions. Since there are so many issues, and at least two solutions for each, the permutations and combinations of political patterns are numerous indeed. It is this variety that constitutes the fascination and the challenge alike to those who practice the art of politics, and to those who systematize its study into a body of organized knowledge. No group of men can establish a government without being confronted by these five issues, nor can they avoid the necessity of including a decision about each in the pattern of the state they choose. Every kind of state embodies an institutionalized answer to the basic problems with which the five issues are concerned. A student of politics cannot find any governmental system of non-nomadic peoples in any place or at any period that does not provide its solution of these issues. Wherever the Great Issues are, there is found the political process. Wherever the political process is, there are the Great Issues. Such an analysis, moreover, has the merit of interpreting the processes of politics in terms of dynamic motion. For no solutions are ever fixed or final. All government has a touch of the experimental and the tentative. Men change their preferences. They oscillate from one pole to another. Ceaselessly they reconstruct the outer facade and inner floor plan of their state.

Synthesis of the Great Issues. Such changes are conditioned, however, by another fact. It was suggested above that each issue is unique and can be distinctly analyzed. In logic that is true. But in practice the issues are not entirely isolable and separate. Instead they are mutually connected and interacting. Nobody is able, therefore, to say precisely where one stops and another begins. Their edges are ragged, not sharp. Their contents somewhere merge together. Analysis of political complexities into five issues, each having its varying solutions, is an aid in simplification. Yet it would be over-simplification, and hence distortion, if politics were finally represented as an amalgam of five categories tacked on to each other. Perhaps the analogy of a watch will help to explain this. The dial of a watch is divided—quite arbitrarily—into twelve hours and sixty minutes. These partitions are necessary because they show us the time at a given moment. But time itself is a continuum. It is a ceaseless, unbroken, flow. And so it is with politics. When all analysis is finished, the need for resynthesis remains. As governments operate in reality, the five issues act upon and interact with each other, just as the minute hand moves simultaneously with the hour hand. Indeed, whatever choice is adopted under the heading of any issue in politics, it can scarcely fail to have some effect on decisions concerning the remainder. Thus a change anywhere tends to promote accompanying changes elsewhere. The history of politics, described in one sentence, consists in trying out alternative solutions for the basic issues in altered combinations.

It is in this light that the meaning of the term "politics" and its relation to the kindred concept of "the state" can best be viewed. The state is the institution in and through which men make up their minds on the five issues and choose between the possibilities available. But the process of selection, the nature of the decision, the reasons and reasoning that prompt it—all this is the material of politics. It is through politics that men formulate their preferences, determine the goals for which they strive, and appraise the values that they cherish or reject. Politics, so conceived, is wrapped up in all five issues, since each requires an act of choice, more or less conscious and deliberate. Hence the common etymology of the words "politics" and "policy" is no accident. If the latter implies a selective judgment about the merits of a social ideal or program of action, then assuredly politics consists in picking and charting a policy.

An analysis of governmental problems into five great issues can, if successfully conducted, yield the following advantages:

(1) It serves to break down complex relationships into simple components.

(2) It provides a dynamic understanding of government because it reveals the factors that undergo change and the area of choice within which the changes occur.

(3) It makes the political process meaningful by interpreting the actual forms and functions of the state in the light of valued ideals.

The next ten chapters will be devoted to discussion of the great issues.

CHAPTER 5

FIRST ISSUE:

(1) THE RULE OF PRIVILEGE

Citizens or Subjects. Since the state consists of members associated together, there must be some rule to determine who are to be recognized as members and how their membership is acquired. If membership produces opportunities for certain kinds of action, and expectations of certain kinds of treatment—or, what amount to the same, rights and responsibilities—these must be allotted according to principles, the choice of which endows a state with its special character. The politically inevitable division of society into government and governed raises a flock of queries about their mutual relations. What persons, for instance, should be picked to compose the government? Are all people fit and entitled to serve in that capacity? What rights do the governed possess? Should there be the same fundamental rights for everybody? Or is the community to be divided between first and second class citizens, between citizens and subjects? All such matters are variations upon a single theme. They involve an inquiry into the nature of citizenship and the relations between those who compose a state.

Aristotle's View of Citizenship. The first European thinker to reduce this concept to systematic analysis was Aristotle.[1] His formulation, therefore, because of its priority in time and the significance of his argument, is a suitable opening for discussion. "What makes a person a citizen?" is his initial question. He mentions, but rejects as inadequate, answers that define a citizen by residence in a certain

[1] *Politics*, bk. III, chaps. 1-5.

place or by birth of parents who are citizens. Residence is not a satisfactory explanation since aliens and slaves reside in a community, but are not its citizens. Nor is it helpful to derive citizenship from one's parents, since this will not explain how their citizenship was obtained. In any case, Aristotle makes plain that he seeks to explore citizenship in terms of functions rather than origins. At once, by shifting the emphasis to the functional side, he invests his answer with a dynamic quality. For when a citizen is characterized by performance, it is as an active doer that he is judged. What then is his function?

The reply subdivides into two parts. The citizen is "a man who shares in the administration of justice and the holding of office." [2] What Aristotle means is that citizens must be both subjects of authority and holders of it. They must serve in the twin roles of government and governed. They are to make the law, obey the law, and share the chores of enforcement. But to this doctrine, that a citizen is one who participates in ruling and being ruled, Aristotle attaches a corollary. Those so described must possess capacities that qualify them for playing both parts. The citizen cannot be merely an obedient subject. He should also be competent to rule. The latter requirement, however, is one that in Aristotle's view calls for special abilities of character and intellect not necessarily found in all people. He even classifies some human beings as "slaves by nature." He considers others, by reason of their occupations, incapable of leading a life of virtue. Consequently, as he insists on defining citizens functionally, his logic compels him to exclude those whose personal failings debar them from adequately performing the duties essential to citizenship. Hence the conclusion that "one need not class as citizens all those without whom there would be no city." [3] Citizens, in other words, form an exclusive group. They do not and should not embrace all members of the state. Such is the Aristotelian argument. Its main steps, briefly summarized, are contained in three assertions:

(1) A citizen is a person who performs certain functions.

(2) One such function is to participate actively in the exercise of authority.

(3) The number of persons competent to share in this is limited.

[2] *Ibid*. bk. III, chap. 1, secs. 5-6.
[3] *Ibid*. bk. III, chap. 5, sec. 2.

His chain of reasoning evidently depends on the connections between the three links. A break in the sequences must bring a breakdown in the consequences.

No matter whether one agrees or disagrees with Aristotle's analysis, admittedly it contains that merit which is characteristic of much in Greek philosophizing. Aristotle goes straight to the heart of the problem. He concentrates upon the issue that is fundamental. He asks the right question, irrespective of whether he supplies the right or wrong answer. That question may be variously phrased. Is membership in the state synonymous with citizenship? Is a common status to be given to all who are necessary to the state's existence? Is politics so different from other social activities that citizens ought to be a class separate from subjects? Let us consider more fully what is implied in these queries. For in the answers they receive everything is at stake.

The Argument for Inequality. Broadly speaking, one may distinguish between two contrasted answers. One line of reasoning proceeds from the assumption that government is an expert undertaking that requires a highly specialized technical competence and consequently demands of its practitioners more than ordinary qualities of character of mind. Government is not then considered an activity appropriate to the common run of men. Its "secrets of empire," in so far as these may be revealed, are variously pictured. Those who conceive of ruling as a skill that springs from intuitive imagination speak of government primarily in aesthetic terms. To them it is an art,[4] more or less fine. Others consider that politics is conducted according to a body of rules that are knowable and can be studied and learned. They therefore place it in the category of the rational and dub it a science. Still others, viewing human strivings in relation to a Supreme Being or superhuman forces operating in the universe, envelop their concept of politics with the aura of magic or theology. To them government is a mystery, indeed a fragment of the greater mystery of life. But, whether art, science, or mystery, government in any case is deemed the reserve or preserve of the chosen.

If these assumptions are accepted, certain conclusions flow natu-

[4] See Jacob Burckhardt, *The Civilization of the Renaissance in Italy* (New York: Oxford University Press, 1945), where Chapter 1 is entitled "The State as a Work of Art."

rally. It is evident, for example, that as soon as the process of government is viewed primarily from the standpoint of the expertise needed for its performance, only a minority of the population are likely to be judged as meeting the required standard. If such were not the case, the standard set and the skill prescribed would have little meaning. Thus the chosen turn out to be few in number, and government becomes—in the literal sense of the Greek word—an "oligarchy." [5]

In opposition to this view, however, it can be urged that while the task of ruling, namely the actual making of decisions and exercise of authority, is not a job for Tom, Dick, and Harry, nevertheless Tom, Dick, and Harry, are competent at least to judge and, if necessary, to criticize what their betters do. Should this be conceded, the chosen few must somehow be answerable to the vulgar many; and the way is open to argue that those who by definition are less wise and less worthy should nevertheless control their betters. In the long run this could imply the subordination of the few and their ultimate loss of caste. Those who shrink from such a conclusion resist the insertion of the wedge which cracks their logic. Not only do they argue that government must be conducted by experts, but they deny that the quality of their work can be appraised by anybody less skilled. Excluded from participation in ruling, the many cannot be allowed to judge their rulers. The chosen few are not merely the practitioners of politics. They are also the sole judges of their own handiwork.

This view, which may be called "hard-boiled," adopts many guises—some sophisticated, others crude. An example is this opinion of Thomas Carlyle: "Aristocracy and Priesthood, a governing class and a teaching class: these two, sometimes separate, and endeavoring to harmonize themselves, sometimes conjoining as one, and the King a Pontiff King:—there did no society exist without these two vital elements, there will none exist. It lies in the very nature of man. You will visit no remotest village in the most republican country of the world, where virtually or actually you do not find these two powers at work. Man, little as he may suppose it, is necessitated to obey superiors.—He obeys those whom he esteems better than himself, wiser, braver; and will forever obey such; and even be

---

[5] Oligarchy means rule (*arche*) by the few (*oligoi*).

ready and delighted to do it." [6] Next to this may be placed a statement of Hitler: "The parliamentary principle of decision by majority, by denying the authority of the person and placing in its stead the number of the crowd in question, sins against the aristocratic basic idea of nature." [7]

Arguments of this character are themselves founded upon a number of assumptions, which add up to a picture of human nature. Here is one of many examples of the connection between political science and psychology. It is impossible to theorize about politics without formulating ideas about human behavior, and such ideas must embrace a psychological doctrine. Common meeting ground for all doctrines of the chosen few is the position that mankind must be separated for political purposes into two groups. These are supposed to be distinguished by certain fundamental differences that are both qualitative (that is, superiors vis-à-vis inferiors) and quantitative (that is, the few vis-à-vis the many). Implied in this division is the belief that among the differences between human beings are some that are basic, and that should consequently weigh more heavily in politics than any over-all resemblances. Inequality thus becomes the cardinal principle on which the relations between members of the state are patterned. Their rights and duties are then apportioned, not uniformly, but according to their differences in status and function. The chosen few, who constitute the ruling circle, refer to their system of government as an aristocracy. [8] Seen from the other side, the same appears a regime of privilege.

A Classification of Elites. Any theory of aristocracy, or advocacy of government by an elite, must face two associated problems. It has first to justify the power that a few exercise over many, and explain why these few are the worthier to govern. Second, it must devise a means of separating lions from lambs. This requires some criterion of inclusion in the elite and exclusion therefrom. The two problems are closely connected because the success of any justification depends largely on the nature of the criterion adopted. In practice, types of aristocracy have been numerous for the reason that so many criteria have been used at one time or other, as a list will show. Here are the principles invoked to select the chosen few

[6] *Past and Present*, bk. IV, chap. I, on "Aristocracies."
[7] *Mein Kampf* (New York: Reynal and Hitchcock, 1939), p. 103.
[8] Literally, "rule by the best."

and reject the inferior masses: race, ancestry, age, sex, religion, military strength, culture, wealth, and knowledge. This classification of types of aristocracy can be represented pictorially in a chart such as appears below.

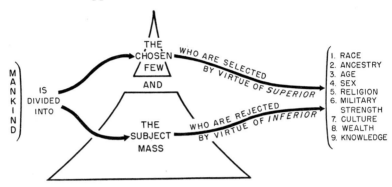

So that misunderstanding may be avoided, two comments on the classification should be added. These nine criteria, though distinguishable, are not in all cases mutually exclusive. On the contrary, most elites known to history have exhibited two or more of these criteria in combination. For example, those of reputedly superior ancestry may also be the wealthiest; or a self-styled superior religion may be that of a conquering people who excel in military strength. Actual elites may thus turn out on examination to be mixed kinds, and not simple. Further, it should be noticed that, while these nine criteria and their permutations differ, all have an essential feature in common. However they may vary on other matters, they invariably glorify inequality. To this principle all doctrines of aristocracy, or "lions and lambs" formulae, are inexorably committed. With those reminders, let us now explore each of the nine criteria as postulated in theory and applied in practice.

The Myth of Racial Superiority. One way to distinguish between individual human beings is to classify them into the racial groups of which mankind as a whole are composed. If this be tried, and if the distinctions are to be valid, the term "race" should be defined with exactitude, so that in distinguishing one race from another everybody may know what is being described. Unfortunately the word has often been employed with a looseness and imprecision— sometimes innocent, sometimes deliberately misleading—that impair its usefulness for scientific discussion. In writings, as in daily speech, examples abound of references to "the human race," "the Negro race," "the British race," "the Jewish race," "the White race," "the Indian race," and so on. It is evident that not all these usages are correct since some include, contradict, or overlap with others. What sense can be made, for instance, of the term "British race"? If pigment be the test, then the British belong to a wider grouping of people with white skins. If the test be religion, then the British, who are overwhelmingly Christian and predominantly Protestant, can hardly be separated from other Protestant Christians. If it be language, the use of English in the British Isles (where there are many dialects and accents) does not mark off its inhabitants from the English-speaking people of the United States. If, however, the determinant be political, and "the British race" refers to a group that shares a common historical tradition and lives under the same government, at least the meaning becomes clearer—but then some other term, possibly "nation," had better be substituted.

Race can receive only one connotation that is clear, and it will be used here in that sense alone. An anthropologist calls it "a principal division of mankind, marked by physical characteristics which breed true. In this sense," he points out, "the word race is a biological term, and is restricted to the bodily characteristics that distinguish one group of human beings from another." [9] Thus defined, one may properly apply the word to Caucasians, Mongolians, or Negroes, and to subdivisions of these main stocks; and one can proceed objectively to discover and describe the physical traits peculiar to each. When all facts of this sort are collected and classified, what is revealed? That there are differences. Yes, but how should these be interpreted, and what is their social relevance? Admitting that differences do exist, can anybody assert that one kind is superior to another? This is not possible except on one condition, namely that certain traits are demonstrably related to the better performance of certain functions. Take the human nose, for example. The purpose of a nose is to smell. So, if it can be shown that broader or longer nostrils are definitely correlated with a keener power of scent, then the wider or lengthier nose is manifestly superior.

[9] Melville J. Herskovits, *Man and His Works* (New York: Alfred A. Knopf, 1948), p. 133.

But can the argument about the part be transferred to the whole? On the analogy of noses, this would be possible if men, by virtue of being human, could be shown to have a function that certain racial stocks are better equipped to perform than others. In that case —and only then—would it be arguable that a particular race is superior or supreme, a doctrine which reaches its climax in the assertions that the inferiors are not really human but sub-human, or that the master-race is made up of supermen (*Uebermenschen*). This is exactly the reasoning of so eminent a philosopher as Aristotle when he justified the institution of slavery. According to him, a man's goal or end (*telos*) is to maintain happiness by leading a life of virtue under the governance of reason. Since it is reason that makes virtue possible, and virtue that makes happiness possible, anybody insufficiently endowed with reason can be neither virtuous nor happy, unless he is placed under the control of someone who is so endowed. In this way, both master and slave would benefit. The former, who needs to own property in order to develop his potentialities, possesses the slave as "an animate tool." [10] The latter lives the life that is best for him by obeying the dictates of his superior in wisdom.[11] Slavery is therefore a natural institution, because it is rooted in and conforms to physiological and psychological differences in human nature. The entire argument is one that flows logically from premises to conclusion, provided that its major assumptions be accepted. These are: (1) that man, as man, has a definable function; (2) that happiness, virtue, and reason are understood in the Aristotelian sense; and (3) that differences between individuals, inherited at birth, are too great to be modified by learning afterwards.

The argument is not of interest, however, only as a theoretical exercise in logic. Its political importance lies in the efforts made to apply such principles in practice, or rather in the attempts of those who practice discrimination anyway to borrow from Aristotle the color of justification and respectability. While virtually every historical period, continent, and civilization yields its harvest of examples, some of the most significant may be gleaned from the nineteenth and twentieth centuries. The enslavement of human beings was permitted by law in the British Empire until 1833; in the

[10] *Politics*, bk. I, chap. 4, sec. 2.
[11] *Ibid.*, chap. 5, sec. 9.

United States until 1863; in Russia, where it assumed the form of serfdom, until 1861; in Brazil until 1888. In the decade or so before the American Civil War, the South's defense of its "peculiar institution" was often couched in Aristotelian terms that confidently asserted the permanent inferiority of one human group to another. At the close of the nineteenth and beginning of the twentieth centuries, when colored peoples stirred restlessly in resentment at the imposition of alien white rule, there were European and American writers who reaffirmed a belief in racial differences and their own preordained supremacy. Such was the spirit of Rudyard Kipling's ballad *The White Man's Burden,* or his *England's Answer* where he wrote:

Truly ye come of The Blood; slower to bless than to ban;
Little used to lie down at the bidding of any man. . . .
Thus for the good of your people—thus for the Pride of the Race.[12]

A similar attitude inspired the Frenchman, De Gobineau, and two American writers, Madison Grant and Lothrop Stoddard.

But it is a twentieth century German who sought and has rightfully earned the dubious credit of formulating the doctrine in its starkest manner and applying it with most systematic thoroughness. Before seizing power, Adolph Hitler, dictator over the Germans from January 1933 to April 1945, had expressed this philosophy in *Mein Kampf:*

> Any crossing between two beings of not quite the same high standard produces a medium between the standards of the parents. . . . But such a mating contradicts Nature's will to breed life toward a higher level. The presumption for this does not lie in blending the superior with the inferior, but rather in a complete victory of the former. The stronger has to rule and he is not to amalgamate with the weaker one, that he may not sacrifice his own greatness. . . . Just as little as Nature desires a mating between weaker individuals and stronger ones, far less she desires the mixture of a higher race with a lower one, as in this case her entire work of higher breeding, which has perhaps taken hundreds of thousands of years, would tumble at one blow. . . . What we see before us of human culture today, the results of art, science and techniques, is almost exclusively the creative produce of the Aryan. . . . For the formation of higher cultures, the existence of inferior men was one of the most essential presumptions because they alone were able to replace the lack of technical means

12 From *The Seven Seas* by Rudyard Kipling. Reprinted by permission of Mrs. George Bambridge and Doubleday and Company, Inc.

without which a higher development is unthinkable. The first culture of mankind certainly depended less on the tamed animal, but rather on the use of inferior people.[13]

For more than a decade, while the National Socialists ruled Germany, these beliefs were promulgated as the official policy of the government of a major European state. In their name were enacted the so-called "Nurenberg laws," prescribing the conditions of citizenship and proscribing all marriages between those of "superior" and "inferior" blood. In their name were committed atrocities against people of the Jewish religion that resulted in the mass extermination of six million Jews. In their name the German government prepared and unleashed a war for the domination of Europe where millions of Europeans and Americans perished.

The sin of racial arrogance is no monopoly of whites. Each race, it seems, fashions its idea of excellence after its own kind. There have been Chinese and Japanese spokesmen who have pronounced that yellow-skinned people are racially superior to others. Similar notions have not been lacking among the redskins. The western poet [14] who wrote so condescendingly about "the poor Indian" and his "untutored mind" would have been astonished to learn that some Indians at least believed the boot to be on the other foot. Among the Cherokees, whose knowledge of mankind extended to Europeans and Negroes, this delightful myth is related about the origin of races. The Great Spirit created Man out of dough, modeling three figures that he put in an oven. Overanxious to see the results, he opened the door and took out the first figure too soon. It was whitish, half-baked, unattractive. But the act was irrevocable, and a white race descended from this sorry specimen. Next he drew out his masterpiece, a figure perfectly cooked to a rich reddish-brown, which of course became the progenitor of the redskins. So proudly did he admire his handiwork that he forgot all about number three, until alas! he smelled something burning. Too late, he removed it from the oven, a blackened cinder—ancestor of the Negroes.[15]

[13] *Mein Kampf*, pp. 390, 392, 397, 404, 405.
[14] Alexander Pope, in the *Essay on Man*.
[15] The story, cited in Herskovits' *Man and his Works*, pp. 68-69, was reported by a Belgian anthropologist. The identical theme has also been found among the brown-skinned Malayans.

The Aristotelian assertion that by nature some men are masters and others are slaves lends itself too readily to the Nazi perversion: "All that is not race in this world is trash." [16] This statement of Hitler, which incidentally is a good example of his own advocacy of the "big lie," is itself pure trash and is refuted by much evidence.

The Cult of Ancestors. The doctrine that human beings are to be divided into superiors and inferiors by virtue of inborn physical and psychological differences may take another form. The emphasis can be placed on the family, rather than the race to which a human being belongs. In other words, the line of division between human beings is still surveyed in terms of hereditary factors that are transmitted at birth and are not supposedly acquired or modified afterwards; but the smaller family group is substituted for the larger one of race. According to this way of thinking it is a person's lineage or pedigree that counts. His ancestors' merits rather than his own may secure him, without effort on his part, a lofty position in the social order; or may relegate him, possibly contrary to his abilities, to a lowly status. [17] The lions and lambs become the well-born and ill-born, the upper class and lower, the aristocrats and masses.

When an elite is constituted on this basis, one must distinguish between its central feature and the attendant consequences. The central fact is the perpetuation of an aristocracy over successive generations by the hereditary principle. A group of families recognize each other, and are respected by the rest, as members of a charmed circle. In any one generation the odds are heavily against the demotion of any of these families or the admission of a new one. At the outset, of course, and before its hereditary character becomes fixed, such a system must originate in some alternative scheme of differentiation. The families that eventually emerge as superior may have succeeded earlier in accumulating greater wealth or conducting a military conquest. Thus they win an initial position of privilege that they pass on by inheritance. Furthermore the

---

[16] *Mein Kampf*, p. 406.

[17] See Chapter 6, pp. 144-5. The connection between the concepts of aristocracy and lineage is revealed in the Spanish word *hidalgo*, and the corresponding Portuguese *fidalgo*, meaning a "nobleman." The former is an abbreviation of *hijo de algo*; the latter of *filho de algo*. Both expressions mean "son of a Somebody."

members of a family that belongs to the charmed circle can accumulate possessions through social influence, just as they may enhance their personal abilities because of their opportunities and experience. In judging the merits of a hereditary aristocracy, however, one is not primarily concerned with their wealth, their powers, their polish, or their knowledge of affairs, since these factors are either the cause or the consequence of the point that is really in issue: the acceptance of kinship as the determinant of a social classification.

The basic assumption of such an aristocracy is the belief that planned, selective, breeding among human beings can produce characteristics that parents will transmit to their offspring, so that a "higher" type may be evolved and preserved. Whether this view be true or false only the specialist in genetics can venture to assert. The student of politics, however, can observe that no actual aristocracy has ever conformed to this ideal. Indeed, if experience warrants any hypothesis, it can just as well support a contrary generalization. The aristocracies that have survived the longest were those which, like the Roman and the British, were willing to accept periodic or continuous infusion of new stock; while from excessive inbreeding once famous lines, like the Hapsburgs or Bourbons, have run to seed. But, quite apart from genetic difficulties, the hereditary principle involves social consequences that are open to major objections. One of these is its rigid application to circumstances that are highly variable. For the principle ignores the fact that no one stratum of society has a monopoly of great ability and that its reproduction in successive generations cannot be guaranteed. A second obnoxious feature is its system of ancestor worship, which classifies the living, not for what they are, but for what their forefathers were. Too often has the luster of a noble house conferred an inflated valuation upon an ignoble scion. Too often have the talents of those less fortunately born been denied creative outlets. To base distinctions upon heredity is to predetermine the lives of all by a criterion in no way related to their personal efforts or exertions. One's parentage cannot be chosen, altered, escaped, or denied.

Be this as it may, examples of the hereditary elite may be found in almost all periods of history and all parts of the world. The Homeric poems, which present in blended fact and fiction one of

our earliest literary pictures of a European society, relate the deeds of
a cluster of eminent families acknowledged in war and peace as the
leaders of the Hellenic World. Their prerogatives come to them
by right of birth, and, since their lineage is illustrious, they may be
addressed by their own name (for example, Achilles, Agamemnon,
Odysseus) or by the patronymic (for example, Son of Peleus, Son
of Atreus, Son of Laertes).[18] The same status that creates their
rights demands connected duties. Chieftains are under obligation to
be champions of the army and fight in the front line. They receive
the greater rewards of an exalted position, but run the greater risks.
And what of the rank and file? They are the ever-present background, but nameless and nondescript. If individualized at all, they
appear in the favorable role of the faithful and humble servant
(for example, the swineherd Eumaeus, who stays loyal to his master,
Odysseus). Only once does Homer portray them in protest, and
in that single instance the poet, whose epics were composed to
glorify heroes and to be chanted in princely palaces, offers an
unflattering characterization. Thersites, criticizing Agamemnon in
the council of the chiefs, voices the first revolt of the underdog in
occidental writing. For this the poet has him thrashed by Odysseus
while the onlookers laugh.[19]

In subsequent centuries, for which more exact information is
available, the same pattern recurs of a ruling aristocracy that faces
an acquiescent or at times rebellious populace. Athens was controlled
until the seventh century B.C. by an oligarchy of families known
as the Eupatridae ("of good parentage"), and most of the other
Greek city-states never evolved beyond this to the more equalitarian
society and politics that appear in the Athens of the fifth and fourth
centuries. In the Roman Republic the most momentous domestic
controversy of the fifth, fourth, and third centuries B.C. was the
famous Struggle of the Orders that has enshrined the names of the
patricians and plebeians in our everyday vocabulary. The gulf
between the two consisted of differences in social status, civil

---

[18] All of these are kings (*basileis*). But kingship has degrees, and some chiefs
are kinglier than others (*basileuteroi*) and Agamemnon is kingliest of all
(*basileutatos*).

[19] Homer, *Iliad*, bk. II, ll. 211 ff. Similarly unsympathetic portrayals of spokesmen for the under-privileged are the pictures of Cleon (the fifth-century
Athenian) by Aristophanes and Thucydides, and that of Jack Cade in Shakespeare's *Henry VI*.

rights, religious ceremonial, and political power. The aim of the plebeians was to abolish privileges in which they did not share and to win equality. But, even when this was achieved, the grant to the plebeians of substantial equality with the patricians reformulated, rather than terminated, the domination of Rome by an aristocracy. What happened was that certain plebeian families were admitted to the clique of dominant clans, who monopolized for themselves and passed around among their own number the principal offices (*honores*) of the Roman republic. Once anybody was elected to a major office, he and his family became ennobled (*nobilis*). Within the nobility so constituted, families were scaled in importance by the number of such office holders they had produced and were conventionally ranked as praetorian, consular, or censorian according to whether the highest office reached by one of their members was that of *praetor, consul,* or *censor.* Thus by the second century B.C. the odds were as strongly in favor of a Marcellus, Claudius, Julius, or Metellus, to secure the office he desired, as they were against a "new man" (*novus homo*) from a family outside the *nobilitas.* Cicero, the orator without equal in Rome, relates with complacent pride that he was the first new man for a long time to break through the barriers of the nobility and obtain a consulate.

Whatever variation there may be in detail, the common feature in this type of political organization is the division of the population into two classes. One is composed of relatively few members, the other contains the great majority, and the former dominates the latter. Membership in each class is hereditary. Only rarely does movement occur upward into the preferred class or downward into the lower. A simple division of society, however, into two levels is in many instances an oversimplification. A cross section of certain communities would show three strata and sometimes more. Indeed, it is possible for the entire community to be organized on the familiar military pattern with a ladder or scale of ranks on which people are assigned their respective places in a hierarchy. A famous example of this is the system that evolved in western Europe after the strife and turmoil following the dissolution of the Roman Empire, namely, feudalism. Its essential feature was to erect a fabric of personal relationships on the basis of land ownership and tenure. The relations of men to land governed the relations of men to men. A man received land as a fief from another, to whom on his knees he swore an oath of fealty. The two thus became lord and vassal; and while it was the responsibility of the lord to protect his vassal, it was the latter's duty to serve the former. This system of horizontal stratification was applied to both the spheres, temporal and ecclesiastical, into which medieval Christendom was split. But though government was hierarchical in State and Church alike, the elite that controlled the latter was prevented from being hereditary by the requirement of celibacy. A social order so built on hierarchical principles, and extended to cover the universe, is described by Shakespeare in an eloquent speech of Ulysses in *Troilus and Cressida.*[20] The same conception is philosophically defended in the essay of a late-Victorian British ethicist A. C. Bradley, who wrote approvingly on the theme: "My Station and Its Duties." [21]

Submission to the Elders. Along with race and ancestry, two further methods for differentiating between human beings and assigning them a superior or inferior political status may be mentioned. These are, respectively, age and sex. The idea that the right to govern is a prerogative of age has underlain the practice of many communities. It is of course associated with the belief that ruling is an art involving a high degree of judgment; that judgment in practical matters is largely acquired by experience; and that older persons necessarily possess an experience that is longer, riper, and therefore more trustworthy. In addition, a system that entrusts government to the aged because of their age is normally built upon a social base that attaches great importance to the family and, within the family, stresses the authority of the father. The rule of the Elders is patriarchy writ large.

Examples are not lacking of political institutions whose *raison d'être* was to embody the authority of age. Such a system in a very primitive community is thus described by J. G. Frazer:

Let us begin by looking at the lowest race of men as to whom we possess comparatively full and accurate information, the aborigines of Australia. These savages are ruled neither by chiefs nor kings. So far as their tribes can be said to have a political constitution, it is a democracy or rather an oligarchy of old and influential men, who meet in council and decide on all measures of importance to the practical exclusion of the younger men. Their deliberative assembly

[20] Act i, Sc. 3, ll. 75 ff.
[21] *Ethical Studies* (1876).

answers to the senate of later times: if we had to coin a word for such government of elders we might call it a *gerontocracy*. The elders who in aboriginal Australia thus meet and direct the affairs of their tribe appear to be for the most part the headmen of their respective totem clans.[22]

But the authority of age is by no means confined to primitive forms of society. In the governmental machinery of Sparta there was a powerful body called the Gerousia, or Council of Old Men, membership in which commenced at the age of sixty. A more celebrated instance is the Roman Senate, a word that means in Latin exactly what Gerousia does in Greek. Composed of past and present holders of the higher offices in the Republic, this body for over four centuries was the nuclear force in the government of Rome. Likewise, the institutions of the Anglo-Saxon tribes distinguished between the Folkmoot, or meeting of male citizens, and the influential Witanagemot, or council of wise men who were the tribal elders. Modern Japan under its Meiji Constitution (adopted 1889) developed a similar council of elders, called the *Genro*. To it belonged the senior statesmen who had twice held the office of Premier. The Genro acted informally as a consultative body to which the Emperor might turn for advice on the formation of a new government, or on issues of high policy.

The Unfair Sex. More common however, than distinctions based upon age have been those derived from sex. Although anthropological research has established the existence of numerous matriarchal societies, patriarchy is the more usual mode of family organization. Politics, similarly, have normally been a function or monopoly of the menfolk. This was most probably due to the primary connection between government and defense, which endows the able-bodied male with importance. But it is also to be explained in terms of the specialization that assigned child-rearing and domestic matters to the female and took the male out of the house as the hunter, farmer, or breadwinner. For over two thousand years the traditional forms of western society excluded women from active participation in government, save when the operation of the hereditary principle conferred a crown upon one who reigned as queen in her own

---

[22] *The Golden Bough*, Part I, vol. I (New York: Macmillan Co., 1919-35), p. 335, 3rd. ed. Italics in original. Gerontocracy means government by the aged.

right (as Elizabeth of England or Catherine of Russia). Not until the twentieth century did the fair sex succeed in challenging the monopoly of government by the unfair.

Systems that discriminate against half the population, or more, on such grounds as age or sex, are open to the same objection as systems based on heredity. They classify entire groups as politically adequate or inadequate in a wholly arbitrary manner, since they assume a connection between fitness for government and some other circumstance that may prove completely irrelevant. Of course, it can be true that older persons, with more knowledge of the ways of the world, may be more competent to run the state. Likewise, because in most societies the menfolk have traditionally done most of the work outside the home, they have acquired an experience denied to women. But this does not mean that age is synonymous with political wisdom, or that any male is fit to govern. Still less can it be argued that persons whose ages are between twenty and forty-five have nothing useful to contribute to government in the way of ideas or energy. If so, how should we explain the achievements of Alexander the Great or Thomas Jefferson, Alexander Hamilton or the younger Pitt? [23] Correspondingly, the belief that no woman has a talent for politics is a gratuitous and false presumption. Who, for instance, could argue thus about Queen Elizabeth I of England or Catherine the Great of Russia? What makes for capacity in government is the merit of the individual concerned, whether young or old, man or woman, as developed by the opportunities that society affords to gain experience.

The principles examined so far are race, ancestry, age, and sex. These have been discussed first because they differ from the remainder of the list and can be appropriately grouped. The feature in which race, ancestry, age, and sex resemble each other is that all four lie beyond our control. We cannot choose our race, our ancestry, our age, or our sex; and though one's age, unlike the other three, does alter during a lifetime, the process of growing old and

[23] Alexander of Macedon, born in 356 B.C., became king at the age of 20. When he died in 323 B.C., he was master of the region from Greece to the north-west portion of India. Thomas Jefferson, born in 1743, was 33 years old when he wrote the Declaration of Independence. Alexander Hamilton, born in 1757, was 30 at the time of his contributions to the convention that drafted the United States Constitution. William Pitt the younger, born in 1759, was only 24 when George III first appointed him as Prime Minister in 1783.

the rate of change lie beyond our power. A community is free to decide whether it will distinguish politically between a few superior members and an inferior majority. If it does so, it is also free to decide whether to select one of these four principles as the criterion of division. But once such a choice is taken and any of these criteria is adopted, an individual has no say about the place to which he or she is assigned and no means of influencing the assignment. The application of the rule to particular cases cannot be modified, still less overruled, by the efforts of the person concerned or the discretion of others.

In the classification of elites presented earlier in this chapter, nine types were listed. Those not yet considered are religion, military strength, culture, wealth, and knowledge. These five differ from the preceding four in that a community that selects its ruling elite by any of these criteria may conceivably permit its members to join the charmed circle by their own volition and exertions.

The Dominance of a Religion. Religion must be considered in this connection, not for the theology or faith it adopts (that is beyond the scope of this book), but for the reason that religious movements become organized in institutions that have social consequences for human beings in this life. Many, indeed, are the instances where religion has sanctified a separation into upper and lower castes, though whether religion was the originating cause of such practices in every case is not always clear. Sometimes it would seem that religious doctrines have been responsible for introducing a stratification and rigidifying the strata with the cement of divine sanction. One illustration is the effect upon Vedic India of the invasion of Aryans from the west who brought to a darker-skinned people the creed of Brahmanism and Hinduism.[24] Under its impact, Indian society was grouped into the four classes of Brahman, Kshatriya, Daishya, and Sudra—a hierarchy in descending order of priests, rulers, artisans, and slave-laborers. These became the hereditary castes which prescribed an individual's occupation as well as his social status. The fourfold grading was based upon an authoritative text of the Hindu scriptures, the Rigveda.[25]

At other times, religions whose creeds were fundamentally equali-

[24] The word "Hindu" is not indigenously Indian, but came in from Iran with the invaders. It is a variant of the Iranian river-name "Sindhu."
[25] *Rigveda*, bk. X, Hymn 90, verse 12.

tarian have condoned and conformed to pre-existing social cleavages that they have helped to reinforce and justify. A case in point is the spread of Christianity. The spirit of the Christian religion in its pure form consists in emphasizing equality,[26] since affairs of the soul are held to be more important than those of the body and all souls are deemed equally worthy in the eyes of God. But when the Emperor Constantine embraced Christianity as the official religion of the Roman Empire, the Church accepted—for this world—the existence of a hierarchical society including the institution of slavery. Similarly the medieval Church tolerated the system of serfdom. As R. H. Tawney has written:

> The canon law appears to have recognized and enforced serfdom. Few prominent ecclesiastics made any pronouncement against it. Aquinas explains it as the result of sin, but that does not prevent his justifying it on economic grounds. Almost all medieval writers appear to assume it or excuse it. Ecclesiastical landlords, though perhaps somewhat more conservative in their methods, seem as a whole to have been neither better nor worse than other landlords. . . . The disappearance of serfdom . . . was part of a general economic movement, with which the Church had little to do, and which churchmen, as property-owners, had sometimes resisted. It owed less to Christianity than to the humanitarian liberalism of the French Revolution.[27]

Correspondingly, the catechism of the Church of England in the eighteenth century gave its blessing to the division of society into classes; serfdom was fully sanctioned by the Russian Orthodox Church; slavery was defended by the southern branches of some American Churches in the 1840's and 50's, as it was also approved in South Africa by the Dutch Reformed Church.

There are other ways in which religion may lend itself to the political stratification of humanity. Sometimes the group who controls the government is closely identified with an ecclesiastical organization which maintains that it alone has the true faith, and that non-believers, or infidels, cannot commune on terms of equality with the faithful. Those who profess an alternative faith may then find themselves relegated to a position of political inferiority and be denied equality of rights. Thus, in Britain the Protestant Non-

---

[26] See Chapter 6, pp. 131-2.
[27] *Religion and the Rise of Capitalism* (New York: Harcourt Brace, 1926), chap. I, "The Medieval Background," sec. iii, "The Ideal and the Reality."

Conformists who dissented from the Church of England were so treated from 1689 to 1828, as were Catholics until 1829. In other countries Catholics have meted out similar treatment to Protestants by imposing disabilities, or inflicting persecution, on those regarded as heretics. Jews, even when not subject to pogroms and inquisitions, were normally denied equality of status in Christian countries until the nineteenth century.

A further example of the connection between religion and the rule of an elite is the form of government known as theocracy.[28] There have been peoples who deified their rulers or ascribed to them some attributes of divinity. Until 1946 the Emperors of Japan claimed to be descended from the Sun-God. Homeric Kings traced their lineage back to Zeus the Thunderer, King of the Gods. Those of the Roman Emperors who did not arouse the ire of their subjects were customarily worshipped (at least in the eastern half of the Empire) while alive, and after death were officially deified with the title *Divus* and placed on the ceremonial roster of gods to whom prayer was due.[29] The Dalai Lama who until 1950 reigned over Tibet from Lhassa was regarded by his subjects as a living reincarnation of the Buddha. Alternatively, while the human character of the ruler may be recognized, he may be considered a prophet or priest acting on behalf of the Deity, ruling by his authority and thus mediating between God and man. In that sense, the people of Israel, when governed by Eli or Samuel, were a theocratic state. Their formal transition from theocracy to secular government is described in the Book of Samuel.[30] Other such theocracies were the city of Geneva when under the control of Calvin; or the Papal States in Italy before 1860; or the Vatican since 1929.

Control by Conquest. Government by physical might is apparently in sharp contrast with government by divine right. Yet for purposes of our present classification, they belong to the same category since both have the result of separating humanity into a superior and an inferior group. Because of the intimate bond between the need for protection and the origin of government, prowess in war has frequently served as a basis for inclusion in the favored

[28] Literally: government by a god, or gods.
[29] Hence the famous saying of the Emperor Vespasian on his death-bed: *Ut puto, divus fio.* ("I suppose I'm becoming a God.")
[30] I Sam. 8.

few.[31] A community that exists in constant fear or suspicion of
hostile neighbors, and that inhabits an area where terrain and topography offer no natural barriers for defense, is likely to place a
premium on fighting ability. Whoever excels in the military art will
be accorded privileges by those who need his services and can exact
obedience from them. No dividing line is then drawn between the
military and civil sectors of government. Or rather, it is the
military that absorbs and embraces the civil. Service in the armed
forces then becomes not merely a vocation or career, but a high-
road to social influence and political power.

The warrior elite, however, while it responds to the group's need
for protection, is liable to the defect that is the corruption of its
virtues. For dominance of the military can degenerate into the
excesses of militarism. The history of Prussia yields a classic illustration of this danger. Living in an exposed position in the center of
the north European plain, with no obvious defensive frontier to
west or east, the Prussians have traditionally thrust outward or been
hemmed inward according to the relation of their striking power
to that of their French and Slavic neighbors. By tight organization
and by building an efficient army, they contrived to be secure
until the army, instrument of their might, took the bit between its
teeth and plunged through wars of aggression to its own and its
people's destruction.

While it is the need for protection that brings a community to
accept the authority of military experts, in yet another way the
practice of warfare results in differentiation between human beings.
The victors may follow up their conquest by imposing their rule
upon the vanquished. Thus the militarily weak are subordinated to
the strong; and the strong, if they seek to maintain their rule, must
preserve their military power.[32] A notorious example is provided
by the ancient Greek state of Sparta. The people whose discipline
has become a byword were trained under the regimen, and lived
according to the pattern, of an army barracks. Their fighting qualities, of almost legendary renown in the Greek world, were dis-

[31] See the characterization of the Condottieri as state-builders in fifteenth
century Italy by Jacob Burckhardt, *The Civilization of the Renaissance in
Italy* in Chapter 1, "The State as a Work of Art."

[32] This is a further illustration of the point discussed in Chapter 3, pp. 62 ff.
that the force which is required for protection may be perverted by abuse.
Internally, that takes the form of despotism; externally, of aggressive conquest.

played at their finest in the heroism of Leonidas and the Four Hundred, holding the narrow pass at Thermopylae in defiance of the invading Persian multitude. But what is significant about the Spartans is that they employed in their domestic affairs the kind of organization appropriate to an army in the field. The reason was that they never lived entirely at peace, but always in a condition of suspended or expectant warfare. The Spartans had migrated into Greece later than many other Greeks and made their home in the Peloponnese when it was already occupied. They took their "living-space" by force, and reduced the earlier inhabitants, Messenians by name, to the level of serfs, or *Helots*.[33] From that time, under the compulsion of their own policy and in fear of their subjects who outnumbered them, the Spartans were condemned to militarize their mode of life and stay permanently on guard against uprisings. They adjudged proper all means to this end. The government maintained a secret organization (*Krupteia*), the equivalent of a Gestapo, whose duty it was to forestall revolt. On one occasion during the Peloponnesian War the *Krupteia* was responsible for the sudden rounding up and slaughtering at night of several hundred *Helots*. Such methods were incapable of doing more than prolonging a static despotism, where the master-people eventually succumbed to internal dry-rot. By contrast, the most successful empires of history are those like the Roman and the British which, though founded in large part by force, subsequently developed the policy of elevating subjects to partners, and which, at least in the case of Britain, upheld at home the supremacy of civilians over the military.

The Claims of Cultural Leadership. Military conquest may be accomplished by one people at the expense of another who differ from them in culture as well as in fighting capacity. In this case the conquerors may assert their right to rule the conquered by virtue of their cultural, as distinct from their military, superiority. Used in this context the term "culture" requires some explaining. It is perhaps best understood in contrast to the term "race" with which it is too frequently, and quite erroneously, confused. Race,[34] properly defined, describes those human traits, both physical and psychic, which are inborn and derive from heredity, while culture refers to

[33] From a word meaning "captive."
[34] See p. 103 above.

other characteristics acquired by learning after birth and representing the influence upon the individual of his environment. To anthropologists and sociologists, culture means the whole way of life of a person or group. To them it is the broadest possible of categories, embracing all aspects of social organization—political, economic, religious, and the rest. A political scientist, however, may be content with a less inclusive formula. For him, "culture" can be defined to exclude politics, economics, and religion, which are more conveniently treated as distinct categories. Everything else, that is, the social remainder, is culture.

What is there in this remainder that is politically relevant? Probably the element in culture that is closest to politics is language. Anything can produce an effect on government that serves to bind people together in a group and dissociate them from other groups, and this assuredly is what language does. Among literate peoples, furthermore, language is a medium for transmitting and communicating the shared experiences of the group. A people's literature is a deposit of their history, and writers (no less than statesmen, soldiers, prophets, and inventors) can be venerated as heroes, as is Shakespeare by Englishmen, Dante by Italians, Cervantes by Spaniards, Goethe by Germans, or Pushkin by Russians. Nevertheless, it is common enough for an alien ruling group to base its right to govern upon the assumed superiority of its culture. Thus did the British rulers of India argue throughout the nineteenth century about their Asiatic subjects. Thus did Manchus behave towards Chinese. Thus did Spanish *conquistadores* regard the Aztecs and Incas. Thus were pre-1918 Austrians disposed to the Slavic inhabitants of their Empire. The paths of empire-builders are strewn with the results of vaunted cultural pre-eminence.[35]

Money Power. If it is not leadership in culture that distinguishes the lions from the lambs, the leadership may come from wealth. In this case, the criterion by which human beings are differentiated is economic. People are classified as better or worse by reason of their possessions and according to the index of riches that is in vogue within a given society. That index can be land, livestock, gold, precious stones, slaves, shares or bonds—anything, in fact,

[35] For a further discussion of the relation between culture and nationhood, see Chapter 12, pp. 343-5, 348-9 ff.

that is conventionally accepted. Whoever succeeds in accumulating a large amount of these is assured of admission to the charmed circle. Whoever has too little to qualify, or owns nothing, is assigned an inferior status and excluded from participation in political functions. The name for this type of state is plutocracy, the Greek for "government by wealth." [36] On what theory is the ownership of riches regarded as justifying a right to rule? This question has been variously answered. Sometimes it is argued that possessions constitute "a stake in the country"—with the implied corollary that the more one owns, the greater one's stake. The wealthy not only have a larger investment in the community, but stand to lose more if misgovernment occurs. Their concern to safeguard their fortunes makes them the more prudent custodians of the public interest. Or it may be argued that if government is to be conducted by "the best," then a man's possessions can be taken as an objective yardstick of his abilities as an individual and of his services to others. The wealthiest are to be adjudged the worthiest. Or again the view may be advanced that an ample fortune emancipates its owner from the daily anxieties of earning a livelihood and enables him to be more fully dedicated to public affairs. Hence the well-to-do enjoy the leisure and the detachment that make them a "natural" ruling class. Finally—and using somewhat different premises—those who call themselves realists may contend that, since wealth does in fact breed influence and power, to acknowledge the authority of the rich is merely to recognize the actual structure of power in society.

The doctrines that the distribution of political power will tend to correspond to the distribution of wealth, and that the difference between "haves" and "have-nots" creates political as well as economic cleavage are, of course, among the well-worn commonplaces of political thought. When Plato drew up a ranking of states on a scale that proceeded from perfect goodness to utter evil, he placed plutocracy in the middle of his five types.[37] He considered its main defect an over-addiction to the amassing of wealth and a general acquisitiveness.

[36] The Japanese term *zaibatsu*, meaning "financial clique," is similar though it does not include the notion of government.

[37] His ranking, from good to bad, was: (1) rule of philosopher-kings; (2) timarchy (government by soldiers conforming to a knightly code of chivalry); (3) plutocracy; (4) democracy; (5) tyranny. *Republic*, bks. VIII-IX.

"Then when in a city wealth and the wealthy are honoured, virtue and the good are slighted?"

"Obviously."

... "Then in process of time, from men who love victory and honour they become lovers of money-getting and of money; they give their praise and admiration to the rich man, and elect him to rule over them, but the poor man they slight?"

"Certainly."

"Then they lay down a law which is the distinguishing feature of an oligarchic constitution. They prescribe a sum of money varying in amount as the oligarchy is more or less extreme, and proclaim all disqualified for office whose means do not amount to the prescribed sum. ... Such a city must of necessity be not one but two— the city of the rich and the city of the poor—rich and poor dwelling within the same walls, and always conspiring against one another." [38]

To similar effect is the judgment expressed by James Madison:

The latent causes of faction are thus sown in the nature of man; and we see them everywhere brought into different degrees of activity, according to the different circumstances of civil society. ... But the most common and durable source of factions has been the various and unequal distribution of property. Those who hold and those who are without property have ever formed distinct interests in society. Those who are creditors, and those who are debtors, fall under a like discrimination.[39]

However, although each was well aware that the economic distinction between rich and poor assumed a frankly political character, neither Plato nor Madison developed his analysis to the lengths that were reached by Karl Marx. For Marx and the Marxists have gone far beyond their predecessors, and beyond the evidence, in asserting that the economic factor controls and determines all other aspects of society, and in interpreting all recorded history as a series of struggles between economic classes becoming more sharply differentiated into exploiters (that is, owners of the means of production) and exploited (that is, those who toil on behalf of the exploiter). This doctrine, which claims to be a descriptive statement of fact, says both too much and too little. Too much, because it exaggerates the influence of the economic factor out of proportion to its true size and significance, and because it pretends to discover

[38] *Republic*, bk. VIII, sec. 551, pp. 246-47 trans. A. D. Lindsay (Everyman's Library).

[39] *The Federalist*, No. X, Everyman's Library, p. 43.

in all places and in all periods of history a polarization between hostile economic classes that has existed in fact less generally than Marx imagines. It says too little, because it fails to allow for the effect upon society as a whole of factors operating independently of economics, and further because it depicts with distortion, or overlooks completely, any actual situation that does not neatly fit the doctrine.

But he who refutes the validity of the Marxian theory could easily lapse into the same error as Marx himself if he leaned too far backward and denied the existence or the political relevance of economic divisions. There are many states that have proceeded from the assumption that the right to participate in government should be correlated with the ownership of property. Of innumerable examples that could be picked, two will suffice. One is the governmental system that prevailed in Britain through the eighteenth century and the first third of the nineteenth. Prior to the Reform Act of 1832, political power was firmly concentrated in the hands of an oligarchy of landowners and merchant-financiers who had a grip on every key institution. Identifying themselves with the prerogatives of the monarchy, they were unassailably entrenched in the House of Lords through the device of hereditary peerages, as well as in the officer ranks of the Navy and Army and in the higher clergy of the Established Church. Over the House of Commons, before its reform, their control was almost as secure as elsewhere. The antiquated apportionment of districts was heavily biased in favor of rural areas and the ancient boroughs and ignored the shifts of population. The method of nominating and voting for candidates gave all the advantages to the lords and squires influential in the locality. Qualifications for the franchise were based primarily upon property with the result that even in 1831—only four generations removed from the present—those entitled to vote in Britain numbered a bare 3 percent of the population.[40]

A striking parallel, in the sense that it was designed to correlate political power with wealth, is the electoral organization adopted in the Kingdom of Prussia and in force there until the year 1918. Representatives to the Prussian *Landtag* were chosen in districts, each of which returned one, two, or three members. These were elected, not directly by the voters, but indirectly by an electoral

[40] See Chapter 6, pp. 136-7.

college. For picking the latter body, every district was divided into sub-districts, to which was allotted one member of the electoral college for every 250 inhabitants. To choose the members of this college, the voters in the sub-district were themselves grouped in three classes, composed of those who paid direct taxes. The first class consisted of the wealthiest who contributed one-third of the tax-quota of the sub-district; the second class, of those who paid another third; the third class, of the remaining tax-payers. Each class chose by absolute majority one-third of the electoral college membership of the sub-district. Those so picked in all sub-districts, acting together as the electoral college of the district, voted for the representatives to go to the *Landtag*. The actual effect of these ingeniously complicated details can be seen in the figures for the year 1908, when the first class contained 293,000 voters (4%); the second class, 1,065,240 voters (14%); and the third class, 6,324,079 (82%).

The Rule of the Wise. Of the types of oligarchy so far discussed, the two most likely to establish themselves in practice are government by warriors and government by wealth, for these possess ample means of "persuasion" and are the hardest to resist. There remains one final type. It is the rarest and most difficult to establish; but, if ever employed, would be in principle the least objectionable of all oligarchies. This is the government of the wisest. The argument in its favor consists of a series of essentially simple points. It asserts that the process of ruling—like the art of medicine or the science of engineering—calls for the professional knowledge of experts. It supposes that there is a body of knowledge concerning the subject-matter of politics that can be discovered and learned. It then calls for an educational system that will impart the "right" knowledge to the "right" people. Perhaps there is no little irony in the fact that the earliest systematic treatise of political philosophy now surviving is devoted to this hypothesis. The whole of Plato's *Republic* rests upon two fundamental assumptions. One is the metaphysical doctrine that a distinction must be drawn between knowledge and opinion; that the subject-matter of the former is reality, whereas that of the latter is appearance; and that the reality that is knowable includes the true forms or models of political ideals that must serve to guide the statesman. The second is the psychological assumption that human beings differ fundamentally in their intel-

lectual endowment, and that only a small number are qualified and
can be trained to reach the highest levels of philosophical inquiry
and know the ideal. It is these superior minds, in Plato's view, and
these alone, which deserve to be entrusted with political power:

> Unless philosophers bear kingly rule in cities, or those who are now
> called kings and princes become genuine and adequate philosophers,
> and political power and philosophy are brought together, and unless
> the numerous natures who at present pursue either politics or phi-
> losophy, the one to the exclusion of the other, are forcibly debarred
> from this behaviour, there will be no respite from evil for cities, nor,
> I fancy, for humanity.[41]

To judge such a system of government is impossible because it
has never been tried. True, there have been sporadic instances where
individuals of superb intellectual and ethical standards have held the
highest office in the state. Witness Marcus Aurelius and Antoninus
Pius in the Roman Empire; or, in modern times, Gladstone in Britain;
Masaryk in Czechoslovakia; Smuts in South Africa; Wilson in the
United States; and Nehru in India. Civil services, too, when they
have sought to recruit their officials according to the ability each
displays in competition, have recognized the connection that should
exist between powers of government and powers of mind. But nothing has ever been attempted in practice that comes anywhere near
the rigorous and uncompromising logic of Plato's grandiose educational curriculum. The elite of the all-wise philosopher ruler remains
in the realm of hypothetical fantasy. There let it remain!

Enough has now been said to demonstrate the point that elites,
or oligarchies, or aristocracies appear in many guises. All constitute,
however, an assertion that the best government is the one that the
few best control. All take for granted the existence of a certain kind
of superiority. All are dedicated to the principle of inequality, which
is the law of their being. Nor are these aberrations, rarities, or de-
viations, that have been considered in this chapter. On the contrary,
most of the governance of men that is known to history has corresponded to one or other of the major types delineated here.

[41] *Republic*, bk. V, sec. 473, p. 166, trans. Lindsay.

CHAPTER 6

FIRST ISSUE:

(2) "ALL MEN ARE CREATED EQUAL"

The Humanity that Unites Us All. "Human beings are divided into two groups; those who divide human beings into two groups, and those who don't. I prefer the latter." This statement deserved to be quoted, because of its satire on the attitude discussed in the preceding chapter, and because it keynotes the contents of the present one. After a review of principles and practices that confine the right of governing to first-class citizens and demote the remainder to second class status, it is appropriate to study the alternative. This consists in rejecting the assumptions of elitists. It does not envisage the relation of government to governed as if it were analogous to that of lions to lambs, of doctor to patient, of brain to body, of potter to clay, of shepherd to sheep, or any of the countless similes of this kind. Instead, it affirms the principle that for purposes of politics the same basic rights are to be accorded to all. If any are to be excluded from full participation, they should be the exceptions, not the rule. They should be as few as possible in number, and their exclusion should require special justification (that is, those under a certain age, those committed to institutions for mental illness, those serving jail sentences for a criminal conviction, those owing allegiance to a foreign state, and so forth).

The purpose of this view is to affirm and promote equality. This involves shifting the emphasis to factors the opposite of those that attracted the elitists. The elitists were preoccupied with singling out and exaggerating features by which human beings may be distin-

guished and segregated. They placed their accent upon differences
and wove their theories around a pattern of dissimilarities. Anything
might then be called into use that could serve as an index for discrimination. The contrary doctrine puts the stress elsewhere. It
searches for what men have in common. Its accent is put upon likenesses, similarities, resemblances. It speaks in terms not of classes,
but of humanity; not of ranks, but of equals. Within its categories
there is no room for the concepts of subhuman or superman. All are
placed on one level, encompassing the whole of mankind.

In describing these contrasts, let us be clear about what is in issue
and at stake. Those who prefer the aristocratic doctrine do not deny
that even between superiors and inferiors certain over-all similarities
exist. The advocates of all-inclusiveness concede that side by side
with the resemblances they observe there are also differences. The
disagreement then resolves itself into a dispute over priorities.
Granted that all men are alike in some respects and different in
others, which factors should be considered more important? You will
be an elitist if you think that the points on which people differ are
the fundamental ones. You will be an equalitarian if you hold that
the features wherein men resemble one another are primary. As the
premises vary, so will the conclusions. The outcome of the former
view is to emphasize whatever elements in human nature divide men;
of the latter, those elements that unite us.

The Case for Equalitarianism. But even when stress is laid upon
unifying similarities, how and why is the right of everybody to
participate in government explained and approved? If the exponents
of aristocracy conceive of ruling as a science, art, or mystery, what
counter-formulation is offered by their opponents? In a nutshell,
what gives Thersites the right to talk back to Agamemnon? When
we proceed to examine the foundations of the equalitarian view, we
shall find that it rests on many pillars. Just as there are numerous
species of oligarchy even though their central feature is identical,
so do numerous roads lead to the unique goal of universal humanism.
For a start one could cite the old words: *Quod tangit omnes ab
omnibus approbetur* ("Let all approve what touches all"). But to say
this without proof is like asserting that the square on the hypotenuse
of a right-angled triangle equals the sum of the squares on the other
two sides without detailing the logical steps that led Pythagoras to
such a conclusion. They can be outlined thus: Each has a right to

determine his own welfare. Each, therefore, has the right to seek control over anything external to himself that affects his welfare. The actions of government do impinge on human welfare and they leave nobody unaffected. Consequently all have the right to participate in controlling the state and contributing to its decisions.

The argument is impressive. By itself, however, it is insufficient to rebut the contentions of the elitists. For their attack exposes one weak link in the chain of reasoning: the statement that "each has the right to seek control over anything external to himself that affects his welfare." To affirm the right, they would say, is one thing; to exercise it, another. The right to control what touches your welfare depends first on knowing how to detect it; and second on being able to master it. The mass of men, so the oligarch will argue, are not equipped intellectually to perform the first task and they lack the power to carry out the second. Hence the assumed right is meaningless.

To this the equalitarian presents a countercharge. In effect he asserts that the analogy drawn between government and science or art is not complete and can become misleading. To look only at the qualifications needed by rulers is to overlook the other side of the equation. If government consists of services provided by the rulers to the ruled, it is wrong to think only of those who produce the services and to ignore the consumers. Granted that I am not able to compose like Beethoven, write like Shakespeare, paint like Rembrandt, or invent like Edison, I can still appreciate the worth of their music, poetry, paintings, or inventions, or even criticize a great master when he occasionally lapses from his highest flights. A man who could not design an automobile can nevertheless learn to drive one and can judge its performance on the road. Government, in other words, is not merely an affair of skilled technique applied by expert practitioners. It is above all else a problem of providing services to people who need them. In politics, as in business, the start and finish of the entire process are consumer need and consumer satisfaction. Traditionally, this truth is summed up in the everyday saying that "only the wearer knows where the shoe pinches." [1] But the theory that embraces all men as citizens has been placed on a yet higher plane. For the arguments of the equalitarians involve basic

[1] For an excellent discussion of this, see A. D. Lindsay, *Modern Democratic State*, vol. I (New York: Oxford University Press, 1947), pp. 269 et seq.

beliefs concerning the nature of man. As such, they cannot be divorced from larger issues of ethics, metaphysics, and theology. If this broadening of the scope of our inquiry occasions any surprise to the student of political science, let him reflect that there are many branches to the study of mankind; that these are all related; and that no single specialization can boast all the answers.

The Classical Roots of the Doctrine of Equality: (1) the Stoics. In the history of western political ideas the doctrine that emphasizes human equality is practically as old as its opposite. After Aristotle's death in 322 B.C., the most prominent star in the Greek philosophical firmament was Zeno of Citium, founder of the Stoic school. Against the background of turmoil that followed Alexander's conquests and early death, amid the breakdown of the once autonomous city-state and the overthrow of kingly dynasties, Zeno's theories were formulated to help men bear their trials with fortitude and lift their hopes toward new loyalties and wider horizons. The central theme of the Stoic philosophy was to equate rationality and deity. The divinity that shapes our ends is a rational one and reason, conversely, is divine. The universe is the product of a divine purpose, manifesting itself throughout nature in a rational plan. Deity is not something external to the universe, inscrutably watching its creation and uncomprehended by its creatures. It is instead all-pervading, since wherever there is reason is God. From these metaphysics the Stoic proceeded to draw conclusions with a social relevance. All human beings possess reason. It is true that the power to reason exists in different degrees in each of us. But wherever it is, and whether it shines bright or dim, the light of reason is a spark of the divine fire. All men, because they share in reason, share in the godhead. It is less important that the reasoning ability of individuals is differently developed than that everyone alike possesses some ability to reason. Thereby all mankind is differentiated from other animals and is united. On this account—and the point is fundamental to the Stoic— the concept of humanity (that is, the quality of being human) does not admit of degree. As men, all are equal. To assert that any human beings do not "belong," or to deny their equal title to consideration, is to exclude a fragment, however infinitesimal, of divinity.

(2) *Roman Law.* With its various additions and popularizations, this philosophy competed successfully with the contemporary doc-

trines of Cynics and Epicureans and acquired a general vogue among educated and professional people in the Mediterranean world. In the period when Roman military and political power was absorbing Greece, and Greek culture and philosophy were humanizing Rome, Stoicism was imported to Rome under the influence of the Scipionic circle [2] and was imparted to Roman audiences by the philosopher Panaetius and the historian Polybius. What followed is an instructive episode in political and intellectual history. The century that marked the introduction of Stoicism coincided with the extension of Roman military power over the lands that fringe the Mediterranean. Newly conquered territories—Sicily, Greece, Spain, Libya, Gaul (France), Asia (Turkey), and the rest—were organized into provinces and absorbed into the empire of Rome. The inhabitants of these areas, so diverse in their cultural traditions and political maturity, their economic resources and religious doctrines, became the subjects of Rome, but not, at first, its citizens. To enforce the peace, Rome was obliged not only to safeguard the frontiers of its empire from external menace, but to establish internally a system of order and trust in human relations. Contact and commerce between inhabitants of different provinces led to transactions involving trade, contracts, property, marriage, inheritance—transactions covering the whole gamut of social activities. A Gaul and a Spaniard, a Greek and a Sicilian, a Libyan and an Egyptian, might be involved in a dispute and seek to have their rights determined by litigation. But whose law would be applied in such cases? Not necessarily the law of Rome, for the civil law was applicable to citizens. Confronted with a practical problem, the Romans responded in a practical manner. They established a new court to hear those cases where the rights of foreigners were involved. The presiding judge considered the legal principles that were in force in the territories of both parties to the dispute. If he could discover some common ground between them, he would adjudicate accordingly. If not, he would propose a solution based upon equity, that is, upon a conception of right and justice that conformed to an abstract standard of fairness. The decisions rendered in particular cases and the principles they embodied were

[2] The Scipionic circle was a group of political leaders, literary men, and philosophers, assembling in the middle decades of the second century, B.C., under the influence and patronage of the great soldier-statesman, Scipio, the destroyer of Carthage.

re-adopted annually in an edict that the judge issued to govern the proceedings of his court. Eventually, the accumulation of precedents hardened into a body of case-law, which Roman jurists came to call the "law of the peoples" (*jus gentium*).

The stage was then set for a brilliant climax. Acting empirically without any preconceived plan or foreknowledge of their goal, the Roman jurists developed from particular cases a coherent framework of general principles. In these were included the legal concepts that the various peoples of their empire were found to possess in common, as well as principles of equity that satisfied a sense of justice. Where the Romans had been thinking inductively and went from the particular to the general, the Stoic philosophers worked deductively. Arguing from metaphysical assumptions and moving from the universal to the particular, the Stoics concluded that all men were united through their common possession of reason. But the two systems of the Stoic philosophy and the Roman *jus gentium*, though they set out from opposite poles, drew close together and ultimately came within hailing distance. What was then easier than to suppose that the common concepts which the Romans discovered and applied by use of reason were actually the product of that same all-pervading reason which the Stoics had divined as a law of the universe? It is true that the correlation was never exact. There were important points of divergence, as when the *jus gentium* condoned the institution of slavery that Stoic reason rejected. But the approximation was sufficiently near and neat for jurist and philosopher alike to assume that their tracks were converging. Speculative metaphysics and pragmatic imperialism led jointly to the desired goal of the equality and unity of mankind.

Nor was the construction of the *jus gentium* the only way in which the Romans attempted to give effect to the principle that all men are equal. No less momentous was the extension of their citizenship, which was granted in stages both to individuals and entire communities, first among the Latins living nearby in the center of Italy; then to their allies in the rest of Italy; and afterwards to inhabitants of the outlying provinces. The climax was reached in 212 A.D. when the notable edict of the Emperor Caracalla conferred the citizenship of Rome upon all free (non-slave) inhabitants of the empire. The nations of contemporary Europe are still far from possessing the common citizenship that Rome accomplished at the beginning of the third century. But idealistic as Caracalla's achievement sounds, it was not lacking a materialistic side. The imperial treasury at that time was depleted and required new revenues. One lucrative source was the tax on the estates of the deceased, but this was levied by Rome only on its dead citizens. Enlarging the citizenry had the result of replenishing the treasury.

(3) *The Gospel of Jesus.* The trends initiated by the philosophers of Greece and the jurists of Rome were reinforced by the preachers of the Christian gospel. Jesus and the Apostles, like many of their early believers, came for the most part from humble origins. The appeal of the new religion was what could be expected of those who spread its message. Christianity spoke first to the underprivileged; to the lowly of this earth, not the mighty; to those who were rich only in hope and faith. Its social teaching in consequence was inclined heavily towards equalitarianism. Human society in this life might display the contrasts of luxury and poverty, power and weakness, eminence and lowliness. But the worth of the individual soul, which would outlive its bodily habitat, was to be judged not by man, but by God whose universal fatherhood made all men brothers. Measured on the infinite scale of divine goodness, justice, and compassion, all human distinctions were insignificant. As St. Paul said to the Galatians: "There is neither Jew nor Greek, there is neither bond nor free, there is neither male nor female, for ye are all one in Jesus Christ." [3] The philosophy here is Stoic. The legal doctrine—apparent to the Apostle who affirmed "I am a Roman citizen"—is Roman. The religious aura is Christian. In that trinity the intellect, the politics, and the faith of antiquity found their culminating union.

It should not be forgotten, however, that the equality on which Christianity insisted was more pertinent to the next world than to this. It was in terms of their souls, which could be lost or saved, that all men stood an equal chance. Or, if not equal, the rich and the mighty were the ones handicapped in the race for salvation, since their earthly power exposed them to greater temptation and made them more liable to fall from grace. This shift of the scene of equalitarianism to the hereafter made it possible for Christianity to accept, and either overlook or minimize, the inequalities existing

---

[3] Epistle to the Galatians, 3:28.

here and now. Let men be content with their earthly lot, though it may be disagreeable, in expectation of glory in the life after death. Since "the powers that be are ordained of God," the Christian should submit to the wrongs inflicted by his fellow men with the certainty of being compensated by a justice that is divine.

The Modern Rebirth of Equality. In the history of the West there have been two periods in which mankind has made notable advances in the direction of equality. The one just reviewed lasted for five hundred years from the rise of Stoicism to the Edict of Caracalla. The second, commencing in the mid-seventeenth century, has persisted through the middle of the twentieth and does not yet seem to have run its course. The circumstances that started and accelerated this modern movement are as interesting as the theories it has evoked. Chronologically these circumstances fall into three phases. The earliest dates from the middle of the seventeenth century to the end of the eighteenth. The next corresponds more or less exactly to the ninety-nine years (1815-1914) between the final defeat of Napoleon and the German invasion of Belgium in World War I. The third phase has lasted from that time to the present. A survey of all three, by discovering whence we have come and where we now are, may help us to understand better whither we may be bound.

The English, American, and French Revolutions. The first phase coincides in time and space with the three great revolutions in the countries that are the standard-bearers of the Atlantic community: the revolution in Britain from 1640 to 1688, in the United States from 1776 to 1791, and in France from 1789 to the present day.[4] Each of these had somewhat similar objectives and therefore produced doctrines with many similarities. The aims of the revolutionaries, whether British, American, or French, included the overthrow of governmental regimes not controllable by the governed. To justify rebellion against the legal order, it was necessary to show that right was on the side of those who rebelled. This could be done either by arguing that the state is founded upon a contract, and by asserting that the contract had been broken by the government; or by insisting that over the laws enacted by governing authorities there reigns some higher law, to which men may make appeal. The rebellions, furthermore, were directed against an established ruling class who

[4] For further discussion of these revolutions, see Chapter 11, pp. 274 ff.

based their position upon doctrines of legitimacy,[5] aristocracy, and hereditary right. To justify their replacement, it was important to contend that the authority to govern did not belong exclusively to the monarch or the nobility, but was the common birthright of mankind that had been stolen from them.

These needs explain why the philosophies of Locke, Voltaire, Rousseau, Jefferson, and Paine place so much emphasis upon the hypotheses of a social contract and a law of nature, and upon the vindication of individual rights to liberty and equality. The insertion of nature as one of the links in the chain of reasoning had a special purpose. Men who were dissatisfied with the existing order wanted a yardstick or standard of comparison. They found it helpful to suppose that there was a state of nature that preceded the organized civil state. This natural state was blended of a medley of advantages and inconveniences, and governments were instituted in order to escape the latter—but not so as to lose the former. Of the advantages, the greatest appeared to be the relative equality of conditions existing among men and their consequential equality of rights. As Locke expressed it: "To understand political power aright, and derive it from its original, we must consider what estate all men are naturally in, and that is a state of perfect freedom to order their actions. . . . A state also of equality, wherein all the power and jurisdiction is reciprocal, no one having more than another." [6] If the actual conditions of organized society differed from this, if there were king and subjects, masters and slaves, luxury and penury, it was not from nature that these differences derived. Rather, they existed in contravention of nature, being the handiwork of political man, not of natural man. Let mankind therefore reconstitute their governments so as to be guardians, not violators, of natural right. Such were the sentiments embodied in the great declarations of the American and French republics. The first of the truths that Thomas Jefferson pronounced self-evident in 1776 was "that all men are created equal." With similar effect the *Déclaration des Droits de l'Homme et du Citoyen*, adopted in 1793, proclaimed: "Governments are instituted to guarantee to men the enjoyment of their natural and imprescriptible rights. These rights are equality, liberty,

[5] Legitimacy meant, in this context, a right to govern based upon ancestry.
[6] *Second Treatise of Civil Government*, chap. 2, sec. 4, Everyman's Library, p. 118.

security, and property. By nature and before the law, all men are equal."

It is significant that such statements were not merely enunciated by individual thinkers but were affirmed officially by public bodies: by the Continental Congress of the United States and by the National Convention in France. No less impressive is the insistence upon equality as a basic ideal, since this concept was truly revolutionary in relation to the social and political facts of the world at that time. Nor are any weakening qualifications inserted into the phrasing. All men, without reserve or ambiguity, were included. The range of equality was universal. What was ambiguous, however, was the appeal to nature as the basis and justification of the desired rights. Men might dispute about the circumstances of the assumed state of nature (whose details were derived from the imagination, rather than from fact), and also about the law of nature that was supposed to prevail therein. Proof and evidence concerning natural law and natural rights were sought by reference to "reason," which was not always a sure guide to government if it gave different answers to different men; or if not to reason, then the reference was to God, the Creator of nature and, therefore, of its rights and law. Once again, however, the interpretations were at variance, since not only did Christians disagree with non-Christians, but Protestants and Catholics themselves disputed the character of the divine dispensation. There were too many prophets who claimed to have heard the voice of God and tried to translate it into the vernacular. When a state contained among its citizens adherents of various faiths, which revelation should it accept?

Problems of this kind made it desirable, if equality and universality were to be upheld, to discover alternative doctrines as substitutes or supplements for natural law. At this point aid was forthcoming from moral philosophies, which, though disagreeing in other particulars, confirmed the same central principle. This was the reassertion of the belief in the equal worth, fundamentally, of all men. In the mid-seventeenth century during the debates in Cromwell's army a Colonel Rainboro, one of the group known as the Levellers, declared: "Really I think the poorest he that is in England hath a life to live as the richest he." The same thought was echoed more than a century later by the German philosopher, Immanuel Kant, who enunciated respect for human dignity in the somewhat cryptic command: "So act as to treat humanity, whether in thine own person or in that of any other, in every case as an end withal, never as means only." [7] With greater clarity and less mysticism, the founder of the English Utilitarians, Jeremy Bentham, remarked that each person should count for one, and nobody for more than one—which is perhaps the most succinct and least equivocal formula for equalitarianism ever expressed in a few words.

Some Effects of Equalitarian Ideas on Government. The relation of the Stoics, who formulated the abstract principles, to the Romans, who broadened outward from the particular to the general, is paralleled in both method and timing by the relation of the nineteenth century to its two predecessors. If it was the achievement of the seventeenth and eighteenth centuries that they hammered out the fundamental philosophies and the resultant declarations, the task of the nineteenth century was to start from actualities and bring them by degrees into closer approximation with those grand abstractions. When surveying these events that are closer to our own time, we have the advantage not only of fuller historical records, but also of more precise statistical description. The concepts of an inclusive or exclusive citizenship can be measured with some precision by reference to the franchise and its gradual extension to those not previously qualified to vote. In countries where the legislature is accepted as a crucial and central agency of government, the number of citizens entitled to vote for their representatives is one of the pointers indicating whether privilege or equality prevails.

The main precipitating cause in this nineteenth century development was undoubtedly economic. The economic factor, however, assumed different guises in different regions of the world. Thus in Britain the movement to broaden the franchise was certainly an offshoot of the industrial revolution, which increased the social power of the urban middle class and converted a large section of the population into factory workers. In the agrarian community of the United States, as also in Canada, Australia, and New Zealand, equalitarianism issued largely from the psychological effect upon Europeans of emigrating from overcrowded lands to spacious undeveloped territories where new vistas beyond the outer rim of settlement beckoned the enterprising. On the frontier and beyond,

[7] T. K. Abbott, trans., *Fundamental Principles of the Metaphysic of Ethics,* 10th ed. (London: Longmans, Green, 1929), p. 56.

where there was more than enough for each, and where muscle and nerve were a man's primary resources and stock of capital, that equality of conditions existed that makes for freedom.

Extension of Voting Rights in Britain. The impact upon politics of these changes deserves description since within a century they were responsible for writing a spectacular new chapter in the history of the state. It is relevant to include the experiences of Britain for the reasons that in the nineteenth century she was the world's most powerful nation; she was ahead of others in industrialization; and simultaneously she was in the vanguard of democratic development. At the time of her mortal clash with Napoleonic France, which for two decades dammed up the domestic currents of reform, Britain did indeed possess a potent legislature, but one that represented only a minority of the population. The House of Lords, filled for life by hereditary peers, was the entrenched stronghold of the land-owning aristocracy who, along with a minority of merchant-financiers, enjoyed a virtual monopoly of wealth, prestige, and political skill. The control of governmental power by this oligarchy embraced a House of Commons whose personnel were in large part the kinsmen of the nobility and were elected from antiquated districts by voters with ancestral or property qualification. That this system did not preclude the possibility of opposition to the government is proven by the rise of the party system towards the end of the seventeenth century, by the conflicts between Whigs and Tories, and by the careers of such men as the two Pitts, Burke, Fox, and Canning. But institutional change was necessary if Britain intended to absorb industrial urbanism into its politics at home and to organize its gigantic empire abroad. A decade and a half of discontent and agitation after the defeat of Napoleon led to the enactment in 1832 of the first of the Reform Acts. Its general aim was to initiate a closer relation between the Parliament and the people. With this in view, the constituencies were redistributed and the franchise was altered. While a property qualification was retained, the necessary amount was set at a lower figure than before, which resulted in the enfranchisement and formal entry into politics of the urban middle class. The electorate in 1833 was 75 percent higher than what it had been two years earlier; but it was still a mere 4½ percent of the whole population.

During the three middle decades of the nineteenth century, the suffrage remained exactly as it was defined in 1832. Indeed, as late as 1866, less than 6 percent of the British population were registered as voters. Government was of the people; but it was certainly conducted by a minority and, on the whole, for that minority. The two major barriers that excluded the majority of adults were wealth and sex. When would the electoral law abandon the disqualifications of poverty and femininity?

TABLE II

THE GROWTH OF THE BRITISH ELECTORATE

Date of Law Extending Suffrage	Registered Voters		Population at Nearest Census		Percentage of Voters to Population
	Date	Number (ooo's omitted)	Date	Number (ooo's omitted)	
1832	1830	440	1831	16,261	2.7
	1833	725			4.4
1867	1866	1,200	1861	23,128	5.6
	1869	2,250	1871	26,072	8.6
1884	1883	2,590	1881	29,710	9.9
	1886	5,000			16.8
1918	1910	7,200	1911	40,831	17.6
	1918	19,500	1921	42,769	45.6
1928	1924	20,650	1921	42,709	48.3
	1929	28,500	1931	44,795	63.6
	1950	34,500	1951	50,000	69.0

The middle class could not avoid the issue of sharing with the working class the privileges that they had themselves wrested from the aristocracy. In the agitation for political reform that shook British politics to its foundations in the years 1830-1832, the working class gave their support to middle class demands without insisting prematurely on a share for themselves. But eventually they were bound to press for their share. It then remained to be seen whether the middle class would acquiesce and reciprocate their support or would, as radicals of yesterday who had gained their desires, become the conservatives of tomorrow. Such queries erupted in the revolutionary year of 1848 when autocratic regimes were challenged or overthrown on the continent of Europe and new constitutions were proposed or established in France, Prussia, Austria, the Italian states, and elsewhere. At a critical stage in those movements, the middle class took alarm at working class aspirations and swung to the side of the conservative elements. Thus the liberal blossoming of Germany's Frankfort Assembly, elected in 1848 by universal manhood suffrage, ran quickly to seed in the Bismarckian reaction. In France, the liberal-democratic constitution of November, 1848, which contained a similar suffrage, gave way to the empire of Napoleon III. Hence, a British historian has tersely commented: "The year 1848 was the turning point at which modern history failed to turn." [8]

In Britain itself the year 1848 did not witness the same upheaval as occurred on the opposite side of the English Channel. This was because the British had been wise enough or fortunate enough to conduct in the seventeenth century the kind of political revolution that others were attempting in the nineteenth,[9] and also because the crisis of 1832 had been weathered successfully from the reformers' standpoint. All that happened of moment in 1848 was that the Chartists, who had been pressing for further changes (including universal adult suffrage), reached the climax of their movement in the peaceful presentation of their Charter to Parliament. Liberalism was now forced to decide whether its acceptance of Bentham's precept would be extended in practice to an all-inclusive doctrine of citizenship. If the desire of the working class for equal voting rights were conceded, the middle class would have to welcome as full participants in the political process those who were poorer, less educated, and on a lower social level, than themselves. The conflict in their reasons and emotions is typified in the candid avowals of the leading intellectual of mid-nineteenth century liberalism, John Stuart Mill. When the first edition of his classic treatise, the *Principles of Political Economy*, was published in 1848, he stated with characteristic frankness: "Of the working classes of Western Europe at least

---

[8] G. M. Trevelyan, *British History in the Nineteenth Century* (New York: Longmans, Green, 1922), p. 292.

[9] Macaulay, in a passage of his *History of England* that was penned in 1848, compares British and continental experiences in a series of rhetorical contrasts that exude no little complacency. Vol. I, p. 412.

it may be pronounced certain, that the patriarchal or fraternal system of government is one to which they will not again be subject. . . . The poor have come out of leading-strings, and cannot any longer be governed like children. . . . The prospect of the future depends on the degree in which they can be made rational beings. There is no reason to believe that prospect other than hopeful." [10] To him, the ultimate goal was not debatable. Only the timing was in question; and he, for one, was prepared to consider the maturity of the working class to be conditional upon their education.

These same anxieties were repeatedly voiced in the years immediately preceding and following the second extension of the franchise in 1867. When Mill's *Considerations on Representative Government* appeared in 1861, he again expressed his fears in this way: "But even in this democracy, absolute power, if they chose to exercise it, would rest with the numerical majority; and these would be composed exclusively of a single class, alike in biasses, prepossessions and general modes of thinking, and a class, to say no more, not the most highly cultivated." [11] Similarly Walter Bagehot, who added a new introduction to the second edition of his *English Constitution* in 1872, commented with even more candor: "As a theoretical writer I can venture to say, what no elected member of Parliament, Conservative or Liberal, can venture to say, that I am exceedingly afraid of the ignorant multitude of the new constituencies. . . . Their supremacy in the state they now are, means the supremacy of ignorance over instruction, and of numbers over knowledge." [12] Nevertheless, British democracy did take the plunge, and dived into the deep seas of mass enfranchisement. In 1867 the vote was first accorded to members of the urban working class; and within less than two decades it was conferred upon their rural confrères. Two years after the Act of 1884, the enrolled voters numbered some five million, or roughly 17 percent of the population.[13]

---

[10] John Stuart Mill, *Principles of Political Economy* (Boston: Little & Brown, 1848) vol. 2, bk. IV, chap. 7, sec. 1.

[11] *Considerations on Representative Government*, Everyman's Library, pp. 276-77.

[12] *The English Constitution*, World's Classics (London: Oxford University Press, 1928), pp. 272, 276.

[13] Enrolment of voters, be it remembered, was voluntary. There were many who could qualify to vote under the law, but who for some decades neglected to register.

The barriers were now breached and the sequel of the story is a march toward the foregone conclusion. The focus of the final struggle was shifted from the working class to the womenfolk. Feminists, like Mill, had already pleaded their cause; and a nation that romanticized its Queen Victoria could not long and consistently deny to woman a place in government. After the turn of the century, the Suffragettes added a militant warhead to the movement, which gained its victory as one of the political offshoots of World War I. The Acts of 1918 and 1928 marked the culmination in a century of orderly evolution toward the ultimate goal of universal adult suffrage. When the British nation went to cast their ballots in the spring of 1951, as many as thirty-four million out of a fifty million population (69 percent) were registered on the electoral rolls and of these, twenty-eight and a half million voted.

The Suffrage in American Democracy. The experience of the United States in the sixteen decades since the Constitution came into force has run a course parallel to that of Britain, with one country or the other taking the lead in the race for equalization of voting privileges. But the American development has been more complicated than the British. This is due in part to the greater heterogeneity of America's population, which has contained a large racial minority, and has owed much of its increase to the immigration of adults whose mother tongue was not English and whose assimilation took time. In part, the complication has arisen from the relation between the electoral laws and the federal system. The regional diversities that have been present in America from its founding precluded the drafting of uniform qualifications for the franchise at the Philadelphia convention of 1787. Instead, the convention adopted a provision that applied to national elections whatever franchise the states respectively chose for electing the lower houses of their own legislatures.[14] Hence every extension of the suffrage within a state has automatically broadened it at the federal level.[15] For this reason, and also because systems of registration of voters have not yet been established in all states, it is impossi-

---

[14] "The House of Representatives shall be composed of members chosen every second year by the people of the several States, and the electors in each State shall have the qualifications requisite for electors of the most numerous branch of the State legislature." *Constitution of the United States,* Art. I, sec. II.

[15] Conversely, any restriction of the franchise within a state automatically narrowed the federal franchise, as happened in states that have a poll-tax.

ble to trace the exact stages in the growth of the American electorate with the same precision as can be done for Britain. We can therefore say how many persons actually voted in the presidential contest, but not how many were qualified to vote under the varying electoral laws of the different states.

According to the estimate of Charles A. Beard, when elections were held in 1787-1788 to choose the delegates to the state conventions who would ratify or reject the United States Constitution, only a small percentage of the nation, then numbering almost four million, participated. "It seems a safe guess to say," he summarized, "that not more than 5 per cent of the population in general, or in round numbers, 160,000 voters, expressed an opinion one way or another on the Constitution. . . . We may reasonably conjecture that of the estimated 160,000 who voted in the election of delegates, not more than 100,000 men favored the adoption of the Constitution at the time it was put into effect—about one in six of the adult males." [16] In the presidential election of 1952, however, when the population had risen to over 155,000,000, there were 61,500,000 citizens who actually recorded their ballots. What happened between 1788 and 1952 to make this possible?

One hundred and sixty years ago there were in America three principal barriers, besides age, that excluded the majority of the people from the polls: wealth, color, and sex. The history of the equalization of the franchise is the story of the total elimination or progressive reduction of these barriers. All states at the beginning had legal requirements that confined the franchise to the well-to-do. Sometimes the method was to insist that the voter must own a minimum amount of property. Sometimes the tax assessment was used as the criterion. Such limitations, in vogue along the Eastern seaboard, lost their meaning when population moved west of the Alleghenies and carved out new territories that were admitted as new states. Here was free land for the taking. Here everyone who worked could become a man of property. Here were intrepid and hardy souls who would not accept a lower class citizenship. The barriers of wealth, like the walls of Jericho, fell before the trumpet blast of the all-levelling frontier, and under the fluid social conditions of the early nineteenth century new ramparts could not long be sustained.

16 *An Economic Interpretation of the Constitution of the United States* (New York: The Macmillan Co., 1935), p. 250.

Benthamism, firmly planted in the West, spread back to the East bringing constitutional change and electoral amendment. As the contemporary French observer, Alexis de Tocqueville, presciently remarked: "The further electoral rights are extended, the greater is the need for extending them; for after each concession the strength of the democracy increases, and its demands increase with its strength.... The exception at last becomes the rule, concession follows concession, and no stop can be made short of universal suffrage." [17] As early as 1832, when less than 5 percent of the people were registered as voters in Britain under the new Reform Act, nearly one-tenth of America's population voted in the election that gave a second term to Andrew Jackson. In the presidential contest when Abraham Lincoln was first victorious, actual voters were 15 percent of the population, a number that compares favorably with the 5 percent who were then registered as voters in Britain.

The failure of the property-line to provide an adequate defensive position in the resistance of quality to equality was followed by inroads upon the color-line. If it was the West that spearheaded the attempts to nullify the electoral predominance of the wealthy, it was the North that began to minimize the political relevance of distinctions in race and color. In the birth certificate of the United States was inscribed the clause: "*All* men are created equal." Written by a Southerner, these words were now to receive a literal and liberal interpretation. Although the northern states did not permit the institution of slavery, they did not universally accord to the Negro the right to vote. By the time of the Civil War, this right was available to colored citizens only in four of the New England states, where they were few in number. The most important of the legal changes resulting from the Civil War were the three new amendments inserted in the supreme law of the land. The thirteenth abolished human slavery from the United States. All American territory henceforth was to be "free soil." The fourteenth clarified the meaning of American citizenship, which had been at issue in the Dred Scott case, and based it primarily upon the fact of birth within the United States irrespective of parentage. The fifteenth spelled out further the status of citizens in the political sphere. It affirmed that the right to vote could not be denied by the federal

[17] A. de Tocqueville, *Democracy in America*, Henry Reeve trans., Part 1, chap. IV.

government or by any state for reasons of "race, color, or previous condition of servitude." By these amendments the principles of the Constitution caught up with the philosophy of the Declaration of Independence.

What was left to be determined was whether "all men" included "all women." Again it was the West that proved itself the radical innovator, and for reasons that are sufficiently evident. The women who braved the hardships of the untamed West earned the respect of their menfolk. What is more, there were fewer of the fair sex in the states and territories between the Mississippi and the Pacific, and rarity supplied a scarcity value. It was in the western region therefore that America's women were first enfranchised. The movement to nationalize what the states were doing piecemeal was stimulated by the events of World War I, which brought more women into public life and economic activity. The climax came in 1919 with the adoption of the Nineteenth Amendment.

Despite these challenges to the barriers of wealth, color, and sex, it remains true, of course, that not all adults are qualified to vote in the contemporary United States. The phrasing of the Fifteenth and Nineteenth Amendments is significantly negative. To declare that the right of citizens to vote may *not* be denied or abridged on account of race, color, previous condition of servitude, or sex, implies that the right may legally be denied or abridged on some ground other than these four. As a matter of fact, various methods are employed constitutionally, for excluding some citizens from the polling booth. The age limitation is sufficiently obvious not to need discussion. The requirement of a certain length of residence in the voting district is justifiable as a means of permitting proper registration and enrollment of voters and thereby of restricting a number of fraudulent practices. The literacy tests that exist in not a few states may be defended on the ground that a citizen who exercises within a democracy the precious right of the franchise ought to possess enough information to cast an intelligent vote. This argument, moreover, applies with special force in a nation where many citizens were sometime immigrants who became naturalized. But such tests are indefensible if the state does not provide for all its citizens adequate public facilities for obtaining the requisite knowledge, or if the system is administered with the ulterior aim of establishing some preconceived pattern of discrimination. The most objectionable by far of the devices employed to deny or abridge the right to vote is the poll tax still in force in 1953 in five southern states. This has succeeded in its avowed purpose of drastically reducing the number of poor voters, whether they be colored or white, and of perpetuating unsavory political machines.

For reasons of this kind, which are largely associated with the heterogeneity of the American population, the number of citizens registered as voters in the modern United States forms a smaller percentage of the total population than is the case in contemporary Britain. Nevertheless, the figure, though it is susceptible of further increase, constitutes the largest example in the world of an electorate that periodically exercises a free choice between rival parties and personnel. Indeed, the acceptance of the principle of universal adult suffrage, not only in the United States and Britain but also in a great many medium-sized and smaller countries, stands out as one of the great political triumphs of the last hundred years in human history. It is a new fact, without precedent in earlier times, to find all or nearly all adult citizens possessing the right to take part in the election of their government. Never before, if a Churchillian saying may be adapted, have so many had so much opportunity to choose so few. In those modern states where the mass of the population are now entitled to participate in the electoral process, the formulae of Kant and Bentham, and the broad humanity of the great Declarations, have been translated into practical effect.

Breaking Down Man-made Discrimination. To approve and apply the policy that differences of wealth, sex, or race should not result in a second-class citizenship has meant a profound political advance. It has also signified a moral advance because it has made a person's civil status depend, not on the group to which he or she was born or inadvertently belongs, but on his or her individual worth. For the United States to inscribe the Thirteenth, Fourteenth, and Fifteenth Amendments into the Constitution, for Britain to enfranchise the working class—these are great achievements. The responsibility remains in the twentieth century of continuing and completing this process of breaking down the man-made barriers of segregation and of according to all individuals the opportunities that their respective merits deserve. If there is any conclusion to which the findings of the majority of anthropologists and sociologists point, it is this: in comparing whole groups of human beings of different race, religion, culture, wealth, or sex, no proof can be offered that any group is inherently superior and any other inherently inferior. The differences that may be observed between the average of one group and that of another are attributable to man-made, socially fostered, discrimination that has enlarged for some and has restricted for others the avenues that lead to education, income, and advancement. When such discrimination is removed, however, experience has demonstrated that individual members of formerly underprivileged groups can reach the level appropriate to their abilities in the same fashion as members of groups that once were privileged.

Furthermore, the belief that intermixture between previously segregated groups results in general deterioration is not borne out by the facts. As was noted in the previous chapter, the aristocracies that have been the most successful and have lasted the longest are those that have replenished themselves with fresh stock. History provides similar conclusions with regard to inter-racial unions. Humanity contains no master-race, nor race of slaves. Many peoples that have considered themselves racially unmixed, and therefore "pure," are not so in fact. Communities that have accepted, or even welcomed, miscegenation have frequently gained in the quality of their human material. A contemporary witness to this truth is the Brazilian nation, which is the outcome of inter-breeding between Europeans, Indians, and Negroes. In that country, the ultimate merging of races—the direct opposite of South Africa's *apartheid*—is generally regarded as a desirable goal.[18]

There remains to be mentioned the final phase in this process of applying equalitarianism universally. Once it was established within the state, the reign of equality could be extended outside. If in domestic politics differences of color, wealth, sex, and religion were disregarded in granting citizenship, might not universalism encompass in its scope the numerous races, cultures, and regions of mankind? Was equality to be intranational only, or could it be international? To this question, ever since the League of Nations was organized in 1919, the world has been groping for an answer. The appropriate place to discuss it, however, will be in Chapter 14,[19]

[18] On this point consult the writings of the Brazilian sociologist Gilberto Freyre. For example, his *Brazil: an Interpretation* (New York: Alfred A. Knopf, 1945), Chapters 4 and 5.

[19] See pp. 371 ff.

where relations between states and the implications of global organization will be considered.

These two chapters, in which the exclusive and inclusive views of citizenship have been surveyed, can now be concluded with a historical comment. Between these two broadly contrasted doctrines, there can be no uncertainty about which has been prevalent. Most political history and most operative constitutions have been the work of oligarchies. Normally and customarily the many have been governed by the few for the benefit of the few. Humanity as a general rule has lived under regimes of inequality and privilege. Efforts to the contrary have been rare and exceptional, but they have been made both among the ancients and among the moderns. To proclaim in theory the basic equality of all men and to establish a system that recognizes in practice the like rights of all is unusual and abnormal. But since the trend in this direction has been more pronounced during the last hundred years than in any century of the past, there is some ground for hoping that what once was rare may yet become the fashion.

CHAPTER 7

SECOND ISSUE:

(1) THE STATE AND SOCIETY

The Unity of Society. Governments exist because we want certain results that they are able to provide. To know, therefore, what the state is, we must look at what it does. Hence we turn from the citizens it serves to the nature of its services. All associations, as we have seen, are differentiated by the functions they perform. In the case of the state, those functions admit many alternatives and, since they embrace a wide range of choice, are debatable. Controversy thus extends beyond what the state does to what it might do. Human beings inject into discussions concerning the state their preferences about the activities that properly belong to it, which makes the study of governmental functions not merely descriptive, but normative. For the state is what its functions are, as influenced by men's conceptions of what they ought to be.

If one is to make a rational choice, the alternatives must be understood. Consequently, it is important to grasp the issues involved in the debate concerning the activities appropriate to the state. What is at stake here? Why do men struggle so strenuously to extend or confine the volume of governmental activity? Since the state germinates within the matrix of society, what is its relation to that society once it has matured? The answer to these questions can best be attempted by picking up the threads of the argument begun in Chapter 2. There the point was stressed that cooperation and competition between human beings give rise to a plurality of groups, and that individuals are variously associated and reassociated according to the aims they share or the ambitions over which they clash. The fact that society is a complex whole, wherein individuals are members of many groups, creates for each of us a problem of competing loyalties. The outward schism between the groups that compose society is reproduced internally by what Toynbee calls "schism in the soul." If people are to feel at one with themselves, and if there is to be harmony among groups, two requirements have to be met. Subjectively, human beings must feel that what unites them is superior to what separates them. Objectively, they need some institutional means for organizing those feelings. For the term "society" to be more than merely a handy generalization, something is necessary to bind the mixture. Can that "something" be identified?

Pluralism versus Monism. The relations between the groups that make up society have been viewed in two ways. Some influential thinkers have held that associations spring spontaneously from the free play of human activity. They are not summoned by fiat, nor are they the product of one central source. In their origins they are independent of one another; and as the stimuli to associate differ, so do the associations themselves. Therefore, it is concluded, they must be allowed to operate with the same freedom that permitted their birth. Since to be free they must be equal, they are to be regarded as co-ordinate with one another. No association can be accorded a special prerogative of superiority over the rest. The strivings of mankind cannot, it is argued, be folded within the embrace of one supreme good or final end. Men reach out for ends in the plural, not for one end in the singular; and as their purposes are plural, the structure of society must be likewise.[1]

To the pluralists comes the rejoinder of the monists. In their view society is, or ought to be, a unity; and for it to be unified, there must be a tie that binds. While it is true that human drives spontaneously produce numerous groupings, once these exist they cannot, though independently born, act in independence. Groups impinge upon each other, as they pursue their aims, and create a need for order and harmony. Men are distracted by the conflicting claims upon their allegiance of separate, and often rival, associations. The

---

[1] For examples of this viewpoint, consult Harold J. Laski, *Grammar of Politics* 3rd ed. (London: Allen and Unwin, 1934), pp. 25-28, 37, or Robert M. MacIver, *The Modern State* (New York: Oxford University Press, 1926), pp. 7, 182.

remedy for this is to discover some highest good that includes and supersedes the lesser. Next, it is necessary to recognize one association as responsible for attaining that highest good. To this let the remaining associations be subordinated. Thus society can become, and stay, unitary in purpose as in organization.[2]

Each of these views is evidently strong where the other is weak. One lays stress on the role of society as a richly creative matrix of varied behavior. To advocates of this way of thinking, any proposal for central control or unified direction spells death to the kind of society they idealize. Spontaneity, freedom, variety, autonomy—these they consider the cardinal virtues of groups and group action; and the society they most applaud is the one in which such qualities are maximized. But the price of diversity is the impairment of unity. The more the pluralist exalts and exaggerates the independence of associations, the more "the great society" [3] vanishes—until, as with the Cheshire cat, a face lingers on without a body, then a grin without a face, and lastly the grin fades away.

Contrariwise is the position of the monist. He is all for unity and for the virtues he hopes will accompany it—order, harmony, and singleness of purpose. To attain these is impossible, as he sees it, unless the many cohere around one focus. Nor does this coherence result from subjective attitudes alone. To unify society, it is not enough for people to feel that they belong together. The sentiment must be fortified with organization that establishes orderly and harmonious relations between groups by institutional procedures. Though this consummation be devoutly wished for by the monist, he too encounters difficulties that stem from his position. For he invites the question whether his insistence upon unity is so excessive that groups, other than the supreme unifying agency, will lose meaning, character, and identity to the extent that their autonomy is impaired. The penalty for unity can be the imposition of uniformity.

There is, in addition, a special difficulty facing the monist that does not confront the pluralist. The former, desiring to provide society with an integrating focus, must designate what this is to be. He must select, in other words, an institution that is most appropriate

---

[2] The monists, curiously enough, exhibit contrasts no less marked than the pluralists. Witness Aristotle, in the paragraph with which he commences the *Politics,* and Mussolini in *The Social and Political Doctrine of Fascism.*

[3] This is the title of a book by Graham Wallas.

to embrace, oversee, or absorb the rest. Which is he to choose? And how can its task be accomplished?

Unity through the Family, Church, or Business. That a choice does exist, and that the answer is not cut and dried, is substantiated by historical evidence. Several social institutions have, as a matter of fact, essayed this role of being prime co-ordinator for society. One of these, at various places and times, has been the family. In such a case kinship becomes the chief determinant that governs every relationship. Because human beings are connected in certain ways by birth, their other group activities are cast within the mold of heredity. Thus the family becomes the economic unit, where each works for all and is entitled to a share of the total output. The family takes care of its weak, its aged, and its incapacitated. The family provides education; and, for religion, worships its ancestors. The family determines marital unions. The family establishes rules and administers its discipline with rewards and punishments. In some instances it even levies a death penalty on one of its members or wages war upon some neighboring family in the form of a blood feud or vendetta.

Similarly, religious associations have sometimes extended beyond their primary function of worship and have encompassed under spiritual authority the general direction of society. In fact, the system of government named theocracy is evidence in point. When Calvin and Calvinists controlled Geneva in the seventeenth century or when the Jesuits ruled Paraguay in the eighteenth, church-government regulated in minute detail the conduct of individuals and groups. Religious, no less than secular, bodies can declare and enforce the law by reference to divine sanction; can maintain and direct an economic system as proprietors and managers; can supervise the family by granting or withholding its rites; can educate the youth; can organize charities for the needy; and can supervise the arts by control over their themes and forms. Religions can likewise launch crusades, proclaim "holy wars," and place armies in the field. Men have bled and died for the Cross, the Crescent, or the *Mogen David*, as they have for Old Glory, the Union Jack, or the Tricolour.

The same has been true of business firms. Occasionally the association paramount over the rest is economic. A group that originates for purposes of commerce, manufacturing, or trade may discover in a certain *milieu* that it cannot fulfill these functions unless it extends its control over other institutions. Whether Napoleon was right or wrong in describing the British as "a nation of shopkeepers"; or whether President Coolidge did full justice to his fellow-countrymen with the remark that "the business of America is business"; the fact remains that society can be integrated not by kinship, or religion, but by control of productive resources, by entrepreneurial technique, and, in Carlyle's phrase, by the "cash nexus." Indeed there have been corporations clothed in the full panoply of governments; and, if one mentions the celebrated East India Company that ruled Britain's Empire in India until 1858, this is merely to cite a conspicuous, and not a unique, example. When business organizes society for business ends, it too can make and apply the law of its choosing, establish the ethical code, and define the standards of right and wrong in relation to such concepts as "property," "profit," or "labor." By prescribing the conditions and hours and wages of work, business can make or break the family. By its influence over occupations and careers, it can mold the policies and curricula of education. By paying the artist and purchasing his products, it can regulate aesthetic style and taste. Lastly, by promoting or preserving a trading or industrial empire, business can mobilize military force and fight its battles at so much outlay *per caput* and for such and such *per cent*.

These facts warrant an inference. Because the family, church, and corporation have made efforts of this kind with more or less success, it would appear that, in the absence of a coordinating institution, society contains a vacuum that there is an opportunity to fill. If various associations have made the attempt, it is reasonable to assume that a genuine need exists which they seek to satisfy, and that they can then be judged by how well they fill it. That need was seen earlier to arise from the competition between associations and the rival claims they make upon the allegiance of their members. The relations between groups create the occasion for control, supposedly by some super-association. But there is more to it than that. If the unity of society means anything, and is not an empty phrase, more may be required than a mechanism that merely mitigates the effects of conflict. Since society is built upon cooperation, as well as on competition, a case can be argued for a positive policy of promoting harmony between groups.

Furthermore, since a group is more than just the sum of its

separate members, so is society more than the mere addition of the component groups. The structure of society has been described by some writers as federal. This is a helpful analogy if it is understood in two senses: first, that society is not properly a collection of individuals, but rather of groups of individuals, and, second, that the groups collectively constitute more than they do separately. Considered by itself, each association is concerned with human interests that are fractional, these fractions being called economic, educational, religious, and so on. Functioning in its primary sense, an economic association performs activities that are economic, a religious association pursues aims that are religious, and similarly with the rest. No one association, if all are co-ordinate in rank and limited in function, has the responsibility or means to see that these fragments of human life are fused into a whole. In other words, there is no way of ensuring that the economy functions, not as a thing apart, but as the economic aspect of society; that a school or university is no cloistered academy, but a training ground for the use of intelligence in the workaday world; that the particular, in short, be treated within the framework of the general.

Defects of a Single-track Society. But while the monist who wants an integrated society has many weapons to use against the pluralist, at the same time he runs a risk. If any association is to succeed in co-ordinating society, it must graduate from a bit part to the lead role. Thus it must broaden the necessarily narrow interest, from which it started, into a comprehensive concern for the whole. The question is whether an association will in fact be capable of growing to the stature of its wider responsibilities, or will instead remain the prisoner of its origins and of the limits they impose. The problem can be illustrated by some examples that are by no means hypothetical. Suppose the institution that attempts the general co-ordination of society is the family.[4] Then it must be expected that a group, created by kinship and sustained by living together, will transfer to other social spheres the characteristics that spring from its primary functions. Thus relations between human beings will correspond to

---

[4] Some Oriental cultures provide examples of the transfer of the family relationship to an entire society. See an analysis of this attempt in Japan by Robert A. Scalapino, *Democracy and the Party Movement in Prewar Japan* (Berkeley: Univ. of California Press, 1953) pp. 120 ff.

those that exist between husband and wife, or parents and child, or sibling and sibling. Authority will be parental in form. Status within the family circle will determine status within the social circle. Family dictates will be the overriding consideration in the economic realm. Thus, for instance, the ownership and inheritance of the family homestead, the provision for a son to marry and support a wife, production for subsistence only or for exchange—these and similar matters will be settled by the prevailing conceptions of the family as the unifier of the social order. The great society will become an association of kinsmen, writ large.[5]

Likewise, when the integrating agency is religious, its theology will be extended to every secular activity. If the religion asserts the existence of a soul that survives the death of the body, men will be taught to prepare themselves in this world of mortal things for the eternity hereafter. The rules of daily conduct will be construed as a life-long consecration to the Deity. The social contacts of the individual will be confined to the ranks of his co-religionists. Those who do not belong to the established communion—call them heathen, pagan, gentile, infidel, heretic, or what you will—will be the low-caste or outcasts of society. These are "the stranger within thy gates," "the untouchables," "the internal proletariate," [6] living witnesses of a house divided against itself, with religion as the divider. Holy Writ becomes law in the form of the Gospel, the Torah, the Koran, the Vedas; and the supreme lawgiver is the Holy Man, Prophet, or Son of God—a Jesus, Moses, Mahomet, or Gautama. Within this frame of reference, criticism of authority is equated with blasphemy. Opposition itself is sin.

Similar in principle is the result that befalls the economic group that seeks to integrate society. In this case the basic elements of the economic order will extend a pervasive influence throughout the social order. Thus the rights that are vested in the ownership of property, and the human relationships arising from it—such factors of production as the control of natural resources, the use of tools and equipment, the structure of the wage system—all this and more will affect the rest of man's estate. Humanity will be preoccupied

[5] Many peoples have expressed this idea in the form of a story that they are descended from a common ancestor.

[6] This is A. J. Toynbee's phrase in his *Study of History*.

with material concerns: with living standards, the distribution of goods, the struggle for acquisition, the maintenance of employment and of purchasing power. The world will be converted into a market. Language itself will take its connotations from the categories of economics. "Enterprise" will be synonymous with business; ideas that one seeks to impart will be commodities one "sells"; human beings will be specified as "managers," "consumers," "hands." The great society, if it knows no other god than Mammon, will strike the balance sheet of its civilization in pecuniary terms. For what shall it profit a man if he gain his own soul and lose a whole market?

The point of the foregoing paragraphs can thus be summarized: When an association that originates with a finite function broadens out to the indefinite horizons of society, it tends to apply to its larger task the criteria of its initial limits. To the extent that this is so, its efforts provide society with both integration and straitjacketing. To subordinate all aspects of life and all kinds of groups to the single principle of kinship, religion, or economics can yield an unwholesome monism. If then its results are to be beneficial, the unifying association must meet this acid test: while retaining its original functions, it must rise above them and change its own character. It cannot integrate society merely by refashioning every other association in its own image.

This survey of the arguments in issue between monists and pluralists and of the problems peculiar to each facilitates a better understanding of the controversy over the functions of the state. The analysis so far has indicated that the question of what activities are appropriate to the state is not narrowly political, but broadly social. It has also become clear that two issues are involved, since a choice must first be made between pluralism and monism; and, if the latter is preferred, a second choice must determine which of many associations can best co-ordinate the whole. The answer to the second question is, in a vital sense, relevant to the first, because if no association can perform the job of integrating, the case for pluralism wins by default. If, on the other hand, some one association is competent to do the job, then the case for the monist is proportionately strengthened.

The State's Relation to Society. In this controversy the state is directly involved. Wherever there is government, questions must arise concerning the activities it is to undertake. This means that the relations of the state to the other associations that men form must somehow be defined. If the pluralist is to have his way, he must explain (1) why it is necessary to limit the functions of the state, (2) where those limits should be placed, and (3) how society hangs together, or achieves integration, in the absence of a unifying agency. If, however, the monist is to get the better of the argument, he must demonstrate (1) that society is in need of unification, (2) that the state is able to undertake this, and (3) that any dangers which may ensue from confiding this duty to the state are either outweighed by the attendant advantages or can be safely forestalled.

As everybody knows, both viewpoints have been put forward at various times by those who wished to advocate or resist this or that manifestation of governmental power. Nor have the rival philosophies been confined only to the realm of theoretical debate. Under one guise or another, each has been translated into practice and has received concrete expression. Hence the discussion and evaluation of each can be based both on the reasoned hopes of their advocates and on the performance that results from their application in practice. Like the family, business, and church, the state has entered this field of controversy because there is an opportunity existing for it to grasp. If society is ready for integration, the state is as well placed to provide it as are associations based upon kinship, economics, or religion. Or possibly, it is even better placed. This is so because of the character of the primary function from which the state originates. Every human being is in need of protection. All, therefore, need, and to a point depend on, the association that provides it. Furthermore, the state controls the force that assures protection. Through this same force, the government is able at times to impose itself upon the other institutions of society. Indeed the state can be more effectively monistic than either businesses, families, or churches, because of the sanctions it employs. Those who do not bow to family control may be excluded from the kin group. Those who defy their employers may lose their bread and butter. Those who resist sacerdotal authority may be excommunicated. Such sanctions are not completely compulsive unless the victim is left with no other alternative. But in some societies a man may sur-

vive without a family; he may earn his living in new ways; he may
embrace a new faith or do without one. Universally, however, the
sanctions of the state are a gun pointed at your temple. If, as is ordinarily the case, the state has a monopoly of the available force,
there is no choice but to submit or die.

The modern debate over the proper sphere of governmental activity trails behind it a history of at least twenty-five centuries. For
that reason the best way to understand current controversies about
the functions of the state is to review them in chronological perspective. The story forms a sequence of alternating episodes, with the
emphasis shifting from one pole to the other. The city-state of the
Graeco-Roman period was primarily monistic in spirit and organization. The counter-doctrine, that the sphere of the state must be
limited, was advanced in idea and reality by the Christian Church
after it became the official religion of the Roman Empire and a
partner in the established order. This principle continued to prevail
through the Middle Ages, but lost ground with the advent of the
Reformation and the emergence of the nation-state. The ethos of
the latter at its inception was as strongly monistic as the city-state
had been. It remained so until the economic ferment of the Industrial Revolution once more brought into vogue the concept of the
limited state, with business now cast in the role formerly played by
the medieval church. The twentieth century, in this matter as in
others inheriting its legacy from the nineteenth, has both imitated
and reacted against its predecessor. Midway in this present century,
it is certain only that both viewpoints—the one which insists on
limits and the one which does not—are still embattled. It is uncertain
which is at the moment dominant or likely to become so.

The five periods may be roughly identified as follows:

(1) First Period: approximately from the tenth century B.C. to
the fourth century A.D. Monistic State.

(2) Second Period: from the fourth century A.D. to middle of the
fifteenth century. Limited State.

(3) Third Period: from middle of the fifteenth century to 1776.
Monistic State.

(4) Fourth Period: 1776 to 1914. Limited State.

(5) Fifth Period: 1914 to middle of twentieth century. Monistic
and Limited States in conflict and crisis.

A survey of these periods,[7] and a review of their problems, will help to explain the advantages claimed for each doctrine and the difficulties attending its fulfilment.

The Graeco-Roman City-State: an Experiment in Monism. In its fully developed form, the *Polis* or city-state, such as Sparta in the sixth century B.C. or Athens in the fifth, demanded of its citizens the whole of their allegiance. All human activities and associations were either actually controlled or liable to control by the state. Society—meaning the sum total of all groups—was regarded, not as separate from the state, but as subordinate to it. Even the Greek language, that flexible instrument for conveying the subtlest nuance of thought, had no word to signify the concept of society any more than it had a term to distinguish between state and city. The one word *Polis* sufficed for city, state, and society combined. Within this context of ideas, the state was the paramount social institution when and where it chose to intervene. Thus, the economic field was subject to political ordering as the public interest seemed to require. Religion consisted of state worship to the patron hero or deity of the city and to the pantheon of the Olympian dynasty. The glorious cultural achievements that have made that age immortal were in large part evoked or produced under the stimulus of state demand. The architects, sculptors, and painters—an Ictinus, a Pheidias, or an Apelles—dedicated their genius to the temples and other civic buildings that the state constructed for its adornment. It was the public market place that served as classroom for the interrogations of a Socrates; the citizens' assembly that inspired the oratory of a Pericles or a Demosthenes; the official festivals and contests that promoted the staging of dramas by the great tragedians and of comedies by Aristophanes.

In order not to be misleading, one must point out that, while the above account correctly describes the general tendency, certain aberrations or exceptions did nevertheless exist. There were religious cults, such as the Eleusinian Mysteries, which did not belong to official state ceremony. There were creative artists, lyric poets for

---

[7] This breakdown into "periods" is offered with the necessary caution that any such subdivision contains an element of arbitrariness. The beginning and ending dates are averages, rather than precise points. Few periods, moreover, are all one thing or all another. Usually, contemporary instances of the opposite to the prevalent tendency can be discovered.

instance, who produced their works to satisfy an inward urge rather than a public audience. In actuality, not everything was prescribed and ordered by the state, save possibly in Sparta and Crete. But what is important is that, if the state chose to extend its authority to any sphere, there was no rival institution strong enough to resist its advance and no social philosophy delimiting the bounds of state action. Indeed, the classic pronouncements of thinkers like Plato and Aristotle are wholly couched in terms of the omnipotent state. These two men, somewhere or other in their major treatises, touch on practically every one of the great issues that occupy the forefront of political theory and practice in the modern world. Significantly though, they omit to raise the questions of the relation of the state to society and the possible limits of state power. The reason for the omission is that such queries did not even arise in Greek experience. It therefore never occurred to Plato and Aristotle to examine an alternative to monism. This they took for granted. On this point, however, in the interests of clarity and accuracy the distinction between state and government must be borne in mind. There was a notable Greek tradition that condemned a certain type of government as tyrannical, justified resistance to it, and made heroes of tyrannicides. Some of the men who employed this line of thought—Plato, for instance—were convinced monists. Prepared to resist a tyrannical government, they were nevertheless not prepared to circumscribe the sphere of the state. Were these viewpoints self-consistent? How can a government be termed tyrannical, and opposition to it be upheld, save on some theory that it is exceeding its limits and doing what it ought not to do? Otherwise, why call it tyranny?

The answer is that the Greeks resolved their inconsistency and saved their logic by accepting another major assumption. They distinguished between true and perverted kinds of government. The former were those wherein the rulers ruled in the interests of the whole community (inclusive of the governed). The latter were those where rulers governed for their own interest only. This distinction explains why Plato and Aristotle could logically accept a monistic theory of the state provided it were of the true kind, and yet support resistance to the perverted kind.

One further clarification should be added. Both Plato and Aristotle are monists in the sense that they view the state as supreme among human associations and set no bounds to its activities. But their mon-ism is not identical. Or, to be more precise, the supremacy of the state reveals itself in different ways. Aristotle asserts his monism in the opening paragraph of the *Politics*, where he says that the state is the paramount association, embracing all the rest, and pursuing the highest good. Yet this conception of the state does not lead him to undervalue, still less to abolish, the remaining associations. These retain their place within the fabric of society and even serve to strengthen the bonds of social cohesion. But ultimately, and in case a conflict arises, it is to the state that all are subordinate. Plato differs from Aristotle in his utterly uncompromising emphasis upon unity which in his belief is best safeguarded by the destruction of competing associations. All loyalties and affections are to be focussed on and drawn towards one center. If other institutions, such as the family or the ownership of private property, are potential rivals, they must be eliminated. The monistic state of Aristotle is one that per-mits other groups to exist, but stands supreme over them. The monistic state of Plato prefers to abolish the other groups and absorb their functions.

Apart from the preferences of the philosophers, however, what were the historical reasons why the practice and philosophy of the city-state were monistic? Two reasons suffice. One is the smallness of the city-state as a unit of government. With an area and popula-tion so confined, there was little room for parallel, co-ordinate, sys-tems. As the Greeks read the lessons of their own history, they could choose one of two clear-cut alternatives: unity with order or faction-fights with anarchy. Closeness of contact, and the pressure of small-sized communities, bred a view of the state as the paramount social organization. In the antithesis between the public and private sides of life, Greek spokesmen gave their preference to the former. Thus their term for private citizen, *idiotes*, has yielded for its modern descendant the word "idiot" and Pericles could castigate persons who did not participate in civic affairs as being useless to the com-munity.[8] Besides smallness, a second reason for monism was the condition of insecurity that plagued the Greeks in their interstate relations. Not only was there the possibility of war between Greek and non-Greek, but the little city-states themselves were often at each other's throats and neighboring settlements were likely to be

[8] See the Funeral Oration in Thucydides' *Histories*, bk. II.

hereditary foes. Seeking protection from these perils, the Greeks were impelled to rally around the institution whose function was to protect.

If monism was encouraged by the smallness of the unit of government and facilitated by the absence of any association rivalling the state, it could be expected that, when these conditions disappeared, the monistic state would disappear also. Early signs of this possibility were discernible in the first philosophies that emerged after the absorption of the *Polis* into the larger political units of kingdoms or empires. The Stoics [9] and Epicureans rejected the outlook of Plato and Aristotle which favored an all-embracing collectivism within the confines of the *Polis*. Instead, they sought to reconcile opposite extremes by finding a place for the individual in the immensity of the universe. Since the politics of the three centuries between the breakup of the empire of Alexander and the consolidation of that of Rome were chaotic and turbulent, men tended to view the state with pessimism, apprehension, or indifference. If the good life were unobtainable through politics, it must be sought in other ways. If the ambitions of governments were prejudicial to the public peace, peace of mind must be cultivated elsewhere. Hence followed a reassessment of the relative priorities of public and private activity, and philosophers now advised that men should compensate for the insecurities around them by building their security inside themselves.

As occurred in the case of equalitarianism, a concept born in the minds of Greeks received institutional form through the acts of Romans. This is, in fact, what did happen after Rome had succeeded in expanding into an empire and Christianity had managed to capture Rome. Previously, when Rome was a small community beset by unfriendly neighbors, it was subject to the same internal and external forces as the city-states of Greece. No sphere of life was exempt from the power of the state, if there were occasion or demand for its exercise. None of the other groups composing society was in a position to withstand the state or claim an independent or higher allegiance. Family relations, religious cults, economic affairs, cultural advances—all could be brought within the ambit of official surveillance. The situation changed when the Roman Empire expanded to a size unparalleled in the earlier history of the Mediterranean area. The tightly-knit, close-packed organization of a small

[9] For the Stoics, see Chapter 6, p. 128.

community could not be transferred or reproduced across the large-scale dimensions of Rome's conquests. Given the means of communication available at that day between the central authority and peripheral regions, the extent of the area to be governed precluded any intensive direction of society by the state. As long as Rome's authority was firmly established in the three vital spheres of military power, foreign relations, and finance, much diversity and autonomy were permitted in other matters to the various provinces and municipalities. Along with this change of scale, an empire that eventually stretched from Persia to Scotland and from the German forests to the Sahara desert, came to embrace a host of religious faiths. Out of the welter of sects, cults, rites, and deities, Christianity through three centuries of growth emerged dominant. When the Emperor Constantine was converted, the *Imperium Romanum* entered into articles of union with the Church. Considered in political terms, this partnership between the Cross and the Eagle brought to the state both gain and loss. Gain, because the spiritual influence of the Christian faith could now be employed to unify the allegiance of Roman citizens. Loss, because the state had admitted to the citadel of power a separate and co-ordinate association.

The Christian Revolution: Church-State Dualism. Thus a new era in political history was inaugurated. The new era was signalized by a different solution to the problem of defining the functions of the state. Where the old order had been content with a doctrine that set no limit to these functions and made the boundaries of politics co-extensive with the whole range of social conduct, the crux of the new order lay precisely in the effort to delimit the field of politics within the larger area of society and thus necessarily establish an adjacent field that the state would have no right to enter. The earlier concept of a society unified by the monistic state was rejected. For it was substituted the notion of a society split in two, with twin institutions separated by a frontier line. Philosophy was now called upon to justify, and statesmanship to operate, a division of spheres. The issues posed by this endeavor were challenging. Reasons had to be discovered for the assertion that dualism was in some ways superior to unity; a line of demarcation had somewhere to be drawn; and finally the separate spheres and the governments of each had somehow to be related to each other. These problems in all their ramifications occupied human ingenuity for over a thousand years.

Whenever it is argued that the state be shorn of a portion of its power, the proposal takes specific form from the nature of the association that offers the challenge to monism. In this case, since religion assumed the offensive, it was the church that emerged as an institution co-equal with the state. Relations between church and state now became a major issue for political theory and organization, which they had not been before. It is, therefore, to the social doctrines of Christianity, as these evolved from the fourth to the fourteenth century, A.D., that we must turn for understanding the theory and tactics of the Dark and Middle Ages. Like all systematic philosophies, Christianity assumed or asserted a view of human nature. Man was thought to be composed of two parts, body and soul. The body, an object of sense perception and known through sensory evidence, exists as a member of the world of material things. It is born, passes through the life cycle, and dies. The soul does not belong in the sensory realm. Proof of its existence is granted by divine revelation that must be accepted on faith. Joining the body when life begins, the soul will depart on the advent of death and is immortal. The soul is, therefore, on a higher plane than the body and a man's most important possession. Hence in the scale of Christian values this world takes second place to the next one. The care of the spirit, which is everlasting, has priority over the care of the temporal and mundane. Man's greatest concern, while alive on this earth, is to save his soul for eternity.

How dualism runs through Christian thinking and theology is evident in the saying of its Founder: "Render, therefore, unto Caesar the things that are Caesar's; and render unto God the things that are God's." The same pattern recurs in the treatise of Saint Augustine, *Concerning the City of God*, where an analogous distinction is drawn between two cities, the earthly and the heavenly. Men should resist the temptations and avoid the perils of the former. Let them seek the eternal bliss of the heavenly city by obeying the counsel to be perfect "even as your Father in Heaven is perfect." To apply these attitudes to actual government was the task initiated by one of the early Popes, Gelasius I, and continued by various of his successors. Since men were compounded of two natures, one mortal and the other immortal, the organization of society—so the argument ran—must correspond to the dualism implanted in humanity by the Creator. The church should be the institution charged with the

salvation of souls and the preparation in this life for the life everlasting. The state should have the responsibility for this-worldly, as
opposed to other-worldly, affairs; that is to say, for the mortal sphere
pertaining to the body. Church and state should be constituted as
separate authorities, each paramount within its own bailiwick and
possessing its own panoply of government. But how were these
twain, the *sacerdotium* and the *imperium*, the ecclesiastical power
and the temporal, the spiritual and the secular, to be related? The
Gelasian answer envisaged them as "two swords" that could not be
grasped and wielded by one hand. As God had endowed man with
a soul separate from his body, so must church and state exist independently of each other. It would therefore be as wrong for an
Emperor to exercise spiritual power as for a Pope to hold secular
sway. What God had put asunder, let no man put together.

It is evident that the application of these formulae in practice depended on the validity of two assumptions: one, that the spheres of
the ecclesiastical and temporal jurisdictions could in fact be separated, and the other, that the two institutions would respectively
adhere to the status of equals and co-ordinates. Failure to fulfill
either assumption would mean the death of dualism. How did the
medieval Christian world meet these acid tests of its dogma?

The Theory of Dualism versus the Condition of Unity. The separation of the spiritual realm from the secular was more easily stated
as an ideal than realized in actuality. The things that are Caesar's
may be distinguishable from the things that are God's, yet both are
in many areas intertwined. Thus, there were ceremonies and official acts of the state that were accompanied by prayer or required
solemnizing by some religious affirmation. Treaties between rulers,
for example, were signed and sworn under oath that called for the
presence of the Bible and a priest. Governments were staffed by
human beings who possessed souls, and who, being Christians, were
sons of the Church. The Church could therefore call them to account if their governmental acts violated its canons of Christian
duty. By the weapons of excommunication and interdict, the Popes
could even subdue a temporal ruler, as in the cases of the Emperor
Henry IV or King John of England. The long drawn out investi-
ture controversy revolved around the question of whether a Bishop
should be invested with the insignia of his office by the secular authority of the area or by an ecclesiastical superior. Conversely, while

the church was involved in various functions of the state, so was the state immersed in matters vital to the church. The church, as its power waxed, became an integral part of the established order that the state existed to protect. The church acquired land and buildings and other forms of property. It had large numbers of people, including serfs, working in its employ. It used for its own needs the revenues that accrued from its possessions and claimed to be exempt from contributing to the temporal treasury. If the state failed to maintain internal order, or was unable to protect its territories from invasion, the church ran the risk of looting and pillage. Hence, in a thousand ways lay matters were interlocked with spiritual. The two spheres were separated by a metaphysical, not an iron, curtain, and it was not practicable to make them self-contained.

Similar difficulties were encountered with the effort to place the two institutions on that footing of equality that the Gelasian theory enunciated. Each of the partners, as occasion permitted or demanded, pressed its attack on the other. Each, at one time or another, struck at the foundations of Gelasianism by attempting either to subordinate one sword to the other or to grasp both with one hand. In this tussle for supremacy between church and state, the initial advantage, strategically and tactically, lay with the church, and the first major blows at the doctrine of Gelasius were dealt by his Papal successors. There were various reasons why this happened. For one thing, the theoretical postulates of Christianity were not easily reconciled with the concept of equal jurisdictions. To a Christian the soul was clearly on a higher plane than the body, life in the hereafter more important than the life here and now, eternity more significant than three score years and ten. Hence in the hierarchy of Christian values the church outranked the state. If churchmen argued that the spiritual sword should precede and overpower the temporal, who could gainsay such a contention? Furthermore, quite independently of theoretical beliefs, there were practical considerations that favored unity rather than dualism. This was especially so in the troubled times that followed the breakdown of the Roman Empire in the West, when Teutonic peoples invaded its territories and carved out new kingdoms. While the secular power was at the worst in dissolution, or at the best in flux, the sole focus and rallying-point for society often proved to be the church. If there were instances when

Popes gratuitously clutched at both swords, there were also times when the church seized both through the state's default.

The Papal Rejection of Dualism. The Papal attacks on the Gelasian doctrine were occasioned by two of the most prolonged and harassing issues of the medieval period: one concerning the claim of secular rulers to invest bishops with the symbols of their office, and the other arising over royal demands that clergy pay taxes to the state treasury. During the former of these controversies, which at one stage witnessed the capitulation of the Emperor Henry IV to Pope Gregory VII, the latter insisted that within the church the bishops were subordinate to the Pope, and that in church-state relations a defiant ruler could be excommunicated and his subjects absolved from their oaths of allegiance to him. This was tantamount to claiming for the Papacy a power to depose a monarch, employable at the Pope's discretion. Implicit in this, of course, was the view that of the two swords the *sacerdotium* was mightier than the *imperium*, a doctrine which, whether justifiable or not, was not Gelasian. But Gregory went even further. Mindful of the distinction which St. Augustine had drawn between the city of God and the earthly city, he proceeded to suggest—which Augustine had not —that the city of God was synonymous with the church whereas the earthly city, or kingdom of the Devil, was identifiable with the state, a pair of equations which definitely concluded with a debasement of the secular sphere in the hierarchy of Christian values!

The later controversy over the taxing power was, if anything, fiercer and more embittered. It reached on the side of the church, as its relative position weakened, the ultimate in extravagant contentions. In this struggle the leading protagonists were Pope Boniface VIII and Philip the Fair, King of France. Armed with the doctrine enunciated earlier by Innocent IV, that the Pope enjoyed *plenitudo potestatis* (i.e. "total power") Boniface moved into the logically final ground and expressly rejected dualism. In a Bull entitled *Unam Sanctam*, whose initial word stressed unity, the Pope claimed both swords—though the temporal one could be delegated to the secular arm to be wielded at ecclesiastical bidding. This pronouncement sealed the Papal rejection of the goal of a divided society.

Attack on Dualism by the State. The position of the state during these controversies was one that switched as its power changed relatively to the church. If the temporal authorities were disorganized, as was not infrequently the case during the Dark Ages; if the Empire, reconstituted by Charlemagne in 800 A.D., was more shadowy than real, and the Emperor was insecure in his authority; if kings were weakened by the pretensions and powers of the feudal nobility; then the secular branch was scarcely so consolidated as to withstand a determined Pope. Under such conditions the state was placed on the defensive, which forced its apologists to adhere fairly strictly to the doctrines of Gelasius. Acknowledging the supremacy and monopoly of the church in the salvation of souls, the defenders of the state had to assert that over temporal matters the ruler derived his power directly from God—not indirectly via the Pope as an intermediary. In other words, the things that are Caesar's are entrusted to Caesar by divine dispensation. For the powers that be (and this means all of them) are ordained of God. Upon this assumption, the state could successfully preserve its role as the equal partner of the church.

In the later phases of the conflict, however, especially during the struggles between Boniface VIII and Philip and between Pope John XXII and the Emperor Lewis of Bavaria, the weights were tipped in the balance on the secular side. This was due to the cumulative effect of political trends operating within the medieval system that finally contributed to its downfall. One such trend was the gradual consolidation of monarchical power at the expense of the nobility.[10] Another, associated with it, was the glimmer or dawning of national [11] sentiments—particularly in evidence when on the tax question the French clergy supported King Philip of France against the Pope at Rome. A third was the eventual political weakening of the Papacy because of its own internal corruption and lowered prestige in the period of the Schism. Thus strengthened, the state was able to launch its own offensive, and therewith attack the Gelasian theory from the opposite flank. Its line of argument contended that the function of the church is to teach and preach. As an institution organized on this earth, the church falls within the category of this-worldly affairs. Hence its property is taxable by the state, while its

[10] See Chapter 11, pp. 272-4.
[11] See Chapter 13, pp. 334 ff.

personnel (that is, the clergy) are merely one vocational group within society and, as such, subject to the jurisdiction of laymen. Like the contrary attempt of Boniface VIII, this, too, was a rejection of dualism. But the advocacy of unification now issued from the other direction, with the state casting itself in the paramount role.

All in all, the medieval experiment in these two respects must be judged a failure. Dualism did not work. The two spheres were not kept separate. The two jurisdictions did not continue equal and co-ordinate. The two swords were not brandished in harmony and unison. Too often they clashed against each other. Like a pair of unruly oxen harnessed to the same yoke, both parties sought to be rid of the Gelasian legacy. But the impasse which medievalism had reached by the early fifteenth century marked the end, not of the story, but only of an episode in it. A new epoch was arriving with new facts and formulae.

The Reconstruction of Unity. The political process has a characteristic, of which many examples may be noted, that when a trend in one direction has reached a point of excess, it is likely to provoke a counteraction in reverse. Sometimes the latter movement, too, will be developed to excess. With the breakdown of the attempt at dualism there came a new effort, or rather a second try to reinstate the older principle that predated Constantine's conversion. In place of two spheres, two jurisdictions, two swords, there was now to be one. Instead of the state performing limited functions that covered a fraction of society, its sphere was now to be as wide as that of society. In lieu of limits, the state's range of action was to know no bounds but those of social need or necessity.

The yearning for unity was a not unintelligible reaction to the insecurities and discords of a divided society. There were many who had had their fill of conflicting claims, clashing loyalties, and antagonistic systems. They preferred to accept, with all its risks, a single authority. Unity at least meant that you knew whose laws and which commands to obey. Hence it is that Thomas Hobbes, describing the nature of the covenant on which a state and government are founded, urges the concentration of authority in these words: "The only way to erect such a Common Power, as may be able to defend them from the invasion of Forraigners, and the injuries of one another, . . . is, to conferre all their power and strength upon *one* Man, or upon *one* Assembly of men, that may reduce all their wills, by plurality of voices, unto *one* will...." [12] In keeping with this plea for unity, Hobbes views with suspicion, distrust, or outright antipathy, the development within society of associations other than the state, since these may grow from subordinates into rivals of the central authority. Upon them he vents his displeasure in a wholesale indictment that embraces "the Ghostly Authority" of the church, the accumulation of too much treasure by a few, the loyalty of an army to an ambitious general, "the immoderate greatness of a town," and also "the great number of Corporations, which are as it were many lesser common-wealths in the bowels of a greater, like wormes in the entrayles of a naturall man." For full measure he adds to his list "the Liberty of Disputing against absolute Power, by pretenders to Politicall Prudence; which though bred for the most part in the Lees of the people; yet animated by False Doctrines, are perpetually meddling with the Fundamentall Lawes, to the molestation of the Common-wealth; like the little Wormes, which Physicians call *Ascarides*." [13]

If allowance is made for the extravagant language, a clear meaning emerges. Hobbes is predisposed against a plurality of associations on grounds that are akin to Plato's objection to the family and private property. For the co-existence of other associations alongside the state is considered a weakness to the state and to society, because it subjects each individual, as a member of many groups, to diverse affiliations and potentially rival allegiances. The Hobbesian cure-all for the disorders of pluralism is as drastic, uncompromising, and clear-cut, as the Platonic. All power must go to the state, and, within the state, to its supreme ruling element. Rid yourselves, so runs his advice, of a multiplicity of associations. Rally around the great association. Finally, since not all his readers were rationalists, with a last flourish he inserts the keystone of religious faith into the archway of his "scientific" reasons for the foundation of the state: "This is the Generation of that great LEVIATHAN, or rather (to speake more reverently) of that *Mortall God*, to which wee owe under the *Immortall God*, our peace and defence." [14]

---

[12] *Leviathan.* Part 2, chap. 17, Everyman's Library, p. 89. My italics. See chap. 29 (pp. 174-75) for his explicit rejection of church-state dualism.

[13] *Ibid.,* chap. 29.

[14] *Ibid.,* chap. 17, p. 89. Italics and capitals in original.

These excerpts from the thinking of Thomas Hobbes have been chosen as representative of the new trend because of the rigorous and unflinching character of their logic. They have the simple merit of hewing the issue in sharp outline and high relief. But the ideas were not, of course, carved *in vacuo* or chiseled in thin air. They were excavated from the rock-strata of facts, thrown up into new convolutions by the political earthquakes of the sixteenth and seventeenth centuries. The violence of those circumstances was due to the breakdown of the Gelasian formula and the search for new solutions.

Reformation, Counter-Reformation, or Toleration. Since the church had been partner or rival of the state for a thousand years, and since church-state relations were a bone of contention, it was to this problem that the new era turned its attention. The relative strength of the two institutions, already changing with the emergence of nationalism, was decisively altered in the sixteenth century as the papacy weakened. In this respect, even more important than the internal decline of its organization (which could be, and later was, reconstructed), was the defection from Rome of large areas of western Christendom. The Protestant Reformation, whose influence was most strongly felt in north-central and north-western Europe and more among Teutonic and Scandinavian peoples than among Latins, established in a Christendom already divided between the Roman and Eastern Orthodox rites a further split within the west. From that time to the present, to be a Christian in western Europe or its subsequent colonial offshoots did not necessarily mean acceptance of the Roman rite or allegiance to papal authority. The Catholic Church, whose Greek name literally means "universal," no longer possessed a universal following. The result has been that for five centuries no one church in the West has enjoyed a monopoly of Christianity. Furthermore, when the dissolvent acids of Protestantism commenced their corrosion of the once-monolithic church, the same chemistry could operate within the chinks and crevasses of Protestantism itself. The practice of dissent could react upon its instigators; and the divisive process, once started, set in motion a train of subdivisions, sects, and schisms. Lutherans, Anglicans, Presbyterians, Baptists, Quakers, Methodists, and others besides, held out to mankind the keys to the Kingdom.

The political consequences of a fragmented Christianity were

momentous alike for citizens individually and for the state of which
they were members. In spiritual matters the individual was no longer
faced with the compulsions of monopoly. The doctrine that "there
is no salvation outside the Church" [15] lost most of its effect, since
there were now a variety of churches, each proffering salvation.
Excommunication lacked its former terror, for there were other
communions to join. The interdict, whereby medieval Popes forbade
obedience to a heretical ruler, became an obsolete weapon. Skepticism now had full scope in matters theological, since if many
churches pointed out different roads to Heaven, the curious were
bound to inquire which was the right one.

What effect did all this have upon the state? In what ways was
government impelled to adjust to this new situation? The political
novelty lay in the fact that Christianity, which for a thousand years
had provided a unifying force in western Europe, was now torn
asunder and became a disruptive agent. Previously, if a ruler were
prepared to accept the church as a partner in his power or as his
superior, there would at least be relative harmony. But now a
Christian ruler had to choose between different churches (it being
agreed that he could not be non-Christian or an atheist); and, once
his own personal choice was made, he had to decide whether his
subjects could choose differently from himself· or must adhere to
the same communion. Thus arose the political issue of whether a
person's religious beliefs were relevant to their citizenship and their
allegiance to their sovereign. Could Protestants tolerate Catholics,
or Catholics tolerate Protestants, as equally loyal members of the
same state? Could one Protestant sect even tolerate another? Should
the state, confronted with the fact of differences, exercise neutrality
and ennoble the tolerance of diversity as an ideal of politics? Or
should it require conformity to orthodoxy, if necessary by imposing
it and persecuting heretics? To find the answers to these questions
took more than two centuries in which throughout Europe much
blood was spilled, martyrs were tortured and burned, great treasure
was squandered, savage wars were fought, and bigotry reaped its
bitter harvest of bestiality.

One answer—which was everywhere the first attempt, and in
some places also the final outcome—proceeded on the assumptions
that a person's religion is relevant to the ruler, that church and state

---

[15] *Extra ecclesiam nulla salus.*

must be identified by merger of their controlling authority, and that heresy is therefore treason. These doctrines were summarized in the terse Latin formula: *cujus regio, ejus religio* ("who controls the region, controls its religion"). Both Protestants, in areas where the Reformation was successful, and Catholics, where the counter-Reformation held its ground, applied this formula to their adversaries. In England, for example, the Reformation was launched when Henry VIII, wanting to divorce his wife, obtained the support of Parliament for abolishing papal authority over the Church in England, dissolved the monastic orders, and established a national church with himself at its head as "Defender of the Faith." These decisive events initiated a chain reaction of after-effects, as when Henry sought to exact from the clergy an oath of allegiance to himself as their spiritual superior; when Mary attempted to reinstate Catholicism; when policy was once more reversed under Elizabeth who authorized a new prayer-book and a revised liturgy; and when James II, a century too late, again led England back to Rome and lost his throne in the final assertion of triumphant Protestantism.[16]

The dreadful cost of internecine strife between irreconcilables prompted England at last to apply an alternative answer: that the state, though officially committed to an orthodoxy of its own, could safely permit its subjects to profess different religious beliefs—always provided that this concession did not diminish their political allegiance. Through the eighteenth century only members of the Church of England were allowed by law to hold political office.[17] But in the third decade of the nineteenth century the disabilities of other faiths were removed and all posts, save the monarchy, were opened to their adherents. Gradually the principle of tolerance, at first a hard-won necessity, was elevated into a virtue. In the United

[16] The principle of the subordination of the church to the state is thus described by G. M. Trevelyan: "Bishop Jewel, the best exponent of the ideas of the early Elizabethan settlement, declared: 'This is our doctrine, that every soul, of what calling soever he be—be he monk, be he preacher, be he prophet, be he apostle—ought to be subject to King and magistrates.' The sphere of King and magistrates covered religion. All were agreed that there could be only one religion in the State, and all except Romanists and very rigorous Puritans were agreed that the State must decide what that religion should be." *Illustrated English Social History* (London: Longmans, Green, 1950), II, 34.

[17] Annually, however, after 1727, Parliament passed Indemnity Acts, exempting from legal penalties those who held public office without swearing the necessary oath.

States, from the beginnings of its independent nationhood, public guarantees of private religious freedom, as well as a ban upon establishing an official religion, were incorporated into the legal structure of the governmental system.[18] Jefferson was author of Virginia's notable *Act for Establishing Religious Freedom* that was passed in 1786. Its preamble affirmed that the state stands neutral where matters of faith are involved: "Our civil rights have no dependence on our religious opinions, more than our opinions in physics or geometry." A few years afterwards, when the Bill of Rights was appended to the Constitution of the United States, the opening words of the first amendment declared: "Congress shall make no law respecting an establishment of religion, or prohibiting the free exercise thereof."

Monism again: the Theory of Sovereignty. The quest for a fresh formula with which to cut the Gordian knot of church-state relations did not lack results. In the sixteenth century a new principle took shape to express the departure from Gelasianism. This is the doctrine, of which so much has been heard from that time to the present, called "sovereignty." An early exposition of it comes from the Frenchman, Jean Bodin, who in 1576 published his *Six Books Concerning the Republic*. He writes: "Sovereignty is a power over citizens and subjects that is supreme and above the law." [19] In this phrasing of it, as in others, sovereignty is evidently a complex, embracing several ideas. Some of these, indeed, since sovereignty has many ramifications, fall under different headings among the five classic issues and will be discussed elsewhere.[20] But one aspect is central to the issue now being considered. In rejecting the view that the functions of the state should be exercised within a limited sphere, sovereignty asserted the limitless range of governmental activity. When sovereignty was pronounced to be one and indivisible, this meant that the state was to assume (or resume what it enjoyed in Graeco-Roman days) the general direction and supervision of society. The very force of the new insistence upon unity was a measure of the reaction against dualism.

But a further word of clarification is necessary. It is self-evident that when a King, like Henry VIII of England, proclaimed himself

---

[18] Prior to independence, of course, the leading example of religious toleration, thanks to Penn and the Quakers, was to be found in Pennsylvania.

[19] *Maiestas est summa in cives ac subditos legibusque soluta potestas.*

[20] See Chapters 11, pp. 273-4; 14, pp. 353 ff.

head of the church, he was definitely unifying the two spheres. The church was then in no position to set bounds to the sphere of politics. If, however, as later happened in Britain and the United States, the state was prepared to tolerate religious dissent, did the abandonment of the demand for conformity imply that the state accepted limits to its power? The answer to this question, though arguable, is probably negative. Where the state tolerated diversity, it did so upon one important condition, whether tacit or expressed. A dividing line was supposed to be drawn between matters of public, and those of private, concern. The churches—any number of them—were permitted their freedom, on condition that they confined their activities to worshipping the Deity and teaching religious doctrine. Belief in this field was ascribed to the private conscience, for which reason the state would keep its hands off. But in the public domain the state maintained its claim to be sovereign, and any church that departed from the private sphere and entered the public arena would run the risk and pay the penalty of grappling with Leviathan. Hence if toleration existed, it did so on political suffrance. The state stood neutral because the stings of the churches were drawn. They, for their part, exercised their freedom on the condition of abstaining from designs to wield political power. Any breach of this condition would call down on ecclesiastical heads the full weight of sovereignty, that is, of secular supremacy.

Thus the wheel had swung full circle. The first experiment in setting bounds to the functions of the state ended in a restoration of the *status quo*. From the Greek concept of the all-embracing *Polis* to the Bodinian or Hobbesian theory of sovereignty a connecting thread is woven across the centuries. But the first challenge to the omnipotent state was not the last. It is time now to turn to the second attempt and observe how, when, and why the pluralist cudgels were brandished anew.

CHAPTER 8

(2) POLITICS AND ECONOMICS

The Economists' Case for Limited Government. The second great attempt to limit the functions of the state began with a series of presuppositions largely different from the first attempt, but ended with a curious and unforeseen resemblance to it. This was the effort to restrict the authority of government by appeal to the authority of the individual. Following the train of thought that government maintains order, order calls for law, law requires enforcement, enforcement demands coercion, and coercion is the enemy of freedom, one may reach the conclusion that government and liberty are antithetical. From this it could follow that any enlargement of the functions of government would mean a reduction of liberty; so that those who prize the latter would have to confine their government within limits. Then, once those limits were set, individual human beings would be free to apply their energies at will outside the sphere remaining under the control of the state.

Historically this doctrine, whose result was to create a power-vacuum wherever the state was unable to operate, preceded the Industrial Revolution. But the latter phenomenon released new forces that rushed pell-mell to fill the void. During the nineteenth century the social order of many countries was well-nigh transformed by a series of economic changes. New scientific discoveries, new techniques of production, new forms of corporate organization, made possible the accumulation of new wealth without the inhibitions of political direction. Such wealth, when amassed, formed a reservoir of power, and its owners were accordingly able to challenge the rulers of the state for the leadership of society. In this indirect fashion, due largely to the historical timing, the individualist doctrine that the Renaissance and Reformation initiated laid the ground for what was tantamount to a second venture in dualism. For there arose an economic theory, suited to the interests of businessmen, that pre-empted the individualistic argument and supplied its own twist to the notion of opposition to state authority. The effect of the doctrine—though seldom presented as explicitly as this —was a virtual bisection of society into a political order and an economic order, allotting to business a position within society co-ordinate with the government and carving out an economic sphere that should function as independently as possible of the state.

The similarity between this and the medieval system resides, of course, in the common presumption in favor of a limited government. The difference, however, lies in the source that produced the challenge to the state's monopoly of authority. It is now economics, rather than religion, which leads the assault upon the monistic state. It is now economists, businessmen, bankers, manufacturers—not the clergy—who provide the main impetus and drive towards pluralism. Hence it is in terms of economic policy, and over the relations between economics and politics, that many arguments about the functions of the state are framed and formulated. The state and the economy; government and business; politicians (or officials) and entrepreneurs; these, whether conceived as partners or rivals, resume the controversy where Popes and Emperors left off. Leviathan in the second round grapples with Mammon.

As there was an element of novelty in the problem that Christianity posed for the state from Constantine onwards, so there was an innovation in this changed relationship of the political and economic orders. Prior to the close of the eighteenth century the intimacy of the connection between politics and economics was not seriously questioned. The field of economics, originating as "household management," the literal meaning of the term, became, when writ large, the management of the community of households. As such, this management was scarcely distinguishable from the government of the community. Issues of public policy and choices between alternative social values were undeniably implicit in the nature of the economy that the political order protected. The problems of the economy, though these embraced their specialized and technical aspects, were not considered to be separable from the sphere controlled by the state. Take any of the major economic questions prior to the so-called Industrial Revolution—the tenure of land and its distribution, the accumulation of wealth, the provision of food supply, urban-rural relations, the pricing system, the direction of foreign trade, and so forth—these were treated as aspects of "political economy" dealing with subject-matters that overlapped and finally fused. Opposition might be directed against specific instances of governmental power, controversies might arise about the equity or expediency of this or that policy. But that the power of the state could include the general control of the economy was not an article of dispute.

State Control of the Economy in Antiquity. From Graeco-Roman antiquity down to the eighteenth century the history of all European states provides testimony to support these generalizations. The list of economic functions that the state has performed in various places and periods is lengthy. Besides waging war, three major activities, which long ago drew the government into affairs of commerce, were providing communications, currency, and food supply. There was always, of course, a military motive behind the building of highways, as well as the need for speedier transmission of official edicts and diplomatic documents. Such reasons explain the lengthy Royal Road that the Persians constructed to link their inland capital of Susa with the Mediterranean seaboard of Asia Minor. Of the same character, and far more spectacular, was the famous network of highways the Romans flung across the provinces where their legions trod. But the roads that were of service to cavalry, phalanx, or legion were usable also by the caravan. Under state auspices they provided the means for facilitating the flow of commerce, and for its control by dues and tolls. The supply and issue of currency, too, was early undertaken by the state. When the direct bartering of commodities was replaced by the use of a medium of exchange, or money, the state intervened for two impelling reasons. If there was to be a medium of exchange, men had to know it, accept it, and have confidence in it. Consequently it was best to employ a single medium, common to all transactions, and issued by authority with some recognizable stamp or imprint.

Furthermore, the medium, in order to be accepted, had to be scarce, durable, and not too bulky. Thus metals were generally in demand for currency, and since their mining and coining could be very lucrative the state found an added incentive to enter and then monopolize the business of money-making. The coins of Athens, Corinth, and other states with far-flung commercial interests, spread extensively through the central and eastern Mediterranean. Wider still in later centuries was the dispersion of the *denarius*, financial symbol of Rome.

The concern of the state over food is explicable in terms that are in part economic, but in greater part political. In the era when the city-state was the unit of government,[1] in addition to the natural dangers of crop failure due to drought or flood, the man-made perils of war exposed many communities to periodic risks of under-nourishment or even starvation. A small city would ordinarily obtain its wheat and olive oil from the rural area adjacent to its walls. When states were at war, the contending armies always sought to destroy the standing wheat before it ripened and to cut the slow-maturing olive trees. Even in peacetime the largest cities suffered the insecurities of having to import their grain and oil from distant areas (the great granaries being Sicily, North Africa, and what is now south-western Russia). There was always the chance that political disorders abroad or piracy on the intervening seas might disrupt or curtail the supply. Hence ancient states often took strict measures to control the food market, for example, by bulk purchases overseas, by naval protection for transports, and by regulating the domestic price. To avoid riot and insurrection among the poor, state policy frequently required the sale of wheat at subsidized low prices or even its free distribution. The politics of food, involving direct governmental intervention, was a dictate of humanitarianism, expediency, and plain necessity.

In these three fields that have been discussed, it is evident that different factors with varying influence led to similar results. The motives for state intervention in communications were mainly military; in coinage, mainly economic; in food supply, mainly political. But regardless of variations in emphasis, the feature common to all instances was the accepted view that a widespread social need occasioned and justified action by the government. All that

[1] See Chapter 13, pp. 321-2.

was necessary was for the need to arise and be felt. Given these conditions, no obstacle was presented either in the form of ideas that the state ought not to enter this field or in the form of non-governmental institutions powerful enough to do the job themselves and to resist conduct of the enterprise by the state.

The Medieval Subordination of Economics to Ethics. The infusion of Christian doctrine into the Graeco-Roman tradition did not, in this respect, produce a change of principle. When the church argued that there were limits to secular power, it sought to define these within a theological context. As to economic problems, neither church nor state denied or ignored their existence. But both institutions stood on common ground in believing that economic affairs were part of the general ordering of this world and were therefore merged with, or subordinate to, the jurisdiction which each exercised in its respective sphere. Now this did not mean that among the issues that divided state and church there were none which had economic relevance. On the contrary, such disputes as those over the ownership of land, the use of revenues from the produce of the land, and the taxation of the clergy were economic as well as political, and they were certainly vital to both parties. But the bone of contention was not the question whether economics formed an independent sphere of its own, but whether the control over particular segments of the economy should be vested in church or state; and each institution, in facing the challenge of the other, became more desperately anxious to strengthen and secure the control of its own economic base.

The dominance in the medieval age of theological assumptions and a Christian ethic was a further reason that impeded any measure of autonomy for economic factors. If to charge interest for a loan, or to exact above a certain rate, was branded "usury" and deemed "un-Christian," then an economic matter was being decided on moral grounds. Likewise, when prices rose too high for the poor to purchase the necessaries of life, a policy of price control could be justified by the concept of a "fair price" (*justum pretium*). In this doctrine, economic, legal, theological, and ethical considerations were intertwined. But the ethical category was the most important and was adopted as the criterion for establishing an economic standard.

In connection with this problem there is an aspect of economic organization in the Middle Ages that should be mentioned because it might seem to rest on a theory that the economy forms an autonomous branch of human behavior. What was the significance of the guilds and the place that these succeeded in occupying in medieval society? A guild was a group of persons organized, by virtue of their common interest, for a particular economic activity. The group might be composed of merchants, traveling together in a caravan or stationed in one spot at some great *entrepôt* of trade and commerce (at Antwerp, London, Hamburg, or the like). Again, the guild could be formed, not of middlemen supplying a service, but of those who produced a commodity. In a handicraft economy, artisans might combine together and define their articles of membership. These could be extended to cover the definition of their craft, the maintenance of a standard of skill, the acceptance of apprentices, the rates to be charged, and so on. Where guilds emerged, as, notably, they did in Flanders, the German states, England, and elsewhere in central and western Europe, they came into being from various causes and under pressure of different circumstances. In some places they developed spontaneously as voluntary groupings for mutual protection (which often meant the establishment of a local monopoly). Elsewhere they were made artificially and were brought into existence by the governing authorities. But irrespective of their origins, the guilds are relevant to this present analysis in that some of them operated with a considerable measure of autonomy. The self-regulation that their members attained, often upon the legal basis of charters that granted specific rights and privileges, was tantamount to a high degree of independence in economic affairs. To state the position of the guilds, however, in stronger language, and to equate it with the ideals expounded by nineteenth century economists, is to be guilty of exaggeration and anachronism. A king or a municipality might recognize the right of an association of merchants or craftsmen substantially to regulate themselves in the provision of their service or the application of their skill. If so, this was done for reasons of expediency or utility. The policy did not conform to, or evoke, the notion that economics pursues laws of its own and functions best when independent of the laws of politics or ethics.

Mercantilism and National Power. While the medieval world subordinated economics to ethics, and the latter to theology, in the following period economics was no less emphatically subordinated to calculations of political and military power. When, therefore, the medieval dogma of dualism was replaced by the politico-legal concept of sovereignty, it was to be expected that a corresponding substitution would take place in the field of economic policy and theory. The new doctrines that emerged to supersede those of the Middle Ages, and that provided in economics a counterpart to sovereignty in politics, have been generally known since the time of Adam Smith's critique as mercantilism. This was a system of thought that reacted against the kind of restraints to which the medieval economy was subject—the restraints upon production, for instance, that the craft guilds imposed, and the numerous restraints upon commerce in the form of customs barriers between localities and tolls on rivers and highways. In order to augment the national wealth, the mercantile system considered it necessary to increase the volume of production and exchange, to which end the restrictions of the medieval order had to be modified or eliminated. The new philosophy held that a surplus of exports over imports was a sign of strength, the surplus being measured by the importation of bullion from the purchasing countries. Hence an inflow of gold and silver to replace an outflow of goods was approved as the sure index of a prosperous economy.

To assess the economic pros and cons of such ideas is beyond the scope of the present inquiry. The political implications, however, are relevant and important. The prime objective of policy, as it seemed to the mercantilists, was the furtherance of national power, and their emphasis was thus placed on national, in contrast to local or regional, interests. To this goal, so pre-eminently political in character, economic policy was supposed to contribute. The means that the mercantilist advocated, as distinct from the ends, (that is, the stimulation of exports, and the desire to accumulate bullion), could, of course, be argued as essentially economic propositions. But the employment of such means led directly to political consequences—to trade wars, to struggles for markets and for sources of raw materials, to control of colonial settlements, and the rest. Hence, under the aegis of mercantilism, economics was necessarily the serving-maid of politics. One had only to demonstrate a connection between a particular economic policy and an advantage to national power, and there was no questioning the central assumption that the state had the right to intervene in any fashion in this or that sector of the economy. The difference between the medieval and the mercantilist economies lay not in the latter's emancipation of the economic order from governmental controls, but rather in its substitution of one type of governmental control (particularly if nationwide in scope) for another.

Laissez Faire—the Economists' Declaration of Independence. When the weather vane of economic policy turned in the sixteenth century toward mercantilism, the change of direction, though significant, was not as momentous as that which ensued two centuries later. The new winds that started to blow in the mid-eighteenth century and prevailed throughout the nineteenth veered to the opposite pole. In fact, they pointed to a quarter of the compass previously unexplored in the social organization and theorizing of the West. Judged from the standpoint of political science, the sharpest break in the continuity of economic thought occurs in the swing from mercantilism to its successor. The newcomer, as it then was, has passed under a number of names or aliases. Nowadays it is variously called economic liberalism, conservative economics, classical economics, or laissez faire. Without prejudice to the other terms, the last of those descriptions will be employed here. What manner of novelty did laissez faire, as an economic doctrine, impart to views about the state?

The essence of the novelty consisted in a bias against the state. Once that central point and its implications are grasped, the rest follows with logical consistency and plausibility. The historical reasons which prompted that bias are no less significant than the character of the bias itself, and they help to explain the resulting consequences. For a convenient point of departure one may select the publication in 1690 of John Locke's two *Treatises of Civil Government*. Writing to justify the peaceful English revolution of 1688, Locke advocates a theory of the state that substitutes constitutionalism for arbitrary [2] power, and limited for omnipotent government. To support the latter position, he assumes the existence of a law of nature that "belongs to men as men" [3] and not as citizens of a state. A natural social union, according to his belief, is chron-

[2] For the meaning of these terms see Chapter 6, pp. 132-3.
[3] *Second Treatise of Civil Government*, chap. 2, sec. 14, Everyman's Library p. 124.

ologically prior, as it is logically prior, to the establishment of a
political and legal union. In this state of nature, as he calls it, men
are endowed with rights that, since they derive from natural law,
are also natural. The collective name for these rights is *property*—
an ambiguous usage, since Locke employs it both in an all-inclusive
sense embracing "life, liberty, and estate" (where estate means
material things that one may acquire and use), and in a restricted sense
that equates it with estate only and omits life and liberty.[4] It is to
enjoy their property (in either or both of those senses) more
securely that human beings mutually contract to institute a government.[5] The legitimate powers of government are derived from that
portion of their natural rights which human beings entrust to its care;
and its functions are to preserve intact the rights which the citizens
retain. Such suppositions glide readily to the evident conclusion that
the scope of state activity is confined within the limits of the powers
delegated to it. Should the state exceed those limits, it has passed
out of bounds, becoming an invader of a domain which it had no
right to enter.[6]

This concept, that there is a domain which the state has no right
to enter, carries the corollary that there is a sphere of social activity
that is best conducted either by individuals in their private capacity
or by associations other than the state. (If there were not this
corollary, it would be virtually pointless to argue in favor of limiting the functions of the state.) To pursue this inference and press
it to a conclusion was the task that occupied many thinkers from the
middle of the eighteenth century to the mid-nineteenth. The next
step forward after Locke was taken by a French school, called the
Physiocrats. Their philosophy was conceived in reaction against
the mercantilist system, as that was designed and developed in
France by Colbert, the finance minister of Louis XIV, and his
successors. Whereas the basis of national wealth and strength
appeared to mercantilists to reside in foreign commerce, favorable
trade balances, and international movements of precious metals, to
the Physiocratic view it lay in the land. Land was the primary productive resource and the chief original creator of wealth. Hence the

---

[4] For these conflicting usages, compare the passages in sections 87, 123, 31,
pp. 159, 180, 132.
[5] *Ibid.*, secs. 85, 94, 138, pp. 158, 163-64, 187.
[6] *Ibid.*, sec. 135, pp. 184-85.

prosperity of agriculture was the prime indicator of the national weal, and the interests of land holders should override those of merchants. Such an outlook confirmed the Physiocrats in an anti-state bias. For one thing, their solicitude for farming was linked with the contemporary, romantic, appeal for a "return to nature," since it was easy to identify farming as man's "natural" occupation.[7] Just as Rousseau in the political theory of that period assumed a contrast between man's primitive goodness in an idealized state of nature and his corruption by society and by the state at Paris and Versailles, so the economic doctrine of the Physiocrats employed the same concept for an assault upon the state. To be precise, it was against the functions of the state as Colbert planned them that the Physiocrats protested—against restraints, restrictions, requirements, both negative and positive, which the state imposed upon the economy in the mercantile interest. The Physiocrats' reaction to this was a desire to curb and confine the sphere of the state, to limit it within boundaries, and leave the (mainly agrarian) economy to the operation of "nature." Their specific protest was voiced in the cry: "Leave us alone to produce what we want and to send our products where, and how, we want" (*laissez nous faire, laissez nous passer*). Shortened into *laissez faire*, this was generalized into the crisp injunction addressed to the state: "Leave us alone!" The further cultivation and final flowering of these principles took place in Britain and the United States. We now turn to these countries in the last quarter of the eighteenth century and the first half of the nineteenth.

The Bible of the British movement was the *Wealth of Nations* which Adam Smith, a Scottish professor at the University of Glasgow, published in 1776. The book was an epoch-making one because of its contribution both to intellectual thinking, and to government policies. Its significance is best judged nowadays by the influences and trends it set in motion, rather than by what Smith actually says and teaches. For the contents of the work embrace much that is outdated or has been superseded. Roughly a quarter of it is devoted to an indictment of the faults of mercantilism, wherein some of the strictures are merited, but others are exaggerated and unduly prejudiced. Smith's theory of value, which he bases upon the cost of labor expended in the production of a

---

[7] The title of "physiocrat" means "rule by nature."

commodity, was discarded by many of his followers in the second half of the nineteenth century and would today be accepted in its naked simplicity by few contemporary economists. But, such criticisms aside, the permanent importance of the *Wealth of Nations* may be found in the general picture that it paints of how a social order can function well. It is this picture, whether clarified by Smith in the highlights of the foreground or veiled in the half-shadows of the background, that was reproduced, filled in, and more sharply delineated by such successors as David Ricardo and John Stuart Mill. It was this which became the leading stereotype in economic thought during most of the nineteenth century. It was this which epitomized the revolution in the attitudes toward the state of the economist and businessman.

What was this picture? Essentially it depicted the individual as the true unit and society as an artificial aggregate compounded of individuals in association. Assuming that everybody desires his self-interest; that the latter, translated into economic terms, means material enrichment; that each individual can best judge and choose for himself the means appropriate to his goal—then it follows that, the larger the sphere of action left to the initiative of private persons, the better. Through the enterprise that involves the taking of risks, through the cut and thrust of competition, individuals will reap the best rewards for themselves and, in the aggregate, for society as a whole. So strongly was Smith dedicated to this individualistic doctrine, and so thoroughly did he apply it, that his antipathy for collective endeavors extended not only to various state activities, but also to the institution of the joint stock company. The latter, which has become a major instrument of a modern capitalist economy, he deprecated as having but limited usefulness and as functioning successfully only when it possesses a protected monopoly or conducts some routine operation.[8] If these presuppositions were granted, Smith still had to demonstrate that the results of free competition between individuals could be not only beneficial, but also harmonious. For this he relied upon a belief in "nature." The economic system, if men left it to the interplay of economic forces,

---

[8] *Wealth of Nations*, bk. V, chap. 1, part III, article I, Everyman's Library 2nd vol., pp. 242-45. Smith's attitude to the joint stock company was common to most English economists through the nineteenth century.

would act in conformity with a set of laws of its own. Certain of these laws were based upon psychological assumptions of universal human egoism (for example, Gresham's law that the bad money drives out the good, because people will keep reliable currency and circulate the unreliable). Others were linked to the operation of physical factors, also rooted in "nature" (for example, the law of diminishing returns, which tells the farmer that if he plants the same crop in the same field year after year, without replenishing the soil, he will eventually obtain decreasing yields). The analysis and elucidation of these laws formed the substance of economic science. Thus to discover and know them would assist men in conducting their economy according to nature.

The Bias against the State. Where did the state fit into this order of thinking? As with most doctrines that place their faith in nature, a contrast was implied between what is natural and what is man-made, conventional, or artificial. Since nature, by definition, is right and good, the actions of man, unless conformable to nature, are likely to be wrong and bad. If nature has laws of its own, they must be beneficial. Human laws, when they contravene those of nature, are by that very fact unsound and harmful. From this point it is a short and simple step to conclude that human laws have but a limited use, since they are fruitful only if they assist nature, and fruitless if they do not. The balance is so delicately poised, the interrelations so complex, between economic factors functioning as nature intends, that state direction is likely through clumsiness and misunderstanding to disturb or destroy the natural equilibrium. Hence a policy is adjudged wise when it enlarges the sphere of private activities and correspondingly restricts the range of governmental action. Such was the chain of reasoning that led John Stuart Mill, in the first edition of his *Principles of Political Economy,* to write:

> In all the more advanced communities, the great majority of things are worse done by the intervention of government, than the individuals most interested in the matter would do them, or cause them to be done, if left to themselves.... The preceding are the principal reasons, of a general character, in favor of restricting to the narrowest compass the intervention of a public authority in the business of community: and few will dispute the more than sufficiency of these reasons, to throw, in every instance, the burden of making out a

strong case, not on those who resist, but on those who recommend, government interference. *Laissez faire*, in short, should be the general practice: every departure from it, unless required by some great good, is a certain evil.[9]

This revealing passage expresses the new way of thinking frankly and without equivocation. It asserts the superiority of private over public enterprise. It places upon the state the onus of proving that its functions are justified and beneficial. It supports, prima facie, any opposition to an extension of those functions. In a word, it typifies the bias against the state.[10]

Thus was launched a new attack upon the monistic doctrine of the omnipotent state. With its ramparts battered or breached, the way was open for all manner of inroads upon its supremacy. The main assault upon the citadel of power was, of course, the one conducted by business or in its name. As in the medieval period, when the sphere of the state was curtailed by the claims of the church, the limits of political activity were drawn along a line that simultaneously marked off the extent of religious activity; so now the effect of circumscribing the powers of government was to widen the powers of economic associations.[11] The strategy of the offensive against the state therefore conformed in the main to the dictates of economic policy. If you could determine how much range was required by nature for the operation of its economic laws, you were by the same logic fixing the boundaries of the laws of government. The economic and political orders were thus considered to be co-ordinate and a new species of dualism was accordingly envisaged as the substitute for monism.

As was to be expected, however, the main assault upon the state was aided and reinforced by a variety of flanking movements whose goal was not so much dualism as pluralism. Educational bodies, in their reassertion of "academic freedom"; religious bodies, seizing the occasion to renew their opposition to secular supremacy; these

---

[9] *Principles of Political Economy, op. cit.* bk. V, chap. 11, sec. 5, 7.

[10] An even stronger bias was expressed by Herbert Spencer in his *Social Statics* (1850) and *Man versus the State* (1884).

[11] The parallelism between the medieval relation of state to church and the nineteenth century relation of state to business is epigrammatically expressed by David Ogg, "The Scarlet Woman has been immured, and the Economic Man let loose," essay on The Renaissance and Reformation in *Great Events in History*, ed. G. R. S. Taylor (London: Cassell, 1934), p. 335.

and others, pooling their forces with the economic agitation, formulated theories of society in terms not of a simple dualism but of complex interrelations between many groups of which the state was only one. Such pluralism is evidenced in the late nineteenth century viewpoints of the German theorist, Von Gierke, or the British legal historian, Maitland. It is continued in the twentieth century by the French authority on jurisprudence and political science, Duguit; by the British political scientist, Laski, and the British economist, Cole, in their earlier works; and by the contemporary American sociologist, Robert M. MacIver.[12]

Nevertheless, in the modern statement of the issue the argument based upon economics and its case for dualism has bulked larger than the argument based upon a multiplicity of associations and their case for pluralism. The reasons for this are significant because of what they reveal about practical politics. To impose upon the monistic state limits that will prove effective, more is required than just the elaboration of a doctrine. A contrary power has to be mobilized to confront the power of the state. Under no other circumstances will the state abdicate from its monistic professions. But to organize a counter-force, capable of resisting the state, means in fact that some other association has to marshal its resources and build a following. It was precisely because the church had attained this position by the fourth century A.D. that Constantine's conversion was assured and state and church in effect established a partnership. If the church had not succeeded in mustering a widespread allegiance, it could not have effectively pressed the case for dualism. You have to create two institutions, or you waste your breath talking about two spheres. It was because this indispensable condi-

---

[12] Some of these men provide illuminating examples of the parallelism between medieval and nineteenth century thought on the subject of the state's relation to other associations. Maitland, impressed by the social role of the business corporation, elaborated a general theory of corporate groups and their independence of the state. The sources from which he drew much historical illustration and philosophical inspiration were medieval. Cole, likewise, developed in his early works a socialist counterpart to the businessmen's doctrine of a division between politics and economics. The resulting concept pictured a social order divided into two spheres, one for the production and distribution of wealth and the other for governmental functions. This he called "guild socialism," reviving the name, and some of the theory of the medieval guilds. Cole later abandoned his own doctrine, realizing that a split between politics and economics would be no more practicable than the attempted medieval separation of church and state.

tion was repeated in the nineteenth century that dualism was converted from a potentiality of social theory into a political actuality.

Business Policy in Victoria's Britain. What reinforced the talk of laissez-faire economists was the rise of business firms that were powerful enough collectively to come to grips with the state. In Britain the writings of Smith, Ricardo, Mill, and Spencer, coincided with the social ferment known by the somewhat exaggerated title of the Industrial Revolution. Aided by a series of technological inventions, the methods of manufacturers not only transformed the industrial process, but created an economic structure of new design. Instead of the former handicraft system, where a worker, in textile production for example, could own his fairly simple machine and operate it in his home, the new and complicated power-driven machinery involved a big capital outlay for plant and equipment. This change divorced the workmen from ownership of their machines, and necessitated their assembling in factories that were also owned by their employers. The latter, being called upon to make larger investments of capital, discovered in the joint stock company a flexible device for pooling and risking the savings of other persons along with their own. Flying the flag of the corporation, the business firm sailed on the buoyant crest of the economic tide.

Being first to apply the new techniques and stimulated by the Napoleonic Wars to increased industrial exertions, the manufacturers of Britain found themselves unrivalled in their domestic market and advantageously placed for international competition. Their efforts over the course of a century made it possible for Victoria's Britain to become "the workshop of the world," to treble its population, and to establish its position as the world's top-ranking nation and the center of the most extensive empire yet known to history. But this achievement was accompanied by demands from the business community that they be emancipated both from the requirements imposed upon production and commerce by mercantilism and also from the political control of landowners with their agrarian preferences. This two-pronged drive against the mercantilists and the landed interest merged into a concentrated attack upon the protective tariff that artificially maintained the price of British-grown wheat. After the Reform Act of 1832 had transferred the control of the House of Commons to the urban middle class, it needed only the succession of potato crop failures in Ireland in the early 1840's to bring about the momentous Repeal of the Corn Laws in 1846. Three years later by the repeal of the Navigation Acts, which had set restrictions on the external commerce of the colonies, Britain certified her full adoption of the principles of "free trade." Henceforth, as long as Britain's manufactures could undersell any competition and as long as her navy dominated the oceans, in neat reciprocity Trade followed the Flag and the Flag followed Trade.

The same symbol of freedom, which in the case of foreign trade was invoked to justify abolition of a tariff on imports, was also applied to the domestic sphere, although in two different senses. In a negative sense, the entrepreneur claimed freedom from control, which meant control by the state, as that was the only association capable of restraining him. Let the economic process function in obedience, not to laws of the state, but to laws of economics—a plea that might be rephrased to read: Let the businessman be a law unto himself. Interpreted in a positive sense, freedom meant the provision of opportunity to employ initiative, to take chances, to experiment, to innovate. This was buttressed in the law courts by the special doctrine of "freedom of contract," which became applicable to a variety of economic relationships: for example, those of business partners, of seller and purchaser, of master and servant. The doctrine assumed the like freedom and equal capacity of the contracting parties, voluntarily agreeing as individuals to transactions for their mutual advantage. In any case, either connotation of freedom, the negative or the positive, spelled a warning to the state to keep its hands off.

Jeffersonian Ideals and the American Frontier. The same anti-state bias found a soil fertile for growth in the United States. But the reasons and reasoning were not identical with those that prevailed in Britain. The act of acquiring independence had involved both resistance to a hereditary monarch, who still possessed a wide discretion in picking his own ministers (for example, Lord North) and defiance of a Parliament in which the inhabitants of colonies were not represented. When a government of limited power, based upon the Constitution, replaced a government that appeared in American eyes autocratic and absolute, the memories of opposition to King, Parliament, and royal governors left as part of their legacy a determination to circumscribe the sphere of activity allotted to the state.[13] Hence, when he came to write the Declaration of Independence, being confronted with the same problem John Locke had faced nine decades earlier, Thomas Jefferson adopted a similar solution and used Lockian terms and thoughts. He speaks, therefore, of inalienable rights, which exist prior to the state. He assumes that in joining the state, men surrender to it a fraction only of their rights, while retaining the rest. It then becomes the duty of government to employ its power to maintain inviolate the rights that are reserved. As a consequence, the power of the state must always be limited.

Besides these ethical and political arguments, Jefferson's thesis was strengthened by his economic philosophy. Although the *Wealth of Nations* was given to the world in the same year as the Declaration of Independence, it is probable that Jefferson in the ensuing decade and a half derived his economic theories less from Adam Smith than from the French Physiocrats. Jefferson's personal predilection for an agrarian economy and the values of rural life chimed harmoniously with Physiocratic doctrines about agriculture and the importance of the landed interest. This preference was unequivocally stated in the *Notes on Virginia:*

> Those who labor in the earth are the chosen people of God, if ever He had a chosen people, whose breasts He has made His peculiar deposit for substantial and genuine virtue.... Generally speaking, the proportion which the aggregate of the other classes of citizen bears in any State to that of its husbandmen, is the proportion of its unsound to its healthy parts, and is a good enough barometer whereby to measure its degree of corruption. While we have land to labor then, let us never wish to see our citizens occupied at a work-bench, or twirling a distaff. Carpenters, masons, smiths are wanting in husbandry; but, for the general operations of manufacture, let our workshops remain in Europe.... The mobs of great cities add just so much to the support of pure government, as sores do to the strength of the human body.

Later on, his stay in Europe where he served as American Minister to France (1784-1789), his residence in the capital city of Paris and observation of its citizens, confirmed in Jefferson a distaste for large urban centers, which he regarded as politically unstable, eco-

[13] See Chapter 10, pp. 239 ff.

nomically parasitical, and socially corrupting. Thus, all elements in his make-up—the statesman, the Virginia gentleman-farmer, and the social philosopher—combined in the conclusion that a community of farmers, owning and working their own properties, constitutes the economic base for an ideal society. Let farmers, who live close to nature, be free to follow nature's laws. Let governments intervene only to protect and enlarge the range of private activities. For are not the best governed the least governed?

Seldom has a theory been launched amid conditions more favorable to its prompt acceptance than was the case with these ideas of Jefferson. Not only had the United States succeeded in opposing what it regarded as autocracy, but the young nation, with independence assured, needed to populate and develop a territory of continental dimensions. As settlers flooded west in wave after wave, Jeffersonism was reborn with each extension of the frontier. The pioneers who tamed a wilderness of forest, prairie, river, mountain, and desert were driven by the varied stimuli of quest for adventure, economic necessity, or religious belief. To them the West beckoned as an escape from a secure but humdrum existence, from poverty, from religious intolerance. The movement west was facilitated by the government in countless essentials, through its diplomatic treaties delimiting the international boundaries, its military action against Indian tribes, its grants of land from the public domain, its expeditions like that of Lewis and Clark, and otherwise. But in a very real sense the spread of the United States from the Atlantic to the Pacific was a feat accomplished by private persons and groups. The scouts, prospectors, and lumbermen; the cattlemen, trappers, and traders; Daniel Boone and Johnny Appleseed; Bill Cody and Kit Carson; these men did not act under political directives, nor did their lives conform to a state-directed plan. They were rather the forerunners, blazing a trail along which others followed to do the work of development and settlement. Their efforts took them into regions inhabited, if at all, by Indians and beyond the immediate sway of the Constitution of the United States. They were, therefore, accustomed to fend for themselves, to go armed, and to discharge as individuals some of those functions (for example, the protection of persons and property) that in a longer established society are transferred to the state and its officials. Such conditions, however, bordered perilously close upon anarchy. When no agencies existed to enact and enforce the law, who could say which citizen was law-abiding and which the outlaw? As the population grew in the West, the need increased for a system of order which only the apparatus of government could provide. Huge tracts of land were thereupon organized as territories and later were admitted as states of the Union.

The key to this entire story lies in the timing. The crucial fact is that governments were instituted in the West after a considerable amount of pioneering had already been launched by individuals and private groups utilizing personal enterprise or corporate capital. Was it not natural, then, that they should regard the state as having a limited, though indispensable, function to perform? Was it not natural that they should prefer to exhaust the possibilities of self-reliance and of private associations before resorting to state action? During a large part of the nineteenth century in America the theory of laissez faire reflected and explained with no little accuracy and adequacy the social realities of a transcontinental expansion.

Both in the United States and in Britain, the laissez-faire doctrine, as was noted earlier, expressed a bias against the state. What consequences ensued when these ideas were put into practice? What have been the results of proceeding upon the assumption that a good society is one in which governmental functions are confined to a minimum and economic activities enjoy the maximum of independence? Without attempting a detailed analysis, which would be out of place here, one can summarize at least the highlights and assess their political effect.

The Consequences of Industrial Capitalism. Some of the most notable changes are those that have occurred in the field of production. Never before in history has mankind come within reach of the abundance, actual or potential, that has lain in its grasp during the last century. The techniques of mass production have increased the sheer volume of commodities available to the consumer beyond previously known levels. The freeing of the channels of trade inside the nation-state, and freer trade—when practiced—across international boundaries, have together resulted in great extensions of the market, with many accompanying benefits. The existence of so many potential customers has helped to offset the proneness of mass production to standardize and, under the stimulus of competition, has encouraged diversification of the products offered for sale.

The same factors have also contributed to price reductions, so that in many instances what once were luxuries for the few have become staples for the many. In general, all this has spelled itself out in a series of changes that from the material standpoint have contributed enormously to human well-being, and in various countries, among which the United States is the pre-eminent example, have made possible the highest standards of living in the world.[14]

These improvements, however, have been associated with other changes that are less beneficial. If risk-taking, individual autonomy, and entrepreneurial initiative, have served as stimulants or intoxicants to induce new endeavors, they have also been responsible for some less pleasant after-effects. The great constructive achievements that laissez-faire capitalism has undeniably registered in the productive sphere are not matched by an equal record in the field of distribution. The main preoccupations of the economic order have been to organize the capacity to produce and to increase the gross accumulation of capital rather than to be concerned about the equities of distributive justice. As a consequence, even the wealthiest nations, such as Britain before 1914 or the United States since 1919, have included within their midst a significant percentage of underprivileged people, and the gulf dividing the very rich from the very poor became dangerously large. The same may perhaps be said in another way: An immoderate emphasis on individual freedom can accentuate inequalities between individuals.

Risk-taking and enterprise, similarly, can be responsible for unwelcome consequences. When millions of persons take their several calculations of profit and loss and make decisions accordingly, their actions lead cumulatively to a collective result to which all have individually contributed (though none have willed it) and which may turn out mutually ruinous. A striking example of this is the phenomenon known as the business-cycle. Over many decades under the normal conditions of peace—wars being considered abnormal—statisticians have been able to trace a cyclical movement of

[14] Great and important as these gains are, it must not be forgotten that the credit for them belongs not to the single factor of the laissez-faire doctrine, but to a combination of factors of which this was only one. In the nineteenth century the economic progress of Britain was attributable in large measure to the fact that she was first in the field with industrialization, and thus possessed a competitive advantage. The similar progress of the United States was facilitated by this country's rich endowment of natural resources that laid the foundation for agricultural and industrial wealth.

the economy through a succession of phases. Market conditions offering opportunities for sales and profits create an atmosphere of confident buoyancy, which encourages brisk expansion and new ventures. The desire to ride the crest of the wave tempts businessmen at times to gamble on commitments beyond their immediate resources. The crash comes when too many have over-reached themselves and the economy as a whole slumps into a depression, more or less prolonged, after which by a gradual recovery it returns to the opening phase. Prosperity—depression—prosperity; boom—bust—boom; this recurrent rhythm can be otherwise described as a chronic condition of instability and insecurity.

The application of laissez-faire doctrines, particularly to an economy in the course of change from a mainly agrarian to a mainly industrial base, has included many by-products that are not merely economic but, in the broadest sense, social. For industrialism alters the physical environment in which men move, reshapes their everyday habits of living and working, and produces effects that are more drastic, the less there is of planning and regulation. Under shelter of the maxim "leave us alone," as it was practiced in Britain and the United States during the nineteenth century, the demands for manpower for the factories, mines, railroads, and all the services linked with them, brought into existence huge and sprawling cities where masses of human beings were overcrowded, overworked, underpaid, and underfed. The cities spread upon nature's landscape their blight of dirt and pollution, and upon their human inhabitants the blight of slums, disease, and squalor.[15] For the majority of the urban population, and certainly for its poorest members, the consequences were a life of virtually unrelieved dreariness and drudgery and a helpless feeling of being imprisoned in a vast and impersonal mechanism.

In large and wealthy countries, however, perhaps the most paradoxical result of laissez faire has been its inability to live up to its own principles in certain critical sectors of the economy. The very freedom on which the system prided itself permitted ample opportunities for any who started with an initial advantage or who were unscrupulous in their means, or who enjoyed exceptional luck, to become richer and more powerful than their fellows. Despite its

---

[15] For an analysis of modern urbanization see Lewis Mumford, *The Culture of Cities* by Harcourt, Brace and Company (New York: 1938).

good intentions, the doctrine of freedom paved the road to privilege. The presence, side by side, of very rich and very poor; the concentration of wealth and, with it, of social power; the organization of trusts, cartels, and monopolies; the rise of holding companies and interlocking directorates; such practices, where prevalent, rendered impracticable the ideal of free competition among equal individuals. Indeed, to apply to huge corporations, owning assets that run into eight or more figures, the rights and attributes of a single flesh-and-blood individual is a fiction that does violence to the facts.[16] The point that systems professing laissez faire and dedicated to free competition between individuals have in reality diverged widely from their own doctrines is fraught with far-reaching implications. The central concept of laissez faire that upheld state inaction as a virtue formed an umbrella beneath whose shelter economic organizations could luxuriate and thrive. Since their activities were subject to few restraints, the largest and strongest could press their advantage to dominate the small and weak. Thus society found itself at grips with the problem that President Grover Cleveland expressed in the words: "It is a condition which confronts us, not a theory." [17] This condition was simply the hard, stubborn fact that business corporations of great size had come into existence, wielding incalculable power by virtue of the numbers they employed, the assets they owned, and the services or commodities they sold. In many branches of the economy and of society in general, the paradoxical outcome of a doctrine that glorified the autonomous individual and simultaneously restricted the role of the state was to subordinate the individual to the pressure of these very corporations. Once established, moreover, they were hard to dislodge, and their ability to survive had the effect both of accentuating the differences between rich and poor and of further diminishing equality of opportunity.

The Power of Business in State and Society. In yet another respect did the results of laissez faire belie one of its initial assumptions. Proponents of the doctrine had called for limitations upon state power and the maximum of independence for the economic order.

[16] For a critique of this practice, see Thurman Arnold, *The Folklore of Capitalism* (New Haven: Yale University Press, 1937).

[17] *Annual Message to Congress*, 1887. Cleveland was referring to the issue of free trade versus protection. But his words had a much wider application.

Let government and business stick to their own spheres, so that individual human beings could have a large area for personal enterprise and be equal and free. Practice, however, did not bear out the theory. For business, as it grew big, spelled power; power in any sense you will—the amassing of wealth, the control of men, the dispensing of social influence, and, above all, the mastery of the state. Such, indeed, was the ultimate and inescapable consequence of the success that business had registered. The enforced contraction of the state did not leave society devoid of potent associations. When state power was dammed up, a vacuum was created into which other forces were free to flow. What resulted, then, was not the extinction or even the limitation of power, but the substitution of one form for another—that is, of economic for political power. Men were still subject to controls. Only the controllers had changed.

Nor is that all. The substitution of economic for political power can be rephrased as the conquest or absorption of the political order by the economic order, of the state by business. Power generated in the economic sphere was merely transformed into political power. Laissez faire did not insist that the state wither away, but rather that its branches be pruned and its growth circumscribed, while business plants could spread around and above cutting it off from sunlight and water. In this way political considerations were subordinated to economic ones; and the powers of the state, when employed, were generally made to subserve what business deemed its interest. Hence the net result of the modern attempt to limit the functions of government and subdivide society into two or more spheres was curiously akin to the comparable medieval endeavor to organize in parallel compartments the secular and the spiritual realm. Both of these historic experiments proved to be unworkable. Both came to grief in the same manner. In neither instance was it possible to establish a clear line of demarcation. The medieval priest and the nineteenth century businessman stepped out beyond their original bounds of saving souls or saving capital; and their respective institutions, church and corporation, became deeply involved in the preservation and direction of the entire social order. Each in turn, as the moment appeared advantageous, sought to establish the supremacy of his own functions over those of the state—the church with the claim that the hereafter was of deeper importance to man than the life now, and business with the assertion that a competitive system promoted freedom whereas the work of government rested basically upon coercion. Starting as pluralists or dualists, both ended up as monists—the one seeking to unify mankind through obedience to the Ten Commandments and the Sermon on the Mount; the other, through the division of labor and the laws of supply and demand.

The similarity does not end there. The power wielded by the strongest of the medieval Popes provoked a counter-assertion of secular authority by emperors and kings, so that the aftermath of state-church dualism was the rise of the "sovereign" state. What has been the sequel to the nineteenth century experiment in state-business dualism?

Karl Marx, the intellectual founder of the organized Communist movement, asserted that capitalism contained in itself the seeds of its own destruction. It would, he predicted, be destroyed from within through the irreconcilability of the classes it created. That the forecast has turned out inaccurate is proven by the number of facts whose potentialities Marx either underrated or misunderstood. He did not, for example, envisage the prospect that capitalism would develop a capacity for continuous adaptation in an evolutionary, rather than a revolutionary, manner. He did not expect that the different economic classes of owners and employees—the relation between whom he described as the *Klassenkampf* or class war— might eventually draw closer together instead of drifting poles asunder. Nor did he anticipate that liberal democracy, in his day largely a phenomenon of the middleclass, would be extended to embrace the working class through a new formula for political partnership and a redefinition of citizenship. The suggestion that remedial measures might be employed to correct demonstrable abuses in the social order was alien to Marxian diagnosis and therapy. His cure for the disease was to kill the patient.

But to say that the "inevitable" revolution did not, in the most advanced industrial societies, explode as predestined does not mean that the capitalist economy has persisted unchanged through the fiery trials of the last century. On the contrary, the continuousness of change has been the one constant factor in these dynamic decades. What has differentiated the history of various modern peoples has been the character, the extent, the depth, and the method of changes from which none have been exempt. The prediction of Marx would have been more accurate had he stated that industrial capitalism contained within itself the seeds of its own reconstruction and reform. Let us explore the evidence for this view and see by what mechanism those seeds were watered and nurtured.

Primarily it was industrialization that created the occasion and pre-conditions for new and momentous changes. Two of these must be singled out for special comment since the train of events they set in motion became directly relevant to politics. When the technology of production summoned ever more complex machines into the service of mankind, it became imperative for an increasing number of the labor force to be commensurately skilled. Many phases of the manufacturing process called for human beings who could operate, tend, and repair an intricate piece of machinery; who could understand and follow elaborate instructions, written as well as verbal; who could calculate mathematically, and so on. In a word, industrialization demanded education; and mass production necessitated mass education. The large capital investment tied down in a manufacturing plant could not prudently be entrusted to the unschooled and the illiterate.

The other great innovation that must be laid at the door of industrialism was the geographical redistribution of human beings. For the first time in their history, countries that felt the full effects of the industrial revolution contained more inhabitants in the cities than on the land, more employees in factories and urban occupations generally than in agriculture, and higher densities of population per square mile. These changes in turn led to a spreading contagion of adverse conditions: slum dwellings, unsanitary streets, high death rates, juvenile delinquency, sweated labor, illiteracy, and ignorance. But the physical overcrowding that aggravated these evils made it possible for their victims to combine in searching for remedies. Thus a second offshoot of industrialism was the encouragement given to combination on a large scale. Hence, while laissez-faire doctrine emphasized the virtues of individuality, the growth of an industrial society tended to negate that same philosophy. Because it demanded mass organization, industry paved the way for collectivism, first of a private, and then of a public, character.

The Rise of Organized Unions. There were various ways of mustering opposition to the wealth and power that a relatively small number of people had amassed under the laissez-faire system. One method was to argue that, if the root-cause of the current trouble was the growth of overpowerful business corporations, the solution likewise must be found in the economic field. The proper counter-poise to an economic force was a rival economic force. It is in this light that such organizations as the trade unions, farm groups, and the consumers' cooperative movement can best be understood. Two of these in the sphere of production, and the third in that of con-sumption, have been designed to offset the dominating position of the captains of industry.

Take trade unions as a case in point. The trade union is an associ-ation of employees banding together for their mutual protection and for improvement in their conditions of labor. Union activities may spring out of, or develop into, a desire for higher wages, for shorter hours of work, for employee welfare, for job security, for a share in factory management and production policy, and so forth. Composed of members who are insecure, because individually they are poorer and weaker than their employers, the trade union stands or falls by the degree of solidarity it can elicit. Hence the urgent stress laid by trade unionists upon discipline and cohesion, upon the "closed shop" or "union shop" and their resentment of those whom they designate as strikebreakers, or "scabs."

The history of organized labor has been a checkered one. It was not long ago that the trade union—now a stock character of the modern economic drama—was viewed askance as an interloper on the legitimate stage. British law at the beginning of the nineteenth century allowed working men to contract individually with their employers, the two parties to each such agreement being considered free and equal. Since in fact, however, the bargaining power of an individual laborer was greatly inferior to that of an employer, the former sought to equalize conditions by contracting collectively and presenting a united front to obtain better terms. The employers thereupon besought the state to intervene by prohibiting such asso-ciations. Parliament duly responded with a series of Combination Acts, such as those of 1800 and 1825, which pronounced collective bargaining with an employer to be a combination in restraint of trade and any union formed for this purpose to be, as such, illegal. Not to be outdone, the courts supplemented the statutes by invok-ing against the unions the common-law doctrine of criminal conspir-acy. Labor had to wait for a Trade Union Act of 1871, sponsored by a government of the Liberal party, and for an amended Combination Act of 1875, sponsored by a Ministry of Conservatives, to remove the common-law and statutory bans upon trade unions and accord them a protected status within the law. Even more severe than in Britain was the penalty at one time imposed by the state on trade unions or *syndicats* in France, where they were classified as seditious—a word only one degree removed from treasonable. The *syndicats* of the Third Republic were not fully legitimized until the passage of liberalizing legislation by the Ferry Ministry in 1884.

In the United States incipient unionism fared in one respect better, in another respect worse, than its British counterpart. Here too the unions fell victim to the criminal conspiracy doctrine. But they shook themselves free of its incubus at an earlier date, being largely helped by a decision of the Supreme Court of Massachusetts in 1842.[18] After the Civil War, however, when the rapid expansion of manufacturing multiplied the number of industrial workers and their grievances, and when interstate unionism sought to advance in step with interstate commerce, the courts gave aid to employers by drawing out of their common law arsenal a weapon forged for other uses but easily convertible to industry strife. This was the famous injunction. By means of this an employer threatened with a strike, a picket line, or certain other hostile tactics could go before a judge and after a summary hearing obtain a court order to enjoin or forbid the union from pursuing its course of action. Only with the passage of the Norris-LaGuardia Act of 1932 was the power of the courts to issue injunctions in labor disputes diminished.

Similarly the opposition to combinations in restraint of trade—an opposition wholly consistent with the pure philosophy of competitive individualism—was pressed into an anti-labor shape. This philosophy found statutory expression in the Sherman Anti-Trust Act of 1890. Enacted by Congress under its constitutional authority to regulate interstate commerce, the law prohibited without exceptions all combinations that restricted the flow of trade across state lines. While the law was originally evoked by a public agitation against the power of big business and monopolistic abuses, its phases were sufficiently general for the United States Supreme Court in 1908 to apply it to a union that had launched a strike against a manufacturer and organized an interstate boycott of his

18 Commonwealth v. Hunt, 4 Metc. 111 (Mass. 1842).

product.[19] Although the Clayton Act of 1914 specifically exempted labor from the operation of the anti-trust laws, the federal courts were still able to devise new deterrents on any union activity that would diminish the volume of interstate commerce. Only the circumstance of the economic depression of the early 1930's, and the ensuing change of political climate, secured in 1935 the passage of the Wagner Act definitively guaranteeing to labor its right to organize [20] and to bargain collectively with management.

The trade unions have thus come a long distance. Formerly regarded as criminals holding legitimate business up to ransom, they are now recognized as having a proper place in the industrial process. But this position has raised new problems. It has become necessary to determine how broad are the powers accorded the unions, what positive limits should be set to those powers, and so on. Such issues were acutely formulated in Britain in 1927 and in the United States exactly twenty years later. In 1926 a strike of British coal miners was extended by sympathetic action of other unions into a general strike, paralyzing the nation's economy for nine days. Next year a Conservative majority in Parliament enacted the Trades Disputes Amendment Act, which among other changes made general strikes illegal. In the United States, when price controls were removed after the end of World War II, considerable industrial unrest occurred during 1946 in the efforts of unions to obtain higher wages. Thereupon the Eightieth Congress under Republican leadership adopted the Taft-Hartley Law, imposing a number of curbs upon labor organizations and tactics. In both cases, labor has agitated for the repeal of the statutory limitations, being successful in Britain in 1945 after the electoral victory of the Labor Party, but unsuccessful through 1953 in the United States. In both cases, labor's antagonists could point with some show of justification to what seemed abuses of power on the part of certain unions; [21] while the friends of labor argued that such abuses were being employed as a pretext for curbs of excessive stringency designed to wreck or weaken the bargaining power of organized unionism.

[19] Loewe v. Lawlor (the Danbury Hatters' case), 208 U.S. 274 (1908).

[20] This right the Supreme Court, when it upheld the Act's constitutionality, pronounced "fundamental." National Labor Relations Board v. Jones and Laughlin Steel Corporation, 301 U.S. 1 (1937).

[21] For example, the calling of jurisdictional strikes, the practice known as "feather-bedding," control of some unions by oligarchies or virtual dictators.

Emergence of Big Government. Where has this sequence of events led? The industrial revolution, geared to a doctrine of individualism and sparked by the power of private capital, permitted the business corporation to wax big and strong, and evoked the challenge of its economic counterpart, the union. The latter, however, in order to present an effective challenge, also had to be as big and strong as its adversary. If and when conflict between the two affected the interests of third parties and even disrupted the economy as a whole, who was to arbitrate or override or compose their differences? The same holds true, of course, of the farmers who have likewise organized to further their interests. At times they have been locked in battle with bankers and industrialists, at other times with labor. Indeed, when the economy is operating under strain, as during depression, inflation, or war, the unity of the social order may be impaired by struggles between business, labor, and agriculture. In such cases a still greater force is needed to keep order among elements always spirited and potentially unruly.

The logic of these circumstances pointed to an inescapable conclusion. For remedying evils and adjusting conflicts such as those described, the only institution capable of doing the job was one that embraced everybody, that concerned itself with the general welfare, and that had power to enforce a settlement among the contestants: in other words, the state. Thus, by a converging of political pressures in its direction, the state was invoked as the chosen instrument to master and keep in leash the forces of social change. But not the state as conceived by the philosophers of laissez faire! Not the kind of state where good government was equated with little government! The new state had to be strong. Its functions had to be formulated in positive, not negative, terms. If changes originating in the economic sphere set up repercussions throughout the whole society, solutions on the political level were required to mitigate their effects. Hence the attempt to carve out for economics a sphere of its own, operating under laws of its own, had broken down. The social order was forced to reassert the primacy of politics over economics, of the state over business.

The truth of this assertion is explicit in the struggle of trade unions for recognition, outlined above. What stands out clearly from that account is the evolving role of the state. First, the state appears in a passive capacity as the underwriter of the businessman's predominance; next, as a recording or certifying agency that admits unions to their place in the sun; and finally, as an institution of active authority, arbitrating rival claims, defining spheres of influence, and enforcing at least a minimum standard of cooperation. The more intense the economic struggle, the more strenuously men sought to enlist the power of the state in their support. No major interest in society has been reluctant to appeal to the state for preferential treatment when its advantage would thereby be promoted. Businessmen, for example, who are supposed to speak in character when voicing complaints about government "interference" in this or that sector of the economic process, are not loath to demand a customs tariff for the political protection of their market, or to accept the services of a Department of Commerce, or to influence monetary policy for their own pecuniary benefit. Farmers similarly welcome the work of the state when the price of their produce is raised by subsidies or when rural electrification brings labor-saving appliances to their barns and kitchens. And just as labor and business both turn to the state to invoke its authority against the other party, so farmers have besought governmental aid against the railroads, banks and insurance companies, and equally against agricultural unionism. All theories to the contrary, the truth is that the pressure to enlarge the functions of government is exerted by everybody who needs some service otherwise unobtainable or who wishes to bolster a weak competitive position. If dependence on the state is labeled sin in the decalogue of classical economics, there is none virtuous enough to cast the first stone.

All these reasons explain why in every country touched by the effects of industrialism the functions of the state have since expanded so broadly. To diagnose the causes, however, is one thing; to describe and summarize the effects, another. In so vast and intricate a subject, it is not easy to depict clearly just how the activities of government have increased and what forms that increase has assumed. Nevertheless it is possible to pick one's way through the labyrinth if guided by a map that marks the main routes and directions. The rest of this chapter is intended to serve as such a map.

A convenient point of departure for exploring the new role of the state is to survey its various relations to the economic order. Three such relations should be carefully distinguished. First, the ownership and operation of an enterprise may be vested in the state, rather than in private hands. This is often referred to as "socialism" or "nationalization." Second, the ownership and actual administration may be left to private citizens, but the state lays down its rules and conditions or insists on certain broad policy requirements to which the private management must conform. In addition, the state may attempt to co-ordinate centrally the different aspects of the economy (production, investment, consumption, wages, profits, prices, et cetera) and may prescribe an over-all plan to fit them together. This is called a system of "controls" or "regulation" or "planning" or a "managed economy." Third, the state may accept the obligation for the welfare of its citizens and may undertake to provide them with what are known as "social services." To finance these it must obtain much of its revenue through taxation, taking most from those who have most and thereby, in some measure, redistributing incomes. Each of these developments—state ownership, state regulation, and state-provided social services—must be reviewed in turn.

(*1*) *Pros and Cons of Socialism.* State ownership and operation, as was shown at the opening of this chapter, is not in itself a novelty. The element of novelty consists only in determining whether this or that specific enterprise should be under public auspices or private. Some state-owned undertakings (the post-office, for example) are so long established and universally accepted that they no longer evoke the raising of an eyebrow, or the shrug of a shoulder. Some, such as the generation of electric power, gave rise to classic controversy in the United States two decades ago, but are now less vehemently contested. Others, like the acquisition by the state of the British iron and steel industry in 1950, are among the storm centers of current politics.[22]

If these facts follow any pattern, it appears to be simply that arguments about whether the state should undertake an activity or not are waged more intensely according to the recency and infrequency of its operation by the state and the strength of the opposing private interests. In this, as in other matters political, yesterday's heresies are often tomorrow's orthodoxies.

The number and the character of the enterprises owned by the

---

[22] In 1953 the British Parliament under a Conservative majority enacted a bill to restore the iron and steel industry to private ownership.

state and operated by governments vary considerably from nation to nation. In the continental United States, besides the ubiquitous post-office and its savings bank, the federal government performs such kinds of business as making loans to corporations and home owners, production and distribution of hydro-electric power, manufacture of fertilizers, maintenance of national parks with tourist facilities, development of atomic energy, and so on. Various states have a monopoly of retail sales of liquor; some operate harbor terminals; and North Dakota is unique in having instituted a state bank, state grain elevators, and state crop insurance. At the local level numerous instances exist of municipally owned transit systems and gas, electricity, and water supply.

In the second largest English-speaking democracy the trend toward state ownership is more pronounced and has existed longer.[23] The telegraph and telephone were nationalized before World War I. During the interwar decades the same was done with radio broadcasting, with London's port and passenger transport, the generation and wholesale distribution of electricity and civil aviation. Translated into terms of party politics, these facts mean, of course, that many socialist experiments were sanctioned by governments and parliaments controlled by Liberals or Conservatives. Since the end of World War II, however, while the Labor party was in office, many more programs of this character were instituted than existed previously, and they were adopted in the short space of six years (1945-1951). The state has acquired ownership over the Bank of England, the coal industry, gas supply, retailing of electricity, the railroads and canals, some of the long-haul road freight, overseas cables, and iron and steel works. A story similar in general character but varying as to detail could be told about most of the democracies on the continent of Europe and in the South Pacific.[24]

The arguments adduced in favor of state ownership are worth exploring. One familiar line of reasoning insists that whoever owns or controls a commodity like water or a service like transportation will wield power over his fellow men since everybody needs these things, and such power should be a function of public authority. A second argument contends that certain industries (coal, for ex-

---

[23] See table III, p. 206.
[24] For the example of New Zealand, a highly socialized country, see my *Politics of Equality* (Chicago: University of Chicago Press, 1948).

TABLE III

Undertakings Owned and Operated by the State in Britain

Prior to 1945
  Post Office (including Savings Bank)
  Telegraph
  Telephone
  Radio
  London Passenger Transport
  Port of London
  Central Electricity Board (generation, transmission, and wholesale distribution)
  Civil Aviation

Acquired since 1945
  Bank of England
  Telecommunications
  Coal Industry
  Railroads (and ancillary services)
  Electricity (retail distribution)
  Gas (some of this municipally owned prior to 1945)
  Iron and Steel

"Denationalized" since 1951
  Iron and Steel
  Road Trucking (in process)

ample) are essential to the functioning of all the rest, so that, if it is desirable to plan and co-ordinate the economy as a whole, ownership of a few "key" concerns facilitates the regulation of the remainder. A third point is that certain of these undertakings require so much capital—either to start an infant industry or to modernize an old one—that the state may well be the sole source for obtaining the necessary finance. Fourth, in cases where an enterprise is already a monopoly in private hands or could operate more efficiently if turned into one, the view is advanced that the kind of monopoly least dangerous to the people is that which they own through the instrumentality of the state. This argument, which is wholly political in character, clearly assumes that the state in question is governed democratically and has no applicability to a dictatorship. Finally it is suggested—from a standpoint which is part political and part ethical—that to substitute state for private ownership is to change the guiding motif of the management from individual profit to public service, which some persons consider socially preferable.

The counter-arguments, too, are many in number and stem from different preconceptions. In the eyes of some, an attempt by the state to conduct a business activity is foredoomed to failure. That is because they regard the quest for individual profit as the most powerful of managerial incentives. A salaried state employee will not, they assume, be as efficient as an owner of a private business; and, in any case the enterprise of the state employee is restricted by the ultimate control of a legislature filled with party politicians. Other objections are directed not so much at the feature of state ownership, but at the inherent difficulties of size. Bigness, whether in private or public organizations, is itself a liability, and may eventually be self-defeating because of the complex structure and elaborate procedure it necessitates. As the size increases, and as an undertaking approaches or becomes a monopoly the elimination of competition may reduce efficiency. Finally, it is objected that nationalization is an irreversible act, since to denationalize would be no more practicable than to unscramble eggs. The more the state acquires, the more power is concentrated in its hands until individual liberties may be endangered.

(2) *State Regulation and a Planned Economy.* When the government, instead of owning an enterprise, regulates those who own it privately, the relationship of the state to the economic order raises some different problems. Not all, however, are dissimilar. Certain regulatory activities of the state, for example, are of such long standing or satisfy so universal a demand that they are accepted without question. Codes for safeguarding public health and sanitation fall into this category, as do provisions to ensure the supply of pure food and drugs. Only a generation ago the regulation of railroads and public utilities by public agencies that fix their rates, prescribe their service, and so forth, occasioned fierce political battles in states like Wisconsin and California, and in the halls of Congress. The struggle to regulate some of the conditions of industrial employment was passionately conducted by factory workers when their unions were weak and as passionately resisted by the majority of employers. Today, businessmen who have not always flinched from price-fixing among themselves when it suited their pocket object to price controls if administered by the state, and unions that in the past have invoked the aid of the state to place a floor below wages sometimes resent its efforts to stabilize them by putting a ceiling overhead.

As with public ownership, regulation incites the most acrimonious controversy when the forms it assumes are novel and those at whom it is directed are powerful. Some examples will illustrate the point. Control of farm production, including such details as the acreage sown, crops planted, hogs raised, and cattle slaughtered; control of stock market transactions and sales of securities by an examination of company assets and prospectuses; control of investment and credit; control of prices, wages, hours of labor, essential materials, and manpower; control of foreign exchange, together with the licensing of imports and exports; control of land use together with building permits, zoning ordinances, and rent restrictions—these and more have been for two decades the battlefields or battle cries of parties and pressure groups in their struggle for place, profit, and power.

In this elaborate network of regulation, what pattern is woven? When controls reach so far, not only into broad sectors, but into cracks and crevices of the economic and social orders, what over-all purpose do they serve? Do they possess a rationale that imparts to them collectively a meaning and a purpose? What more can be said about controls other than that it is their tendency to be extended indefinitely?

The traditional case in their favor represents the relation of the state to the economic process as that of an umpire or arbitrator laying down and enforcing the rules of a contest in which private individuals and groups are engaged. When these are left purely to their own devices, experience demonstrates that certain abuses occur. Monopolies can fleece the public. Competition can become mutually ruinous. The weak can be forced to the wall. The drive of an acquisitive society for individual gain can imperil the foundations of the common weal. Thus arises the need for the state to brandish its big stick at the monopolies; to dull the throat-cutting edge of competition; to shield the weak from extinction; and finally to succor that orphan child of individualism—the public interest. The saintly knight who leaps to the rescue and fends off the devils and dragons is the regulatory agency, whether department, commission, or board.

A system in which the state regulates, but private persons own and operate, is often extolled for combining the best of both worlds. While private ownership contributes its vaunted efficiency, because of the profit motive and competitive [25] stimulus, state surveillance ensures that service to the public interest will be considered along with profit. Or again regulation may be lauded as a happy compro-

[25] Except when the regulated undertaking enjoys a monopoly.

mise between two extreme positions—that of outright public ownership and that of autonomous private ownership. Thus the regulated
economy is pictured as a "middle-way" lying between the aberrations of socialism on the left and laissez-faire capitalism on the right.
An additional argument, and one with quite a different slant, ema-
nates from those socialists who are prepared to confine public ownership within certain bounds, but desire to control the remainder of
the economy that is left in private hands. Britain under the rule of
the Labor party from 1945 to 1951 affords an illustration. It was the
official estimate of the Labor government that by 1950 about 20
percent of the economy was "nationalized," the other 80 percent
continuing under private ownership. Labor, however, was dedicated
to the principle of planning the economic system in order to secure
what seemed to them nationally important ends—the prevention of
mass unemployment, improvement in living standards for the poorest
third of the population, expansion of exports, and a more stabilized
economy with its consequent security.

To these objectives were added the immediate stringencies to
which postwar Britain was subjected by virtue of bomb-damage,
war-weariness, overseas indebtedness, and relative decline in strength
in comparison to the United States and the Soviet Union. Hence
besides those types of regulation that were deemed permanent in
character (for example, control of land use) others were set up that
were intended to be temporary and to be removed when conditions
changed (rationing of food and clothing, for example).

As the nature of controls is diverse, so are the criticisms levelled
against them. It is only to be expected that what some consider the
advantages of regulation appear disadvantages to others. Thus if
regulation is praised as a compromise or middle way, it is also condemned by those who find a halfway house less satisfying than
journey's end. Advocates of unrestricted laissez faire blame the system of state regulation for hampering their initiative and limiting
their authority; while proponents of socialism claim that the public
interest suffers if the state confined itself to laying down conditions
and leaves their application to private operators. Thus instead of a
union of public responsibility and private efficiency in harmonious
wedlock, the results may exhibit divided authority and jurisdictional
deadlock. Furthermore, if regulation is justified as a device that
facilitates a planned economy, many will be found to condemn the

means by rejecting the end. Planning in their view is administratively unworkable, economically inefficient, and politically dangerous. It calls for a large number of civil servants, subordinates economic decisions to political calculations, and concentrates enormous power under the sway of the state.

(3) *The Social Service State.* Besides altering the economy by operating businesses of its own and regulating those of others, the state further intervenes with what are called social services. Under this heading belong the activities of the state in the areas of education, health, housing, and social security—to mention only four of the principal items. All these have excited political controversy at the time of their inception because the assumption of such responsibilities by the state involved bigger public expenditures and competition or conflict with private interests. When education in primary and secondary schools was first organized under public authority on a compulsory basis, the private institutions, both lay and ecclesiastical, which hitherto had monopolized the field, did not always welcome the entry of the state into a domain they considered theirs. Even nowadays there are still many countries where conflict between state and church schools continues to be acute. The care of health has long fallen under state purview because disease knows no boundaries and major epidemics can lead to social upheaval. Modern urbanization, with its concomitant crowding has required strict public precautions in such matters as the provision of a safe water supply, disposal of sewage, sale of food, and isolation of the victims of contagious disease. In the middle decades of the present century stiff battles have been waged around proposals to organize medical service under state financing and control, proposals that invariably encounter the opposition of the doctors' professional associations. There has been a similar situation in housing, where governments in recent years have tried to stimulate the building of low-cost homes in competition with the majority of speculative contractors, lending firms, and banks. So, too, with social security, in which field modern states have launched comprehensive insurance programs that take away business from private companies by giving the citizen alternative protection.

Decade by decade the amounts spent on purposes of this kind have increased until more people than ever before have come to depend upon the annual continuation of these outlays and, except in periods when war or the threat of it has necessitated huge expenditures for defense, social services have accounted for rising percentages of national budgets. Nor is it without significance that the term "social service state" is frequently used to characterize the modern functions of government. Perhaps this is only another way of saying that the pressures impelling the state to carry more responsibilities of this character are geared to issues that are basic to contemporary politics. The reasons advanced in favor of social services will show this to be so. It would never have been necessary for the state to undertake such duties if there had not co-existed within the bosom of a single community those "two nations" of whom Disraeli wrote in *Sybil:* the rich and the poor. Through their wealth the rich could provide for the medication of their bodies and the education of their minds. They could reside in homes that were spacious and gracious. The poor could do none of these things. To the rich neither unemployment nor age presented a financial crisis since the revenue from the capital they accumulated did not cease to flow. To the poor the expectation of loss of earnings through age or unemployment was an ever-haunting dread. Those to whom the price of private education, private medicine, private housing, and private insurance was prohibitive could obtain such services from one source only, namely a public agency. This meant an appeal to the state by the use of the political process. But what was the goal to be attained? Some called it equality, since they proposed to extend uniformly to all the benefits that wealth alone had been privileged to buy. Others named it social justice, for they thought that knowledge, health, a home, and economic security, were due to all men and were not to be rationed out in proportion to property or income. Irrespective of label, however, the movement behind social services was concerned with levelling the living-standards of the less fortunate with those of the more fortunate, and reducing the gap between "haves" and "have-nots." For the state to adopt such policies entailed, of course, the expenditure of large sums of money that could only be obtained from the pockets of those who possessed a surplus beyond their own needs. Consequently the extension of social services was accomplished by an increase in tax levies and the rise of tax levels, and by the imposition of new taxes, generally graduated, on personal income. Thus financed, the social services have the effect, up to a point, of redistributing income. Or, to express it in a nutshell, private wealth becomes subordinated to general welfare; economics yields priority to ethics; and it is politics that serves as the instrument whereby such change is accomplished.

The Reunion of Politics and Economics. Thus a historical survey of the relation between government and the economic order leads to a conclusion paralleling the story of relations between church and state. The same attempt was made in both cases to limit the functions of government through a doctrine that facilitated the acquisition of power by rival institutions. Both attempts broke down. In neither case did it prove possible to fix upon a dividing line that could be mutually acceptable. Instead of harmony between the respective spheres, clash and conflict, overlap and intrusion became the order of the day. The pair of experiments ended in a like denouement. The medieval society and the modern were faced with the issue, not of maintaining co-ordinate spheres, but of deciding whether church or business should control the state or the state control them. In each case the same verdict was rendered.

The twentieth century is witnessing the repetition of what occurred in so many parts of Europe during the sixteenth, namely, the reassertion of the primacy of the state over other associations. For these reasons the evidence contained in the historical record bears directly upon the problem that was explored in more theoretical terms in earlier chapters. The mutual relation between the many groups of which human beings are members; the effect of their variety upon the unity of society; the emergence of the state amid the welter of organizations; and the competition of church, family, business, and state, for the role of social co-ordinator; difficulties of this kind, though they may be discussed philosophically, cannot be resolved by this means alone. Solutions, if attainable at all, must pay respect to historical experience, and it would not seem coincidental that the challenge of the church and the challenge of business produced comparable results.

From Justice to Welfare. These results have an important bearing on the discussion in Chapter 3, where it was observed that the functions of the state undergo a progression. From its initial duty of providing protection, the responsibilities of the state expanded into a framework of order that involves a concept of justice. But this latter ideal, deriving from Greek social theory and Roman legal practice, did not mark the end of the quest for a better life through political means. With the advent of the Christian religion, the function of charity was much extolled in the West, and for many centuries was church-administered. The system, however, whereby religious agencies provided education, hospital care, or aid to paupers and aged, could cover only part of the total need, because of the limitations of finance and staff. Hence, if all the needy were to obtain relief and all the ignorant be educated, the task must devolve upon an institution that could mobilize the resources of the entire community. Thus the state entered the field, though not without challenge and sometimes stubborn resistance from churches that did not relish the loss of their monopoly. From another quarter comparable opposition was expressed by thinkers of the Herbert Spencer variety, who saw in social services—and the tax revenues required to finance them—an interference in the "natural" operation of economic laws. The laissez-faire economists were often moral and merciful men, as individuals; but their economics, as a science, was indifferent to ethics and callous to human suffering. When economics was once more united with politics, it was at the same time subordinated to ethics.

What this means, in short, is that the state, converting charity from the private concern of the church into a public charge of government, and injecting morality into the economic order, has itself progressed from justice to the still higher ideal of welfare. For welfare is simply humanized justice. It is the social concept that forms the climactic fusion of the Greek, Roman, and Christian contributions to man's betterment. The protective state, the law and order state, the just state, the welfare state—such has been the aspiration, and in some places an actual trend, in the upward evolution of politics through four thousand years of effort and experiment. Finally it is through this development, when and if satisfactorily accomplished, that the state fulfills the condition required of any association that seeks to unify society.[26] Only to the extent that government enlarges its conception of its responsibilities from a special interest to the general interest, from private good to public good, from protection to welfare, do the claims of the monistic state deserve the allegiance of its citizens.

[26] For this, see the discussion in Chapter 7, pp. 154-6.

CHAPTER 9

THIRD ISSUE:

(1) THE SOURCES OF AUTHORITY

The Justification of Authority. Choosing the techniques by which the government carries out its functions for the members of the state presents the third of the great issues of politics. If the objectives of government evolve from protection to welfare, the means must likewise be transformed. The force that is necessary to guarantee protection is not enough by itself to establish justice, and still less to promote welfare. The state must, therefore, rise to the challenge of modifying its original methods, or else its usefulness to society is vitiated. The question of whether this can be done and how to do it creates the issue.

Decisions of government must be translated into acts of government. These require enforcement, which admits of two alternatives: to impose coercive power or to elicit a willing support. Thus the problem raised in Chapter 3 of the relation between force and consent becomes of paramount concern. It is the selection of means that helps to mold the attitudes of the governed and imparts to government much of its legitimacy and practical effectiveness. Those in office seek to convert power into authority, while the governed ask of authority that it serve their need. "By what right do you claim to do this?" "Whence comes your power?" "Who gives you authority?" These typical questions are more persistently raised concerning the state than any other human association, the reason being that its functions produce such direct effects upon everybody and are so intimately related to life

and welfare. It is precisely because of the character of these functions and because the results of abuse of power can be so dangerous
that controversies occur about authorization. If the state were a "do-
little" body, few would care to search the validity of its title deeds.
But wherever much power is concentrated, those who insist that
might be adequately endowed with right will not be lacking.

Men normally obey the state. That is, nearly all of us do so most
of the time. For its part, the state expects this obedience, can ordinarily count upon it, and exacts penalties for disobedience. Why
does this happen? A common answer is the one for which a school
of psychologists is responsible. A human being, they explain, is the
product of his environment. His conduct consists in the main of
patterns of behavior designed for him, rather than by him. His
parents, teachers, friends, customers, clients, and employers help to
construct within him a strong pressure to conform. To that pressure
he will habitually respond both because he desires their approval and
because to swim with the tide is always easier, as well as more agree-
able, than to battle against the current.

But this, even if correct, is only a partial explanation. It describes
how men behave and states, in terms of motivation, what drives
them. It does not explain two important matters. One is the fact of
opposition to the state, for, even if obedience to constituted authority
is the normal rule, there are notable instances from every age of
protest, criticism, and resistance. How are we to explain the dissenter,
the nonconformist, the unorthodox, the heretic, the martyr? History would have no record of rebels or revolution, of movements
for reform or independence, if its sole determinant were submission
to the powers that are. Second, it should not be forgotten that conformists themselves look for reasoned justifications of what they are
doing. Those who administer the state usually tell their fellow-
citizens or subjects that they have to obey, and also that they ought
to do so. The problem, therefore, is broader in scope than a description of how people behave. It involves the moral issue: Does the state
rightfully command, and ought one to obey? By what means does
power acquire an ethic and officialdom its legitimacy? What is there,
after all, to distinguish between the policeman with a gun at his hip
and the gun-toting gangster?

Domination versus Accountability. To such questions supporters
of different political systems have offered many answers. These can

be sorted into two groups, based upon diametrically opposed philosophies of the relation between government and the governed. If
government is thought of as a procedure whereby a small number
of persons issue orders to a much larger number who are their subjects and, as such, their inferiors, then authority is supposedly vested
in the ruling class by virtue of the superiority they possess and is
handed down from on high to the mass of the community. Civil government, so viewed, is likened to military discipline. As soldiers obey
their commanding officers, so the people obey the state and are accountable to it. A ruler can no more be held to account by his subjects
than a general by his army. The opposite doctrine reverses this relationship. It makes the ruler answerable for his actions instead of the
people for theirs. The source of authority is the mass of the community who are to be regarded as fellow-citizens rather than as subjects. It is they who grant power, they who supervise its use, they
who may revoke it. Authority is not something that a few impose
upon many; it is what many temporarily delegate to a few.

This disagreement leads to results that are far-reaching. The
character of the state and the structure of its government are directly related to this controversy about the origins of political power.
According to whether authority is believed to flow from the governed or to be exercised over them, institutions will be differently
constructed. In the latter case the ruling group will organize to maintain its supremacy and will repress opposition. It will employ techniques of intimidation and coercion. Not daring to allow any
challenge to its pre-eminence, it will use the police, prisons, and
army, as central organs of administration. In all these respects it
will constitute a dictatorship. If the guiding principle, on the other
hand, is to assert popular control, means must be discovered for
making officials govern on behalf of the people, and for keeping
them within the limits of their powers. The people must choose
certain of their number to act as agents for them all. Systems must
be devised to enforce the responsibility of the government to the
governed. For this purpose the state will be rooted in constitutionalism and the rule of law. It will institute an electoral process and
welcome the existence of two or more parties that offer a variety of
programs and leadership. The choice between these alternatives
must be considered in some detail, since it is crucial to the distinction
between dictatorship and democracy.

Types of Authoritarianism. Whenever a government is founded upon the opinion that its authority does not originate with those over whom it is exercised, some alternative source must be contrived. Only two possibilities suggest themselves. Authority can be imagined to descend upon the government, like manna from Heaven, as a gift of some higher power outside of and above the government and the governed. Or it can be believed to inhere in the rulers by virtue of certain qualities with which they are uniquely and naturally endowed.

(*1*) *Divine Right.* The belief that the right to rule over other human beings comes from a higher than human source has lived long and dies hard. Nor must one seek far for the reason why an idea of this kind should have been advanced. Often bewildered by the world around him, not fully understanding the operation of its physical laws and therefore unable to control his environment, man has sought to erect frail shelters of security against the mysteries of the universe that dwarfs him. Before the modern age of experimental science he ventured to bend to his will the concealed and unknown forces whose effects he observed, but whose causes he did not comprehend. If drought were threatening his crops, with solemn ritual he poured water upon a stone, a symbolic act intended to draw rain from the reluctant skies. Desiring to be rid of some hated person, he fashioned an effigy which he then stabbed or mutilated, thinking thereby to bring on his enemy disaster and death.[1] But when the result did not conform to the hope, it occurred to man that he might entreat the forces which he could not command. Prayer might accomplish what magic did not. In this case, however, since man was begging a favor, he must obtain the good will of the power or powers to whom he made appeal. To attain this end certain observances were necessary on his part. He must be careful to give no offence to his deities and incur no displeasure. Thus, he must live righteously, that is, in conformity with divine will, and must approach his deity in a proper manner, that is, with the correct ritual. To know this will and ritual was of supreme importance. Indeed, in such matters as the conduct of war or the assurance of food supply, the life and death of the community might be at

---

[1] See James Frazer, *The Golden Bough* (one vol. abridgement, London: The Macmillan Co., 1941), chap. 3.

stake. To placate and enlist the aid of a deity was therefore no casual affair but an act fundamental to the general welfare.[2]

These are some considerations that explain the close connection so frequently existing between government and religion or magic. Where much depends upon maintaining the right relation with the power pervading the universe, governmental responsibilities like war and welfare become intertwined with the ceremonies of witchcraft or worship. It calls for special skills, and therefore specialized personnel, to mediate on man's behalf between the world that is seen and that which is unseen. He who holds the key to the mysteries that determine human fates wields power.

For the purpose of this analysis, it is unnecessary to inquire which kind of authority, human or superhuman, was the prior and superior. Indeed, the gaps and silences of pre-history do not allow a conclusive answer to the question: Did those who already possessed political power look for reinforcements from magic or religion, or did medicine-men and priests project their influence into the general arena of government? All that can be stated with certainty is that human and superhuman authority have often been found close to each other and are presumably related. The priest-king or god-ruler is a phenomenon widely spread among peoples at different levels of cultural development. Through the centuries and around the world the research of anthropologists and historians has discovered countless examples of rulers who perform magical or religious rites, or are worshipped as living deities, or trace back their lineage to a divine ancestor; of prophets who announce they have heard the word of God and administer His code of commandments; of priests whom the faithful revere as custodians of the True Faith and exponents of divine will. The lives of men like Moses and Mahomet; the use of state-religion to bolster the Emperorship in ancient Rome and modern Japan; the position of the King of England as head of the Church of England; such titles as Holy Roman Emperor and Most Christian Majesty; Calvin's government in Geneva; the long record of the Papacy; the careers of Joseph Smith and Brigham Young and the founding of the Mormon State of Deseret—these cases are inexplicable save as instances of religious organization accomplishing its ends by control of the state or of political power invoking religion to enhance its strength and sanctity.

[2] *Ibid.*, chap. 4.

What consequence does all this produce for the state? How is the authority to govern men affected by being linked with a belief in power that is more than human? The answer clearly is that when humanity thinks its ruler is divine, or has a divine ancestor, or is divinely appointed, it is impossible to expect that the relation of government to the governed can approach equality or even near-equality. In the presence of deity or a representative of deity, men are accustomed to bare the head or bow the knee, to listen submissively, to avert the eye, or gaze with awe and reverence. All of which effectively precluded controls over government! How can a mere mortal demand an accounting from the godhead when criticism is named heresy and opposition is sin? Is not a law firmly founded when men believe it to be given by God, as when Hammurabi, King of Babylon, received the law from Shamash, or when Moses on Sinai was told the Ten Commandments from the mouth of Jehovah? Small wonder that royal monarchs in the sixteenth and seventeenth centuries attempted to fortify their authority with doctrines of the "divine right of Kings" or that Shakespeare could allow a hypocrite and murderer like King Claudius to exclaim

> There's such divinity doth hedge a king,
> That treason can but peep to what it would,
> Acts little of his will.[3]

From the standpoint of those who govern, the great advantage of attributing their authority to divine will is that opposition is made to seem so fruitless. Who dares resist the government challenges a divine dispensation that mere mortals must accept and cannot amend.

(2) *Ancestral Lineage.* The same feeling—that submission to those in power is an unalterable feature of the established order—can be evoked in another way. It may be asserted that the authority to govern issues not from Heaven, but from the past.[4] Government, so the argument runs, consists essentially in superiors giving orders to subjects. The continuity and stability of the state are best assured when human beings are ranked into classes, and, upon birth, are assigned to the same status in society as their parents. Some are

---

[3] *Hamlet*, Act IV, Sc. 5, ll. 122-24.
[4] In some cases the one approximates the other, for example, when people worship their ancestors.

highborn, some low-born. If my grandfather was the inferior of your grandfather, and my father of your father, then I am inferior to you and take your orders. Authority thus becomes a matter of hereditary right, an appendix to a birth certificate. The title to rule is a product of lineage and lapse of time.

Such a philosophy is not merely a conservative plea for the status quo. It is also a defense of a society divided into classes whose membership is determined—or rather predetermined—without any one of us willing it so. Society thus visualized evolves as a loom weaving a seamless web to a pattern made long ago. Heredity, by allotting to each his station in life, selects his environment for him; and this environment may not be altered since it results from the unalterable circumstance of parentage. It then becomes a simple matter to discover the source of authority. Authority is ancestral—and that is all. This principle is plainly one that can operate only in a fairly static society. Furthermore, it can provide but one political advantage, namely stability of government and a sure procedure for the transfer of power, which, though desirable up to a point, is not the sole ideal for which the state exists. But in any case how does an authority, founded on the past, reply to critics who shout that the times are out of joint and that a sick society needs a new medicine and new medicine-men?

(3) *"Might is Right."* Besides connecting itself with deity or antiquity, a third method by which authority demands obedience is the appeal to force. The right of those in power is then defended by virtue of the fact that they are in power and possess the means for enforcing their will. This view, instead of arguing that might is justified by the right it serves, inverts the relationship, deriving right from might. Thus we have such assertions as "Justice is the interest of the stronger," "Obey the powers that be," and "Whatever is, is right." The most that can be said for this point of view is that it offers the governed a counsel of expediency and prudence. But on all other grounds it is open to most serious objections. Any doctrine is morally indefensible that seeks to justify right by might, and legion are the crimes and cruelties that have thus been coated with a glossy polish. Furthermore, to derive a government's authority from the force it commands is to invite any opponent to test its strength and challenge it with counterforce. For those who can

overthrow the existing order by violence are then entitled to succeed to its authority, and some will think the prize is worth the gamble.

(4) *The Communist Party*. When all else fails, a ruling group that does not justify its authority by one of the three methods just described—by reference to God, great-grandparents, or guns—is left with the final possibility of asserting its own inherent superiority. The privileged few may defend their right to govern the subject-many by arguing that they are the best qualified. What makes them "the best" is a problem that was discussed in Chapter 5 where different kinds of elites were analyzed. The best have been variously defined as the oldest, wisest, wealthiest, and so on. If sufficient people accept the view that fitness to govern is associated with one of these attributes, then those who have mustered enough years or knowledge or property owe their authority to this fact. The newest variation on this ancient theme is the one that has provided many examples and much evidence since the end of World War I. This is the dictatorship within the state of a single party, holding a monopoly of power and legal authority. As a technique of government, the system originated with the revolutionary movement from the left that grew out of the central root of Marxism. The one who invented the idea and first applied it was V. I. Lenin. What he initiated was rigorously extended by the man who chose to call himself "Lenin's faithful disciple": Joseph Stalin. Holding the Marxian view that society is irreconcilably split into two fundamentally opposed economic classes, that the relationship between these can only be one of war, and that the revolt of the submerged class and its eventual triumph are inevitable, Lenin concerned himself with the question of tactics for hastening the inevitable and guiding it into the approved Communist channels. Since the revolutionary class (called the proletariat) was large, poorly educated, and politically inexperienced, its victory required, according to him, the aid of a smaller group, firmly disciplined and iron-willed, whose members could fathom and follow the fundamental laws of "scientific" Marxism.

Such was the Communist party that Lenin set out to build and that Stalin and his followers have continued in the Soviet Union or reproduced elsewhere. The character of the party was clearly described by Stalin at the time (1924) when he was its secretary-general. According to him the party "must first of all constitute the vanguard of the working class." As such, it "must take its stand at the head of the working class, it must see ahead of the working class, lead the proletariat and not trail behind the spontaneous movement." The similarity between a revolutionary struggle and war makes it necessary for the proletariat, like an army in the field, to have a general staff. "The Party," therefore, "is the Military staff of the proletariat." From these premises the conclusions follow that the party must be "the organized detachment of the working class"; that it is "the highest form of class organization of the proletariat"; that it serves as "the weapon of the dictatorship of the proletariat"; and that "the existence of factions is incompatible with Party unity and with its iron discipline." [5] When the "Stalin Constitution" was written and ratified in 1936, the principles outlined above were duly recorded in Article 126 as follows:

> The most active and politically conscious citizens in the ranks of the working class and other strata of the toilers unite in the Communist Party of the Soviet Union (Bolsheviks), which is the vanguard of the toilers in their struggle to strengthen and develop the socialist system and which represents the leading core of all organizations of the toilers, both public and state.

Using statements of this kind to explain his actions, Stalin established a remarkable triple dictatorship; that of himself over the Communist party, that of the party over the peoples of the U.S.S.R., and that of the party in the U.S.S.R. over organized Communist movements elsewhere in the world, with the present exception of Yugoslavia. Numerically the ratio of Communist party members to the population they govern is small. Their control is maintained by various devices—by a complete grip on the machinery of government at its highest levels, by placing their members at key points in the community (in factories, collective farms, educational bodies, etcetera) to direct and report on non-members, by a monopoly of all media for influencing opinion, by the forcible suppression of any overt criticism, and by the terrorist activities of a dreaded secret police. Most important of all to the party is the selection and training of its own personnel. Prospective members are carefully observed during a long period of probation and preparation. Once

---

[5] All the above quotations are from a lecture on "Foundations of Leninism" given by Stalin in 1924 and printed in many collections of Marxist writings.

admitted to the party, the Communist's life is completely dedicated to a meticulous discipline of thought and action prescribed by his official superiors. Every now and then a purge is conducted to rid the party of any who are too weak, too half-hearted, or too independent for its tasks. Because of the Communist conception of their mission as an officer class directing a revolutionary upsurge of the masses of mankind, their ethical code knows no greater sin than disunity. Their bitterest hatred is therefore directed, not at those they call their "class enemies," but at any Communists who differ or deviate from the high command (such as the late Leon Trotsky or the contemporary Yugoslav ruler, Marshal Tito) and at socialists of a democratic brand who compete with Communists for the support of the working class. Finally since a dictatorship thrives on continuing an atmosphere of crisis, the Communist leaders pursue the policy of sowing suspicion among their subjects and implanting widespread fear of traitors within and spies from without. If systematically conducted by a watchful secret police who are backed up by concentration camps, this policy is well calculated to keep the opponents of those in power disorganized, demoralized, and therefore harmless.

(5) *Fascism and Nazism.* When Mussolini in 1932 wrote an article on "The Political and Social Doctrine of Fascism" for the *Italian Encyclopedia,* he asserted, "A party which entirely governs a nation is a fact entirely new to history, there are no possible references or parallels." This statement conceals the debt that Mussolini owed to Lenin and Stalin. Although there are significant differences between Fascism and Communism—differences of outlook, origins, and objectives—the systems resemble each other in two facts of fundamental importance. In both cases a minority clique, organized as a party, wields absolute power over a large majority whom it considers and treats as inferior. To preserve its supremacy the minority is pushed to extremes of ruthlessness and fastens on its subjects the coercive fetters of the police state. Under Fascism and Communism alike the dominant group professes to care for "the people," "the nation," "the broad masses," et cetera, but does not concede that its authority is delegated or may be defined by them.

Unswerving obedience to an ironclad autocracy is a hallmark of the Fascist state. In Italy and Germany under the regimes of Mus-

solini and Hitler the dictatorship of the party over the people was
as intense as the pre-eminence within the party of the Duce or
Fuehrer. "Believe, obey, fight" was the motto prescribed by Mussolini for his countrymen. "In the name of God and of Italy I swear
that I will obey the orders of the Leader without questioning"—
this was part of the oath taken upon admission to the Fascist party.
Mein Kampf, the Bible of the Nazi movement, enunciated with
grotesque clarity the contempt that Hitler felt for the mass of
humanity and his determination to subject them to a disciplined
inferiority. "A view of life," he proclaimed, "which, by rejecting
the democratic mass idea endeavors to give this world to the best
people, that means to the most superior men [the Germans], has
logically to obey the same aristocratic principle also within this
people and has to guarantee leadership and highest influence within
the respective people to its best heads." Political organization therefore requires "putting the heads above the masses" and "subjecting
the masses to the heads." Mankind's interest "is not satisfied and is
not served by the rule of the masses who are either unable to think
or are inefficient, in any case not inspired." Such assumptions brought
Hitler to formulate his principle of leadership. "The principle which
once made the Prussian army the most marvelous instrument of the
German people has to be some day in a transformed meaning the
principle of the construction of our whole state constitution, authority of every leader towards below and responsibility towards
above." [6]

The Hallmarks of Dictatorship. To militarize civilian life, to
dress people's bodies in uniforms and their minds with uniformity,
to have one legal party serving as the general staff or officer class
of a browbeaten population—this is the common denominator of
dictatorships of extreme Left and Right. Hitler, Mussolini, Stalin,
Franco, Gottwald, and their ilk are in this respect brothers under
the skin—or under the shirt. For the governed (that is, the majority
of the population) to determine policy or call their rulers to account
is as impossible under Communism as under Fascism. Both systems,
since their government is a dictatorship, exalt the value of leadership
and impose the party as an aristocracy on the nation. Both are

[6] These quotations are all from "Personality and the Conception of the
National State," *Mein Kampf*, trans. Alvin Johnson, chairman (New York:
Reynal & Hitchcock, 1939), vol. II, chap. 4, pp. 661, 665, 670.

authoritarian in the sense that, as in an army, authority resides in a few who are responsible for, but not responsible to, the many. Both maintain their dominance by trial and terror.

Authoritarianism leaves its imprint on politics in many ways. An oligarchy, while it sharpens the distinction between ruler and subject, blurs the distinction between government and state. In order that its authority may not be challenged, the ruling class not only seeks to monopolize the actualities of power, but denies to others their right to power. An effective means to this end is for rulers to assert that those who are the government are in fact the state—thereby obliterating the difference. If their contention is accepted, an attempt to change the government becomes an effort to overthrow the state and political opponents of those in power can be punished as revolutionaries. When, however, the government is viewed as a group of officials authorized for the time being to act in the name of the state, then it is possible to say that the state continues in existence despite changes of government. Hereditary aristocracies of the traditional kind have regarded the state, in periods when they held a monopoly of governmental power, as a species of property that they owned. The people who were their subjects "belonged" to the privileged class by virtue of an inherited status—in much the same way as a mansion, land, crops, and cattle belonged to the individual noble.

A similar outlook pervades the one-party state of the twentieth century. The elite party in a fascist or communist dictatorship absorbs the state, instead of merely acting on its behalf. The party does more than "take over" the government. It abolishes any institutions of the state that might compete for authority with the organs of the party—as the Russian Communists abolished the Duma; and Mussolini, the Chamber of Deputies. Or, instead of destroying, the party emasculates its rivals, permitting them a twilight and ineffectual existence—as Hitler allowed the Reichstag to linger on and as the Communists under Stalin have treated their own Soviets. The state thereby becomes the adjunct of the party; not the party, the servant of the state. Only in this one respect can the state be said to wither away: its life is sucked from it by the cancerous growth of the party.

Besides thus identifying the rulers with the state, authoritarianism also produces a distinctive theory of law. Since every kind of state formulates general rules for its members to obey, the sources and sanctions of law are closely related to the problem of authority. Different governmental systems advance varying answers to the question, What gives law its obligatory character? Under the dictatorship of an authoritarian regime, the answer is unambiguous. Law simply expresses the will of those with the power to issue and enforce their commands. Once the authorities have spoken, what they said is the law—and that is all there is to know. Such a doctrine is well adapted to exempt the rulers' wishes from challenge. If law must be accepted at its face value because the rulers will it so, how can anyone query its validity? As long as the ruling group remains united and speaks with one voice, no alternative is left to the subject but obedience.

The classic vice of all dictatorial systems is their basic assumption of the superiority and infallibility of those in power. Such pretensions are not justified by the facts of history. Though some absolute rulers have been benevolent, though some oligarchies have performed acts of wise statesmanship, these systems generally have been and are still productive of far too much stupidity, waste, and cruelty, to merit the favor of mankind. Dictatorship exaggerates the worthiness of a few and demeans or brutalizes the remainder. With unwarranted arrogance, it identifies the general well-being of the community with the special interest of the ruling group. Even when philosophers, like Hegel, devote their services to its cause, the claims of absolutism remain bogus. Stripped of the veneer and camouflage, dictatorship is essentially a regime of privilege. As such, since it cannot evoke consent from the underprivileged, it must hold sway by force and fraud. The dominant group coheres together for fear of losing its special advantages. It is able to prolong these, because in practice the mobilized force of an equipped and disciplined minority is often superior to the potentialities of an unorganized majority. Dictatorship thus succeeds in diverting a portion of the force, which the whole community needs for its protection, to supply the government with protection from the governed. Hence the familiar characteristics arise of "the police state," which is simply an arrested stage of political development. It is a state that begins with the elementary need of protection and has advanced as far as establishing order. But there it stops, and is unable, while it continues as a dictatorship, to progress toward the law and ethics of justice or the humanism of welfare. Furthermore, the evolution of its techniques, like that of its objectives, is also arrested. The police state is an embodiment of force and power, but has not developed the moral claims of authority.

Foundations of Freedom. What is the alternative to dictatorship? By what means can the authority of government be made subject to consent? How is it possible to grant powers for use and safeguard them against abuse? The beginning of an answer is to reject the doctrine that the government is the source of authority and to embrace the contrary notion that authority derives from the mass of the people who entrust the government with powers to be exercised on their behalf. Although one of the critical issues of the present century is the choice between these two political poles and their resulting forms of organization, the decision that confronts humanity is not a new one. A long tradition supports the view that authority is somehow delegated by the governed to their government, despite the fact that states founded on this principle have been the rarities of history and continue today to be the exception rather than the rule. The assertion of the principle, however, would have had little effect on practice unless institutional means were developed for placing a curb on those in authority. The doctrine that government should be responsible has to be studied in the light of historical efforts to make it so.

The Athenian Democracy. In the oldest democracy about whose institutions anything is known in detail, an elaborate system was devised to ensure that the people, or *demos*, would be self-governing in fact and would possess the upper hand over their officials. From the middle of the fifth century B.C. to the middle of the fourth, the government of Athens rested upon the belief that all power belonged to the people, who exercised it by a many-sided participation in public affairs. The price of Athenian citizenship was activity and versatility. Among the duties of a citizen were service in the army or navy, attendance at festivals and spectacles, and jury-work in the courts of law. But most important of all was his presence at the monthly meetings of the Assembly where he helped to enact laws and decrees, settle questions of high policy, conduct foreign relations, and authorize the financial operations of his state. The work of the Assembly, however, busy though it was, required supplementing by administrative officials. These were selected in one of two ways. The Assembly filled by election offices that required special qualifications and expert knowledge. In other cases, where the duties to be performed simply needed average intelligence and the use of ordinary judgment, the Athenians employed a method that was distinctive to their democracy—the lot. Their favorite practice was to place at the head of a department or agency a board of citizens picked annually by lot. Such a system served many purposes. It ensured that government was conducted, in a literal way, *by* the people. It contributed to public education by enlarging the direct acquaintance of citizens with governmental problems. Through rotation in office it spread a sense of civic responsibility.

Certain safeguards were added, moreover, to forestall the appointment of anybody manifestly unfit and to prevent abuse of power. Before they could assume their posts, those whom the lot selected were made to pass a scrutiny that was a mixture of qualifying test and loyalty clearance. Then ten times during the year, at one of the regular meetings of the Assembly, a standing order of business invited the populace to vote approval or censure of their officials—censure being followed by an indictment in the law courts, tantamount to impeachment. Finally, when the office-holder's year of service came to an end, he was duty bound to present to a special board of auditors the accounts for any public monies of which he was collector, custodian, or disburser. It was this last requirement—the accountability of the official as enforced by a post-audit—that in Athenian eyes constituted the ultimate weapon of popular control. When Athenian statesmen and philosophers contrasted their own political institutions with those of oligarchy or monarchy, two of the features that they most frequently mentioned to highlight the differences were appointment by lot and post-audit. Both practices, in their view, prevented the rise of a bureaucracy, either in the sense of an official caste aloof from and superior to the people or in the sense of an uncontrollable corps of officialdom.

There was, however, another risk to which Athenian democracy was liable. Where matters of such weight were determined at the Assembly of the citizens, much depended on the judgment that the leading orators displayed. Decisions were reached by vote of the majority after free and open discussion, and a proposal could be adopted on the motion, not of some holder of public office, but of

a private citizen with a popular following. That being the case, in
the absence of further safeguards, policies might be settled or reversed by snap votes; majorities could be incited by ranting orators;
the heat of factional fights might inflame the community. To coun-
teract these dangers, of which they learned through bitter experience, the Athenians instituted two more safety devices. One was
the curious and drastic expedient called ostracism. When internal
dissension and conflict between ambitious politicians imperilled the
unity of the state, the Assembly could adopt a motion to ostracize.
This was followed in two months' time by a special election where,
provided at least 6,000 participated, the man who received a
majority of adverse ballots was banished for ten years after which
he could return and resume all his civil, political, and property
rights.[7] A second way in which the Assembly sought protection
against irresponsible leaders and against its own worse judgment
was by drawing a distinction between laws, which contained rules
of general application, and decrees, which dealt with particular
circumstances. A law could not be amended or repealed without
notice in due form and the observance of certain procedural requirements. Likewise, a decree had to fulfill some procedural checks;
but in addition it must conform to existing legislation. The Athenians
enforced these principles by a judicial process.[8] Within a year of
the passage of any law or decree, its proposer could be indicted
on a charge of unconstitutionality, the penalties for which were
severe. Thus an all-powerful Assembly attempted to guarantee a
government under law.

There is more than experimental novelty and a uniquely interesting structure to give merit to this Athenian constitution. It is
distinguished in addition by the quality of wise political realism.
The Athenians were not content solely to proclaim the fine-
sounding doctrines of citizen participation, official accountability,
and rule of law. Such ideas would have been insufficient to mold
political behavior, were they not reinforced with appropriate institutions and procedures. It was the latter that put teeth into theory
and made democracy effective. How vital it is to install the necessary

[7] The last recorded instance of an actual ostracism was in 417 B.C., the victim
being Hyperbolus.
[8] N.B. Judicial process meant a trial in the courts, where the verdict was
returned by a jury who were a random sample of the citizens.

machinery, if ideas are to operate in practice, can be better understood by noting the contrast with other systems that neglected adequately to translate some well-meant formulae into hard fact.

The Roman Sacrifice of Liberty to Empire. Consider the experience of Rome and the political testament which that city bequeathed to its successors. Between the expulsion of the monarchy at the end of the sixth century B.C. and the establishment of the Augustan Principate five centuries later, Rome was a republic. During this period of half a millennium, the Romans accomplished some remarkable political achievements. They laid the groundwork for a system of civil and criminal law that is basic to the jurisprudence and legal codes of many modern nations. By the prowess of their redoubtable legions they absorbed within a single empire all the lands and peoples surrounding the Mediterranean. Under the dominion of Rome almost all southern and western Europe, North Africa, and much of the Middle East, experienced a greater measure of political unity than that region had known before or has ever known since. But these organizers of law and legions; these architects of highways, aqueducts, and central heating; these Caesars and Ciceros whose craftsmanship left Rome the eternal city and Latin a universal language; these men could not for all their political genius construct a democracy. The governmental tradition associated with the name of Rome was and is authoritarian. The major concepts that typify the Roman contribution to politics are expressed in these Latin-derived words: power—*potestas*, authority—*auctoritas*, empire—*imperium*.

The reason for this is plain. The constitution of the Roman republic did embody principles that were potentially democratic. Wanting to avoid a repetition of the tyranny they had suffered under some of their kings, the Romans adopted the device of a distribution and separation of powers and relied upon the various agencies and authorities to balance, and thereby check, each other. Their officials, from the consuls on down, were elected by assemblies of citizens, and for a year at a time. Legislation, too, had to be voted upon by the citizens, whose approval converted a proposed bill into an authoritative law. From this it would seem clear that the Romans intended their government to be subordinate to the governed. But circumstances combined to defeat the intention. The republic seldom enjoyed the luxury of a long, uninterrupted peace. Its response to the challenge of nearby peoples launched it upon a tide of military conquest. Acceptance of an imperial mission, however, brought to Rome an enlargement of size and power for which its earlier institutions proved inadequate. The need for continuous direction of policy and for central supervision of outlying provinces was ill met by the poorly organized popular assemblies and annually changing magistrates.

Only one institution attempted to fill the need: the Senate. But when this body—a tightly-knit oligarchy of past and present office holders and noble families—was itself split through the growing division of Roman society into opposed classes, the state was torn apart by internal conspiracies and civil war. The last century of the republic's existence (133-31 B.C.) comprised a dismal catalogue of revolution, counter-revolution, and coup d'état. Unable to control its powerful commanders in the field, the Senate lay successively at the mercy of Marius, Sulla, Pompey, Caesar, and Anthony, and finally succumbed to Augustus. The system founded by the last of these became an autocracy powerfully centralized in the person of the emperor, who maintained his position by placating the mob in the streets of Rome and controlling the legions in their barracks on the far-extended frontiers of the Empire. Only as a perfumed memory of the past did the theory linger on that the emperor received his authority in a law conferring the imperial prerogatives at the beginning of his reign. That law, however, was enacted merely out of deference to an ancient form. It altered not a whit the political realities of absolutism.

A striking parallel may be observed in the medieval period. The political structure of feudalism exhibited a glaring contrast between the doctrines that government is limited by law and rulers are responsible for their actions, and the absence of effective means of enforcement. Though they acknowledged the principle that they should serve the common good, medieval governments fought shy of control by the common people. For this there is a historical explanation. The Germanic tribes, which in the fifth and sixth centuries A.D. burst the ramparts of the Roman Empire and sliced its sprawling territories into kingdoms, had formerly developed some institutions of a rough and primitive democracy in the forests of Germany. But the urge that drove them west and south was itself the result of pressure upon central Europe from other peoples further east—the pressure of Asiatics, like the Huns, foraging for new supplies of food and plundering as they went. This migration of peoples, the *Völkerwanderung*, had a profound effect upon forms of government. A tribe on the march, or one that has to repel invaders, must militarize itself to survive, which always means that it becomes authoritarian. When in addition the Goths, Franks, Vandals, and the rest, gradually imbibed the influence of the civilization they had overrun, they sought to assimilate their own kingdoms to the pattern of imperial Rome. The democratic folkways of the German forests, like the traditions of the Roman republic, thenceforth continued to exist in a fairyland of remembered ideas to which the brute facts of daily government gave the lie.

The Medieval Order: Fictions and Facts. The medieval world that emerged from the turmoil of these Dark Ages fairly bristled with notions of law as a restraint upon government. Being a Christian, a ruler must conform to the law of God. Being custodian of the community's way of life, he must uphold and preserve its immemorial customs, to which indeed he owed his own powers and privileges. But was there anyone to say whether a ruler had in fact violated divine or human law, and, if so, how could he be called to account? The possibility of curbing a ruler depended, as always, on the existence of organized opposition. In the Middle Ages there were two sources from whence this might spring. One was, of course, the church. If it could be charged that a ruler had sinned against divine law, the church could direct against him its two powerful weapons—excommunication and interdict. When employed by a masterful Pope, these devices could bring to heel a king like John of England, or even such an emperor as Henry IV.

Clerical resistance to royal or imperial power, though it imposed a limitation upon the state, did not necessarily constitute a gain from the standpoint of democratic or popular control. All that happened when the Papacy scored a success was the subordination for the time being of secular to ecclesiastical authority, the latter being as authoritarian in spirit and structure as the former. Hence, toward the close of the Middle Ages a movement developed for the reform of church government. Associated with the names of the Italian, Marsiglio of Padua, and the Englishman, William of Occam, this was called the Conciliar Movement because its aim was to place at the head of the church a general council of elected delegates representing not only the clergy but all Christian believers. The Conciliarists came near to their goal at the end of the Great Schism when, in order to heal the breach in the church and overhaul its organization, two Councils were convoked and did meet respectively at Constance (1414-1418) and Basel (1431-1449). In the face, however, of opposition from the Pope, the Cardinals, and the higher clergy generally, this attempt to democratize the structure of the church met with failure. The "Petrine theory" of Papal power, placing supreme authority in the Pope who governs in consultation with the College of Cardinals, was emphatically asserted. In consequence, as George H. Sabine has written: "The pope in the fifteenth century established himself as the first of the absolute monarchs, and the theory of papal absolutism became the archetype of the theory of monarchical absolutism." [9] From that basis has the organization of the Roman Church proceeded to the present, plus the added reinforcement in the year 1870 of the dogma that the Pope, when he speaks *ex cathedra*, is infallible.

The Struggle between Kings and Nobles. There was only one other quarter besides the church from which effective opposition to a king could come in the Middle Ages. This was the nobility. Much of the political history of those centuries consisted in struggles between the nobles and their monarch, with each side trying to curb the other. When the nobility stood solidly together, they could wring concessions from a king. A notable instance was the triumph of the English barons in compelling King John to sign the Great Charter of 1215 that reaffirmed their ancient rights and privileges against royal encroachment. Still more successful were the Polish nobility, whose prolonged resistance reduced the institution of monarchy to a weak figurehead. In their case, however, success had tragic consequences since the Polish state in the absence of strong direction fell easy prey to Russian and Prussian expansion and was erased from the map. Sometimes a powerful nobleman opposed the reigning monarch in order to dispossess him of the crown and place it upon his own or a kinsman's head. More often than not the rivalries between great aristocrats and their clans sowed a bitter crop of strife and bloodshed. The Wars of the Roses, which for three decades tore medieval England into two hostile camps, were sparked by the clashing ambitions of the Houses of

[9] George H. Sabine, *History of Political Theory* (London: Harrap & Co., 1937), p. 326. See the whole of chap. 16 in that book.

Lancaster and York, as were the political aims of Papacy and Empire respectively championed on the European battlefields by Guelphs and Ghibellines.

From this welter of discord, into which the loose-knit character of feudalism had plunged society, there emerged in one country the beginnings of a constructive achievement that was destined to endure. It was in England during the thirteenth century that the institution of Parliament took shape and acquired, at the hands of Simon de Montfort (1265) and King Edward I (1295), the form and functions that differentiated it from the earlier Great Council. During the thirteenth and fourteenth centuries that form was set into the definite mold of two chambers, one of which, the House of Lords, contained the higher nobility and higher clergy and the second, the House of Commons, represented the lesser nobles (for example, knights of the shire) and commoners. The functions of Parliament are a more complicated story. The reason for its existence in the Middle Ages may be found in two circumstances. The "loyal, trusty, and well-beloved subjects" of the king normally had various grievances of which they wished to complain to His Majesty. These could be more effectively voiced and would carry more weight, if expressed through a regularized procedure. While subjects needed to approach the king for redressing their wrongs, he had a motive on his side for approaching them, for what he wanted was their money. Originally the king's government was conceived of as a branch of his household. As any great landowner managed his estates and supervised the affairs of his tenantry, so a king was supposed to govern the realm and protect its inhabitants. Affairs of state were handled by secretaries and other palace officials who in a literal sense were servants of the Crown, while the costs of administration were defrayed out of the king's personal wealth and income. In all this, no attempt was made to separate what was public from what was private. Or rather, the concept of public interest had disappeared in the smothering embrace of private relationships. Public officials were court functionaries; the public treasury, a private purse.

Such a situation could continue only so long as the functions of the central government were few and their costs remained small. Everything changed, however, when kings endeavored to extend their authority to new fields (for example, the provision of a uniform,

national system of justice) and when they embarked on the most
expensive of all governmental activities—war. To pacify the Welsh,
to drive back the Scots, to crush the Irish, and to conquer the
French,[10] meant retaining and supplying large armies in the field.
No longer could a king "live off his own" as tradition expected him
to do. He must now ask his subjects to contribute in his service
not only their lives but that other dear possession, their money.
Here then was a situation with the makings of a bargain advantageous to both sides. If the king were to appropriate his subjects'
money without their consent, they could have a new and serious
grievance. If he requested them, however, to contribute their money
voluntarily, was not the time opportune for them to request him
to remedy their wrongs, which might lead to legislative action or
to changes in executive policy? Furthermore, when asking for
money, the king would have to satisfy the natural curiosity of tax-
payers who wished to know how equitably it would be collected
and for what purposes it would be spent. Hence Parliament received its start in life from the coupling of two original functions—
the exercise of the power of the purse and the need for a public
forum for the ventilation of grievances. From these roots grew
such other duties as the enactment of law, discussion of public
policy, and control of the executive.

Rise of the English Parliament. Great institutions grow slowly,
however, and, like big trees that put on a new ring annually, store
up their annual accumulation of precedents. Four centuries elapsed
between Edward I's Model Parliament of 1295 and the final, decisive, victory of parliamentarians over royalists in 1688. What was
it that took so much time? The answer consists in a social and
economic, as well as a political, explanation. When Parliament was
constructed to represent wealth and social superiority, when the
dominant interest in the economy was the possession of land, and
when the nobility were among the biggest land owners, then an
addition to the powers of Parliament with its proportionate weakening of the Crown could only mean government of the people by
the nobility for the nobility, and it was doubtful whether anything
was to be gained by rejecting the king's yoke in favor of that of

---

[10] For example, the protracted campaigns of the "Hundred Years' War"
(1337-1453).

the nobles. On the contrary, from the standpoint of the mass of the population there was much to be said in favor of a weak nobility and a powerful king, since, when a king abused his power, his oppression was likely to bear hardest upon the nobles who were the nearest rivals to his pre-eminence.

The politics of this situation were reinforced by the economic developments of the fifteenth century. At that time the structure of feudalism, centering around the ownership and produce of the land, was being remolded by the force of a contrary interest. An expansion of handicraft industries was accompanied by an increase in domestic and foreign commerce. Enterprises of this character stimulated and strengthened the craft guilds, associations of merchants, and credit and banking institutions. For mutual convenience these clustered within the walls of the trading-city [11] *(Handels-stadt)*, which was indispensable as the focal point in the system of production, distribution, and communication. Such cities began to exert their influence upon the political process. What they sought was the preservation of order, because warfare disrupted trade, and emancipation from rural supremacy. On both scores urbanism pitted itself against the feudal aristocracy whose discords disturbed the peace and whose wealth was drawn from the soil. The monarchy, natural foe of the nobility, was the natural ally of the urban *burghers* or burgesses. The grant to cities of royal charters of incorporation, as was done in England, enabled them to be self-governing, that is, to be rid of feudal government by the nobles who dominated the surrounding countryside. Consequently it was this urban "middle" class that rallied to the Crown, that helped to replace the decentralized disorder of feudalism by unified central power, that embodied the new concept of sovereignty [12] in the person of the Sovereign (a word that became synonymous with King), and reaped the economic benefits of the centrally directed policies of mercantilism.[13] In England as in France the monarchy became absolute because there were organized interests approving the powers it wielded.

[11] Witness the growth in importance of the Hanseatic League (including in its membership Hamburg, Bremen, Lübeck, Bergen, Danzig, and others), the cities of northern Italy (like Venice, Milan, and Florence), and Antwerp, Amsterdam, and London.

[12] See above, Chapter 7, pp. 172-3.

[13] See above, Chapter 8, pp. 179-81.

The Revolution in England. It is the style of political change, as was observed earlier,[14] to proceed from excess in one direction to counter-excess. If feudal disunity was the prelude to royal absolutism, the latter too outlasted its original justification and by abuses of its own invoked new opposition. A monarch who was steering a dangerous course—witness Henry VIII piloting the English Reformation, or Queen Elizabeth holding the Spaniards at bay with zigzags of dalliance and defiance—wisely employed the institution of Parliament for enlisting public support; and Parliament's members, their appetite for authority whetted with each taste, would not willingly be denied a further share once the immediacy of crisis was past. The cooperation between Parliament and the Crown, which was fairly well maintained by Tudor monarchs, broke down under their unhappy successors, the Stuarts. A variety of circumstances turned a rift into a revolution. Chief blunders on the royal side were the decisions of Charles I to dispense altogether with Parliament, to levy taxes without parliamentary consent, and to administer secret and arbitrary "justice" in the Court of the Star Chamber. The price that England paid was a civil war of ten years duration (1641-1651). Charles paid by defeat and the loss of his head. Even this example did not deter King James II, thirty years later, from attempting to restore Catholicism to a predominantly Protestant people. Again an aroused Parliament formed the focus of opposition. In 1688 a second revolution was won without bloodshed, the King being forced to flee with his neck intact. It was Parliament that then invited William of Orange and his wife Mary to occupy the throne, and in an Act of Settlement laid down the terms and limits by which the monarchy has since been bound.

Thus was consecrated the first of the series of revolutions that delivered a new birth of freedom. By the end of the seventeenth century England had secured the essentials of political liberty by creating at the apex of its government an institution representative of the governed. In this way the English people established for themselves, and by their example demonstrated to others, a method through which the effectiveness of power could be legitimized with the moral sanction of consent. Then, with parliamentary supremacy assured, the theoretical explanation followed. These stirring events required a justification, and the occasion fortunately

[14] See Chapter 7, pp. 167-8.

found the man. It was in 1690 that John Locke published the two *Treatises of Civil Government* to which reference has already been made in this book. The first he devoted to the negative task of destroying the fatuous doctrine of the divine right of kings. In the second he constructed a positive theory to take its place. Governments, he asserted, may rightfully exercise only those powers to which the people give their consent. Authority is conferred as a trust, being simply "a fiduciary power to act for certain ends." [15] The wishes of the community are represented and formulated by the legislature that ranks supreme among the organs of the state. Should those in power abuse their trust and a conflict break out between the government and the governed, the latter retain the ultimate weapon of revolution since they can never surrender the right to save themselves.[16] In any such dispute between the citizen-body and authority, no third party can serve as judge. The people are always their own final court of appeal.

The supremacy of Parliament, which had resulted from military victory in the civil war and political triumph in 1688, accorded well with these doctrines—subject to one proviso. It was one thing to assert that the monarchy should henceforth be limited, not absolute, and that Parliament (the legislature) should be paramount over the Crown (the executive). It was something else to assume that the dominance of Parliament was the same as control by all the people. The franchise at the time when Locke wrote was limited to a small number of property owners who were but a fraction of the population. Nor did Locke propose that this be changed. Thus the consent of the governed boiled down to the consent of a class. Nevertheless, it was Locke's glory that, wittingly or unwittingly, he had sown a seed, and there was no stopping its growth. What is more, there were other soils besides that of England in which it could take root. This was what an English government learned in 1776, with results that are explored in the next chapter.

[15] *Second Treatise of Civil Government*, chap. 13, sec. 149.
[16] *Ibid.*

CHAPTER 10

THIRD ISSUE:

(2) THE FREEDOM OF THE GOVERNED

Principles of the American Revolution. "To secure these rights, Governments are instituted among Men, deriving their just powers from the consent of the governed." The key word in this sentence is the adjective "just." Jefferson's problem, when he drafted the opening to the Declaration of Independence, was similar to what Locke had faced one century before. He was expounding the right to rebel against any kind of authority that was unresponsive to the governed. He wanted a society of free men, since liberty to him was a supreme good. Free men, he recognized, must accept certain restraints upon their behavior and must enforce their rules upon offenders. Like the other fathers of the American revolution, Jefferson was no anarchist. His purpose was not to sweep all government away, but to substitute authority that could be held to account for authority that could not. How was this to be done? Was it possible to argue for freedom and yet acquiesce in some coercion?

Jefferson's answer began by reasserting the principle that the consent of the governed is the foundation of all legitimate government. It is consent alone that gives moral sanction and legal validity to the physical force employed by the state. Powers, therefore, which are derived from consent are just, that is, are justified. But suppose a government acts in defiance of consent. What then? "Whenever any form of government becomes destructive of these ends," continues the Declaration, "it is the right of the people to alter or to abolish it, and to institute new government, laying its foundation on such principles and organizing its powers in such form, as to them shall seem most likely to effect their safety and happiness."

To assert, however, the inalienable right of a people to win back their freedom by revolution is to describe an ultimate weapon for use in the last resort. Revolution can be a method—excusable when directed against despotism—of founding a government in the first instance. It is not a method for continuous popular control over regular government activities. For this, something else is required. The achievement of Jefferson's generation was that they not only formulated abstract ideas but also constructed the appropriate institutions. While the ideas have never ceased to yield inspiration, institutions were required to translate them into practical results. The foundations of the latter were laid between 1787 and 1803.[1]

Supremacy of the Constitution. In the American solution to the age-old problem of keeping government under control the distinctive feature is the special role assigned to the Constitution. Whereas the English revolution of the seventeenth century left Parliament supreme, the American revolution resulted in the supremacy of the Constitution. How was this ensured? Various measures have been employed to guarantee that the Constitution would occupy the paramount position in the American system of government. Its drafting was undertaken by a special convention of delegates, presided over by George Washington. The adoption of the finished product was referred to the states, in all of which, except Rhode Island, delegates were elected to special state conventions that debated and voted on the issue of ratification. Ever since it went into effect, the Constitution has possessed the unique status that its contents intended it to have. The preamble announces unequivocally that "We, the people ... do ordain and establish this Constitution," thereby affirming that the government is founded upon popular will. While it is the people who create the Constitution, it is the Constitution that creates the institutions whereby government is conducted. All of these—the Congress, President, and Supreme Court, as well as the State Constitutions and their officials—are subordinate to the Constitution of the United States, to laws that

---

[1] 1803 was the date of the decision in *Marbury v. Madison.* See pp. 241-2.

conform to it, and to treaties made under its authority, which together comprise "the supreme law of the land." [2]

Besides being asserted, the supremacy of the Constitution must be enforced. How is this accomplished? In the first place, by the requirement that all governmental officials—federal, state, and local, elected and appointed—take an oath or affirmation to support the Constitution. Second, by the provision of judicial procedures and penalties, including impeachment, in case any official betrays the people's trust. Third, by the institution of a special system, distinct from the ordinary process of legislation, for amending the Constitution's written text. Further, for good measure there is a fourth method—the judicial review of legislation. Under it, any statute enacted by the legislature and approved by the chief executive or repassed over his veto, may be challenged on the ground of unconstitutionality. A case will then be heard in the courts where it is the judiciary who determine whether the contested statute is to be obeyed as law or regarded as null and void.

The Practice of Judicial Review. The system of judicial review of legislation, involving as it does the two points that statutes must conform to the Constitution and that the judges will decide whether they do conform or not, is nowhere explicitly mentioned in the Constitution.[3] In a partial [4] sense, however, the practice was known in the period before 1776, and certain of the Founding Fathers did assume that it would be employed under the new Constitution.[5] It was, therefore, left to the judges to pick an occasion for asserting this power, if they were so minded, and exercising it successfully, if they were able. Their occasion was the case of *Marbury v. Madison*, decided in 1803. Chief Justice Marshall there used a relatively minor incident as an opportunity for proclaiming the momentous

[2] *Constitution of the United States,* Article VI.

[3] However, the point that laws should conform to the Constitution can be inferred from the wording of Article VI: "This Constitution, and the laws of the United States *which shall be made in pursuance thereof,* . . . shall be the supreme law of the land." My italics.

[4] Prior to independence a colonial statute could be disallowed by the Privy Council if it contravened the colony's charter or an Act of the British Parliament. In such instances, an agency of a legally superior government was supervising the legislation of a government legally inferior—as when the United States Supreme Court now reviews a state law.

[5] For example, Alexander Hamilton in *The Federalist,* No. LXXVIII.

power of judicial disallowance of legislation enacted by a co-ordinate branch of the same government. His words deserve to be quoted:

> It is a proposition too plain to be contested, that the constitution controls any legislative Act repugnant to it; or, that the legislature may alter the constitution by an ordinary Act. Between these alternatives there is no middle ground. The constitution is either a superior paramount law, unchangeable by ordinary means, or it is on a level with ordinary legislative Acts, and, like other Acts, is alterable when the legislature shall please to alter it. If the former part of the alternative be true, then a legislative Act contrary to the constitution is not law; if the latter part be true, then written constitutions are absurd attempts, on the part of the people, to limit a power in its own nature illimitable. Certainly all those who have framed written constitutions contemplate them as forming the fundamental and paramount law of the nation, and consequently the theory of every such government must be that an Act of the legislature repugnant to the constitution is void. . . . It is emphatically the province and duty of the judicial department to say what the law is. Those who apply the rule to particular cases must of necessity expound and interpret that rule. If two laws conflict with each other, the courts must decide on the operation of each.[6]

The Rule of Law. The cumulative effect of this reasoning and these principles is impressive. Added together, they form a special derivation from the broader principle summed up in the phrase that has become symbolic, "the rule of law," and, because the offspring of the same parents are related to one another, an affinity also exists between Marshall's logic and other specific points deducible from the same general source. Some of these points are the following:

(1) that governments shall exercise their powers in conformity with known laws enacted through a regular procedure;

(2) that no laws be passed to convert into offenses actions that were lawful at the time when performed;

(3) that no one may be convicted on any charge save after a fair trial in open court;

(4) that the judiciary, when applying the generalities of the law to particular cases, must be independent of external pressure and control. Such maxims, while arguable on theoretical grounds, are chiefly derived from hard facts and bitter experience. Each was

---

[6] *Marbury v. Madison,* 1 Cranch 137 (1803).

formulated as an ideal contrasting with the proven practices of many governments in the past and present. When a state does not enthrone the rule of law, the governed have no adequate protection against the whim and caprice of those in power. Tyranny, despotism, or dictatorship exists when a government makes and unmakes the law without permitting public criticism or challenge; when it imprisons an individual without public hearing and an equal opportunity for defense; when judges decide cases under the intimidating shadow of executive power; and when laws are enforced arbitrarily, that is, so as to discriminate on grounds of political or personal favoritism between citizens who deserve like treatment.

The Constitution that the State of Massachusetts adopted in 1776 contained the hope "that it may be a government of laws and not of men." This antithesis, of course, cannot be taken too literally. No legal system can operate with automatic, impersonal, machine-like precision. Laws, unlike men, are not self-made. Still less are they self-enforcing. It is men who must draft, enact, interpret, and apply the law. A human—indeed, a humane—discretion must scale down the broad classification to the narrow particulars. But though the Massachusetts statement is a rhetorical exaggeration, the contrast between a government of laws and a government of men serves to emphasize an important distinction. A state may be of a kind that acknowledges and observes certain restraints upon its activities. Or it may flout and defy all efforts at restraint. In the former case, the government's power is bridled and harnessed. In the latter, the powers of government are absolute, and therefore uncontrollable.

Conformance of Law to Custom, Nature, or Utility. The attempt to impose restraints upon government through the medium of the law manifests itself in different ways and has evoked a number of principles, each with attendant merits and difficulties. One example is the concept that law is the product of immemorial custom. Just as the activity of millions of minute crustacea eventually surrounds an island with a coral reef, so the acts of millions of human beings, repeated in patterns that become habitual, erect a ring of custom around a community and its government. Custom is then thought of as a barrier confining the operations and powers of officials within limits they may not overstep, and law is merely the collection of practices that custom has confirmed. Discover the usages of the past, and you find the law of the present. This done, the duty of government becomes the simple one of preserving unbroken the links that unite the circle of custom. Such a view of the relation between law and government is admirable if its purpose is to maintain stability and continuity in a static or imperceptibly-changing society. It accords ill with the problems of government under circumstances of rapid flux when experimentation and flexibility are more at a premium than traditionalism.

Another device for subordinating the state to the restraints of law is the belief, referred to in earlier chapters, in a law of nature or law of reason. Once the preliminary assumption is accepted that such a law exists—which is itself a matter of faith rather than reason—various consequences can be readily deduced—for instance, that nature embodies principles that are in themselves rational and can be understood by reason, that these are universal in scope and eternal in duration, that the state governs well when it assists men in conforming to natural law, and that acts that violate such law are therefore invalid. The "higher law" theory here outlined, like the doctrine that derives law from custom, is appropriately adapted to a certain goal. By appealing to a higher law (that is, higher than that proclaimed by the state) men may justify resistance to authority or outright revolution, since it is always psychologically necessary for people who resist or rebel to make their opponents, and not themselves, appear in the wrong. Alternatively, the higher law doctrine suits the needs of other institutions that fear the state or are its rivals, since these can affirm that men do not live by politics alone and that in nature's house there are many mansions. For such reasons, both churches and business organizations have heavily subscribed to the natural law philosophy.

But this same philosophy abounds with unsolved problems. For who is to say which principles are natural or what is reason's law? When different interpretations are offered, whose shall be adjudged correct? Because of these uncertainties the net practical effects of appealing to natural law doctrines are often unfortunate. One outcome is for men to flee from one type of authority, that of the state and its laws, and seek refuge in the arms of another, for example, that of the priest, pastor, or businessman. The law of nature is then respectively translated into the law of nature's God, as clerical authority affirms it, or the natural laws of economics as some economist expounds them. Alternatively, if men shrink from substituting new authoritarianism for old, they will escape into the skepticism that rejects every interpretation of natural law on the ground that anybody's guess may be right and none can be definitely proven. In this case there is a flight from reason; decisions are reached through force; and the more powerful proclaim themselves the rightful.

There is a third and equally celebrated formula for using law to place restraints on government. It is the one coined by Jeremy Bentham and popularized into a slogan by the Utilitarians—the notion that governments must promote the greatest happiness of the greatest number. The Utilitarians were the British reformers of the nineteenth century, who, seeking to modernize their political machinery and legal code, applied to each established law and institution the test: What is its utility? Whatever statute or executive act helped to increase the sum total of happiness in the community was considered good. Whatever diminished that stock of happiness must be removed or reformed. A government merited support or opposition according to how it influenced happiness. Such a yardstick subjects the state to a different standard. To appraise a government's action by its degree of conformity to custom or nature means referring to the source of authority. To test an act by its relation to happiness means studying its effects and comparing one set of results with another. In spirit at least, this latter approach is experimental and scientific. Applied in practice, however, Bentham's formula fails to be as scientific as one would wish because it is impossible to measure a quantity of happiness with precision. People will therefore wrangle endlessly about whether a particular governmental action, compared with possible untried alternatives, produces more happiness or less.

Constitutions and Constitutionalism. Besides these specific methods of restraining government by law, there is the more general argument that the state will not tyrannize over its citizens if it is imbued with respect for constitutionalism. What is meant by this? A distinction should be made between the terms "constitutionalism" and "constitution." A constitution is the basic design of the structure and powers of the state and the rights and duties of its citizens. In that sense there is a constitution in every state that has a settled form and an established government—in the United States, Canada, and Britain, as well as in Nazi Germany, Franco Spain, and Stalin's Russia—and to say that a state possesses a constitution contains by itself no implication about its democratic or dictatorial character. Constitutionalism, however, is a term that does have definite implications. It is bound up with the notion of the rule of law. It embraces the idea that a government should not be permitted to do anything its officials please, but should conduct itself according to equitable and agreed procedures. The purpose of this restriction on its freedom of action is of course to safeguard a fundamental area of freedom for its citizens. For tyranny is most probable where power is total.

Clear though it is that constitutionalism is incompatible with dictatorship, and that political freedom requires some curbs on power, the nature of these limits calls for more discussion. It is one thing to harness a horse, and another to hobble it. It is one thing to control a government, and another to cripple it. The difference may be one of degree or emphasis. But it is all-important. It stems from contrasted attitudes towards power. Some thinkers are so preoccupied with the abuses of power that their whole interpretation of constitutionalism is a series of negatives. Their rule of law degenerates into a bundle of prohibitions. A government must be prevented from doing this, that, and the other. To devise checks, controls, restraints, and limitations becomes the very essence of constitutionalism and the prime guarantee of human freedom. But is it really necessary to lean so far backwards? May not this overattention to abuses defeat its own purpose? Since government is indispensable, and since no one can govern without power, it ought to be evident that constitutionalism should first be concerned with how power must be used, not with how it may be abused. The state should be envisaged as a canal through which political power may flow, releasing its energy for the benefit of mankind, rather than as a dam to hold it back. After all, the basic task in any philosophy of government is to figure out what the state must do, not what it should be prohibited from doing. Nor is it to be forgotten that, while tyrannical governments destroy freedom, other governments may enlarge it. Many of the functions which the modern state undertakes are designed to make opportunities more nearly equal for everybody and to protect weaker individuals from the rapacity of the strong.

But there is a still more basic objection to those who develop their photograph of constitutionalism in the negative and neglect to print it in positive colors. If constitutionalism is approved on the ground that it causes restraints upon government, the inquiry has to be thrown one stage further back. Constitutionalism is itself the result of other factors that are its causes. What are these? Essentially, as can be demonstrated, their character is political. This is an assertion that has the effect of switching the discussion onto another track. Hitherto in this chapter the problem of making government accountable to the governed has been viewed in a predominantly legal light —in terms of the rule of law, of legal curbs upon power, of constitutionalism—so that political freedom appears as the consequence of a certain legal situation. But this is an illusion, for the image has been turned upside down. Although there is always some interaction between law and politics, it is primarily politics that controls and determines law and not law that controls and determines politics. It is not any rule of law or respect for constitutionalism that gives birth to a politically free society, but rather the politics of freedom that creates the sanction for constitutionalism and law. What has been called "the firmament of law" [7] is not self-supporting. It is propped up on political pillars. Without them it would topple.

The Political Roots of the American Constitutional System. To understand this better, let us take a closer look at the framework of government in the United States. The Constitution stands at the center and is the chief symbol of the American form of government. Because the Constitution is a supreme law, because it contains a list of judicially enforceable rights, and because of the practice of judicial review of legislation, it has become customary in many quarters to think of the Constitution as a lawyers' document to be construed in legal fashion.[8] But this is to overlook the political context that gives law its significance and judges their status. The ultimate power under the Constitution is lodged, not with the Supreme Court, but with the people. It is "We, the people" who "ordain and establish" the Constitution. It is the people's elected representatives who amend it and may by amendment express disapproval of a Supreme Court decision, making it inapplicable to future cases.[9]

[7] By Robert M. MacIver in *The Web of Government* (New York: Macmillan, 1947), chap. 4.

[8] A cynic has observed that "a government of laws, not of men" becomes a government of lawyers, not of men.

[9] There are several instances of amendments that reversed decisions of the Supreme Court. To wit, the Eleventh, which recorded the indignation of the States at *Chisholm v. Georgia;* the Thirteenth, Fourteenth, and Fifteenth, which

It is the political branches of the government, the President and the Senate, that nominate and confirm appointees to the Court and, by choosing its personnel, influence the general trend of future decisions. If the rule of law exists, that is because a political will wants to have it so.

This point is reinforced by a further reflection. As every practicing politician knows and every student of government soon discovers, there are many essential features of the American system of government that cannot be learned from a reading of the Constitution. The Constitution is a concise, compact document, its brevity being one of its many marvels. On few issues does it elaborate in any detail, and these few are mostly concerned with electoral machinery or the procedure for a presidential veto of legislation. For the rest, as a Constitution should be, it is broad in scope and general in its terms. Since the addition of the Bill of Rights (the first ten amendments) in 1791, the text has been changed only twelve times in a hundred and sixty odd years. But the nation, over whose growth to greatness the Constitution has presided, has changed almost beyond recognition. From a community of four million souls living in thirteen states along the Atlantic seaboard with an agrarian economy and a precarious military position, the Union has expanded into more than one hundred and fifty-five million spread over forty-eight states from ocean to ocean, exhibiting the world's most highly developed industrial technology and living standards, administering distant territories and possessions, and wielding the mightiest single contemporary aggregate of military strength. Of all these changes there is scarcely a trace or record in the written text of the Constitution. But such social transformations cannot fail to have their effects upon the basic design of the powers and structure of government and the rights and duties of citizens—to repeat the definition of a constitution suggested earlier.[10] It stands to reason therefore that these effects have been registered in other ways than by the formal method of constitutional amendment. What are they?

The first is by legislative enactment. It is true that much of the output of Congress is of no fundamental importance. Legislation runs the whole gamut from private bills that concern a particular

repudiated the principles of the Dred Scott case; and the Sixteenth, which overthrew the opinion of the Court concerning federal inability to levy income tax.

[10] See above, page 245.

person or mere municipal ordinances for the District of Columbia to the weightiest measures affecting national and international prosperity and security. But although opinions will differ in certain cases, some statutes, as judged by their subject-matter and content, clearly occupy a crucial position in the governmental process. Laws, for example, that organize the federal district and appellate courts, that establish such agencies as the Defense Department or the Interstate Commerce Commission, that provide freedom from want through a program of social security, that regulate the franchise or the conduct of elections, these and others like them deal with matters no less fundamental than some sections of the Constitution itself. The continuous labors of over eighty Congresses have done much to shape the primary patterns of American government.

The same may be said of the work of the Supreme Court. Because the Founding Fathers were writing a Constitution rather than a statute, they wisely drafted many a critical clause in language so vague and broad as to permit diversity of future definition and detail. In innumerable instances it has been left to the Court to supply the guiding principles for Congress and the executive branch to follow. Take the federal powers over interstate commerce and general welfare.[11] The terse and simple wording of the clauses in which these are described has lent itself to wide possibilities, as may be seen from the questions that the Supreme Court at some time or other has been forced to decide. Does the power to regulate interstate commerce permit the federal government to prohibit certain commodities outright (for example, impure foods, unsafe drugs, or pornographic publications); or certain business practices, such as competitive methods that are specified as unfair; or certain forms of corporate organizations, such as trusts and monopolies? Does the definition of commerce include the channels of transportation (such as navigable waterways, highways, railroads, and airlines) and other means of communication like the telephone, telegraph, television, and radio? Does commerce mean only the exchange of a finished article, or does it extend backward to cover manufacturing and forward to include retail prices? From the kind of answer given to

[11] In its list of subjects on which Congress may legislate, Article I, section 8 of the Constitution includes the powers "to regulate commerce . . . among the several States" and "to lay and collect taxes . . . and provide for the common defence and general welfare of the United States."

these questions there follows, in accordion fashion, either a sharp contraction or a huge enlargement of federal authority with its consequent effect upon the relation of government to business. The same has happened with other critical clauses of the Constitution. By interpretations of such clauses as those that deal with general welfare, due process of law, equal protection of the laws, or freedom of speech, the Court is virtually engaged in amending the basic law by giving more precision to its generalities. Judge-made definitions [12] have thus added essential portions to the foundation work of the Constitution.

Nor is this all. Many of the fundamental facts of the American system of government can be explained only in political, not in legal, terms. There are some sections of the Constitution that are not applied in practice because political considerations do not permit their enforcement. Thus the Fourteenth Amendment declares, in section 2, that if a State denies voting rights to any of its citizens, the congressional representation to which its population entitles that State shall be proportionately reduced. No effect has ever been given to this provision because, if it were enforced, both major parties and many states, northern as well as southern, would take a loss of representation. By "gentlemen's agreement," therefore, the Constitution is tacitly ignored. The same is true of many state governments. Normally a state constitution contains a requirement that after each decennial census the legislative electoral districts must be reapportioned. In various States this requirement is persistently flouted by farmer-controlled legislatures that deny to urban areas their fair share of representation. Again it is politics that controls law, and not vice versa.

This truth becomes yet plainer when one reflects upon other features of American government that have developed in political practice and of which the Constitution remains entirely innocent. Many examples of this can be cited; but there is none more revealing than the rise and organization of political parties. The party system that grew and matured in the nineteenth century was antithetical to the ideals of the men who drafted the United States Constitution.

[12] Many doctrines have been enunciated by the Court that, until modified by a later majority of judges, have controlled the legislative and executive branches, for example, the doctrines of "original package," "business affected with a public interest," "the flow of commerce," "clear and present danger," et cetera.

Thus the institutions they constructed did not anticipate the emergence of parties, were not designed to admit them, and have not always dovetailed with them in a harmonious fit. What is more, James Madison and other leading spirits of his generation would have regarded government by parties as an evil since they habitually described their eighteenth-century equivalents by the unfavorable term, "factions." Modern democracy, however, has taken the parties into the inner sanctum of power and its political process is nowadays unthinkable without them. Voting for a President by means of a college of electors; the organization, procedures, and output of Congress; cooperation or friction between chief executive and legislature; the people's choice of policies and personalities; none of these would be as they are if parties did not profoundly influence the result. No small slice of American government is composed of political customs whose content is as important, whose character as enduring, as what is written in the Constitution.

All this suggests a fresh approach, couched in realistic terms, to the problem of explaining constitutions and what they stand for. The basic pattern of government in the United States can be compared to a broad river created by four streams flowing together. One is the document we call the Constitution. A second is made up of certain legislative enactments. A third of judicial opinions. The fourth is political custom. If a name is needed to describe the sum total, a convenient term is "the constitutional system." It is this that underpins the entire structure of government, deriving its strength from the bedrock of political power rather than the sands of legal formulae.

The Politics of the British Constitution. If more evidence is needed to sustain this view, it can be furnished from the case of Britain. To many writers of political science the British form of government affords a paradox, especially when compared with that of the United States. Some striking differences exist between the American and British constitutional systems. In Britain there is no document analogous to the United States Constitution. Parliament, unlike Congress, is empowered to make any kind of law it chooses. The courts have no authority to nullify legislation. From the purely legal standpoint, therefore, it is impossible in Britain to specify which rules, procedures, and institutions are part of the constitution and which are not; and a constitutional lawyer, reasoning solely from legal assumptions, can never satisfactorily explain the nature of the constitution and its sanctions. Much nonsense has consequently been written about Britain by those who, starting with false premises, arrive at wrong conclusions. Thus the Frenchman de Tocqueville asserted that because of the legal supremacy of Parliament, which may change the constitution at any time by simple legislative act, there is in reality no constitution at all.[13] An odd argument this one, since it involves defining a constitution so narrowly and restricting it to those states where the power of the legislature is limited by a superior law.

Equally queer was the reasoning of A. V. Dicey, the English jurist, who wrote a classic book on *The Law of the Constitution*.[14] Dicey there distinguished between what he called the law of the constitution and its conventions (customs). The former consists of rules that the courts will recognize and enforce, the latter of rules that are binding in political usage. Both kinds of rules, legal and political, are, as Dicey observes, habitually obeyed and occasionally breached. What is the explanation? For a constitutional lawyer it is easy to understand why legal rules are observed. The courts are there to enforce them. But what is it that secures respect for political rules and why should these be obeyed? To Dicey this is a major difficulty. And how characteristic is his answer! Political rules, in his opinion, are followed because, if they were not, some breach of law would be included among the consequences [15]—which brings him happily back to the courts and to a legalistic interpretation of the Constitution.

As a general statement, that is an error. It is true of some political customs, but inapplicable to many others. It does not apply, for instance, to various well-established rules that are essential to Britain's cabinet type of government: that the King must assent to all bills passed by Parliament; that he should grant a dissolution when requested by the Prime Minister; that the Prime Minister and the majority of the Cabinet should be members of the House of Commons; and that all Ministers should belong to one of Parliament's two

[13] Alexis de Tocqueville, *Democracy in America*, Part I, trans. Henry Reeve (New York: J. & H. G. Langley, 1841), chap. 6, p. 103.

[14] First published in 1885, this work went through eight editions in thirty years and has been many times reprinted since its author's death.

[15] *Law of the Constitution*, 8th ed. (London: Macmillan, 1931), chap. 15, pp. 441 ff.

Houses. If these rules were violated, as some have been, there would be a serious departure from settled political practice, but no offense punishable in a court of law.

The failure of Dicey's explanation does not mean that the British constitution is inexplicable. It indicates that the constitution is primarily a political instrument, and not a legal charter. What the British refer to as their constitution is simply a way of summarizing the popular consensus about the principles to which their government should conform and the institutions with which to make them effective. The consensus is political in character because it embodies the will of an overwhelming majority in favor of a certain governmental system and their determination to preserve its basic features. This will, of course, find varied forms of expression. One way is for Parliament to enact a statute, or for the courts to render a decision acceptable to Parliament, in which case a political will is dressed in the outer raiments of law. Another way is to leave it to usage to build a system of rules, creating the expectation that what was done under like circumstances in the past will ordinarily be followed in the present. Each method has merits of its own. To write a political agreement into legal form normally results in greater precision and definiteness and thereby reduces the area of controversy. To leave decisions to the formulation of custom may permit a change, when desirable, to be speedily accomplished without the need for overcoming legal impediments.

The American and British Systems Compared. A comparison of the two constitutional systems, those of the United States and Britain, will now make it possible to view the whole question of constitutions in true perspective. Misunderstanding has been responsible for a number of false contrasts and exaggerated distinctions. Thus the American constitution has been described as a written one; the British, as unwritten. If these words are taken literally, they are incorrect. If figuratively, their meaning is anybody's guess. The truth is that both constitutional systems include portions that have been committed to writing and portions that have not. Statutes and judicial decisions, as well as the document we call the Constitution of the United States, are put in written form—as if the mere form were the decisive factor in determining the character of a constitution! That certain topics receive written statement, while others are left to informal understanding, is of itself a somewhat trivial difference.

What surely matters more is the choice of the content that receives
expression in one medium or in the other.

Another contrast calls the British system flexible, the American
rigid. The point at issue here is not trivial. It concerns the ease or
difficulty of the method by which the constitution is changed in
each of the two countries. The belief, however, in the flexibility of
the one vis-à-vis the rigidity of the other is a glaring example of
fallacious inferences, as an analysis of the reasoning will show. The
British constitution, it is argued, consists of two parts, law and custom. The law may be changed at any time by ordinary Act of
Parliament. Custom, too, may be altered by statute, or by the simple
device of breaking away from precedent. In either case, a procedural
green light aids the possibility of change. The American constitution, however, consists of the document drafted in 1787 and amended
only twenty-two times since then. The amending process, enshrined
in the constitution itself, presents a formidable obstacle to innovation.

The errors and omissions in this argument are numerous. For one
thing it rests upon a myopic view of the American constitution, excluding from sight the statutes, judicial opinions, and political usages,
which in a broader, but truer, sense are integral parts of the constitutional system. It further assumes that amendments to the Constitution of the United States can be obtained only with the greatest
difficulty; that Parliament will dare in political reality to proceed as
far as its legal powers extend; and that rules of custom are more readily modified than rules of law. But all this is nonsense. When the people of the United States after a dozen years of nationwide prohibition
decided that the experiment was unworkable, they adopted the
Twenty-First Amendment with remarkable ease and in record time.
On the other hand, the tradition that no President should serve more
than two terms was maintained for a century and a half with a rigidity that only the grim menace of Hitler and the demonstrated
greatness of Franklin D. Roosevelt could shatter.[16] As for the use
by Parliament of its theoretically unlimited authority, it will be
shown later that obstacles and limitations do exist—but of a political,
rather than a juridical, nature.

This does not mean that on the subject of rigidity or flexibility

[16] What was a rule of custom has now been made a rule of the Constitution
by the adoption of the Twenty-Second Amendment.

the two constitutional systems are indistinguishable. There are some genuine distinctions to be drawn, but the reasons for them have been wrongly stated. Any portion of a constitutional system, whether legal or customary, is likely to be rigid if expressed in exact and minute detail and supported by an active and organized sentiment. Conversely, any provision, legal or customary, can be flexible if its terms are vague or general and if sentiment in its favor is lukewarm or disorganized.

Some examples will illustrate these points. One of the most rigid features of the American Constitution is the clause that prescribes a four-year term for the President and an election for a new term in every fourth year. Never yet have the American people deviated from the requirement of conducting the presidential election at regular and identical intervals. In 1864 when civil war was still being waged, and again in 1944 when the nation was locked in mortal conflict with deadly adversaries, the election was not postponed but took place at its appointed hour. Likewise in the gloomy years from 1930 to 1932 when the economy was paralyzed by depression, the people had to wait their opportunity to give their verdict on the stewardship of President Hoover and to vote for a new man and a New Deal. Only by amendment to the Constitution can a President's term be shortened or lengthened and a special election be held. Rigidity on this point is mainly due to the exactitude with which the Constitution expresses itself. On the other hand, where the wording is general and imprecise, the same Constitution (though "written"!) can prove conveniently flexible. Look for instance, at the interstate commerce clause, whose text has never once been amended. This clause has proved adaptable to vastly different interpretations that reflect the changing will of the majority of voters, of Congressmen, and of Supreme Court Judges.

The same story can be told about the rules that are the product of political custom. As was mentioned earlier, the rise of parties is a subject about which the Constitution is entirely silent. Yet its operation has been profoundly influenced by them. For purposes of contrast let us note two examples. The President of the United States is not elected directly by the people. He is chosen by members of an electoral college whom the people in their respective states elect for that specific function. When people wish to vote for their party's candidate, they vote in fact for others of the same party who will subsequently cast their ballots in the electoral college for the presidential candidate. Nothing in federal [17] law compels a member of the electoral college to give his vote for the party nominee. In political obligation, however, he is forced to do this. The member of the college performs this one duty under a rigid compulsion, whereupon his office immediately terminates. How different is the system of voting in the two houses of Congress! Nearly every Senator and Representative is elected under a party label and continues during his term of two or six years to be a party member. But he does not consider himself, and is not considered by his constituents, under obligation to vote on every issue with the majority of his party or to support every measure that a President of his own party proposes. Indeed, on many a legislative division, a minority of Republicans will be found voting with the majority of Democrats, and vice versa. What this means is that the party system requires absolute discipline on the one specific matter of getting its candidate into the White House, since control of the presidency is deemed vital to the power of the party. The parties do not yet, however, regard the enactment of legislation or the acceptance of a President's program as equally vital. They therefore tolerate some independence in the halls of Congress. Thus rules of custom, it appears, like rules of law, may be rigid or flexible according to the precision with which they are formulated and the force of opinion that backs them.

Before the argument moves on, this is an appropriate point from which to retrace the steps that have led hither. The present chapter opened with the question: How may the people control their government? Since many attempts have been made to control political power by subjecting it to the restraints of law, it was necessary to examine some concepts of law that were propounded for this purpose. From these the transition to the problem of constitutionalism, viewed as a system of legal limitations, was simple. This in turn called for an inquiry into the nature of constitutions in general and of the American and British types in particular. What is ordinarily construed in legalistic terms was seen on closer inspection to possess a political character. In other words, a certain kind of political order was found to sanction the legal rights of individuals and to guarantee due process of law. Such a conclusion, however, bears directly upon

---

[17] The laws of some states, however, place certain restrictions on presidential electors.

the initial question of how a government may be made responsible to popular control. For the answer, as is now evident, must be discovered not in the realm of law, but in that of politics.

The Key to Freedom. What then is the political method whereby the people can control the powers they grant? How can a populace that reposes trust in its officials be sure that they will not overstep the limits of their authority? A clue is suggested by the events that were discussed in Chapters 7 and 8. The efforts of medieval churchmen and modern businessmen to curb the power of the state produced competing institutions that rivalled the state in the interests they mobilized and the loyalty they exacted. The peculiar significance of those ventures lay in the attempt to construct within society, but outside of the political framework, an association capable of resisting the state. When dualism led to discord, and discord to conflict, the unity of the social order was in both cases eventually reaffirmed under the aegis of the political order. The triumphant assertion, however, of the primacy of the state over the rest of society could permit a tyrannical abuse of power, if no corrective existed. The secret of the new solution is to limit political power not from outside, but from within; to make the state safe for its citizens not by an external, but by an inner, check.

The method by which this is done is ingenious. It consists of an argument in various stages. Stage one asserts that the state belongs to all its members, whether they are of the government or of the governed. This is a flat rejection of the authoritarian, elitist view that the rulers are the state and that the people are subjects who belong to them. The contrary belief is contained in the two famous terms, *republic* [18] and *commonwealth*. Both have essentially the same meaning, that the state is possessed by the public who own it as wealth that they share in common. The second stage is a logical corollary of the first. If the state is the property of the whole people, including both government and governed, a distinction exists between the state and the government. The government is not identical with the state. It is a few chosen from the whole people who act in the name of the state and on its behalf and for a while dispose of its authority. The implication is that the same state can have a succession of different governments. These may change while the state continues.

[18] From the Latin *res publica,* "a public possession."

From Factions to Parties. But how can the government change
and one group of rulers take the place of another? By a device that
is perhaps the most notable of modern contributions to the art of
politics, the organized party system. In itself, the existence of parties
is not distinctively new. Their genealogy can be traced across the
centuries. A single theme, a single thread, unites the attacks of
Thucydides upon Pericles in Athens in the fifth century B.C. and
the opposition of Taft to Truman or Churchill to Attlee. What is
novel, however, is the place that parties have come to occupy in
the political process and the attitude that now prevails towards them.
Not so very long ago the organization of parties was viewed with
disfavor. A party was regarded as a menace to the unity of the state.
Because men had banded together in resistance to despotic kings, a
party was associated with the taint of treason. Because schisms had
split the church, the whiff of heresy clung to parties. The very name
of faction, by which a party was commonly described, possessed
unsavory connotations. Hence it was not only because of his anxieties for a Union still in its infancy, but also because he reflected
the dominant thought of his time, that Washington in the Farewell
Address uttered this solemn warning:

> I have already intimated to you the danger of parties in the State,
> with particular reference to the founding of them on geographical
> discrimination. Let me now take a more comprehensive view, and
> warn you in the most solemn manner against the baneful effects of
> the spirit of party, generally. This spirit...exists under different
> shapes in all governments, more or less stifled, controlled, or re-
> pressed; but in those of the popular form it is seen in its greatest
> rankness, and is truly their worst enemy. The alternate domination
> of one faction over another, sharpened by the spirit of revenge,
> natural to party dissension, which in different ages and countries has
> perpetrated the most horrid enormities, is itself a frightful despotism.
> But this leads at length to a more formal and permanent despotism.
> The disorders and miseries which result gradually incline the minds
> of men to seek security and repose in the absolute power of an
> individual.... There is an opinion, that parties in free countries are
> useful checks upon the administration of the Government, and serve
> to keep alive the spirit of liberty. This within certain limits is prob-
> ably true, and in governments of a monarchical cast, patriotism may
> look with indulgence, if not with favor, upon the spirit of party.
> But in those of the popular character, in governments purely elective,
> it is a spirit not to be encouraged.

Since Washington's day political developments in democratic countries have produced a complete about-face on the subject of parties and their value. While nobody would deny that a system of government by alternating parties contains imperfections and invites risks, a superior method of ensuring political freedom has yet to be discovered. So strongly is this opinion held throughout a large portion of the contemporary world that the existence of more than one party is nowadays considered an essential criterion to distinguish a regime of liberty from one of dictatorship. For wherever there is an opportunity of choice, there is some freedom. Where no choice exists, there is coercion. Hence when the nature of the state is appraised, an all-important test is whether more than one political party is tolerated. When the connection between party politics and the principle of freedom is studied, the difference between a two-party or a multi-party system appears far less significant than the gulf between one-party government and any system permitting more than one. Indeed if language has any meaning, the term "one-party system" is a misnomer. For a party is by definition a part of the whole and therefore implies the presence of an alternative and an opposition. To speak of the "one-party state" is to employ a contradiction in terms. Such a state, whether it is fascist or communist, whether its capital is Moscow or Madrid, Bucharest or Lisbon, exhibits a tyrannical monopoly of power. Its proper name is dictatorship.

The Requirement of Two or More Parties. A genuine party system, that is, that which contains two or more parties, is a major step in the attainment of political maturity. Historically the emergence of the modern party has accompanied the growth of the modern electorate. Indeed, it was the latter that made the former possible. As the right to vote was extended to more and more citizens throughout the nineteenth century, party organizations, which previously had been mainly based upon legislative cliques, undertook to attract and mobilize the ever-increasing electorate. Parties then acquired their new character. They became mass organizations, linking together a large body of citizens with their representatives in the legislature; they developed institutions of their own; and, to fight and win elections, they besought financial contributions. In this way the parties responded to a genuinely felt need. Without them, the millions who composed the new electorate, would have become a disorganized crowd, unable to formulate their aims or debate the vast issues they confronted. By means of parties, the voters obtained a medium that, to state it in no stronger terms, afforded a chance of rational and coherent action.

Nothing in the entire conception of the party system is as crucial as the requirement that there be more parties than one. It is this condition that sanctions the right of criticism and opposition as a legitimate and necessary element in the political process. The government of Britain symbolizes this situation with a unique terminology. There the Ministry is officially styled Her Majesty's Government. In like manner the minority party is Her Majesty's Opposition—its loyal duty being to oppose in the name of the Crown what the majority is loyally doing in the name of the Crown. The result of this remarkable concept is that resistance to constituted authority—so long as it confines itself to words, not deeds—is brought within the scope and shelter of the constitutional order. No longer is it necessary for men who seek a change of government to launch a revolution. No longer does the prevention of political tyranny depend upon the erection outside the state of institutions capable of opposing it. Through a two- or multi-party system the means of curbing an overpowerful government is a built-in fixture of the political order. In a word, the party or parties that fill the role of opposition supply the modern equivalent and take the place of the captains of industry and finance in the era of unregulated capitalism or the popes and cardinals of a still earlier age. But the relation of the state to society, and the nature of the state itself, are vitally different when that which prevents abuse of power derives from inside the political order, not from outside. Freedom is not primarily the legal concept that jurists depict. Nor is it, as Robert M. MacIver holds, solely the consequence of a pluralistic [19] society. In the modern state freedom is basically political. It permits and is then perpetuated by a two- or many-party system.

The Ins and the Outs. Saying this, however, does not exhaust the complexity of the relation between a party that governs and a party that opposes. The peculiarity of this relationship is that the party in power does not eliminate those opposed to it; and the latter, while opposing, obey the declared will of the majority. Each side recog-

---

[19] For the meaning of this term, see Chapter 2, pp. 36-7. See MacIver's *The Web of Government* (New York: Macmillan, 1951), chap. 8, 13.

nizes that it is a member of a system requiring, as a permanent feature, the existence of an opponent. Each accepts the principle of "live and let live" in the certain knowledge that the system allows to each in turn and in time its fair share of power. This means, of course, that parties which are thus prepared to alternate in office do not disagree on everything. On certain points there must be a consensus that overrides their differences on other matters. It is evident, for example, from what has already been said, that the agreement must extend to the basic features of the system to which they belong. This, however, is only another way of describing the constitution, which, as was noted earlier in this chapter, must be understood as a political instrument. The contents of the constitution include those principles and procedures about which the parties are in the main agreed. Conversely, the parties give their general support to the constitutional system that embodies some of their wishes and guarantees each its place. A revolutionary party is, of course, one that wholly rejects these fundamentals and operates either from outside or inside the constitutional system in order to destroy it.

More proof of the way in which parties, otherwise opposed to each other, are prepared to sink their differences can be discovered in the field of foreign policy. The conduct of external relations is an activity of government that puts a premium on the maximum display of internal unity. When it represents the state in international affairs, a government is ordinarily able to appeal to the solidarity of common interest and loyalty that welds a group together. A bipartisan foreign policy, therefore, is more likely to lie within the realm of the practical than a bipartisan policy on domestic issues. Evidence for this can be observed in time of peace. But it is plainest to the eye in time of war when the survival of the state itself is in issue and the motivation for strength through unity is greatest.

Some further reflections are invited by the character of the party system. The preceding paragraphs have shown that it is the nature of parties, where two or more co-exist, to work within the same constitution, yet to be rivals in the contest for political power. Expressed differently, this means that parties cooperate on some matters and compete over others—which is precisely the crux of the problem discussed in the second chapter of this book. There it was stated that human beings and the groups they form are thrown into social relationships by the contrasted, yet complementary, influences of cooperation and competition. The relation between parties and the constitution, and the manner in which government and opposition reciprocally contribute to freedom and to constitutionalism, afford a clear example of competition within a framework of cooperation. The forces that operate at the core of the political process are the same ones that explain the formation of groups and the development of society itself.

Flaws in the "Iron Law" of Oligarchy. There is one final problem that has purposely been left to the conclusion of this chapter. To the view here presented, a serious objection has been raised that, if valid, strikes at the root of the argument. As against authoritarian doctrines that subject the governed to a ruling elite, the principle of freedom proclaims that the governed must and can control their rulers. For this to be realized in practice, the many have to be able to control the few. But can they? An emphatic answer denies that they can. There is an influential school of writers who hold that any social activity requires organization; that organization evokes leadership; that leaders must be in command over their followers; that so it has always been and ever shall be. Two Swiss are notable among the modern founders of this school.[20] One of these, Vilfredo Pareto, is author of the saying: "In fact, with or without universal suffrage, it is always an oligarchy which governs, and which knows how to give whatever expression it likes to the 'popular will.'" The other, named Roberto Michels, formulated what he called "the iron law of oligarchy." Its central assertion is that in every human association power gravitates by an inevitable tendency into the hands of a few. By the force they wield, the fear they instill, the prestige they possess, and the propaganda they spread, the superior few outwit and overawe the mass. "Majority rule," "responsibility to the people," "popular sovereignty," these and like phrases are merely samples of the illusions that cunning rulers pour into the minds of their unwitting dupes.

This point of view is backed by enough evidence and wears enough plausibility to have gained many adherents. Nobody, after all, would deny that human institutions of every type abound with examples of oligarchical rule. Scan the records of churches, clerical

---

[20] A contemporary writer of the same outlook is James Burnham. See his *Managerial Revolution* and other works.

orders, armies, navies, universities, business corporations, trade unions, governments, political parties, civil services—this list is by no means exhaustive—and the same story of controlling cliques, power monopolies, and autocratic bossism can be illustrated in almost identical terms. The social history of the human race includes several upheavals against tyrannical authority that were designed to set men free, but did not always turn out as planned. The Gospel of Jesus was a challenge to the might of Rome. Its teaching was pacifist and equalitarian; its political ideal, anarchic. But in a later century the church became wedded to power and then showed itself ready to do what seemed necessary for maintaining its power. The French Revolution was initially dedicated to the principles of liberty, equality, and fraternity. Yet its attempts to usher in a new birth of freedom delivered the military autocrat, Napoleon. The Bolshevik Revolution was once greeted with the plaudits of many an idealist who hailed it as a landmark in the liberation of man. But Stalin's relentless rule forged the fetters of a new despotism.

What does all this add up to? That the larger part of the government of mankind has been oligarchic? That many a movement conceived in freedom has degenerated into its opposite? This much is true and cannot be gainsaid. When Michels, however, spoke of an "iron law," he was asserting its universal applicability. In one sweeping formula he sought to summarize the whole range of mankind's experience in constructing institutions to serve their needs. But this effort, as all such, could not avoid the pitfalls of error, exclusion, and exaggeration. It is not true that all species of organization, political and other, have been and inevitably must be oligarchic. Apart from two exceptions—the military and the civil service, both of which are everywhere built on the authoritarian pattern from the top downwards—every kind of institution offers some instances of genuine control by the mass of the membership. As far as the state is concerned, it is perhaps not surprising that Pareto and Michels should have been ill-acquainted with the democratic achievement of the Anglo-Saxon peoples, but it is quite inexcusable for them to have ignored the traditions of their native Switzerland. One may grant that democratic governments are themselves imperfect and do not yet fully attain the high standards of their own ideal. Nevertheless, to dismiss as a sham and a delusion the record of what has been accomplished in countries, great and

small, like the United States, Britain, Switzerland, Norway, or New
Zealand, does violence to realism. The fact that in any community
power tends to gravitate to a few and that authority is ordinarily
exercised by a minority does not refute the possibility or genuineness of democracy. What makes the vital difference between dictatorship and freedom, between responsible and irresponsible power,
is the method whereby authority is acquired, the conditions under
which it is wielded and the manner in which it is forfeited. The
nature of power is changed—not merely in its external apparatus,
but in its inner character—when its holders must run the gauntlet of
periodic elections and must respond to the charges and criticisms
of a free press. Nor are such phrases as majority rule and popular
control empty of all meaning. A system that invites its citizens to
believe in these principles often ends by bringing the beliefs to life,
for people will demand of their government that it pay more than
lip-service to its professions. Moreover, there is the corrosive effect
upon the "iron" law of oligarchy of a two- or multi-party system.
It is not so difficult for a fascist or communist party in a one-party
state—or any monopoly for that matter—to be authoritarian. But
where a choice exists, the knowledge that people may select an
alternative is itself a deterrent from oligarchy. A party's rival is
likely to create trouble for a controlling clique by encouraging its
followers to rebel against their leadership; and such revolts, outside
of a police state, are not so easy to suppress. Those who formulated
this iron law did not pay enough attention to the mutual interaction
of competing organizations. For nothing does so much to make men
free as a chance to choose.

Civil Liberties. Finally it must be remembered that, where the
opportunity exists to choose between two or more parties and to
oppose a government within a constitutional framework, certain
related liberties are found that negate or mitigate the strength of
oligarchy. The state can be subordinated to popular control, instead
of the people being subservient to the state, when freedom of
association and the right to criticize are preserved inviolate. Without freedom of association men could not organize a group of like-
minded individuals as an alternative to those in power. Without the
right to criticize, genuine debate of public issues, such as those
analyzed here, could never be conducted. These rights are in turn
buttressed by the accompanying freedoms that prevent enslavement

of one's person or one's mind. Freedom from arbitrary arrest, from secret trial, from seizure of one's belongings, from cruel and unusual punishments, these and the like protect the liberty of the person. Equally important are the particular rights that add up to liberty of thought in general, the right of access to information and to publish without censorship, the right to read whatever one wishes, and the right of free speech.

For those who cherish the values of a free society such rights are as indispensable as the air we breathe. The reasons for them are written in clear type in the annals of every police state, old and new, and in the long uneven record of men's intellectual progress. There would today be no Bill of Rights in the United States, or its equivalent in any other democracy, if dissident minorities and individuals had not clashed with past wielders of power in the name of truths they held to be self-evident. There would be none of our modern achievements in pure and applied science, no betterment in our methods of living together in organized society, if some of our ancestors had not been willing at times to express unconventional ideas or challenge the established *mores*. The memory of Socrates before his Athenian accusers; of Jesus before Pilate; of the library at Alexandria whose books the Arabs destroyed; of Roger Bacon, Copernicus, Galileo, and Darwin, whose scientific method demolished untruths sanctioned by the religious orthodoxy of their time; of Spinoza excommunicated by his synagogue; of beliefs in sorcery and burning of "witches"; of propaganda and persecution as practiced by Joseph Stalin, Joseph Goebbels, and the Japanese thought-controllers—these are salutary warnings to prove that it is not the punishment of men that guarantees which ideas shall perish and which prevail.

But though political liberty depends on these accompanying freedoms, it is no simple task to dovetail them in the structure of the state. If a passion for order, pushed too far, can degenerate into authoritarianism, so a zeal for liberty can become license by excess. All rights involve responsibilities and there is no right exercised within society that is absolute and admits no exception. Even the right to life itself can be forfeit in those states whose criminal code provides for capital punishment and whose defense policy includes conscription. The same holds good of freedom of speech. On the principle that my right to swing my arm ends where the other fellow's nose begins, the right of free speech must similarly avoid infringement of the rights of others. Hence it is appropriate to have laws against libel and slander, against obscene publications, and against incitement to violence.

Added to the difficulty of definition is that of enforcement. The rights of a citizen may be invaded by other citizens or by his government. They may therefore require protection by the government or against it. Rights produce their impact upon government, as does government upon rights, through the medium of institutions or agencies. How vigilantly these operate, how they are staffed, what precedents they develop, to what pressures they bow—this can make all the difference between paying lip-service to freedom and practicing it. Traditionally, the branch of government that has encroached the most on civil rights has been the one whose opportunity is greatest—the executive. That was so under the regimes of absolute monarchy, and continues to be true of the modern dictatorship. Naturally, since the executive administers the law and has military force, police, and prisons at its disposal, threats to liberty will always come from this source if such powers be abused.

For that reason, in countries where civil liberties have nurtured political freedom, the other branches—the legislature and judiciary —have often been called upon to champion the rights of citizens against executive invasion. But institutional history may vary so from one state to another as to place a different emphasis on the respective roles of legislators and judges. In the United States, where the hierarchy of law subordinates a statute to the Constitution, where the Constitution contains a Bill of Rights, and where it is the judges who say what the Constitution is,[21] the courts have become the inner citadel in which the defense of civil liberties is conducted. Political factors, moreover, reinforce this arrangement. The courts —and more particularly the federal judiciary headed by the Supreme Court—have a deservedly high reputation among the American people for dignity, impartiality, and scrupulousness. The same reputation is not enjoyed by Congress and the legislatures of the states. The legislative branch in general has shown considerably less zeal than the judicial to uphold civil rights and not infrequently it endangers them. What holds true in one democracy, however, does not necessarily obtain in all. In Britain, on the whole, the boot

[21] This is the observation of former Chief Justice Charles Evans Hughes.

is on the other foot. There the judges are accorded high social prestige and are rightly respected for their integrity and learning. But the court system is so complex, its costs are so high, and its delays so notorious, that few persons in fact can obtain the substance of justice when a wrong needs to be righted. Parliament, on the other hand, has earned a secure place in the respect and affections of the British public, not the least for its continued championing of popular liberties against encroachment from any source. A question raised by a member in the House of Commons is far more likely than litigation to bring prompt and proper redress.

Finally, there is the problem of determining the ultimate sanction that guarantees that civil rights will be operative. Though it is valuable to have basic rights spelled out in classic formulae and constitutional definitions, those are not self-enforcing. Many a constitution has been drafted to include the finest sounding liberties that in practice have not been worth the paper on which they were written. Nor does the secret of the defense of rights lie solely in such institutions as courts and legislatures, indispensable though these be. Again it is necessary to remember that institutions, like rights, will vary in effectiveness, that courts may function under the shadow of intimidation, and legislatures may be maintained as a convenient fiction. The truth is that institutions are strong to the extent that a large enough section of the public feels keenly enough to have them so. Exactly the same applies to civil liberties. If enough people are sufficiently determined to preserve and exercise their rights, those rights will be exercised and preserved, and the institutions will then be found to do the job. But where that determination is lacking, no Court, no Congress, no Parliament can fill the gap. The ultimate sanction, therefore, of all civil liberties resides in the same source that creates the constitution initially and renders it effective—the political will of the people. Freedom in any society is what the people earn and guard for themselves.

CHAPTER 11

FOURTH ISSUE:

(1) CONCENTRATION OF POWER VERSUS DISPERSION OF POWERS

Power, Functions, and Institutions. The difficulties surrounding the problem of authority are not limited to the controversy over its source that was discussed in the two preceding chapters. Regardless of how authority originates—whether from the government that wields it or from the people who entrust it to the government —there still remains the question of its organization and use. As the electric energy, generated at a mighty dam, is released and distributed through a complicated network of transmission lines, so the current of political power is conducted from its source to the various points and outlets where the business of government is carried on. The machinery for doing this consists of an elaborate structure of institutions and procedural arrangements, whose design may conform to one of a number of patterns. The choice of the pattern creates the issue.

For understanding the nature of the issue, two points that emerged in the earlier discussion are relevant—first, that people have certain needs which they want the state to satisfy, and, second, that power seeks recognition as authority. In an important respect the two factors converge since they have a common bearing upon an identical problem. Both the provision of services by the state and the organization of authority have the like effect of stimulating the growth of institutions. Law-enactment, for instance, produces a law-making body—for example, the legislature; the establishment of justice evokes a system of courts; the mail is administered through the post office, and so on. Similar consequences follow from the mobilization of power. For the latter also operates through institutions in order to obtain its results. The Roman Senate and the later Emperorship; the British Monarchy, Parliament, and Cabinet; the American Congress, Presidency, and Supreme Court; the Japanese Shogunate; the Nazi Fuehrer and the Italian Duce; the Presidium of the Central Committee of the Communist Party in the Soviet Union; all these are examples of institutions whereby the political power generated within society is canalized and exercised.

The machinery of government thus varies in design according to the needs of its consumers or the plans of its engineers. The framework that fits a period of prosperity and full employment may be ill-adapted to a time of economic stringency. The structure that suits the more leisured tempo of peace may have to be streamlined amid the urgencies of war. If those in power desire to act with a minimum of delay and to forestall any challenge to their supremacy, they will weaken or destroy whatever institution can be a rallying-point for opposition. This will involve the concentration of authority to facilitate decisions, together with an unimpeded line of communication from the authority that decides to the subordinates who execute. But if the overriding aim of constitution-builders is to put a brake upon the government, to restrict its functions to a minimum, and to prevent abuse of power, then institutions will be constructed upon different principles. In any case, and irrespective of the kind of government, the ever-present problems are to devise machinery appropriate to whatever functions men expect from their state and to see that political power and governmental institutions are meshed together. For those institutions are strong in fact which serve the citizens' need and faithfully reflect the realities of power. But woe betide an institution that retains the shell of authority from which the content of power has departed! Where revolutions occur, that is, where one form of political power is substituted for another, there is generally some change in the functions of government and always an overhauling in its institutions.

Centralism or Localism, Separation of Powers or Integration. There are two angles from which the question of the concentration or dispersion of authority needs to be viewed. One kind of power relationship exists between a central government, possessing jurisdiction over the entire territory of the state, and the various localities into which the whole is subdivided. In some states local government is merely an extension of the center, and local officials resemble the fingers at the end of a long arm controlled by a single brain. In other states local governments enjoy varying degrees of autonomy and independence of central direction. A second power circuit arises from the relations between the various governmental agencies constituted on the same level. It is possible to have one focal institution or office, to which the rest are inferior. Or powers may be distributed among several co-ordinate branches so designed as to maintain an equilibrium between one another. The choice between strength at the center and strength in the localities is the difference between centralization and decentralization; the alternatives of having one integrating agency or several that are co-ordinate is the contrast between integration and separation of powers.

These contrasts must be carefully distinguished. The government of the United States combines a separation of powers with decentralization. But in Switzerland decentralization is combined with integration. France supplies an example where power is not only centralized, but also integrated at the center. In Costa Rica, however, a separation of powers is associated with centralism.[1] How these different combinations occur and what results they yield forms the subject-matter of the present chapter.

The Contrast between Athens and Rome. The fact that such questions are not confined to contemporary states, but were raised in bygone centuries, is proof enough—were proof required—that they comprise an issue basic to governments everywhere. The politics of antiquity provide in this respect a preview for many a modern controversy. There was a period in Athenian history when the city was governed by a dictatorial ruler, Peisistratus, in whose hands all power was gathered. After his system broke down under his sons, a major stride was taken toward achieving popular self-government through the assembly of citizens. Its authority was, however, limited in certain respects by the veto of a court, the Areopagus, which represented oligarchical, rather than democratic,

---

[1] All four countries cited here, it will be noted, are democracies. Presumably, therefore, democracy may co-exist with any of these four patterns.

influences. A more fully democratic system was instituted in the middle of the fifth century, B.C., when the Areopagus was stripped of many functions and the power to declare legislation enacted by the people unconstitutional was transferred to the ordinary law-courts where mass-juries formed a cross-sample of the citizen-body. Thus a decision approved by a majority of the Assembly could be taken on appeal to the majority of a jury—an appeal presumably from the people drunk to the people sober. With this single exception—that the people serving as a jury could be a check upon the people serving as legislators—the structure of Athenian government was tightly consolidated under the authority of the Assembly.

The experience of Rome offers an instructive comparison with that of Athens. The Romans, too, retained a vivid memory of a past spent under despotic rule, their despot being a king named Tarquin the Haughty. After he was driven into exile, so intense was the feeling against the title of *Rex* (king) and any type of one-man rule, that the Romans devised a constitution in which authority was elaborately subdivided and distributed. Instead of one popular assembly, there were several, with different functions and powers. Instead of one consul (the most important of the annually elected officials) there were two, who had equal status and could check each other's actions. And as if this were not enough, for protection of the plebeians from the upper class (the patricians), ten tribunes were instituted with power to veto a consul or any lesser official. Hovering between the assemblies and the magistracies was the Senate, combining enormous influence in practice with slender legal authority. Under such a system it is small wonder that when the Romans faced a military crisis, their constitution allowed for an emergency office that could produce a temporary integration of powers. This was the office of the *dictator*, who for a six months' period was granted supreme command over the army and could virtually dominate the civil government through martial law.

Such institutions proved inadequate for the government of the extensive empire that Rome acquired. Neither the annually elected officials, nor the assemblies, nor the Senate itself, could maintain the necessary continuity of policy or keep a rein on distant commanders in the field. A repetition of civil turmoil led to the drastic expedient of converting a republic into an empire under an emperor.

The wheel thus turned full circle; and after its lack of success with dispersion of powers, Rome went to the extreme limits of integration.

Over the companion issue of centralism versus decentralism the experience of the Greek states was also divergent from that of Rome. A city-state was ordinarily so small and compact in area that problems of internal decentralization were scarcely pressing. Larger states, like Athens, might contain smaller units (the *demes*) for purposes that were tantamount to local government. But such units were strictly subordinate to central jurisdiction. Indeed, it was this heavy emphasis on centralism that contributed to the ultimate downfall of the city-state system, since the Greeks were unable to invent a workable method of consolidating their small states into larger and stronger units.[2] To this problem, however, the Romans did find a solution. The vexed issue of how the central government should control the governors of imperial provinces was settled, as has been seen, by the emergence of an emperorship that swallowed up the divided institutions of the republic. But along with integration at the center, the emperors made it their policy to promote a measure of autonomy (or local self-government) in the cities of their empire. While fundamental questions of foreign relations, military security, and to some extent finance, were reserved for the jurisdiction of Rome and its proconsuls within the province, on a wide variety of other matters local diversity and discretion were tolerated. The grant of special privileges of home-rule to the *municipia* was one of Rome's outstanding accomplishments and partially explains the long duration of its empire.

The Medieval Dispersion of Powers. The Roman way of combining some measure of decentralization with strong integration at the center was abandoned in the centuries that followed that empire's collapse. Though municipal autonomy was permitted and encouraged, the rule of Rome, at the times when the empire was firmly knit, did tilt the balance to the side of central supremacy. The medieval world, however, developed a social and political organization in which the scales dipped heavily on the other side. Decentralization was the chief characteristic of that period, despite its theory of universal unity. Few facts indeed impress the student of medieval government more forcibly than the contrast between

[2] See Chapter 13, pp. 322 ff.

the strength of localism and the weakness (sometimes the impotence) at the center. To this end some of the weightiest forces in medieval society jointly contributed. The principal resource in the feudal economy was land, and its ownership and tenure were closely bound up with the character of feudalism. Much of the land was parcelled out in large-sized estates that were assigned as the property of a nobleman. The labor of production was carried on by tenants who occupied the lord's land, paying their rent in services and kind. In rural England under the manorial system [3] these formed a community that was largely, though not completely, self-sufficient. All tenants owed allegiance to the lord, while he owed them protection. For the nobility, besides being land-owners, were also a political and military elite. The lord extended his influence to protect each of the vassals dependent on him. If able to bear arms, he was expected to don the heavy suit of mail, which only the wealthy could possess, and which made the armored knight on his mount the heavy tank of the medieval battlefield. Since the nobility occupied a strategic role in the administration of justice, and in the mustering and supply of armies, since good highways were infrequent or non-existent, and since the economy was organized around tightly knit local units, the political structure consisted less of a state than of a collection of estates. Consequently, in the struggle between king and nobles—the key conflict of medieval politics [4]—the decentralized fragments were normally more powerful than the institution that represented centralism. And as for the government that did exist at the center, the king, though he bulked largest, was by no means omnipotent. Wherever any Council or Parliament or Estates-General was organized, even though its functions might be mainly consultative and its structure rudimentary, such a body was likely to limit the king, since in it the nobility were the mainstay. Furthermore, the presence of the church, in the Middle Ages virtually a state within the state, posed another obstacle to an ambitious monarch.

Sovereignty and Absolutism in the Nation-State. When the changeover occurred from the medieval to the nation state, and from a feudal to a mercantilist economy, the attempt was made in

---

[3] For a detailed study, see E. Lipson, *The Economic History of England*, Vol. I (London: A. & C. Black, 1937), chaps. 1-2.

[4] See Chapter 9, pp. 233 ff.

theory and in practice to construct government upon the opposite principles. In place of localism, the accent was put upon centralization, drawing its breath of life from the new sentiment of nationality. To achieve this, it was, of course, necessary for the king to triumph over the aristocracy, a feat that was accomplished in every state that succeeded in making the transition from medievalism. But royal supremacy over the nobles brought an additional consequence besides centralization. The power that redounded to the king at the center was there concentrated in his office. Monarchy became the magnet, attracting local loyalties to the capital and the court, and overriding the separatist tendencies of competing institutions. With centralization, therefore, came integration. From both of these the king was the gainer. In theoretical terms these facts were synthesized in the new doctrine of "sovereignty." [5] The consolidation of power, which this term signified, meant the recognition of one supreme will, paramount over other central agencies and local particularisms. The identification of the symbol of sovereignty with the office of monarchy was easily brought about. The king was "the sovereign" personified. What could be more simple?

Thus was inaugurated in Europe a period in which monarchy attained its zenith, accumulating so much power as to merit the description "absolute." Never was this absolutism more fittingly epitomized than by Louis XIV of France, the Sun-King, in his remark: "L'Etat, c'est moi," a comment whose boast of personal pre-eminence exceeds even the claim of Adolf Hitler, "For twenty-four hours I was the supreme court of Germany," or the statement, "I am the law," attributed to a sometime mayor of Jersey City.

But as so often occurs in politics, a tendency that is originally justified as a response to a public need can with lapse of time breed faults of its own. Exaltation of the monarch, who served as a foil to the obnoxious nobility, outlasted its usefulness when the power of the nobles was reduced or when a corrupt and incompetent prince sat on the throne. In various countries, therefore, resistance developed to royal absolutism and to the identification of sovereignty with monarchy. It was this opposition that culminated in the series of three revolutions out of which the modern democratic state was born. What bearing did these revolutions have upon the age-old issue of concentration versus dispersion of power?

[5] See Chapter 7, p. 172.

Parliamentary Supremacy in Britain. Because the British revolution, which opened in 1640 and finished in 1688, was the earliest, and therefore provided an example for others to copy or alter, it will be discussed first. It was from the membership of the House of Commons and within its chamber that much of the protest against the autocracy of Charles I was voiced. Parliament, therefore, spearheaded the rebellion against the king. But to fight Charles and his supporters an army was needed. The occasion produced an Oliver Cromwell who organized the "New Model Army" on the parliamentary side. When the battle was fought, however, and Charles had been sent to his execution, Parliament found itself the servant of a new master who preferred to govern without assistance from the legislature. Not until after the death of Cromwell, the restoration of the Stuarts, and their final expulsion in 1688, was the supremacy of Parliament over the Crown irrevocably established. What was thus politically accomplished duly received formal legal recognition. The sovereignty that once belonged to the monarch was transferred to Parliament, which thereby became the omnipotent law-maker. Integration, therefore, continued to be the keynote of the British political system, but with the important difference that the supreme institution was henceforth a legislature and not a king. The supporting theory was penned by John Locke when he declared: "In a constituted commonwealth standing upon its own basis and acting according to its own nature—that is, acting for the preservation of the community, there can be but one supreme power, which is the legislative, to which all the rest are and must be subordinate...." [6]

Nor was the supremacy of the legislature diminished in 1700 when permanence of tenure was granted by Act of Parliament to the judiciary. During the constitutional struggles of the mid-seventeenth century, the position of the judges vis-à-vis King and Parliament was much debated. Against a royalist like Bacon, who contended that judges were "lions *under* the throne," the famous Chief Justice Coke argued for judicial review of the constitutionality of parliamentary acts and royal actions. To him the principles of the common law imposed a restraint upon both and it was the judiciary who expounded those principles. The result of Parliament's successful rebellion against the monarchy was that the legis-

[6] (Second) *Treatise of Civil Government,* chap. 13, sec. 149.

lature insisted upon the subordination of judges to itself, but approved their independence of the executive. Judges were not to be intimidated by the Crown or its representatives or to be subjected to any pressure in deciding individual cases. On the other hand, they were to accept as definitive the law that Parliament enunciated and they were never to invoke any other or higher law. To these arrangements Britain has steadily adhered, even since the time when the political power of the Cabinet absorbed the legal authority of Parliament.[7]

The French Pattern of Unified Power. The French Revolution, though it postdated the American, can be conveniently discussed next, because in this respect it developed institutions of a pattern similar to the British. Through the many stages of France's revolutionary agony runs one persistent theme—the concentration of all power in a single supreme body. Whether that were the Convention or the Directory made little difference from the standpoint of integration. The new rulers of France were conducting a revolution, and the revolutionary temper and tempo do not brook opposition, delays, or checks and balances. One critical difference did exist, however, between the British and French situations. The European repercussions of France's revolution brought upon that country the threat of invasion and before long its domestic upheaval embroiled the nation in foreign war. Whereas Britain's revolution produced a civil war and required a military dictator to bring Parliament to victory, the revolution in France, which lacked the advantages of an island, led to prolonged and deadly conflict with her neighbors and discovered the military genius of Bonaparte. His dictatorship, however, was imposed for longer on the French than that of Cromwell on the British, first because the survival of the nation was more imperilled by foreign than civil war, and then because of Napoleon's far-reaching ambitions and greater longevity. So deeply was the mark of Napoleonic statecraft imprinted on the government of France that when his Empire was replaced by constitutional monarchy, and that in turn by a democratic republic, the principles of integration and centralization remained as his permanent legacy. The philosophical implications of these historical facts might be summarized in the comment that the French followed

---

[7] See below, pp. 289-92.

primarily the course laid down for them by Rousseau, rather than Montesquieu. Montesquieu, however, was not without influence. Less heeded by his own countrymen, his ideas helped to shape the government of the new republic of the United States.

Separation of Powers in the United States. The American Revolution resembled the British and French in being directed against authority uncontrollable by the governed. Moreover, in practically all the constitutions that the states adopted within the first decade of independence, and in the machinery set up by the Articles of Confederation, clear provision was made for legislative supremacy. That the legislature should have been designated for this role is understandable in the light of the part played by the colonial assemblies in resisting British authority. "Thus in a typical revolutionary manner," writes William Anderson, "all powers of government were brought for the time under a single control, that of the convention or congress in each state. Perhaps in no other way could the quick and decisive measures have been taken that were needed to sever the bonds with Great Britain. Surely it was no time for a separation of powers and checks and balances in government." [8]

A short experience, however, with legislative predominance convinced the leading spirits of the generation that concentration of power in any one institution is fraught with abuse. Consequently, it was Jefferson who wrote thus about the first constitution of Virginia: "All the powers of government, legislative, executive, and judiciary, result to the legislative body. The concentrating these in the same hands is precisely the definition of despotic government. It will be no alleviation that these powers will be exercised by a plurality of hands, and not by a single one. One hundred and seventy-three despots would surely be as oppressive as one." [9] The same point was observed by Madison who issued this warning: "The legislative department is everywhere extending the sphere of its activity, and drawing all power into its impetuous vortex. . . They [the founders of our republics] seem never to have recollected the danger from legislative usurpations, which by assembling all power in the same hands, must lead to the same tyranny as is threatened by executive usurpations." [10]

[8] *American Government* (New York: Henry Holt & Co., 1938), pp. 39-40.
[9] *Notes on the State of Virginia*, Query XIII.
[10] *The Federalist*, No. XLVIII.

If concentration of power was the evil to be avoided, was there, besides executive or legislative omnipotence, some third possibility? The answer was provided by the introduction of what has come to be called "the separation of powers." The republic of the United States has followed the model of the republic of Rome in the respect that its institutions have been intentionally constructed with the idea of dispersing authority. Let us see how this came about and what the results have been.

Prior to its adoption as the architectural design of American governmental machinery, the doctrine of separation of powers had evolved in a long, slow sequence. Its origins may be traced back to Aristotle, if not indeed to earlier writers. In the *Politics* is found an analysis of three "parts," or branches, of government—the deliberative, executive, and judicial.[11] Aristotle confines himself to a description of their personnel, organization, and functions, and is content to leave his account at that. The modern phase of the doctrine opens in seventeenth century England and forms an aspect of the philosophical inquiry into the fundamentals of politics that the Puritan revolution stimulated. Locke's *Treatise* distinguished between three powers that exist in every commonwealth. These he called legislative, executive, and federative—the last-named being equivalent to the conduct of foreign relations.[12] The executive and federative powers, he pointed out, "are always almost united," and to this union he expressed no objection. But it was otherwise with the relation of the executive power to the legislative. The latter "in well-ordered commonwealths, where the good of the whole is so considered as it ought" is placed in the hands of an assembly that convenes at intervals. But since the administration and enforcement of law is a continuous task, a power distinct from the legislative must remain "always in being." In practice, therefore, "the legislative and executive power come often to be separated." In principle, however, there is also a good reason why this should be so "because it may be too great temptation to human frailty, apt to grasp at power, for the same persons who have the power of making laws to have also in their hands the power to execute them."

The Ideas of Montesquieu. It was the suggestion contained in this last sentence that formed the central theme in the next development

---

[11] Bk. IV, chaps. 14-16.
[12] (Second) *Treatise of Civil Government*, chap. 12, sec. 143-48.

of the doctrine. The French writer, Montesquieu, visited England in the middle of the eighteenth century and compared favorably the independence of the judges and the strength of Parliament there with the subordination of the judiciary to the French monarchy and the virtual extinction of the Estates-General. Not foreseeing the rise of the cabinet system in Britain, and wanting to substitute political liberty for royal absolutism in France, Montesquieu advocated the separation of powers as a device to make government safe for the governed. The division of powers that he envisaged was similar to Locke's conception. But in his insistence that they must be entrusted respectively to different personnel he went considerably beyond his predecessor.

> In every government there are three sorts of power: the legislative; the executive in respect to things dependent on the law of nations; and the executive in regard to matters that depend on the civil law. By virtue of the first, the prince of magistrate enacts temporary or perpetual laws, and amends or abrogates those that have been already enacted. By the second, he makes peace or war, sends or receives embassies, establishes the public security, and provides against invasions. By the third, he punishes criminals, or determines the disputes that arise between individuals. The latter we shall call the judiciary power, and the other simply the executive power of the state.... When the legislative and executive powers are united in the same person, or in the same body of magistrates, there can be no liberty; because apprehensions may arise, lest the same monarch or senate should enact tyrannical laws, to execute them in a tyrannical manner. Again, there is no liberty, if the judiciary power be not separated from the legislative and executive. Were it joined with the legislative, the life and liberty of the subject would be exposed to arbitrary control; for the judge would be then the legislator. Were it joined to the executive power, the judge might behave with violence and oppression. There would be an end of everything were the same man or the same body, whether of the nobles or of the people, to exercise those three powers, that of enacting laws, that of executing the public resolutions, and of trying the causes of individuals.[13]

While the framers of the American Constitution were profoundly influenced by Montesquieu's argument,[14] their own political expe-

---

[13] *Spirit of the Laws*, Book XI, 6. ed. Franz Neumann, trans. Thomas Nugent (New York: Hafner, 1949), pp. 151-52.

[14] Note Madison's remark in *The Federalist*, No. XLVII: "The oracle who is always consulted and cited on this subject is the celebrated Montesquieu."

rience reinforced the persuasiveness of his theory. For the governmental system with which they had the longest and closest acquaintance—that of the colonial period—embodied a species of separation. Prior to 1776 the executive branch under its governor was distinct from the legislature, and controversies between them were rampant in the two decades that led up to independence. With the principle of judicial review, at least when applied to an inferior legislative body, the statesmen of that day were equally familiar, since the constitutionality of colonial enactments could be challenged before a British court, the Judicial Committee of the Privy Council.[15] History, therefore, joined hands with philosophy in writing a separation of powers into the federal Constitution.

Design of the American Constitution. To be more precise, however, the separation of powers was not explicitly stated in the Constitution. For an enunciation of the principle one must turn to such a Constitution as that of Massachusetts which affirms: "In the government of this commonwealth, the legislative department shall never exercise the executive and judicial powers, or either of them; the executive shall never exercise the legislative and judicial powers, or either of them; the judicial shall never exercise the legislative and executive powers, or either of them; to the end that it may be a government of laws and not of men." [16] In the United States Constitution the principle is implied rather than asserted. Hence a special need arises to understand exactly what kind of separation is intended and what is not. Clarity, however, is obscured by the traditional use of the ambiguous term "powers." The meaning of the doctrine can be better analyzed if one drops the reference to powers and distinguishes instead between "branches" of government and their "functions." A branch is an organization of agencies with their personnel. The services they undertake are their functions.

If this distinction is borne in mind, the doctrine can be redefined and its logic expressed in the following manner. The activities of government group themselves into three divisions. That these divisions exist is a plain matter of fact which observation may verify, for they arise not from preconceived theory but from the character of the functions themselves. It is one thing to legislate, another to

[15] See Chapter 10, p. 241, n. 4.
[16] Preamble, sec. 30.

administer, and a third to judge. Such is the nature of the governmental process, as one finds it. How then can these three activities be embodied in the institutions of the state? If separation is the guiding aim, that can be achieved by establishing in the government three branches composed of separate personnel. Assign to one of these the whole function of law-making; to a second, the entire function of administration; and to a third, the full judicial process. Thus by creating a division of branches to correspond with the division of functions one may transfer separation from the realm of theory into the structure of political fact.

To what extent were these principles incorporated into the federal government of the United States? The Constitution completely achieved the formation of three branches, each with its distinct personnel. Expressly, it prevents any legislator from simultaneously holding either an executive or a judicial office.[17] Simultaneous tenure of two such offices as those of administrator and judge is not explicitly forbidden. But on this score the text could afford to be silent because judicial independence of the executive, secured in England in 1700, had already entered into the American tradition and, being no longer controversial, did not require statement in writing. The question whether a senator or representative could administer an agency was controversial. Therefore the solution had to be recorded in black and white.

The threefold division of functions, however, was not designed to correspond with the organization of the three branches. Instead of assigning each function in its entirety to one branch, the Constitution adopted a pattern of distribution. The lion's share of a function was apportioned to one branch, but smaller slices were given to each of the other branches. In the field of legislation, for example, the bulk of the law-making power was placed in the Congress. But the President received his share in the powers to recommend measures, to summon Congress in special session, and to veto their bills. The Supreme Court, likewise, by exercising the power of judicial review, asserted its claim to a portion of the legislative function. Similarly with the judicial process, although most of this is undertaken by the courts, Congress acts in a judicial capacity in cases of impeachment where the House is empowered to prosecute and the Senate sits in judgment. The President, too, can inter-

---

[17] *Constitution of the United States*, Art. 1, sec. 6.

vene in the business of the courts through his power of pardon for all offenses except treason.

Hence the term "separation of powers" oversimplifies a somewhat complex set of facts. Though many people have misunderstood the doctrine, the leading lights at the Philadelphia convention did not deceive themselves about what they were doing.[18] Because portions of each function were distributed among agencies of different personnel, the "separation of powers" was intended to result in a system of checks and balances. Ordinarily, unless the members of the three branches saw eye to eye and cooperated harmoniously, none of the principal functions of government could be adequately performed. Conversely, a branch or pair of branches that sought to overstep their constitutional authority could be restrained by the refusal of a third to connive.

The Tradition versus Modern Dynamics. It was only to be expected that an institutional framework which emerged from the political upheavals of the seventeenth and eighteenth centuries must undergo later adaptation. As the age of Jefferson, Napoleon, and Nelson receded into history, western societies faced fresh problems, or new forms of old problems. An industrial revolution, geared to a novel technology that harnessed unprecedented quantities of energy for men's productive enterprise, upset the equilibrium of primarily agrarian economies. The extension of occidental influence around the world, first under European and then under American leadership; the ambitions of new states, such as Germany; the impact of two global wars; the growth of a mass franchise and demands for social reform; changes like these were bound to impose a strain upon structures designed originally for different loads.

Two other factors were responsible, however, for more direct and immediate effects upon the relation between legislature, executive, and judiciary. These were the increase in the functions of government and the rise of organized parties with a mass following. As the state enlarged its activities, it was inevitable that the burden on all branches should increase. Law-making bodies had to debate new issues of public policy, discuss fresh objects of expenditure and modes of revenue, and provide more grants of statutory authority. The courts found their dockets crowded as they were called upon

[18] For example, Madison in *The Federalist,* Nos. XLVII-XLVIII.

to interpret legislation and review administrative acts. But the greatest expansion of all occurred in the executive branch, for there lay the responsibility of translating policy into practice. Every new service that the voters thrust upon the state, every additional power that the government sought, redounded to the advantage of the executive. New programs brought more agencies and bureaus into being, thus multiplying the number of civil servants. Huge sums of public money were theirs to disburse. Broad legal powers were entrusted to their discretion. In their files and records a treasure-house of specialized information was garnered. The administrator's status was converted from that of amateur to professional. He became an expert in the art of managing the relations between men.

These changes resulted in shifting the foundations on which the doctrine of the separation of powers was built. Locke had conceived of the relation between the three powers in terms of legislative supremacy. Montesquieu and Madison preferred to see an equilibrium between three co-ordinate branches. Despite such differences, however, all of them were united in their opposition to executive predominance, which they associated with royal absolutism. But though no longer linked with monarchy, executive predominance or something close to it has become customary in the twentieth century. This is to be explained not only by the contrast between the small number who compose a legislature or a judiciary on the one hand, and the huge staffs engaged in administration on the other, but by some further advantages that the latter possess. The strength of a judiciary, for example, lies in their mastery of the content of law—a mastery that requires skilled and trained practitioners and familiarity with elaborate forms. On these counts the civil service based on the merit system of appointment and promotion—that great governmental invention of the late nineteenth century—has nothing to yield to the judges! The complexity of public administration, its large-scale character, its technical content and intricate procedures, its opportunities for career service and the system of recruitment and promotion by merit, these have made public employment a profession comparable to the practice of law. Neither one is more or less scientific than the other, and each is as much of a mystery to the uninitiated. The role of the legislator, however, has not become as professionalized. Because he comes to his office by public election, his masters are the majority of his constituents; and since some of these may switch favorites, he cannot be sure of steady employment. Though his legislative service, if continued long enough, acquaints him with governmental problems, his relation to civil servants is that of amateur to expert. While they depend on him for political backing, for legal authority, and for financial resources, he is in need of their technical know-how. He may supervise them, conduct inquiries, watch, and castigate. But in the final analysis, if the state is what its functions are, a government becomes what its functionaries do. It is the administrator who makes or mars the policy. Power resides in the hands that execute and enforce. Small wonder, therefore, that much modern government has come to be realistically described as "bureaucracy," [19] or rule by the bureaus.

There is still another respect in which modern developments have upset the original concept of the separation of powers. Besides changing the relation of the three branches, the needs of modern government have also blurred the distinctions between the three functions. Administration and adjudication, for instance, no longer seem as different as they may have once appeared. Both judges and administrators apply broad rules of law to individual cases, each possessing within limits some discretion in fitting the particular facts under the general principle. Bureaus and courts are alike engaged in the same task of law enforcement,[20] the essential difference being that the former take the initiative in administering law whereas the latter wait until a dispute arises and one party seeks a judicial settlement. Nor is the function of law-making as dissimilar from that of law-enforcing as it was once thought to be. Owing to the intricacy of modern social problems, the formulation of general principles and the administration of concrete facts are no longer clear-cut and sharply separable. Many intermediate steps must be taken before broad rules are narrowed down to the particular circumstance. A good way to visualize the process of government is to think of a series of concentric circles. Each circle represents a field of choice among a number of possible policies. When one

[19] Like the term "politician," bureaucracy has acquired some unfavorable connotations. But it can be used neutrally and descriptively, as above.

[20] Courts in earlier periods performed many administrative services, and still perform some.

of these is adopted, the next smaller circle provides for a new choice—limited and bounded, of course, by the previous decision—and so on. Most legislation nowadays has to be supplemented by a series of rules, regulations, or orders, that spell out the generalities of a statute in finer detail. Certainly at the higher levels of any executive department, the work of officials is primarily concerned with matters of policy, on which subject they render advice to members of the legislature and give instructions to their own official subordinates. Between a people drafting a constitution and a mail-man delivering a letter to the correct address, there are rings within rings within rings of diminishing fields of choice and ever-narrowing decisions. The moulds have broken in which the thought of Locke, Montesquieu, and Madison were cast and their contents have spilled together.[21]

Effect of Political Parties on Institutions. The rise of the executive branch to pre-eminence, however, and the blurring of the traditional division of functions are not due solely to the increase of governmental activities. Besides the organization of the career civil service a second great innovation of the nineteenth century was the new kind of party system with its mass following. Political parties had no place in the calculations of those who espoused the doctrine of the separation of powers,[22] an omission which, though regrettable, is not altogether surprising for a period when parties were despised as factions. But their impact on the separation of powers was bound to be felt after the extension of the franchise had encouraged the electorate to mobilize under the banner of parties and thus compete for control of the state. Being a newcomer to the political scene, the mass party lacked restraining inhibitions about the sacrosanctity of separation. Avid for power, it was less scrupulous about the nicety of distinctions between powers. It would not willingly exempt any segment of authority from its grasp. What constitution framers had divided into three and put asunder, the party was prepared to reunite.

[21] A familiar example of this is the so-called regulatory agency (for example, the Interstate Commerce Commission or Federal Trade Commission). Under an Act of Congress these issue rules, enforce them, and serve as tribunals to hear disputes and complaints. Their work, exemplifying the unity of the governmental process, marks a fusion of powers rather than a separation.

[22] See above, Chapter 10, pp. 258-9.

Thus it was that in mid-nineteenth century America, from the time of Jackson roughly to Cleveland, the parties made their onslaught upon the institutions of government. They regarded jobs in public offices as the spoils of political warfare, to be looted after an electoral victory. The patronage thus obtained was used to grease the party machine. But simultaneously it filled the civil service with partisan employees of uncertain tenure and dubious qualifications. Almost the same treatment was accorded to the judiciary. Control of the courts was necessary to the party because of the key role they played in law enforcement plus their power of judicial review. Where judges were elected to the bench, as in many state and local governments, the parties determined the selection of candidates and ensured the support of the voters. Otherwise, if judicial office was filled by appointment, the party could influence the chief executive who made the nomination and the senate that confirmed. The capture of the legislature, and of elective posts in the executive branch, was achieved through the electoral system, where the parties maintained a firm grip on nominating procedures and methods of balloting. The extreme point in this series of developments was reached when, like an octopus extending its tentacles, the party fell under the domination of a boss. Often without holding any public office himself, a boss was able by his unchallenged mastery of the party machine to achieve a concentration of power that violated the fundamental concepts of American democracy.

The popular reaction, however, to the scandals, which in this instance, as always, accompanied excessive power, ushered in a trend of reforms, designed to purify the processes of government and restore to the people their birthright of political authority. Slowly, but surely and inexorably, the evil of bossism, entrenched in so many sectors of American public life, has been attacked and, if not completely eradicated, at least reduced to smaller and safer proportions. Slowly but surely, around two institutions, the civil service and the courts, a *cordon sanitaire* of political neutrality is being drawn. Since law must be applied by both bodies with fairness and honesty, there is no room for spoilsmen in the bureau or partisans on the bench. Administrators and judges, therefore, must be kept independent of party pressure—in one case through security of tenure and appointment by merit, in the other by non-partisan election or selection.

While dikes and dams were thus erected to hold back the flood-waters of party power, alternative channels had to be provided in which the new pressures could usefully and legitimately flow. Since parties inevitably brought politics in their train, any place in the governmental system that fitted one was appropriate for the other. Plainly then, the correct fields for parties to penetrate and occupy were the legislature and the elective offices of the executive branch. These areas were rightfully theirs. Nobody [23] would want to see the parties ejected from the institutions that represent and translate the preferences of the voting public on broad issues of economic and social policy. But that being so, if it were permissible for the parties to capture the presidency and governorships and to organize majority and minority caucuses in Congress and the state legislatures, the structural separation of the executive and legislative branches was certain to be modified by the party tie. Though discipline within the party may not always be strong, though there may be opposition to the leadership of the chief executive, nevertheless a common interest of a sort—even if it is no more than the desire to keep their side in power—unites all those who bear the same label. At least they know that, if they do not hang together, they are more likely to hang separately!

Government by Party and Civil Service. Thus a study of the party system and its consequences suggests that modern government can be viewed in a fresh way. In the eighteenth century an elaborate attempt was made to explain government in terms of three powers with their corresponding branches. The nineteenth century, under the stimulus of expansion both in the electorate and in state activities, witnessed the formation of two potent institutions—the political party and the civil service based on the merit system. When these were superimposed upon the existing trio of branches, the junction of two such newcomers with the three older bodies produced at the outset much friction and disturbance because the older institutional framework had to accommodate itself to the intruders. In the twentieth century the governmental process has consisted increasingly of a partnership between party and civil service. Between them they have harnessed administrative technique

---

[23] Exceptions are the two states of Nebraska and Minnesota, whose constitutions require non-partisan elections of members of the legislature.

to political strength, and it is in their hands that effective power lies. Most of the work of the modern state is accomplished by a party and a civil service together.

New Role of the American Presidency and Governorship. In the American system the clearest evidence of the joint impact of party and civil service is revealed in the exalted new status of presidents and governors. When the potentialities of each office is fully developed, the man who fills them ceases to be, in any narrow or restrictive sense, a chief executive. He becomes, in addition, a party leader, chief legislator,[24] and general mobilizer of public opinion. This is an accurate description of the role played by outstanding Presidents of this century, such as Wilson and the two Roosevelts, and by successful Governors like the elder LaFollette of Wisconsin, Smith and Lehman of New York, and Warren of California. The leadership provided by these men has been dual since it has embraced both the legislative and executive branches. To them may be applied, not inappropriately, the words that Walter Bagehot used to describe the British Cabinet in the mid-nineteenth century: "a *hyphen* which joins, a *buckle* which fastens, the legislative part of the state to the executive part of the state." [25]

A variety of circumstances have combined to thrust the chief executive, whether of the state or of the United States, into a more prominent role. A new dynamism was infused into politics by the readjustment to a continent-wide expansion, a rapid industrialization, and the absorption of immigrants. With the mounting demands of underprivileged people, both actual voters and potential, for a more secure status, the governments of states and nation assumed increasing responsibilities. As a consequence, people who had some common interest to promote formed pressure groups to influence legislative action. Issues of public policy were aired in public debate. Party organizations had to decide what course of action to endorse—or even of inaction, since dodging or straddling an issue was itself a decision. Inevitably such a situation created the need and the opportunity for some person or agency to take the initiative and give a lead. It was possible for that leadership to emanate from

[24] This is a phrase used by Howard L. McBain in *The Living Constitution* (New York: Macmillan, 1937), Chapter IV.

[25] The English Constitution, *World's Classics* ed., (London: Oxford University Press, 1928), p. 12. Italics in original.

within the legislature, but difficult, because in a bicameral body there were usually several members in each house with independent influence who competed for the limelight. A tactical advantage thus lay with the chief executive, since in the White House or the Governor's mansion there could be only one occupant and, if he chose to dive into the center of the fray, he could immediately command an audience and something of a following. For this, the constitutional powers of his office provided a springboard. The President, and many of the Governors, had a direct entrée into the legislative field through their powers to send messages, to recommend measures, to summon special sessions, and to veto bills. In addition, however, they could harness other techniques to supplement their political strategy. By the use of patronage, jobs could be traded for votes.[26] By effective appeals to the voters through the spoken word, press, radio, and lately television, chief executives have been able to dramatize their programs and compel consideration of their views. In this way, the Presidency and Governorship became the focal offices in state and national politics so that through them the force of public opinion and the power of the party system have been funnelled into the structure of the Constitution.

Cabinet Dominance in Britain. The analogy with the contemporary development of British institutions is instructive. It is one of the ironies of political science that Montesquieu based his support of the doctrine of separation of powers in large part upon his study of the British system wherein he believed it to be embodied. He omitted to notice, or failed to consider significant, the rise of the cabinet in the reigns of George I and II, and the emergence under Sir Robert Walpole of the Prime Minister as the cabinet's presiding officer. It is precisely the cabinet, however, that has become the unique and distinctive agency of British government, and that has made the fusion [27] rather than separation of powers its central principle. In the course of two and a half centuries the cabinet has evolved by stages, owing its modern pre-eminence to precisely the same factors as have modified the American system—

---

[26] This technique was formerly more effective than it is nowadays because of the extension of civil service protection to large numbers of government jobs.

[27] The only exception to this statement is that the judiciary, though subordinate to Parliament, is independent of the executive.

on the one hand, the extension of the suffrage and of governmental functions, and on the other, the organization of the party and the civil service.

The stages through which the cabinet has passed are briefly these: the first phase lasted from the accession of George I in 1714 to shortly after the close of the Napoleonic Wars in 1815. During that period the cabinet successfully emancipated itself from royal domination. In so doing it was aided by the lucky circumstance that the first two Georges, being German immigrants from Hanover, were ill-acquainted with the English language and British politics. They, therefore, discontinued the practice of presiding in person at cabinet meetings and left this duty to a leading Minister, who was designated Prime Minister. In the absence of the Monarch it was easier and safer for the Ministers to oppose his wishes and strengthen one another by assuming collective responsibility for decisions. When George III, being English-born, sought to revive the king's power, the total failure of his policies in 1776 and the insanity to which he fell victim in the later years of his reign enabled the cabinet to reassert its supremacy over the Crown.

The second stage opened with the beginnings of parliamentary and electoral reform in the early 1830's. In the middle decades of that century the extension of the franchise encouraged the growth of a party structure among the voters, whose allegiance, particularly when newly enfranchised, the parties were eager to capture. Increasingly, therefore, candidates were elected to Parliament because of their affiliation with a party and support for its program. This was a process, however, that took time to consummate because economic and social conditions were fluid and the size of the population and the electorate was expanding. Hence, although party discipline was crystallizing within the legislature, there were still minority blocs and a number of independents whose political fluctuations could determine the rise and fall of governments. Cabinets in this period, therefore, were dependent upon the House of Commons and it was there that they could be made and unmade.

The third stage commenced around 1884, when the adult male franchise was obtained. The consequent increase of the electorate made stronger party organization both desirable and imperative. The heavier expense of canvassing and campaigning in a larger constituency made local candidates depend upon central endorsement and assistance. Since the central organization of the party was controlled by its parliamentary leaders, they had the wherewithal to determine the votes of the parliamentary rank and file. As the two-party system became more firmly established, and the number of independents in the legislature dwindled into insignificance, the majority and minority in Parliament were predetermined by the effectiveness of party discipline. Only in the rare and unlikely event of a split within the major party, or during the temporary existence of a three-party system [28] can Parliament nowadays reassert its power to make the cabinet. The rule in modern times has been that the people determine at the polls which party shall have a legislative majority, and the party leaders determine the composition of the cabinet. A mid-twentieth century British Parliament records the popular decision in much the same way as the electoral college ratifies the American people's choice of a President.

Nor is this all. The cabinet's functions are not limited to the legislative sphere. They extend to the executive branch by virtue of the fact that members of the cabinet are Ministers of the Crown. Severally, they are responsible for administering the various departments of state. Collectively, they must weave together the countless strands of administration and decide the broadest issues of national policy. To accomplish this they have at their command the skill and resources of the superb civil service that staffs the agencies which Ministers direct. The role, therefore, of the cabinet is essentially dual. In that body resides the ultimate responsibility of leadership in the legislative and executive spheres alike. The cabinet has proven itself the convenient and flexible institution where the potencies of party and civil service are fused.

A century and a half ago the American and British systems were poles apart in important respects. Moving by different routes, the two democracies have lately been converging upon the same destination. This does not mean, of course, that the distinctions have been obliterated. There is still an important contrast between a leadership that is exercised within the legislature and one exerted from outside. There are divergencies due to dissimilar electoral patterns, since in the United States it is possible for the party opposed to a President or Governor to have the majority in one house or even in both.

[28] As occurred in Britain in the 1920's, when the Liberals were declining and Labor were gaining strength.

Furthermore, the highly disciplined character of the British parties makes parliamentary action much more predictable than the actions of American legislatures. Nevertheless, it is true that the similarities between the two systems are now at least as significant as their differences; and at certain periods—still admittedly the exception rather than the rule—they function alike. President Franklin D. Roosevelt's relations with Congress in the first three months of his first term strongly resembled a Prime Minister's relation to the House of Commons. Conversely, during the war years from 1940 to 1944, Prime Minister Churchill's relation to the House—which he attended infrequently and where he spoke only on major occasions—was not at all unlike the contact between Congress and the President. Affected by the operation of the same influences, both systems have certainly changed and it is arguable that they may now be approaching a common denominator.

The Legislature and the Courts. At this point, however, a word of caution is necessary if misunderstanding is to be avoided. To say that the party and civil service have been superimposed upon the organization of the three branches does not mean that the latter have been replaced or obliterated. Likewise, the argument that presidents and governors have risen to a new peak of power, or that the cabinet has become pre-eminent over Crown and Parliament, does not imply that legislatures and courts are nullities and no longer perform a useful function. It is true that there has been a change in relative power. It is not true to state that institutions, which are now less influential than they once were, have been placed in the discard.

Courts of law continue to be indispensable bulwarks of personal freedom, since they offer a tribunal where citizens who are involved in a dispute with each other or who have a case against their government may sue for justice. To this end it is essential that courts be immune from outside pressure, that they prevent an arbitrary use of executive power, and that, under the American system, they prohibit violations of the Constitution by a legislative majority. If courts be guardians of personal freedom, it is the legislature that safeguards political freedom. In countries that recognize that there is a proper place in the governmental process for discussion, criticism, and opposition, the interplay of rival parties is deemed valuable and constructive. The institution designed for this very purpose is, of course, the legislature. Here the parties meet and test each other in public debate as it is intended they should. Here alternative policies are proposed and analyzed and popular grievances are ventilated. The party and the civil service could wield power and perform their jobs without the presence of a judiciary and legislature. But their regime would not be one of liberty; and if efficient at the outset, it would, if history is a safe guide, end in corruption.

Ultimately, therefore, it is on the legislature that political freedom depends, since it is here that government and the opposition to government are both rightfully represented. The legislature constitutes the public forum where the power of leadership confronts the power of criticism. Not a little is at stake, therefore, in the manner wherewith the legislature discharges its responsibilities. If the legislature does not merit the people's respect, if it succumbs to the pressure of special interests, if it fails to strike a balance between the roles of a rubber-stamp and of a negative obstructionist, then it does democracy no service, since it forfeits its claim to be the unique institution differentiating democracy from dictatorship.

The Power Pattern of Dictatorship. Unfortunately the evidence on this point is not taken only from the pages of the past. Modern dictatorships—Nazi, Fascist, and Communist—supply corroborative testimony. There, too, the executive branch has acquired enormous new power and the work of government is carried on through the twin media of party and civil service. But these institutions, though employed by democracy and dictatorship alike, differ radically in the two political contexts. The spirit and status of any party are completely changed when it alone has the legal right to exist and therefore possesses a monopoly. Likewise a civil service, organized to serve a one-party state, must itself share a partisan loyalty and does not dare maintain the political neutrality that is expected when two or more parties may alternate in power.

A dictatorship, furthermore, goes to extreme lengths in subjecting other branches to the domination of the executive. The courts may not, in any case that has political relevance, give a decision contrary to the will of the party leadership. Judges must be mice under the throne. So too with the legislature, which in a dictatorship is a superfluous and dangerous institution since it could be a rallying point for opposition. Dictators sometimes permit the outward form of a legislative body to survive. But it is a hollow shell, with the kernel removed. By packing it with party stalwarts, by convoking it at long intervals, and by controlling its agenda and procedure, the dictator turns it into a receptive sounding-board for his own and his party's propaganda. Such was the fate that befell the Italian Parliament after 1925 and the German Reichstag after 1933, and the history of the Soviets in Russia has been similar. That system of councils or representative assemblies was constructed in 1917 by the revolutionary movement both as an instrument of opposition to Czarism and as a nucleus for a new government. But the Soviets, just because they were representative and elected bodies, contained within themselves a seed of democracy that Stalin did not permit to grow. Under his rule, therefore, the Soviets were reduced to a nullity. Any possibility of their independence was throttled by the stranglehold that the Communist Party secured over them.

As examples of a concentration of power, pushed to its utmost, the following may be grouped together: the autocracy of the Russian Czars prior to 1905, the dictatorship of Stalin as boss of the Communist party in the U.S.S.R., the Hitlerite regime in Germany, Mussolini's Fascist system in Italy, and the oligarchy of militarists, bureaucrats, and businessmen who controlled Japan from 1931 to 1945. All the modifications that have occurred of recent decades in the American and British governments seem, when compared with such cases, meek and mild indeed. Such dictatorships aptly illustrate and justify the remark of Madison: "The accumulation of all powers, legislative, executive, and judiciary, in the same hands, whether of one, a few, or many, and whether hereditary, self-appointed, or elective, may justly be pronounced the very definition of tyranny." [29]

[29] *The Federalist*, No. XLVII.

CHAPTER 12

FOURTH ISSUE.

(2) LOCALISM, CENTRALISM, AND FEDERALISM

Areas and Government. Some of the same causes that have impelled the party and the civil service in the modern state to remold the relations between the three traditional branches have also affected profoundly the choice between a concentration of power in one place or its decentralization. There are additional factors, too, such as the revolution in transport and communications, that bear specially on this particular problem. It is the purpose of this chapter to continue the discussion of the issue presented in the previous one in order to see to what extent and by what means the powers pertaining to central and local governments have lately been redistributed.

No modern government, not even the smallest, can transact all its affairs in one place. Because the territorial range of the state must be co-extensive with that of society, wherever there are social relationships between individuals, situations will arise that call for governmental regulation on the spot. Thus any modern political system, whatever its nature, must provide for local administration. Two questions then inevitably arise: What functions are to be assigned to which level? Which authorities are or should be preponderant, the central or the local?

The issue posed by such questions has several ramifications that are fundamental to statecraft. Ever since governments began to be organized upon a territorial basis, their structure has necessarily been influenced by considerations of area. The state is conditioned by geography as well as by history. Its operations extend continuously over space and over time. Hence the problem has arisen—and always will arise—of relating its functions, institutions, and jurisdiction to the area that has to be served. This is no easy puzzle to solve because the boundaries that would be the fittest from the standpoint of any one governmental activity are seldom identical with those that are appropriate from another. A large-sized city will obtain its water-supply from one place; its electricity and other forms of power may come from a second; its sewage will, or should, be disposed of in a third. The plan of a transportation system, connecting the various districts of a city, and linking it with adjacent dormitory suburbs, will assume one shape, but the organization of districts for school construction or crime prevention may require yet a different plan. Food for the urban population will be drawn from nearby farms, and also from distant flour-mills, stockyards, fruit orchards, and fishing-grounds. The livelihood of the city-dweller, who must find employment in a factory, business office, or retail store, depends on the intricate relationships of complex economic mechanisms whose boundaries are sometimes national, sometimes international, in extent. Finally, military defense, which in the middle ages was provided by the thick stone wall that ran around the city's perimeter, is today secured by bases flung halfway around the world. In short, each function of government, when envisaged geographically, projects itself on a map corresponding to its own needs; and if all the maps were superimposed, scarcely two would coincide.

That being the case, how is the structure of the state best adapted to interests and services that spread themselves so differently in space? The answer is a common-sense solution. Since it would be impossible to organize separate governmental systems with different areas for each function, and since identical areas would be unworkable, a compromise has to be adopted. This consists in drawing a distinction between needs or problems of general concern, and those whose range is essentially limited. Hence the familiar division between a central agency and units of more circumscribed jurisdiction.

The Community of Interest. Besides this argument of convenience, the case for separating local from central authorities is reinforced by further political considerations. It is an undeniable fact that proximity creates a community of interests. People who live in the same neighbourhood have many ties with one another. They are equally concerned about sanitation and public health, about water and similar essentials, about transportation to and from their work, and about shopping and recreational facilities. What is more, the inhabitants of the same area are in constant contact. They meet each other face to face and have direct communication. Their daily activities bring them together; their children go to the same school or playground; they find their friends, for the most part, among those who live within easy reach. In circumstances such as these, many elements that are basic to the community are present, for a community consists in that sense of solidarity that springs from common interests and shared experience.

But it is also politically possible for that feeling of oneness to extend beyond the small area of face-to-face relationships, provided that common interests exist and that similar experiences are shared. The experiences may assume a variety of forms. Men can be united, for instance, by the problems of growing and selling the same crop, as the Old South paid homage to "King Cotton" or Canadian prairie farmers to wheat, or São Paulo *fazendeiros* to coffee. Membership in the same religious faith may serve as a bond between persons such as the Catholics, Jews, or Moslems who are scattered among different localities, or nations, or even continents. So may people be drawn together who speak the same language, or who have similar systems of government, or who acknowledge one cultural tradition. However, all such wider unions—or extended communities, as they may be called—are reinforced politically when the territory they occupy forms a physical continuum. What gave the Old South its strength and made secession, even at the risk of civil war, seem practicable was the compactness of the Cotton Kingdom. What consolidates the French-speaking Canadians, besides their Church, is their concentration and dominance in the Province of Quebec. An extended community is always stronger when its members are contiguous than when they are dispersed. For like reasons, because proximity makes organization easier, a concentrated minority is generally more effective than a scattered minority of the same size. If this was not so, it would be impossible to explain such political phenomena as the separation of Ulster from Eire, of Norway from

Sweden, of Pakistan from India, of Israel from the Arab states.[1] Decentralization, local autonomy, states' rights—such terms and all
that they imply are grounded in the fact that proximity does make
a difference to politics.

Boundaries and Psychology. Moreover, it must not be forgotten
that the very existence of a political boundary is itself a major contribution to a sense of solidarity. To assume that a community of
interests is a result, transferred to politics, of causes that always
originate in other social groupings, would be erroneous. Among the
most important of the experiences which can unite a group is that
they share the same unit of government. The structure of the state
has no less intimate an effect upon the organization of society than
has that of society upon the state. When territorial areas are de-
limited so that jurisdictions and services may be clearly distributed,
symbolic associations tend to cluster around the selfsame boundaries.
Cooperative sentiments of pride and loyalty, competitive attitudes
of jealous rivalry, attach themselves readily to spatial units. Thus
it is that cities, big and small, can evoke a city-centered patriotism of
their inhabitants. People may then become very conscious of their
identity as Londoners, Parisians, New Yorkers, Bostonians. Or they
may identify themselves with some wider, yet politically articulated
areas. A county, perhaps, or a province, or a state within a union,
will acquire an individual character. Witness the traditions, and the
folklore, of the Vermonter, the Texan, the Bernese, the Gascon, the
Castilian, the Yorkshireman. Or again the area may broaden out into
regional dimensions, as long as it is endowed with recognizable
features, real or supposed; for example, New England, Dixie, the
Border Country, the Highlands, the Midi, the *Sertão*,[2] the Out-
back.[3]

It is the purpose of boundaries to divide. Physical separation lends
itself to psychological alienation. All who are on "your" side of the

---

[1] However, the geographical concentration of the minority, though a vital
factor in all these cases, is not the sole explanation of such splits. Sometimes
the resistance that the local minority offers to the majority is fortified by a
potent group outside. Thus the support of Protestant Britain was indispensable
to Ulster; that of the Moslem peoples in the Middle East, to Pakistan; that of
American and British Jewry, to Israel.

[2] The arid area of northeastern Brazil.

[3] The interior of Australia.

line belong to "your" group; those beyond it do not. This feeling is heightened by the opposition that so often arises mutually, between different communities. A pair of cities may develop a strong rivalry, as in the cases of San Francisco and Los Angeles, Toronto and Montreal, Sydney and Melbourne, Madrid and Barcelona. So may a pair of counties, like Yorkshire and Lancashire in England; or two cantons, such as Bern and Zurich; or two provinces, like Ontario and Quebec; or two sections, like North and South develop strong rivalry. It is precisely because of the psychological significance which attaches to boundary lines that common speech confers a symbolic meaning, of deeper import than their literal one, on such terms as "crossing the Rubicon," [4] "beyond the Pale," [5] "the Chinese Wall," "the Mason-Dixon Line," and "the Iron Curtain." [6]

The Case for Local Liberties. Local loyalties, regional rivalries, separatist sentiments—these, where they exist in force, are barriers to unity and therefore to centralization. But there is a further factor, sometimes working in conjunction with these influences and sometimes operating independently, that also produces a decentralizing effect. It is the fear that power is always susceptible to abuse, and that any accumulation of power which is not counterbalanced by an independent power can become dangerous. This is the core of the argument against monism, since the net result of ecclesiastical or business autonomy was to create social groups largely exempt from the control of the state and therefore capable of resisting or obstructing it. This is equally the logic of the "separation of powers," since there can be no omnipotent state to fear if the institutional structure of the government is dispersed in the form of co-ordinate branches. Likewise, this is the rationale of a preference for federalism and for "local liberties," the assumption being that Leviathan's grip is weaker when its skeleton is loose-jointed. Local or state

---

[4] This river formed the boundary line between Italy proper and the province of Cisalpine Gaul. Caesar, in 50 B.C., led his army south across it, which the governor of a province was forbidden to do. Thereby he declared war on the central authorities of Rome.

[5] When English power was expanding in the Middle Ages, the area where English law and jurisdiction prevailed (for example, in France, Scotland, or Ireland) was called the Pale. Those outside it were not subject to England.

[6] Compare the expression that describes the gulf between social and economic classes in an urban community, "the other side of the tracks."

governments, on this theory, can to some extent be made independent of the center, so that they may provide foci of resistance if tyranny should ever be established there.

The nature of such tyrannies has been too vividly exemplified in modern times for any doubts as to their character to be left remaining. Modern dictatorships are a product of aggressions, attaining control by the use of violence. Because their regimes are founded primarily on force, and not on right, they continue, even after they have come to power, to feel insecure, and hence they continue to display aggressiveness. This they vent against those individuals who are their opponents and against any institutions where opposition can rally. It is obvious that, if the government at the center is dictatorial, men may turn to local parties as a medium for criticism and to local government as a vehicle for organization. To prevent this happening is important to the modern dictatorship that never feels safe if its control is not total. Hence it is characteristic of the authoritarian regime to eliminate any aspects of local autonomy and to subordinate completely all local authorities to the central will.

Dictatorships, Fascist and Communist. That decentralized autocracy would be a contradiction in modern political logic is a truth exemplified equally in both extremes of right and left. Before Mussolini's supremacy was established in Italy, a system of local self-government was in operation that, with all its shortcomings, did allow for manifestations of local sentiment. This was particularly so in the regions of Tuscany and Lombardy, where so many famous cities flourished, where great men had lived and worked, and where historic events were cradled. A dictator, however, prizes in his fellow citizens the quality of dependence, not independence. The Municipal Council of Milan, for instance, had been controlled by Mussolini's political opponents, the Socialists, and he could not permit such a possibility. Hence he abolished the locally elected councillors and substituted for them an official appointed from, and responsible to, the center—the *Podestà*. The same method of organization commended itself to Adolf Hitler, an authoritarian centralist by temperament and conviction. In the German Empire that Bismarck made by Blood and Iron, and in the Weimar Republic, which the moderate left and center parties created after World War I, the structure of the state followed a federal pattern. Hitler would have none of this, for federalism and dictatorship do not make harmonious bed-fellows.[7] As his power was consolidated after the summer of 1934, he proceeded to abolish the Lands (or states) that composed the federal system. Then, applying the *Führerprinzip*, he organized the German government from the top downwards, and placed in regions and in districts a hierarchy of officials (*Gauleiters* and others) whose power derived from his.[8]

The Communist dictatorship in the Soviet Union, as Stalin practiced it until his death, conformed to this inexorable tendency. In semblance, at least, a federal structure was adopted that outwardly diverged from the centralization of the Romanoffs. Moreover, in reaction against the Czarist policy of "Russification"—a requirement of cultural uniformity that had been imposed on Poles and other minorities—the Bolsheviks initially sponsored a program of cultural diversity. But circumstances conspired to suppress these decentralizing influences.[9] In the economic sphere a centralizing factor of great importance was the series of plans, prepared and directed in Moscow, and encompassing the entire Soviet Union. To the exigencies of these national plans the policies of the component "republics" and "autonomous states" were subordinated. At the same time, in the political sphere, the monopoly of power by a single party prevented that interplay between the union and its components that is so characteristic of federal politics. In the face of the discipline of the Communist Party and its hierarchical command no unit of government was able to deviate from the central line. Finally there was the incalculable force of Stalin's personality, which did not brook opposition and which would not see authority delegated. A Georgian from the Caucasus, Stalin had made himself supreme over all the Russians, and, like many a leader who emerges from a minority group, he evolved into the super-centralist. Comparable cases—to an equivalent or smaller degree—are those of Napoleon, the Corsican who became Emperor of the French; Hitler, the Austrian who subjugated the Germans; Mussolini, the peasant-boy from

[7] The same truth can be observed in the changes introduced into the Brazilian system between 1937 and 1945 when Getulio Vargas established his dictatorship and controlled the states through "interventors."

[8] It should be noted that in the Italian Fascist and German Nazi cases, this excessive centralism represented in part a reaction to the lateness of both countries in achieving national unification. See Chapter 13, pp. 344-5.

[9] Soviet publicists themselves recognized this aspect of the facts by describing their system as "democratic centralism." Centralism it certainly is; democratic it certainly is not.

Italy's northeast coast who strutted as the would-be Caesar of the New Rome; Lloyd George, the Welshman who galvanized the British nation in World War I; and Poincaré the frontiersman from Lorraine, who typified French nationalism in the middle of the 1920's. Such a list would appear to indicate that minority sections, which may be breeding-grounds for separatism, not infrequently give birth to the ultra-nationalist.

Because of this natural affinity that has developed in modern times between centralism and despotism, the question must arise whether centralism and liberty are compatible. Some indeed argue that political liberty positively requires a substantial measure of decentralization. The theme has been developed by both statesmen and scholars that local self-government spells local liberties, and these, when added together, make up a sum total of national liberty. Historically there is some evidence to support this view. In the case of England, for example, it is undeniable that the grant of corporate privileges to London and lesser cities, and the growth of a rural administration in which the country gentry (as distinct from the higher nobility) played a major role were factors that encouraged a sturdy spirit of resistance to anything that smacked of oppression from the center. Moreover, it is true that in the arena of local politics and administration many persons discovered a preparatory training-ground where they were initiated into the art of government before deploying the experience thus gained in the national sphere. These are important considerations that should never be overlooked.

But if a true perspective is to be secured, one must remember that sin is no monopoly of the center and virtue no monopoly of the localities. Examples of despotism emanating from the center can be matched by just as many cases of local dictatorship. "There are village tyrants as well as village Hampdens." [10] People have often sought the aid of a distant protector to defend them from a nearby oppressor. The local bully—whether landowner, ecclesiastical potentate, captain of industry, or political boss—cannot in all cases be opposed by the people of the locality where he dominates. If they are to be freed, he must be overawed by some greater power from outside. In short, dictatorship can reign at the center; but so can freedom. There can be local tyrannies; or, alternatively, local liber-

---

[10] Justice Jackson, in *West Virginia State Board of Education vs. Barnette,* 319 U.S. 624 (1943).

ties. Local independence may defy a central dictator; and freedom, centrally organized, can defeat a local autocrat. Political chemistry is a rich amalgam of the same basic elements in diverse formulae that make new compounds.

Unitary and Federal States. Though it is true that modern dictatorships prefer a centralized structure of government, it does not follow that all contemporary democratic states have decentralized systems or are decentralized to the same degree. The fact is that wide differences do exist and are expressed in contrasted institutional patterns. The most familiar of these is the distinction between a unitary state and a federal one. In the former the government is organized on two levels only—national and local, the latter comprising both urban and rural authorities. In a federal state there are three levels instead of two, since between the national government and the local ones there is placed an intermediate level, designated as states in the United States or Australia, as provinces in Canada, or as cantons in Switzerland. Intergovernmental relationships are therefore much more complex in federal systems than in those that are unitary. In the latter, only central-local and inter-local relations need to be considered. But under a federal union there are not only federal-state, federal-local, state-local, and federal-state-local, relationships, but also the inter-state and the inter-local, so that the problem of delimiting jurisdictions and then of meshing them together in a smooth-running machine is vastly more intricate. Federal systems therefore are inevitably more "jurisdiction-minded," more legalistic, and slower-moving than the unitary.

But still another caution is required, lest these generalizations become over-simple and thus inaccurate. Even when federal and unity states are distinguished, it must be remembered that differences still occur among those that fall within the selfsame category. The unitary state may be as highly centralized as France or New Zealand; or centralized, but to a slightly less degree, like Britain. The federal system can embody the amount of decentralization that is found in the United States or Switzerland. Alternatively, the blend, while remaining genuinely federal, may include more centralizing features, as is certainly the case in Canada.

Centralization in Britain. A review of some contrasted types will serve to make these points clearer. Great Britain can be taken as an instance of an unquestionably democratic state that is unitary and centralized. How important in that country are the local governments and what functions do they perform? Being the product of ancient traditions and of continuous adaptation to changing social patterns, the design of British local government is neither uniform, simple, nor entirely logical. Its outline, as a compromise between the practicable and desirable, between old and new, is not wholly self-consistent or clear-cut. But certain features stand out prominently and endow the system with its general character. One of these is the differentiation between urban and rural units—the former being classed as county boroughs or boroughs, the latter as counties. A second dominant trait is the dependence of the great majority of local governments on financial aid from the center, and the complete subordination of them all in matters of legal authority. A third factor of importance is the method by which functions are distributed between the two levels. Let us see what bearing this has on the dispersion or concentration of power in the British system.

Even when the structure of the state is specifically designed to avoid excessive centralization, it is never easy to determine the best allocation of powers. In Britain the decisions about what functions "belong" respectively to the national or local level have been influenced by such considerations as social convenience, political pressure, fiscal resources, and historical tradition. In certain cases a dividing line between local and national concerns can be drawn without too much difficulty. For example, the provision of public transport for an urban population inside municipal limits is clearly appropriate to local authority. On the other hand, the organization of a police force to protect both persons and public and private property has remained under local control,[11] largely through a series of historical circumstances hardening into a tradition. The social and economic changes of the last century have, of course, evoked a national concern in many matters where the original emphasis was primarily local. In a complex of contributing factors, the root-cause can undeniably be traced to the expansion of industry with its consequent stimulus to population growth and to urban concentration. Britain nowadays has roughly one-third of the population

---

[11] The nature of modern crime detection, however, and the problems of apprehending criminals have enlarged the activities of Scotland Yard as a nationwide police service.

of the United States in one-thirtieth of the area; and even within that small space (about equal to the state of Oregon) a high proportion of the people are densely congested in and around London, in the "Black Country" of the Midlands, the Industrial North, and the "waist" of Scotland. The larger cities have further increased in size. Their suburbs and satellites have sprawled into the nearby countryside. Their economic urgencies and opportunities, acting as a magnet, have drawn the rural economy into their orbit. The culture of the capital, transmitted by newspapers,[12] magazines, books, and radio, continues to pervade the village. The automobile—that "magic carpet" of the modern family—brings urban tourists, sightseers, and holidaymakers to "Ye Olde Tea Shoppe" and the parish church. Equally, it permits Farmer Giles to take his wife and children for an outing so that they may savour the throngs, hubbub, and sooty air of city streets.

Economics, congestion, and mobility have necessitated many readjustments in central-local relations. Programs of public assistance to the poor, for example, were once regarded as a local responsibility. But when the realization dawned that poverty (especially if associated with inadequate education or prolonged unemployment) was mainly a consequence of nationwide economic circumstances, when furthermore the areas hardest hit by a business depression were unable out of local resources to offer sufficient public relief to needy families, the conclusion was inescapable that the responsibility for assistance must be spread over the entire community. In this way, and for these or similar reasons, many a governmental service has literally been "nationalized." Some functions have therefore been wholly transferred from local to national jurisdiction. In other instances a partnership has evolved whereby national and local governments cooperate in a specific activity (for example, education, health, housing).

Under such a system, as is evident, the partners are not, and never can be, equal. A government that represents the whole is inevitably more powerful than those that represent the parts, irrespective of whether it deals with the parts severally or collectively. The realities of their relationship, as these exist in political power

---

[12] Britain's small territorial expanse, and the integration of the railways that radiate from London, permits the London morning newspapers to circulate throughout the country.

and financial resources, are faithfully mirrored in the law of the United Kingdom. Only one institution in Britain has the legal authority to decide how to distribute governmental functions between the center and the localities, and when to add or take away. That institution is necessarily the supreme law-making body, Parliament. At law, every local government is subject to the Parliament, which has created most of them, can reorganize any of them, and has clothed them with authority and defined their areas and powers. In this sense, because of the legal omnipotence of Parliament, the form of the British system is highly centralized. Moreover, the difficulty of financing the social services has reinforced the centralizing principles of constitutional law. The increase in governmental functions has been felt at both levels, local as well as national. But many of the newer local activities cost more than local resources can afford, particularly in the less wealthy areas where the need of governmental aid is so much greater. With most sources of taxation engrossed by the national treasury, there is a limit to the revenues of local bodies, which must thus depend on annual grants from the center. These are given subject to conditions and programs and standards determined in Westminster and Whitehall.

Nevertheless, despite the potency of centralizing pressures, the practices of Britain continue to be more decentralized than its formulae would indicate. Historically, the tradition of local self-government has maintained an unbroken continuity. Though far fewer voters are interested in local affairs than in national, local politics are often vigorously conducted and the locally elected councils, which appoint their own officials and disburse large sums of money, are far from negligible. Local government provides a valuable training-area for acquiring governmental experience, as the careers of Joseph Chamberlain and Herbert Morrison bear witness. All in all, the cities, boroughs, and counties that crowd the map of Britain contrive to modify, in part, what might otherwise be an excess of centralization.

American Federalism, the Start of an Invention. Much more decentralized, however, both in form and fact is the government of the United States. In this respect, as when following Montesquieu and separating the three branches, the framers of the Constitution displayed their preference for dispersion of powers. Their accomplishment was the novel and ingenious one of federal union, which has undoubtedly been the most distinctive, enduring, and influential contribution of America to the art of government. In what did the novelty consist? Prior to 1776 the thirteen colonies were severally and separately bound to Britain. In no way were they connected together. But to declare independence, to fight and win a war, and to build a new nation, required union. The first framework designed for this purpose and proposed to the states by the Continental Congress, was experimental and its construction was imperfect. Under the aegis of the Articles of Confederation a government was organized for the United States. When faced, however, with the urgent problems of postwar development, its powerlessness was quickly revealed. The Congress resembled not so much a legislature as a conference of ambassadors, acting under the instructions of the governments they represented. Its most important decisions required a majority of at least nine states; and the Articles themselves could not be amended without unanimity. The central authority was weak in its executive arm and altogether devoid of a judicial branch. For revenues and troops it depended upon what the states contributed from their resources.

Only a few years of experience with such a system were needed to demonstrate its inadequacies. The Congress lacked the authority to weld the states into a unity, to mitigate their commercial rivalries, to establish a sound currency, to remove the causes of domestic disorders,[13] and to foster American interests abroad. The delegates to the Philadelphia convention of 1787 were, therefore, sent by the states for the purpose of preparing a revision of the Confederation. Fortunately they went beyond their instructions and drafted the constitution of a federal union. As Hamilton saw it, the Articles had failed to meet the need of the United States because the parts predominated over the whole. The principal weakness that he diagnosed was the dependence of the government at the center upon the governments of the states that acted as intermediaries between it and the individual citizen.[14] It was precisely this defect that the Constitution removed, thereby inaugurating a more perfect union. The new central government was endowed with a Congress, whose powers are genuinely legislative; an executive, with adequate means of enforcement; and a judiciary, with authority to preserve an

[13] Such as Shays' Rebellion in 1786.
[14] *The Federalist*, No. XV.

equilibrium between the whole and the parts and to uphold the supremacy of the Constitution. The federal powers include that of levying taxes. Above all, the federal government derives its support and mandate directly from the people as voters, and carries its services directly to them as individuals.

When George Washington was inaugurated as President of the United States, something else was inaugurated along with him. This was the principle of a new and stronger type of federal union, the like of which was unknown in the previous history of the world and was unfamiliar to the generation that witnessed its birth. Leagues were no novelty, nor were confederations. But all of them, and the Articles of Confederation, were alike in the essential feature that real power lay with the parts, and the institutions at the center provided machinery for cooperation rather than for government. The feature that distinguished a federal union from leagues, confederations, and unitary states is that everyone in it is subject to and served by three levels of government. This is because every parcel of land in the continental United States falls under three jurisdictions—federal, state, and local.[15] What further distinguishes a federal union from leagues and confederations is that in the former the law and procedure of the constitution make it impossible for the federal government to abolish the member-states or for them to eliminate the federal government. The reason is that the governments at both the higher levels are derived directly from the people, and the Constitution not only creates a national authority, but guarantees to the states their permanent position within the federal union. Thus, Chief Justice Chase in an opinion [16] rendered after the Civil War described the American system as "an indestructible union composed of indestructible states." By the first part of this phrase he meant that the states could not break up the union or the federal authority which embodies it; by the latter, that the federal government may not destroy the states and replace them with a unitary state.

Variations on the Federal Theme. Once the example of the United States had demonstrated that a federal union could work

[15] An exception is the District of Columbia, which comes solely under federal jurisdiction. Its residents are denied the right to vote in federal elections and do not control the city government of Washington, which is directly supervised by Congress.

[16] *Texas v. White,* 7 Wallace 725 (1868).

successfully, a precedent was established that others whose situations were similar could follow. Thus in 1847 the Swiss Confederation was convulsed by an attempt of seven Catholic cantons to secede. The Protestant majority crushed the secessionists (the *Sonderbund*) in a civil war of short duration. Next year the victors rewrote their constitution and created a federal union closely patterned on that of the United States. For the first time [17] since 1291, when the Confederation was launched in a mutual defense pact between the cantons of Uri, Schwyz, and Unterwalden, the Swiss organized for themselves a genuine central government, which has now lasted for more than a century.

It is interesting to speculate whether the Swiss would have copied the American model so faithfully if the civil war had already broken out in the United States. But a possible clue is provided by what happened in Canada in the middle of the 1860's. A Canadian federal union was brought into being by the combined forces of three powerful reasons. An economic depression had hit the maritime settlements of Nova Scotia, New Brunswick, and Prince Edward Island, which sought recovery in a wider political framework. A unitary government had proved unworkable for the French and English inhabitants of Quebec and Ontario. Cool relations with the United States [18] and a determination to hold the West for Canada enforced the argument for a national authority. Federal union seemed the obvious solution, since it would permit the incorporation of the Atlantic seaboard with the upper St. Lawrence region, the separation of Quebec from Ontario, and the eventual inclusion of western territories when adequately peopled. But the recent experience of the near-dissolution of the American union in the Civil War led British and Canadian statesmen to the conclusion that the central government of Canada must possess more powers than belonged to its counterpart in the United States. Thus, whereas the federal government of the United States was organized on the principle that its powers are delegated to it by the Constitution

[17] A partial exception is the unitary state that Napoleon imposed on the Swiss shortly after conquering them. This was accepted, however, only under foreign duress and proved so unworkable that Napoleon himself aided the Swiss in restoring confederation.

[18] These were due to the British government's unfriendliness to the North during the Civil War, and to intimations of possible expansion by the United States in the north and northwest.

while the residue are retained by the states, the Canadians reversed
the distribution by delegating powers to the provinces and re-
serving the rest for the Dominion.[19] In Canada, moreover, the
national government (in effect, the cabinet) has authority to veto
the legislation enacted by a province, an ultimate weapon clearly
intended to bolster national supremacy.

Centralization in American Government. The great merit of a
federal union is its flexible capacity to extend a single jurisdiction
over a bigger area and more people than previously and to allow
at the same time for diversity and decentralization. But federalism,
like all systems that succeed in enduring, has not, and could not
have, remained the same as it was in 1789. In the United States, for
example, it has had to keep pace with the expansion in numbers and
power of the American nation. Federalism in this country has
presided over, and responded to, the industrialization of the American economy and its social after-effects; the migration of tens of
millions from Europe who filled a continent with farms and cities,
like water trickling through irrigation channels; participation in
two world wars; the growth of a national loyalty, and acceptance
of international responsibilities. Events such as these have inevitably
led to the changes that one author has called "the new centralization," and another "the rise of a new federalism."[20] The immediate cause of modifications in the federal structure has been the
assumption by governments of new functions, described in Chapter
8.[21] This trend has been felt at all three levels with the result that
federal, state, and local authorities have undertaken in the twentieth century far more activities than they ever did before. The
amount and rate of growth, however, have differed from one level
to another, so that the equilibrium formerly existing between the
three has altered.

It is an important but inadequately known fact that until quite
recent decades more than half of the American system of govern-

[19] On this point compare the Tenth Amendment to the Constitution of
the United States with the British North America Act, 1867, secs. 91-93. The
Swiss copied the American pattern in their Federal Constitution, Article 3, as
did the Australians later, Commonwealth of Australia Constitution Act, secs.
51, 52, 107.
[20] These are the titles of books by George C. S. Benson and Jane Perry
Clark, respectively.
[21] See pp. 202 ff.

TABLE IV*

PUBLIC FINANCES AND PUBLIC EMPLOYEES IN THE AMERICAN FEDERAL SYSTEM, 1890-1950
(THOUSANDS OMITTED)

	Government Revenues			Government Expenditures			Government Employees		
	Federal	State	Local	Federal	State	Local	Federal	State	Local
1890	403	107	455	318	72	488	—	—	—
1902	562	176	846	485	182	888	—	—	—
1913	724	345	1,326	724	378	1,460	470	—	—
1932	2,006	2,317	6,004	4,535	2,734	6,501	622	368	2,299
1938	5,855	4,754	—	7,239	4,765	—	900	544	2,510
1945	46,456	6,775	7,667	100,405	5,822	—	3,569	471	2,666
1950	38,354	11,863	13,545	40,166	13,183	—	2,117	1,057	3,228

* SOURCE: *Historical Statistics of the United States, 1789-1945* and *Statistical Abstract.* The blanks indicate that the data are not available.

ment was local in character. Prior to the outbreak of World War I local revenues and expenditures and the number of local public employees exceeded the total revenues, expenditures, and employees of the federal and all state governments combined.[22] Even as late as 1932 local revenues and personnel still stood at higher figures than those of the other forty-nine governments together, although by that date the states and the United States were beginning to outspend the localities. What happened thereafter was a spectacular extension of federal activity. On the domestic front this was occasioned by the economic depression of the early 1930's and the political demands for security, relief, and social services to which it gave rise. According to the traditional pattern whereby powers were distributed under the federal system, it was with the local governments that the first responsibility lay for taking remedial measures. Their financial resources, however, proved utterly incapable of meeting their legal and political obligations. Consequently, the cities and counties turned elsewhere for aid. First, to their state legislatures which provided what help they could, but in most cases were themselves too weak financially to underwrite the whole bill. Eventually, it was the federal government alone that in the program of President Roosevelt's New Deal mobilized the resources of a nation to alleviate a catastrophe of national dimensions.

The result of six years (1932-1938) of legislative debate, electoral decision, and judicial review was a federal commitment to such policies as the regulation of agriculture along with subsidies for farm products, unemployment relief, public works, and social security, the generation and sale of hydro-electric power, fixing maximum hours and minimum wages in industry, control of the securities market and insurance of bank deposits, and more besides. For certain of these programs, precedents on a limited scale had been established earlier. In other instances federal intervention was entirely new. In every case, however, the scope of the federal undertakings was unprecedented for peacetime. Nor, throughout the entire period of President Roosevelt's leadership, was any amendment made to the written text of the fundamental law, save one [23] which, ironically enough, diminished federal authority by restoring to the states the power to regulate or prohibit the sale and

---

[22] Consult on this point the figures in Table IV, p. 311.
[23] The Twenty-First Amendment, repealing the Eighteenth.

consumption of alcoholic liquors. Central jurisdiction was extended by the simple device—simplification being helped by the effect of the presidential election of 1936 on some judges of the Supreme Court —of elastic interpretations of the interstate commerce and general welfare clauses and such a liberal use of the Marshallian doctrine of "implied powers" [24] that little meaning attaches any more to the Tenth Amendment.

Equally important from the standpoint of the operation of federalism were some political and administrative techniques now adopted more systematically than before. The New Deal inaugurated and bequeathed as its permanent legacy a new era in intergovernmental relations. Previously the federal system somewhat resembled a three-layer cake. There was some thin icing to hold the horizontal layers together, but little else. Most of the work of government was conducted at the appropriate level with little or no reference to either of the other levels. The states did, it is true, exercise some controls over the localities within their midst. But federal-state relations were few and loose, while federal-local relations were non-existent. Since the New Deal the situation has changed almost beyond recognition. Federal-state relations have become ampler and closer. Federal-local relations have been established. Federal-state-local cooperation is now frequent. Much of this is due to the more generous use of a device employed but sparingly before the 1930's—the conditional grant-in-aid. For running the new model federal machine the fuel and lubricant are the financial grants that a government of wider jurisdiction and broader taxing powers allocates—on conditions—to smaller governmental units. The three-layer cake is thus being cut in vertical slices. Various functions (for example, social security or the regulation of agriculture) are nowadays performed by the governments of all three levels acting in unison.

The root-cause underlying these readjustments can now be understood. Whenever government is decentralized, functions must be assigned to the level at which they are most appropriately conducted. How is this "appropriateness" to be gauged? The problem is to work out a relationship between four factors—people, areas, fiscal resources, and governmental services. The ideal would

[24] Formulated in the opinion of the Court in *McCulloch v. Maryland*, 4 Wheat. 316 (1819).

be to create for any governmental service an area in which the residents possess the fiscal resources to maintain the service. Most of the modern modifications of federalism are due to the emergence of social needs for which the political boundaries drawn in an earlier, pre-industrial society are inadequate. If business corporations and trade unions become big, developing a nationwide organization and producing goods that will move across state lines, it is evident that labor relations can no longer remain within the jurisdiction of the states. If a huge metropolis like New York City requires a daily supply of fresh milk of certified quality to be sold at a price that will remunerate producers, processors, and distributors, a governmental solution has to be reached by agreement between the authorities of the city, of the several states whose farms supply the milk, and of the federal government that supervises interstate compacts and regulates farm production. If a river valley, like that of the Tennessee, in a backward region suffers from periodic floods and chronic soil erosion, only an authority that is wider and wealthier than the states and localities concerned can raise their economic and social conditions nearer to the national average. In the modern world, especially in a relatively young country, population is often mobile. New industries can choose the most advantageous among a variety of sites. Cities attract more people and their suburbs expand over the countryside. The social order, the economy, and its human material, are flexible and dynamic. But political boundaries tend to become rigid. A jurisdictional line, once drawn upon a map, is likely as not to be indelible. To eliminate a county or city, once established, is almost impossible. To abolish a state is utterly unthinkable. The structure retains its decentralized form. Powers continue in theory to be distributed as constitutional law would have them. But the modern requirements of the governmental process are knitting the fragments together.

The Military Impact on Federalism. Even these developments on the domestic front, important though they have been, are dwarfed by what has happened on the international front. The two World Wars that occurred in the first half of the twentieth century were such that no major power could remain outside the struggle. On a federal government the effect of participation in an all-out conflict for survival is indeed drastic. War is always a great centralizer. It increases the control of the state over society, since protection and

security become the nation's paramount concern and these are pre-
eminently the responsibility of the state. In addition it concentrates
in the capital city the authority to plan, decide, and execute in order
to promote a speedy and unified direction of military operations.
These statements can best be proven by the evidence contained in
the nation's budget. In 1916 the expenditures of the federal government amounted to $734,000,000. By 1919 the figure had risen to
$18,515,000,000. With the "return to normalcy" under President
Harding by 1922 that amount was cut back to $3,373,000,000. The
same story was repeated in World War II. In 1940, federal expenditures stood at $8,998,000,000. The effort to defeat Germany and
Japan cost the United States, in 1945 alone, the unprecedented sum
of $100,405,000,000, of which over $80,000,000,000 represent appro-
priations for the War and Navy Departments. Victory over the
Fascist powers was again reflected in a reduction of expenditures,
especially for the military services. Thus in 1948 federal expenditures
amounted to under $34,000,000,000. After that year, however, the
strained relations with the Soviet Union and the outbreak in 1950
of Communist aggression in Korea sent the federal budget soaring
once more to the higher altitudes of public finance. By 1952 federal
outlays approximated $80,000,000,000, of which some four-fifths
was directly attributable to the obligations incurred in past wars,
the cost of operations in Korea, aid to friendly foreign governments,
and military preparedness as insurance against a third World War.

When the modern state, therefore, is required to re-emphasize its
original and primary function of protection, the framework of
governmental institutions must be adapted to the performance of
that activity and to the mobilization of the necessary power. Because
of the military need for unified command, co-ordinated plans, and
prompt action, an era that places the accent upon defense is ill-suited
to the maintenance either of checks and balances between branches
or of rights of states vis-à-vis the government of their nation. A
dispersion of powers is incompatible with the troubled politics of a
world that is scarred by past wars and scared of new ones.

The conclusion seems unavoidable that older patterns of decentralization—whether in the form of local autonomy under a
unitary system or of states' rights in a federal union—were doomed
to dissolve in the corrosive acids of twentieth-century politics,
economics, and technology. Virtually all the great driving forces

in modern society combine in a centralist direction. The political urge for equality of rights and greater equality of treatment; the extension of the market, increased standardization of products and the growing uniformity of taste; the quest for social security and economic stability; the tensions of military preparedness and the technology of warfare in an age of jet propulsion and atomic energy—such conditions do not harmonize with separated powers and scattered jurisdictions. Different levels of government can no longer be thought of as independent in their respective spheres. Either one is dependent on another, or they are mutually interdependent. Though great differences in degree still exist, the unmistakable tendency of our century is to integrate and centralize.

CHAPTER 13

FIFTH ISSUE:

(1) THE SIZE OF STATES AND RELATIONS BETWEEN THEM

Territorial Basis of the State. The subject of the preceding chapter carried the discussion across the threshold of a new domain—the effect upon government of the size of the area it controls. This is the last of the five classic issues that give the state its character and politics its problems. Many questions are wrapped up in this issue. How large is the most desirable and practicable unit of government? Can a state be too small or too big to function effectively? What is the loyalty that inspires the people inside the same political boundaries to feel that they belong together? Must a state have a piece of territory that it can guard as its own? Is there any other basis, besides the territorial, for organizing a state? When many states co-exist, what are the relations between them? What is the meaning of international politics, international law, and international organization, and is there anything that can be called international government?

It is the universal rule nowadays that for a state to exist and be recognized as such by other states there must be an area with boundaries defined over which it exercises jurisdiction. Unless this condition is met, there is no state. Some modern examples will illustrate the point. Until 1860 the Papacy ruled a belt of land in the center of Italy running from the west coast to the east. When Italy was unified in 1860-1861, the new kingdom absorbed the Papal States. The Pope retained only the city of Rome, and this too he lost in 1870. In that year the Papacy ceased to be a state, although it did not cease to have political influence. Half a century later, Mussolini and the Pope reached an agreement (the Lateran Treaty of 1929) about church-state relations. As one of its terms a Vatican State was constituted, covering 109 acres in the heart of Rome, which has since received ambassadors from foreign powers and has sent nuncios to their capitals. Because of its temporal juris-diction over this pocket-handkerchief of territory the Papacy was again recognized as a state. Another case in point is the history of Poland. That kingdom, formerly a great power in eastern Europe, was obliterated and partitioned in 1772, 1793, and 1795 by the joint action of Russia, Prussia, and Austria. No Polish state existed until one was re-established in 1919. That state lasted two decades, but again disappeared in 1939 by partition between Germany and the Soviet Union. With the German defeat in 1945 the state of Poland arose once more from the ashes and has been admitted to the United Nations though its boundaries had not, by 1953, been approved by the western powers. A third illustration of the fact that territory is a pre-requisite of the modern state is provided by Israel. The Jewish religion and culture have survived the dispersion of Jews around the world and their persecution for centuries by people of other religions and cultures. There was no Jewish state, however, until 1949 when the partition of Palestine was internationally sanc-tioned by the United Nations and the new state of Israel earned its right to exist by repelling the armed attacks of Arab and Egyptian forces.

What matters, then, is that a state must have some territory to call its own. How much is immaterial. Consequently, states come in all shapes and sizes. At present, the biggest in territorial extent is the Soviet Union, which embraces one-sixth of the land surface of the globe. Luxembourg, however, is also a state and a member of the United Nations although its area is only 999 square miles—smaller than that of Rhode Island. China contains a population that is esti-mated to exceed 460,000,000. At the other extreme lies Iceland, an independent republic since 1944 and a member of the United Nations —but with a population of only 132,000. The contours and contents of the state vary as the accidents of history, geography, and military vicissitudes rough-hew them.

Kinship the Earlier Basis. The truth that the possession of territory is necessary for a modern state invites the initial question whether this has always been so. Is it possible to erect a government upon some other foundation than area? The answer, of course, is yes. In an earlier stage of social development government was generally based upon kinship rather than territory. A political relationship between men was derived from their physical relationship due to common heredity. Authority was thus a by-product of ancestry. Frequently the unit of political organization has been created by the collection of families into larger groupings of tribes or clans. Historical research on this point is confirmed by linguistic evidence. The vocabulary of politics, ancient and modern, contains many terms whose roots come from words that describe human procreation and birth. The Greek *phule*, meaning "tribe," derives from the verb *phuein* (to "bring forth" or "beget") and has the same etymology as "physique." The subdivision of the *phule* called the *phratria* (that is, fraternity or brotherhood) was a clan composed of kinsmen and was used in Athens for political as well as religious functions. Likewise, the *genos*, or "clan," is formed from a root that means "to be born," as is the identical Latin word *gens* which has yielded the terms "genocide" and "gentile," [1] "Nation," in Latin *natio*, is taken from the verb *nasci* "to be born," which has also given us "nature" and "nativity."

Two conditions could make kinship a possible or appropriate basis for governmental organization. Clearly the size of the group must not be too large. The bigger it becomes, the remoter the physical connection must be, until eventually a belief in a common ancestry is more of a fiction and less of a fact.[2] The state has often resembled the family writ larger. But there are certain inherent limits to the elasticity of the family concept. To enlarge it indefinitely is to cease to take it seriously. Besides its appropriateness to a small group, kinship could serve a useful purpose for people who were nomadic. If military or economic reasons compelled men to

---

[1] Also "gentle" and "gentleman"—though any resemblance between these and politics is purely coincidental.

[2] The political mythology of the Greeks, whose name for themselves was Hellenes, contained the belief that they were all descended from one ancestor, Hellen; just as the ancient Hebrews assumed a common descent from Abraham.

be on the move, around what better principle could they unite? For working or warring [3] together the kin-group was a convenient, ready-made, association.

It is understandable, therefore, that, when these conditions no longer applied, political organization would seek some alternative foundation. Men who gave up the life of the gypsy for that of the peasant found in territory an obvious substitute for kinship. The state was then organized around the fact that men were neighbors rather than kinsmen. The land under them became more relevant politically than the genes inside them. The transition from one principle to the other is a familiar chapter in the early history of many peoples.[4] In some instances even the exact events and time of the substitution are known.[5] Few political changes have wrought so revolutionary a transformation of society as this one. Previously, when the state was an extension of the kin-group, there was a direct and immediate link between person and person through kinship. When territory took the place of kin, one person was linked with another by their common relation to land that acted as the intermediary between them. A new factor was thus introduced into the political equation, raising a host of derivative problems. Since land had become the foundation of government, its ownership and distribution brought political results. Political status depended on whether men were owners or tenants or serfs bound to the soil. Control of the land meant control of the men upon it. Property, rank, wealth, and power, found in land a common denominator.

The Optimum Area for the State. Among the most perplexing of the new problems was the question of the land area over which the jurisdiction of the state could extend. The kin-group, for

---

[3] Shakespeare gives a reverse twist to this ancient principle when he makes Henry V say to his army in the eve-of-Agincourt speech:

> We few, we happy few, we band of brothers;
> For he to-day that sheds his blood with me
> Shall be my brother; be he ne'er so vile
> This day shall gentle his condition.
>
> *Henry V*, Act 4, Sc. 3, 60-63

[4] Thus the Romans, whose original popular assembly was the *comitia curiata* (based on the *curia*, a kin-group), set up alongside of it the later *comitia tributa*, an assembly based upon a territorial unit, the *tribus*.

[5] For example, in Athens the constitutional reforms of Cleisthenes in 510 B.C. replaced the *genos* (a kin-group) by the *deme* (a local subdivision) as a unit for governmental purposes.

obvious reasons, did not admit indefinite extension. If a political
association based on kinship sought to incorporate persons of different stock, some formula or fiction such as "adoption" had to be
invented. A state set up on a territorial basis confronted no such
difficulties. Conceivably it might expand by accumulating more
segments of land and thus acquiring control over those who resided
thereon. But there were obstacles that prevented an indefinite
enlargement of terrain. If the area exceeded a certain limit, could its
military defense be ensured? Could it be administered from one
center? Would its inhabitants feel a sense of union? What would
be its relations with other states similarly organized? From that
time was launched the great debate, still raging, over the optimum
unit of government and the appropriate size of the state. During
the course of twenty-eight centuries the western world has experimented with three solutions to this problem and is currently
groping for a fourth. In chronological order these have been the
City-State, Empire-State, and Nation-State; and perhaps, though it
is still incomplete, the Region-State. Ultimately, there is the possibility of having a World-State. But that ideal is far-removed from
today's practicalities. What light is thrown on the nature of
government by each of these attempts and aspirations?

The Greek Polis. The City-State (or *Polis*) was the characteristic unit of political organization in the Mediterranean region from
about the ninth to the third century, B.C. Typically it consisted of a
central urban nucleus and an adjacent rural area. Food production
in the one supplemented commerce, government, the arts, and
military defense, in the other. Its population, like its area, was small,
anything over one hundred thousand being abnormal. The reasons
for a state on this scale are best explained by the obstacles of geography, the scarcity of agricultural land, and difficulties of communication. Practically everywhere in Greece, in central and southern
Italy, in Sicily, along the coastline of modern Turkey, and throughout the islands of the Aegean, the interior was rugged, broken, and
mountainous. Land forms created barriers, rather than a passage,
and offered plentiful opportunities for road-blocks and ambush.
But the sea was a highway, and an open one as long as piracy was
suppressed. Most settlements were, therefore, located on the coast,
wherever there was a usable harbor; or at some defensible strong-
point, slightly inland but connected with a nearby port (for exam-

ple, Athens and Peiraeus, Rome and Ostia).[6] These were conditions that imposed fairly definite limits on the size of the state, the primary considerations being that its inhabitants must receive physical protection and should not exceed their food supply.

But it was impossible continuously to preserve a stable equilibrium. That ideal was precluded by the growth of population because of a high birth rate—even though offset by a high death rate. When the state could no longer contain its numbers, what were the available outlets? One solution was for a section of the citizen-body to depart and found a new settlement, a colony or "home away from home" (*apoikia*) as the Greeks called it. A second venture was to indulge in widespread commerce and search for distant markets and sources of food. Athens and Corinth were examples of states that did both, and became commercial and colonizing powers. This policy, if successful, might bring prosperity, power, and even luxury. But it involved far-off commitments with long sea-lanes to guard and the risk of starvation if those lanes were cut. The third remaining possibility was to expand by warfare and appropriate the resources of another community. To this practice, states were led by population pressure [7] and commercial rivalries, and also by political ambitions.

Anarchy and Imperialism in Classical Greece. The combined effect of military insecurity and inadequate economic resources impelled the city-states to experiment with wider unions. Various methods of enlarging the scope of political organization were accordingly tried. One way was to establish a league of states. This could ostensibly cluster around a common shrine, as the Amphictyonic League joined in the worship of Apollo. Or it could be frankly constituted for defense with some powerful member for its nucleus, like the Boeotian League over which Thebes presided. In these leagues there lay the rudiments of federalism. But the structures never developed sufficient firmness and were weakened or destroyed by rivalries within or blows from without. Another way of broadening the unit of government was for some unusually powerful state to carve an empire for itself, signing up as allies the smaller

---

[6] From this standpoint Sparta and Thebes were exceptional, since they were inland cities that succeeded in making history.

[7] Plato ascribed the cause of war to the need of a growing population for more land to supply the necessary food. *Republic*, bk. II, 373.

fry who accepted protection and imposing its domination on whoever resisted. Virtually all the big states tried in turn to achieve this leadership (the Greeks called it *hegemony*), as opportunity seemed for the moment to smile in their direction. First it was Sparta, then Athens, next Sparta again, then Thebes, and finally Athens once more. None of these efforts succeeded. All collapsed, because even the mightiest states could not forever prevent their unwilling subjects from trying to throw off the yoke, and because the aggrandizement of one super-state conjured up a coalition of rivals. Thus it was Athens that led the opposition to Sparta. Then, when Athenian leadership menaced the autonomy of others, a powerful alliance of Sparta, Corinth, and Thebes was arrayed against her and Greece was torn asunder in the long agony of the Peloponnesian War (431-404 B.C.). With Sparta again predominant, Athens and Thebes joined to restrain her; but when their success was followed by Theban supremacy, Sparta and Athens sided together. The balance of power, as practiced in modern times by giant states, was no mystery to the Lilliputians of those days.

The worst of this situation from the standpoint of the Greeks was that their jealousies and divisions left them a tempting prey to the powers on their periphery. Their traditional foes were the Persians. The Greeks came in conflict with them when the Persian empire, which Cyrus founded, sought in its expansion westward to engulf the Greek settlements along the coast of Asia Minor and these settlements were reinforced by the Greeks further west (for example, by Sparta). The Persians thereupon decided to strike at the heart of the Hellenic world. The expedition they launched in 490 B.C. was repulsed by the Athenians at Marathon. A decade later came the major invasion by strong sea and land forces commanded in person by Xerxes, the Great King. His offensive power was broken in the series of valiant encounters that have made the names of Thermopylae, Salamis, and Plataea immortal. On this occasion the city-states under the joint leadership of Sparta and Athens reached their high point of unity. But as the danger receded, their solidarity soon melted and Persian diplomacy and military power were able again to take advantage of Greek discord. The same tactics were employed with complete success a century and a half later by the astute and unscrupulous Macedonian king, Philip the Great. By the alternate use of strength and cajolery he insinuated

himself into the chaotic politics of the Greek world. Systematically
he extended his influence until, when Athens was finally bestirred
by the oratory of Demosthenes (that is, the "Philippics") to rally
a coalition against him, the hour was too late. The autonomy of the
city-state was extinguished in the battle of Chaeronea (338 B.C.).
When Alexander took over his father's legacy, he confirmed the
position of the Greek states as a dependency of Macedonian power.

Considering the fact that the loss of Greek liberties was directly
due to an inability to combine in a larger political union, one is
astonished that the political philosophies of the two most eminent
Greek thinkers are scaled to fit the small dimensions of the *Polis*.
Though they were familiar with larger formations (for example,
the kingdoms of Persia, Egypt, and Macedon), Plato and Aristotle
wrote a theory of government that treated the *Polis* as the ideal
for size.[8] Well aware of the economic and military reasons for its
limited territory and population, they provided also a philosophical
justification. Unity, they argued, is the greatest political good. A
people will feel united only if they have a sense of belonging
together. They will lack this if there are too many of them, for
they will then lose the spirit of a single community. What is too
large cannot be understood, since it passes the limits of man's comprehension and is therefore no longer orderly or rational. A community, moreover, must be self-sufficient. If too small to maintain
itself (for example, a family or a village) it must be absorbed into
a greater whole. But if too large, its interests become involved in
the well-being and goodwill of others so that it ceases to be strictly
autonomous. Hence the Aristotelian conclusion that the upper limit
in size for an ideal state is to have a citizen body of adult males who
can all be assembled in one spot at one time and hear the voice of
one speaker.

The most interesting thing about this theory is its startling devia-
tion from so many of the recorded facts of Greek history and its
utter impracticality for the times when it was written. If the
Platonic-Aristotelian doctrine was formulated on the right lines,
then most of the city-state politics known to us proceeded on wrong
lines. Nor could the philosophers plead in excuse that their specu-

---

[8] In Aristotle's case this is still more extraordinary in view of his connection with Macedon. His father had served as physician to Philip and he himself
was tutor to Alexander.

lations were dated to an early stage in the development of the *Polis*, for Plato flourished in the first half of the fourth century, B.C., and Aristotle in the second half. Indeed, when Aristotle wrote the *Politics*, the military conquests of his own pupil, Alexander, had once and for all destroyed the independence of the unit of government about which the master, with his eyes in blinkers, continued to philosophize. What is described and evaluated in the *Politics* is an institution, the *Polis*, which was already receding into history because it could no longer ensure physical security and material prosperity. In this instance at least, philosophy's function was to write the postscript to the end of an epoch, thereby for once exemplifying Hegel's remark that "the owl of Minerva takes its flight only when the shades of night are gathering." [9]

The Roman Peace. But in the movement of history the night that closes one era is followed by the dawn of another. The inability of Alexander's successors to hold his conquests intact, and the rivalries of the kingdoms into which his empire was subdivided made the central and eastern Mediterranean a scene for conflict. It was therefore left to the West to produce a power that could accomplish what all others had failed to do—the military subjugation and political consolidation of the entire Mediterranean world. Such in fact was the achievement of Rome. The means employed by this doyen of empire-builders deserve a scrutiny, not merely for antiquarian interest, but because their effects are still being felt today.

The Romans had one method for founding an empire and another for governing it. New possessions, or provinces, they acquired by a blend of military might and judicious bribery. Their soldiering became renowned for its qualities of sturdy courage and dogged tenacity, and the legions, when commanded by a Scipio, a Sulla, or a Caesar, were invincible. In their initial engagements they were likely as not to suffer defeat. But once they had reorganized and discovered a competent general, they demonstrated their happy knack of always winning the last battle. To their subjects the conquerors presented the gift on which they prided themselves most, the Roman peace (*pax Romana*). But this "peace," though eventually it brought order, security and the reign of law, could be a

[9] This is the famous closing sentence in the last paragraph but one of the Preface to his *Philosophy of Right* (1820).

brutal experience whenever its victim was a formidable opponent or a rebellious former-subject. The Roman was a pitiless foe when he played for the high stakes of empire. Nearby rivals like Alba, Veii, and Capua were crushed or destroyed. Carthage was razed to the ground. Corinth was sacked and blotted off the map. Even the famed clemency of Caesar did not spare from death the brave leader of the Gallic uprising, Vercingetorix. The majestic formulae of the Roman law were grounded in a politics of frightfulness (*Schrecklichkeit*) that even a Nazi could admire.

To govern the empire they had gained, however, the Romans used other techniques. Two of these, the development of the *jus gentium* and the gradual extension of the imperial citizenship, were described in an earlier chapter.[10] But some of their other practices should be mentioned here. Once they had cowed a people into submission, they proceeded by degrees to raise them to partnership within the empire. The process was a slow one. For, whether they constructed a road or an aqueduct, a legal code or a civilization, the Romans built for eternity and were not disposed to hurry. Adroitly they would win over the potential leaders of a conquered community (those of them, that is, who had not been sold into slavery or massacred) by conferring favors on men of wealth and the heads of influential families. These then became the clients (*clientes*) of Rome. In return for their privileges, instead of becoming the instigators of local revolt, they cooperated with the imperial authority.[11] Then with the grant of citizenship, the Latins, the Italians, and eventually the inhabitants of the provinces, found themselves sharing in the benefits of the empire as a common enterprise. Why then rebel when the Roman masters had abandoned their exclusiveness and from every province the roads of opportunity could lead to the city on the Tiber?

Besides peace, law, and citizenship, the Romans scattered the seeds of their civilization among the peoples within their jurisdiction. Throughout the provinces by deliberate policy they planted centers from which their culture might spread. For this purpose, the chosen medium was the city—whether this were of ancient foundation and incorporated by Rome as a municipality, or some new

[10] See Chapter 6, pp. 129-31.
[11] This policy is similar to the one successfully followed for many decades by the British in India.

colony of Roman émigrés, or an army camp on the frontier where the legions kept vigil against the "unpacified" and "uncivilized" peoples beyond. Here one might find the schools that taught provincial children the Latin tongue; the central-heated villas of the Roman administrators; their baths; yes, and their circuses. Rich dividends were yielded by this policy of Romanization. Not only did people far afield become assimilated in their thoughts and ways to the pattern of Rome (witness the Latin culture shared in common to this day by France, Italy, and Spain), but talented individuals from the provinces were drawn to the capital or applied their abilities in her service.

This was especially so in the field of literature. Already, in the closing decades of the Republic (from 79 to 49 B.C.), some of the most gifted figures hailed from Italian cities outside of Rome. Thus Cicero, whose spoken and written words converted the cumbrous Latin language into a vehicle for flowing prose, was a native of Arpinum, and the exquisite lyric poet Catullus was born near Verona. In the Augustan age, it was Italy that gave to Rome her Virgil and Horace, as well as two other poets, Ovid and Propertius, and, among prose-writers, the historian Livy. During the so-called Silver Age in the second half of the first century, A.D., an eminent group of Roman literati were Spanish-born—the two Senecas, the rhetorician and critic Quintilian, and the verse-writers Lucan and Martial. In the following two centuries it was North Africa that contributed much of the greatest talent, as the names of Apuleius and Tertullian indicate. Truly the provincials were apt pupils and their sons repaid the debt to Rome in full!

But this process of cultural assimilation, remarkable though it was, succeeded only in the western portion of Rome's dominions. The Latin language and literature were capable of dominating France, Spain, Italy, and North Africa. But they could not oust the Greek tongue from its ascendancy in the eastern Mediterranean. Politically and militarily one, the empire was cut culturally in twain, with the Adriatic serving as the geographical boundary. It was understandable, therefore, that the structure of government would eventually conform to the unalterable facts of social division. The Emperor Diocletian was accordingly responsible (in 286 A.D.) for slicing the empire into two halves and assigning the administration of one half to a colleague. The unity of the whole was later re-

stored by Constantine, who also moved the capital from Rome to the
City of Byzantium which he renamed Constantinople (330 A.D.).
But the empire once more fell apart at the seams and was partitioned
between the sons of Theodosius, after their father's death in
395 A.D.

Limits of the Roman Empire. The truth was that onward from
the third century A.D. the huge sprawling mass of the Roman
empire could only with the greatest difficulty and by an exceptional
man be ruled from one center. This was due to a mixture of circumstances and an accumulation of changes taking place both
inside the boundaries of the empire and beyond. As Rome added
to her possessions and laboriously cemented the political mosaic
of the Mediterranean world, the question was inevitably posed:
Where should this expansion stop? With every new acquisition
Rome lengthened the frontier she had to defend and the lines of
communication from the capital to the perimeter. A permanent
military establishment was required, as legions must be stationed
at the chief danger points, and their loyalty and that of their
commanders created anxiety for no few Emperors. Besides, the
incorporation of more peoples with alien ways imposed further
strain on the absorptive capacity of the Graeco-Roman civilization.
Where would the Roman Eagle find the limit of its cruising radius?

The limits were set at the two extreme points where the force
that Rome could exert was at last matched by the defensive strength
of another people with a resistant culture. One place where this
occurred was in Germany. With the conquest of Gaul (that is,
France) completed, the Romans fanned out across the Rhine, hoping
at one time to make the Elbe their frontier. But the hostility of
leading German tribes, militarily aided by the thick cover of their
forests, was climaxed in the year 9 A.D. when they ambushed and
decimated an army of three legions. Augustus, the Emperor, accepted this verdict and drew back his frontier to the Rhine. The
other point at which distance weakened the striking power of
Rome was in the East where the civilization of Greece confronted
that of Asia. For many centuries the control of the interior highlands of Turkey, of the Arabian desert and the river valleys of the
Tigris and Euphrates, was hotly contested by rival oriental monar-
chies and by occidental invaders. Here in this embattled region,
the cockpit then as now of East-West relations, the Romans retrod

the paths and refought the issues of the Trojan War, the Graeco-Persian Wars, and the campaigns of Alexander. But the legionary, superb infantryman though he was, could not so readily dominate a terrain whose aridity forced men to be mobile and placed a premium on the camel or the horse. When the army of Crassus was cut to shreds by the Parthians [12] at Carrhae (53 B.C.), it was cavalry that won the day. Sometimes with success, but more often not, the Emperors sought to plant the Eagle on the Euphrates, making it the Rhine of the East. Even when that limit was attained, however, the Romans were never able to recreate the union of occident and orient of which for a brief moment Alexander the Great had seen and left a vision. Albeit a titanic achievement, the empire of Rome was not universal. Before the opposition of Germans and Parthians its expansion halted.

Then came the time when the power that Rome could direct outward was exceeded by the pressures upon her from north and east. The reasons for her decline and fall have long been a topic of debate and speculation among historians many of whom have searched for a single root-cause in the general complex of disintegration. To Christian theologians the humbling of Rome was a sign of the wrath of God for the sins of the city. To Gibbon it appeared that Christianity was itself responsible, for by glorifying meekness and pacifism, it was supposed to have weakened the martial nerve of the population. Economists have, of course, pointed to the evidence of economic decay—to the decreasing fertility of the soil, especially in Italy; to the impoverishment of the citizen-farmers and to the chronic shortage of precious metals and ensuing monetary crises; to the huge corps of imperial civil servants and the fiscal difficulties of the exchequer. Add for good measure the political turmoil created by the ambitions of rival generals, who competed for the succession to the Emperorship, and the insecurity and loss of life and treasure when the control of an empire hung periodically on the decision of civil war. So far had internal dry-rot proceeded that when the empire's outer shell was finally cracked in the West (410 A.D.), the inside substance softly crumbled before the hammer blows of Goth and Visigoth and Vandal. Like the city-state of

---

[12] The "Parthian shot" was their celebrated trick of feigning retreat and, when the enemy gave chase, turning around on horseback and firing a last murderous volley into their pursuers.

the fourth century B.C., Rome could no longer provide for its citizens those two essentials of government—security and prosperity. Therefore it had to fall.

The Medieval Dream of Universal Order. Politics are often molded by the survival of a memory. Few examples of this truth are as striking as the almost legendary spell that the name of Rome has never ceased to shed. Long after its collapse in the West, the empire continued to be an influence in politics because of the remembered fact that it had once existed. The feat of uniting the Mediterranean world, of which Rome proved itself capable, inspired a series of would-be imitators; and autocratic rulers with the title of Czar, or Shah, or Kaiser, have proudly taken the name of Caesar.

The first of these attempts was launched by Charlemagne in 800 A.D. Two circumstances had occurred in the three preceding centuries to make his venture feasible and justifiable. In the first place the "barbarians" from the north, falling heirs to the legacy of Graeco-Roman civilization, slowly imbibed its characteristics. As the Romans before them were educated by the Greeks they conquered, so the victorious Franks, Goths, and Lombards became Christianized and partly Romanized, and such cultural assimilation made easier politically the revival of a single empire. A second factor was the stimulus of a new pressure from outside. This was the militant growth of the power of Islam, which rose out of the Arabian desert and turned the flank of Europe by its lightning spread across North Africa. As André Maurois has written: "Mahomet died in 632; by 635, the Moslem armies were at Damascus, in 641 at Alexandria, in 713 at Toledo. In 725 the Arabs pushed up the Rhone Valley as far as Autun. These new conquerors could not be assimilated as the Germans had been. The Franks had admired Rome and adopted Christianity; the Moslems remained faithful to their own ways and religion. At the beginning of the eighth century, they were virtually masters of the Mediterranean. They occupied the whole of Spain, and a portion of southern France." [13]

The Popes of the eighth century were preoccupied with the fear that the Crescent might supplant the Cross. No less concerned were the Kings of the Franks whose dominions were menaced by the advance of the Saracens. An additional reason impelled the eighth-

[13] *Histoire de la France*, Vol. I (New York: Editions de la Maison Française, 1947), p. 41 (my translation).

century Popes to bid for French support. From their north Italian base in the Po Valley the Lombards were spreading south and threatened to take Rome. The Franks, in the rear of the Lombards, were natural allies for the Papacy. First to Charles the Hammer, and later to Charlemagne, the Pope appealed for protection. When Charlemagne by the close of the eighth century had established his supremacy in western Europe, he struck a mutually advantageous bargain with the Pope. Using his temporal power to bolster the Church, in St. Peter's on Christmas day, 800 A.D. he received from Pope Leo III the title, "Emperor of the Romans."

But words and ceremonies, though in politics they have symbolic value, cannot alone perpetuate the realities of empire. His successors were unable to maintain the unity of the territories that Charlemagne had knit together. In 843 his three grandsons divided their patrimony. One obtained the eastern section, comprising portions of Germany. A second received in the west a large slice of France. To the third, Lothair, was given a middle kingdom, following the direction of the Rhine and extending from north Italy to the North Sea. Much of the subsequent history of Europe is related to that division: the separate political development of the French to the west of the Rhine and the Germans to the east, and the struggle between them for the control of the middle kingdom. Once again, however, the idea of a single empire outlived the disappearance of the fact. This time it moved east, cropping up among the Germans whose efficient ruler, Otto the Great, was crowned Emperor by the Pope in 962. Henceforth, for what it was worth, the title of emperor and the claim to universal empire remained with the Germans. Thus was the stage set for the turbulent medieval politics of a German-based empire and an Italian-based Papacy.

To the problems of the size of the state, with which this chapter deals, the Middle Ages contributed an ambitious dream imperfectly realized. The governing concept of the period was that of a universal society permeated with the Christian spirit. Utterly lacking, however, were the means of making the dream come true. The medieval structure, described earlier,[14] was a dual one, with church and state organized to take care of men's spiritual and bodily needs respectively. On the temporal side, the universal society was a pretentious fiction to which the facts bore no resemblance. Because

[14] See Chapter 7, pp. 161 ff.

of the feudal system, localism was the order of the day.[15] Kingdoms were mostly patchwork quilts, where much depended on the personality of the reigning king. Central authority was frequently defied; with difficulty imposed. The Holy Roman Empire embraced a group of German principalities. But its writ did not run in France or Spain, in England or Lombardy. After the collapse of Rome and the turmoil of the Teutonic invasions, the state had suffered fragmentation and its essential functions were as often as not decentralized. Rather than be without shelter amid the perils of a world in flux, men tried to rebuild security and prosperity in small oases of local order.

On the ecclesiastical side, the dream came a few steps nearer to fulfilment. The Roman Church had a centralized authority, a single canon law, a common ritual and theology. As a citizen of Rome in any province could formerly appeal his case to Caesar, so now in matters pertaining to salvation—and they were many—a Christian could make appeal to the Pontiff, who jealously guarded the principle of uniformity. Stern punishment was meted out to heretics. The Albigenses in the southwest of France and the Waldenses in the southeast, who deviated from the Latin rite and challenged Roman authority in the late twelfth and early thirteenth centuries, were fiercely attacked and all but exterminated.[16] Nor was the Church loath to invoke for this purpose the military forces of the temporal sword. Whoever indeed paid more attention to realities than forms could argue that the imperial mantle had fallen on the shoulders of the Pope, not on those of the Holy Roman Emperor.[17] Certainly many a clergyman, in order to associate his church with the symbols of Roman power, talked and acted as if the most important place in the Christian world were not Jerusalem or Bethlehem, but Rome.

The Cracks in Medieval Unity. Yet there precisely was the rub! One reason for such talk and action was the geographical fact that

---

[15] See Chapter 11, pp. 272-3.

[16] It was at this time and in this connection that the Papacy inaugurated the Inquisition that was responsible for many infamous cruelties in the name of religious orthodoxy.

[17] In a later century such a hostile critic as Thomas Hobbes wrote in the *Leviathan:* "And if a man consider the originall of this great Ecclesiasticall Dominion, he will easily perceive, that the Papacy, is no other, than the *Ghost* of the deceased *Romane Empire*, sitting crowned upon the grave thereof." Part IV, chap. 47 (Everyman's Library), p. 381. Italics in original.

Rome lay in the West, whereas the Holy Land belonged to the East. The split of the Roman Empire into two halves, divided by language and having separate administrative capitals in Rome and Constantinople, outlived the social and military breakdown of the western half. In the east a Byzantine empire based on Constantinople continued in existence. Associated with it was the eastern Church, employing a Greek rite, and further differing from the western Church in being a department, rather than a partner, of the State. Situated closer than Rome to Islam, the eastern Church and empire were harder pressed by the upsurge of oriental power. In 637 Jerusalem passed into the hands of the Moslems, though Christian pilgrims were still admitted to the Holy Places. But in 1071 the Turks of the Seljuk dynasty captured the city from their Islamic rivals and forbade entry to Christians—a decision which the Byzantine empire was too enfeebled to alter.

Then was initiated that series of dramatic events which, more than anything else, reveal in its true light and perspective the medieval assumption of a universal society. These were the Crusades. No less than seven of them were launched in the period between 1096 and 1270. The Turkish policy of sealing off Jerusalem provided a pretext and an occasion. To drive the Infidel from the Holy City and recapture it for Christendom was the mission preached by Peter the Hermit, evangelist of the First Crusade (1096-1100). But the motives and objectives were in fact as mixed as the participants. The various French kings who gave their blessing to the enterprise saw an opportunity to extend their influence in the East and there found a Latin kingdom. North Italian merchants, in cities like Venice, welcomed a chance of creating or reviving a trade with the Levant to which Turks and Saracens offered so serious an obstruction. A motley assortment of religious zealots, adventurers, fortune seekers, footloose knights, and romantics, were lured by the glittering prospect of excitement, mystery, and plunder. The Papacy itself was influenced by three-sided calculations. Under the banner of the Cross, raised by the Church militant, the unity of western Europe could be consolidated. A display of occidental strength on the continent of Asia would check the onrush of Islam by penetrating its own domain. Furthermore, the superiority of Rome over Constantinople, of the Latin rite over the Greek rite Church, would be triumphantly asserted if the Christians of the West accomplished what those of the East could not. That this thought was by no means last or least among Papal hopes seems clear from the historical evidence. Certain of the Crusades were as evidently directed against the Byzantine power as against that of the Seljuks, and the fourth one (1202-1204) actually resulted in the temporary establishment of a Latin kingdom in Constantinople!

Perhaps the most remarkable aspect of these expeditions is that so many were sent and that they were prolonged for nearly two centuries. This can prove only one thing—that those who launched and led the Crusades were convinced of their political value. Despite all the difficulties in that period of transporting an army from western Europe to Palestine and supplying it in the field at such a distance from its home base, despite reverses and failures,[18] the organization of Crusades developed into a medieval habit. They must, therefore, have produced a profit that does not appear on the military balance sheet of gain and loss. Nor is that profit hard to discover. It was the kind of gamble that is expressed in the maxim that a divided community should prosecute a vigorous foreign policy. It would be exaggerating to call the Western Europe of that time a happy band of brothers, and the unity to which the Papacy aspired had to be created through subjective loyalties as well as structured institutions. The Papacy hoped this inner consolidation could be achieved by attacking an outer enemy; by hostility, not only to Islam, but also to the eastern church; by a policy of clenching both fists and brandishing both swords, not of turning the other cheek. The medieval Christian society, in short, was not fully unified and was never universal. Christendom itself was split and against it was arrayed the militancy of a rival faith and culture.

Even a series of Crusades, however, could not cement the cracks in the West's foundation-walls or prevent new fissures from opening up. For reasons that have been mentioned in earlier chapters,[19] the structure of the feudal economy and church-state dualism began to sag in the fourteenth century and broke in the fifteenth. The theories of Thomas Aquinas had been predicated upon an ideal of universality and a social hierarchy reinforced by rural conservatism.

[18] For instance, the First Crusade did succeed in taking Jerusalem (1100). But in 1187 the city once more fell into Moslem hands. Recovered in the Fifth Crusade (1228-1229), it passed again to the Turks in 1239.

[19] See Chapter 7, pp. 163 ff., Chapter 8, pp. 179-81.

But between Thomist doctrine and political and economic actualities the gap grew ever wider, until the one bore as little relation to the other as the Aristotelian *Polis* did to the results of Macedonian state-craft. The same fundamental causes that had brought first the city-state and then the Roman empire to its downfall were again operating in the fourteenth and fifteenth centuries. The unit of government, which men had earlier contrived to yield them the necessary mini-mum of security and prosperity, was no longer adequate for its functions. Because of conflicts among the feudal nobility, the rise of urban centers that desired a wider extension of commerce, and the schism and corruption in the Papacy followed by the Protestant Reformation, a new territorial unit had to be organized wherein people could once more feel themselves safe and work to be pros-perous. Nor should one overlook the effects of the invention of gun-powder. Applied to the art of war, it blew the knight in armour to bits, thus lowering the political status associated with his military importance. Shakespeare has a reference to this when he describes "a certain lord, neat, and trimly dress'd," who enraged the battle-weary Hotspur with his foppish manner and elegant chitchat:

> And that it was great pity, so it was,
> This villanous saltpetre should be digg'd
> ·Out of the bowels of the harmless earth,
> Which many a good tall fellow had destroy'd
> So cowardly; and but for these vile guns,
> He would himself have been a soldier.[20]

Similarly the vanished world of the medieval knight-errant and its illusions form the subject of Cervantes' satire in *Don Quixote*. The windmills at which the superannuated knight tilted were cannons and commerce. Under such sponsors western Europe witnessed the start of its third experiment in the search for the state of ideal magnitude.

Birth of the Nation-State. This third attempt, the nation-state, differed from its two predecessors by reason of its intermediate size. In area it was designed to be larger than the city-state, but smaller than the empire-state of the Roman and medieval pattern. Thus did its architects hope to avoid the extremes of a unit that was too little or too large. The new arrangement had the appearance of a

[20] *Henry the Fourth*, First Part, Act I, Sc. 3, ll. 59-64.

compromise. Perhaps this time Europe would strike the happy medium. Here at least was one angle from which the nation-state could be seen and judged.

But something as complex as the nation-state presents many angles. Viewed in time, the nation-state flourished as the dominant unit of government for almost four and a half centuries. Such a statement, of course, contains an element of the arbitrary. One cannot assign precise dates to the beginning or end of a political category, which takes unconscionably long to be delivered or to die. Nevertheless, it is not unreasonable to place the official birthdate of the nation-state in the later decades of the fifteenth century. In 1469, the year of Machiavelli's birth, a marriage between Ferdinand of Aragon and Isabella of Castile sealed the union, and inaugurated the sixteenth-century greatness, of Spain. Martin Luther was born in 1483, and with him a generation that was to commit the irrevocable acts of the Reformation. Two years later, after his victory at Bosworth Field, Henry VII ascended the throne of England. Himself a Lancastrian, he married Elizabeth of York in 1486, thereby founding the strong Tudor dynasty and healing the feud between rival aristocratic clans that had brought upon England the long travail of the Wars of the Roses.[21] And when did the death-throes of the nation-state commence? Probably in 1914, as will be argued in the next chapter, though it is still too early for death to be officially certified.

Viewed in space, the nation-state illustrates a singular combination of politics with geography. All those that were organized earliest and rose to prominence in the sixteenth and seventeenth centuries—Spain, Portugal, England, France, and the Netherlands— were situated on the coast with direct access to the Atlantic. Interestingly enough, however, the initial reasons for the influence of the seaboard states of the West lay in the East. In 1453 the Turks succeeded in a centuries-old dream by the capture of Constantinople and extinction of the Byzantine empire. Thereupon, with complete strategic command of the Mediterranean's Asiatic fringe, they were able to consummate the policy already applied in Jerusalem and elsewhere. Europeans were denied access to the entire region under Turkish-Arabian control. The caravan routes which for over a millennium had given the West its most direct approach to the trade of the East were cut and blocked. A crippling economic blow was

21 See Chapter 9, p. 233.

dealt to such commercial states as Venice, of whom Wordsworth was later to write:

> Once did she hold the gorgeous East in fee;
> And was the safeguard of the West.

Between Europe and India, Islam had stretched its crescent of steel and cordon of sand.

To this challenge the Europeans replied with a search for alternative routes that would bring them around to the rear of the obstructive Moslems. The Portuguese prince, Henry the Navigator, sent out a series of expeditions to chart a course round Africa. Financed by Isabella in 1492 the Genoese captain, Columbus, sailed west and found what he thought were the Indies.[22] Thus was a New World opened up to compensate for the loss of the Old, so that before long the spoils of Mexico and Peru were replacing the treasure of the East. The effect of this geographical reorientation was to give to the English Channel and the Straits of Gibraltar the significance formerly possessed by the Dardanelles and the Isthmus of Suez. The routes that linked Europe to the rest of the world no longer pointed east, but south and west. The great inland sea, the Mediterranean, ceased to be the main artery for traffic. It became instead a side road, for the Oceanic Age had begun. For centuries past, the calculations of political and military strength had been primarily computed in terms of land-power, since the land-locked Mediterranean could be commanded by armies as the Romans, who were certainly no sailors, had demonstrated. Now, however, it was the sea that figured with equal, or in some cases greater, prominence. The peoples who bordered on the Atlantic began to think of the coast as their front door and, when that door was opened, the corridors of a stale diplomacy were freshened with briny breezes. Upon the wave of sea-power the nation-state floated to its destiny. What started, though, as an Atlantic phenomenon did not remain a preserve of the western seaboard. Not the least remarkable aspect of the nation-state has been its capacity to spread. The city-states, after all, were never able to

---

[22] Besides Columbus, the leading men who pioneered the ways to the future were Vasco da Gama, discoverer of the route around the Cape of Good Hope; Pedro Alvares Cabral, who found South America and landed in Brazil; Amerigo Vespucci, who gave his name to America; and Fernão de Magelhães, after whom the Straits of Magellan are called.

extend over much more than the coastal fringe and islands of the Mediterranean. Even the empire-state and medieval Christendom were stopped in their advance. But the nation-state has left scarcely a portion of the world uncovered. Almost the whole of every continent, except Africa, has been subdivided into nation-states. No unit of government previously known to history has achieved so comprehensive a coverage.

How is this fact to be explained? Probably in three ways. The great advantage of sea-power is its mobility. This facilitated the spread of western European influence in Asia and the Americas. Furthermore, the Europeans, when they came into contact with non-Europeans, were in many fields the possessors of demonstrably superior technical skills. Hence the understandable impulse of non-Europeans to borrow from Europe not only its techniques but its political system as well. The third reason is perhaps more subtle. The nation-state seems to operate with a contagious magic on those beyond its borders. The pressure that one people organized around the principle of nationality exerts upon another has often stimulated a rival growth of national feelings. Thus the attempts of English kings to extend their grip on France and secure its throne assisted the birth of French nationhood, of which Joan of Arc in the years 1429-1431 supplied a flaming symbol. The might of Spain in the sixteenth century was challenged by English seamen in duels that ranged across the Atlantic and the Caribbean and even reached into the Pacific. When the Spanish Armada was defeated in 1588, Elizabeth's England experienced that outburst of national élan to which Shakespeare's *Histories* are testimony. The protracted hostilities of Poland and Russia developed in both an ardent patriotism. Napoleonic conquest set spurs to Prussian re-organization and speeded the pan-German aspirations on which Bismarck rode to power. Austrian resistance to Italian unification boomeranged upon the Hapsburgs by giving Mazzini and Cavour a target to attack. Similar events occurred the world over. British rule in India eventually provoked an Indian national sentiment. The action of the United States in forcing Japan to open itself to contact with the world (1853-1854) aroused the rapid reaction of the overthrow of the Shogunate, industrialization of the economy, and the aggressive nationalism that reached its climax in 1941 and 1942. Likewise Japan's own endeavor to subjugate the eastern Asiatic mainland, coming on top of successive encroachments by European powers, added new motive and momentum to China's revolution.

Components of Nationality. These facts raise a number of queries that require explaining. What is there in the components of the nation-state that has both made it an article for export and encouraged the domestic manufacture of a competing product? What makes a community a nation? What makes a nation organize a state? Above all, what is a nation?

A unit of government tends to inspire and reflect a certain feeling among its citizens. If the state is adequate for its function of providing security and prosperity, the feeling will be one of positive loyalty and willing allegiance. This is the subjective side of government, so-called because it includes the emotions and attitudes, the hopes and hates and sympathies, for which men find fulfillment in the political process. Every kind of state, in order to survive, must breed an appropriate patriotism as the counterpart to its institutions. The city-state had to glorify its own achievements, so that a man might take pride in being an Athenian or a Spartan. The empire-state had to inculcate a loyalty to Rome, just as the medieval society sought to unify mankind through acceptance of the Christian creed. The same has been true of the nation-state. The subjective element in this case is the feeling of nationality, which gives a group of human beings the sense of belonging together. When people do feel this way, that is, when they unite around a national symbol, they think and live and act—and, if necessary, die in warfare—not as Athenians or Romans or Christians, but as Americans or Frenchmen or Russians.

Building the American Nation. How do such sentiments arise? What are the conditions of nationhood? From what has just been said, it follows that, if a nation must have a sense of belonging together, anything that a people share in common may help to weld them into a nation. Conversely, anything that divides them can weaken the union. Hence the foundations of nationality are embedded in the structure of society itself. The various associations, through which men combine or compete in their economic, religious, cultural, and other activities, can be politically significant because of their relation to national unity or division. This truth will be evident from some examples. The slavery issue in all its far-reaching implications precipitated a crisis on which the American nation almost broke. "A house divided against itself cannot stand," said Lincoln quoting the Scriptures. "I believe this government," he went on, "cannot endure permanently, half slave and half free. I do not expect the Union to be dissolved,—I do not expect the house to fall; but I do expect it will cease to be divided. It will become all one thing, or all the other." [23] In that instance a social cleavage culminated in civil war because of the powerful interests and passionate feelings arrayed on the two sides, and their near-equality of strength.

Another American case can be cited, however, that also involved the fundamentals of the social system, but was differently settled because a huge majority confronted a small minority. In 1846 the Mormons trekked to the western wilderness to found their own community under the dictates of their church. Yet their Promised Land could not escape the pursuit of the society they had left. When the hour arrived for Utah to be organized as a state, Congress would not confer statehood until the Mormon Church abandoned polygamy. That raises an interesting point. The Constitution certainly gives Congress exclusive authority over the admission of new states. But on the whole question of the family and its place in the social order the document is completely silent. Nevertheless the members of Congress felt that the Constitution assumes, though it does not specify, a marital orthodoxy that frowns upon the practice of one man having more than one wife simultaneously. This government could not endure permanently, part monogamous and part polygamous. It had to become all one thing, or all the other.

Among the social ties that can contribute to national unity, it is customary to include such factors as a common language, common religion, and common race. People who speak the same tongue, worship the same deity in the same way, and belong physically to the same branch of mankind, clearly possess some important points of resemblance and avoid some potential causes of misunderstanding. One of the great marvels in the history of the United States has been its ability to absorb millions of immigrants from many lands and mold their children and grandchildren to a new design. Out of the "melting pot" has flowed the material of an American nationality. What made this result possible? Much of the credit belongs to cer-

[23] From the speech at Springfield, Illinois, on his nomination to the United States Senate, June 17, 1858.

tain provisions of the Constitution that tolerantly permits the practice of any religion, guarantees to individuals the same fundamental rights, and allows for the naturalization and enfranchisement of aliens. These principles were reinforced by the opportunities of an expanding economy and by the conformist tendencies of the public schools that have taught one language and imparted the same basic beliefs to the younger generation.

That is not to say that such a phenomenon as the creation of a new nationality for more than 155,000,000 people could be accomplished without friction and end in complete assimilation. When Catholics were arriving from Ireland in great numbers during the 1840's and after, some Protestants voiced and organized an opposition. When Italian and Slavic immigration increased in the decades between the Civil War and World War I, many qualms were felt by anxious Anglo-Saxons.[24] Divided by religion, Americans have been united by the English language, which for reasons of economic and social necessity became the common medium of expression. Most difficult of all, however, has been the absorption of America's oldest minority, the Negroes,[25] who have been the victims of more persistent discrimination than any other group. In their case the racial difference has outweighed the fact that they are English-speaking Christians. Nevertheless, of recent decades both north and south of the Mason-Dixon Line a slow, but steady progress has been maintained in lessening the gap between the living standards and social status of white and colored.

Nationhood in the British Commonwealth. The American problem of transforming immigrants into nationals may be compared with the experience of countries in the British Commonwealth. Australia and New Zealand have escaped many of the difficulties of the United States because more than ninety-five percent of their European population were drawn from the British Isles. In Australia the Aborigines were too few and too weak to withstand the onset of the newcomers. The sturdy New Zealand Maoris were a match for the colonists in the early days of settlement; but since the 1870's they have been outnumbered, though relations between the races are formally equal. Both countries, of course, while they enjoy the ad-

---

[24] This problem forms a central theme in André Siegfried's *America Comes of Age* (London and Toronto: Jonathan Cape, 1927).

[25] See Gunnar Myrdal, *The American Dilemma* (New York: Harpers, 1944).

vantages of homogeneity, suffer from its defects since their culture
is inevitably lacking in richness and diversity. That this same diversity, however, may spell division, and impede the building of a nation, is the lesson supplied by Canada and South Africa. Though
the population of Canada is one tenth of that of the United States,
Canadianism is a less potent sentiment than Americanism. The reason is that Canada is an addition of two cultures which have not yet
amalgamated. Canadians are divided by language as well as by religion, and the linguistic boundaries largely coincide with the religious.[26] So do the boundary lines of economics, for in industry and
commerce it is the English-speaking Protestants who predominate.
A further obstacle to nationhood is the geographical concentration
of the French-Canadians, since physical separation always assists a
movement towards political separation. American and Canadian
history alike confirm the generalization that the most dangerous way
in which a nation can be internally subdivided is into two nearly
equal parts, territorially distinct. It was the sectional basis of North-
South rivalry that strengthened the secessionist tendencies of the
cotton economy, the plantation system, and the slaveocracy, thus
making the Confederacy seem practicable. Likewise, it is the solidarity of Quebec, a residue of France's *ancien régime* reinforced by a
tenacious Church with long memories, that retards Canadian unity.
Oddly, but truly, as the motto *e pluribus unum* indicates, it is sometimes easier for many to become one, than for two!

If the United States is more unified than Canada, Canada is more
united than South Africa. The bitter discords of the nineteenth century have left in that unhappy country a legacy of frustration and
antagonisms. As in Canada, the European population is divided by
religion, language, and economics, along lines that coincide in each
case and therefore accentuate the differences. What then maintains
their fragile union? One reason is that the speakers of Afrikaans and
English, though the former are mainly rural and the latter mainly
urban, are relatively interspersed. More important, however, is the
pressure on both European groups to combine in the face of an
African majority outnumbering them by four to one. The color
bar thus counts in the balance for more than everything else put

---

[26] A bridge between the British and the French is sometimes provided by
the small minority of English-speaking Irish Catholics, whose religion draws
them to one side and whose language attracts them to the other.

together. Even so, it is dubious whether one can talk accurately about a South African nation. The most one may assert is that such unity as exists is for whites only and its cement is fear.

The Problem in Europe, (1) The Effects of Cultural Division. Among the nation-states of Europe the problem of race relations is non-existent. But religion and language and the other aspects of culture have served as cutting teeth to shape the pieces of a continental jigsaw puzzle. There are on the continent three principal cultures— Latin, Germanic, and Slavic. With the exceptions of Switzerland and Belgium (the latter being a less successful union than the former) no nation-state has been compounded of Latin and Germanic elements. Similarly, in east-central Europe no nationality has ever been formed out of a Latin-Slavic blend, save in the case of Poland and possibly Yugoslavia. For, though the Poles are a Slavic people, their church until recently was linked with Rome; and in Yugoslavia, if that country can yet be considered to have achieved national unity, the Croats are Latinized and Catholic, while the Serbs are Slavs and follow the Greek rite. A fusion of Germanic and Slavic people into one nation has been even harder to accomplish. The only state that had both the chance and motive to do this, namely Austria, was unequal to its opportunity. The Austrians organized their government upon the principle of German ascendancy, and, in contrast with the Roman policy, admitted none but the Hungarian Magyars to the charmed circles of influence. Slavs were not welcomed as partners in the citadels of power.

The case of Austria is particularly interesting for the light it throws on certain problems of the nation-state in Europe. The empire of the Hapsburgs in east-central Europe originated and continued to exist for many centuries because it appeared to serve a useful purpose. It was the bulwark that kept the Ottoman empire out of central Europe. The Slavs were the subject of a squeeze, and to the extent that they could act for themselves, might choose between a Hapsburg Emperor or a Turkish Sultan. Both alternatives left much to be desired. The odds were by no means always in the favor of Austria whose political stupidities were a fair match for Turkish cruelties. Indeed the Balkan Christians of the eastern Orthodox Church were at times more tolerantly treated by the Caliphate than they were by the Papacy. But to those who thought and felt in terms of a conflict between Europe and Asia, Austria could at least claim to be Europe's champion. Even so, the appeal of Vienna to the Slavs fluctuated in inverse ratio with the strength of the Turks. When Ottoman power was expanding, Vienna might seem the lesser evil. But when the Turks were in a decline, as in the nineteenth century, the Austrian empire lost its *raison d'être* and the Balkan peoples were disposed to say: "A plague on both your houses!" Then came the opportunity that Austria missed. If she were to avoid a series of wars of independence, she must unite her multi-national empire around a comprehensive loyalty and, as Rome had done, turn subjects into partners. This would involve either decentralization of government from Vienna and the grant of more power to Hungarians, Czechs, and other peoples, or a sharing of authority at the imperial capital itself. The former solution was applied only in the case of Hungary. The latter, which meant, of course, a representative legislature and the abandonment of autocracy, implied also the sacrifice of German leadership. To Metternich and his successors, and to the unteachable Hapsburgs, the full consequences of both policies were unthinkable. Hence, amid the babel of national aspirations that intransigeance provoked, the Austrian autocracy in step with the melodies of Johann Strauss waltzed to its own destruction.

The dilemma of the Austrians, caught between their desire for German superiority and the demands of a multi-national population for equality, can be seen from another perspective. It is a chapter in the story of the national consolidation of two neighbor states, Germany and Italy. At first glance it is a puzzling fact that these countries were not unified until some four centuries later than Spain, France, and England, and their unification, when it did finally occur, took place in the same decade (1860-1871). The reasons can be discovered, however, in the policies of Austria and the Papacy and the relationship between them, the roots of which reach down to the Middle Ages. The attempt to organize western Christendom under the Holy Roman Empire and the Papacy was formulated in terms of a universal society. In fact, however, the Papacy was based upon Italy, a portion of which the Popes governed as temporal sovereigns, while the Empire acquired a German base. Even when Pope and Emperor cooperated, it was not in either's interest to permit the other to consolidate his jurisdiction over Germany or Italy respectively. If Italy remained divided, the Pope's position was more precarious and he was less able to dominate the Emperor. If the

Empire was a loose and tenuous union, the Emperor was less likely to control the Pope. Each must therefore support a balance of powers, and prevent a concentration of power, in the other's terrain.

As the Reformation sapped at the foundations of Catholicism by breaking the unity of western Christendom, so did the emergence of the nation-state present a challenge to the Empire by negating its claims to universalism. Not until the conclusion of the Thirty Years' War (1648) were the division of western Christendom and the system of nation-states definitively accepted as irrevocable features of Europe's political order. Both Papacy and Empire in the eighteenth century steered against the prevailing wind and current with just enough power to keep themselves at a standstill. But, in the century that followed, the dominant forces operating within society were those of industrialism, laissez-faire economics, liberal democracy, and a latter-day nationalism that, because belated, was more intense. Against all these movements Empire and Papacy set themselves in opposition; and, being on the defensive and compelled to retreat, found themselves allies in a last-ditch resistance.

Neither Germany nor Italy could be unified except by defying both the Hapsburgs and the Pope. Metternich had condemned the union of all Germans in a single state as "an infamous object." Those who thought in Pan-German terms hoped to include Austria in a German state, but wanted to exclude her non-German subjects. For her part, Austria was unwilling to pay for admission into an all-German state the price of losing her empire; and until the middle of the nineteenth century, while unwilling to unify Germany herself, she was strong enough to prevent anybody else from doing so. A similar situation existed in Italy, of which Austria controlled the northeast. To unify Italy meant the defeat and expulsion of the Austrians. Metternich had declared that Italy was only a geographical expression and he intended to keep it so. The other obvious loser in any Italian unification was the Papacy that would have to surrender its temporal rule over the center of the peninsula. Consequently, when the kingdom of Italy was established in 1860, and when Bismarck's Prussia (Protestant-led) did organize the German Reich in 1871, it was nationalism in both cases that triumphed over a multinational Empire and a supra-national Church.

(2) *The Religious Cleavage*. If it has proven difficult in Europe to create a nationality out of mixed cultures, it has been no less diffi-

cult with mixed religions. The most successful nation-states have been those that contained a big majority of either Protestants or Catholics. The oldest powerful nation-states are witnesses to this truth. In Britain the Protestant Reformation triumphed—and though England could amalgamate with Wales and Scotland, she was never able to absorb the Catholic portion of Ireland. In France and Spain the Catholic Counter-Reformation triumphed. Thus in all three countries nationalism in its early phase was associated with religious intolerance. Only in exceptional cases and under great difficulty has a nation been formed with a blend of Protestants and Catholics in relatively equal strength. On this point the example of Switzerland is instructive. Because of the work of Zwingli in Zurich and of Calvin in Geneva, portions of Switzerland became a Protestant stronghold. Because, however, of its geographical proximity to France, Austria, south Germany, and north Italy, the Swiss were strategically important to the Papacy and the Jesuit Order attempted to recapture their allegiance. In 1847 it was a minority of Catholic cantons that seceded—without success; so that in 1848 it was a Protestant majority who wrote the new federal constitution—which incidentally banned the Jesuits from Switzerland.[27] But though religion has severely split the Swiss, and though they are, of course, divided by language into French, German, and Italian sections, they are able to hold together because the religious and linguistic divisions cut right across each other. While Geneva is French-speaking and Calvinist, Neuchatel and Fribourg are French-speaking and Catholic. While Bern and Zurich are German-speaking and Protestant, Luzern and Glarus and Schwyz are German-speaking and Papist. In this respect the Swiss are more fortunate than the Canadians.

Even this fact, however, would not account for the miracle of Swiss nationhood if there were not also an additional reason. Instead of preferring incorporation into France, Germany, Austria, or Italy, the Swiss have chosen to become Swiss because of their reaction to the pressures of surrounding big powers and because of a geography that has made defense and independence militarily practicable. Furthermore, the survival of their state has been guaranteed by the integrity of their policy of permanent neutrality. The Swiss, therefore, illustrate a point discussed earlier, that a nationality is often a response to a pressure exerted from without. But they illustrate

[27] *Constitution of the Swiss Confederation*, Article 51.

something else. When one is analyzing the nation-state, it is appropriate to ask whether the nation helps create the state or the state helps create the nation. The answer is that examples occur of both, which proves that, while a nation may be molded out of social factors, it can originate in politics as well. Switzerland is an example of a state being organized first, and a national sentiment developing second. So is the United States, where the foundation of a federal government in large part preceded and then promoted the ripening of an American nationality. In other words, living under the same system of government and the tradition that the system acquires with the lapses of generations—all this is something that a people do share in common and that may, therefore, stimulate their sense of belonging together. Thus it is not only the English language, the monogamous family, and the abolition of slavery that have contributed to an American nation, but also the common pride and respect inspired by the Declaration and the Constitution and by such names as Franklin, Washington, Jefferson, and Lincoln.

Conversely, a group that already feels a national unity because of a common language, literature, and religion, may eventually develop such cohesive political force as to found a state. Witness the modern instances of Poland, Czechoslovakia, and Israel. This is especially likely to happen to a minority group who are governed by a repressive majority of different language or religion. Where the government is thus monopolized by an intolerant majority, the minority, unable to share in politics as equals, clings to other associations than the state, seeking through these a medium for its own representation. Often this role has been assumed by religion that has supplied a structure and a voice for a group that felt itself suppressed. Thus the Roman Catholic Church traditionally assisted the nationalism of the Poles and their resistance to the Czarist program of Russification. The same church provided the Irish with a vehicle of opposition to the British and has been the mainstay of the French-Canadians. Jewish synagogues, transmitting the *Torah* from one generation to the next, kept a Hebraic culture alive among a people sorely persecuted in their dispersion. On the island of Cyprus the Greek Church has led the agitation against British colonial rule and espoused the demands for the accession of Cyprus to Greece; just as in Burma the Buddhist priesthood, at odds with Britain on educational policy, lent their support to the independence movement.

Similarly on the South African veld the Dutch Reformed Church has represented the fierce nationalism of the Afrikaner extremists.

Nationalism and the Arts. As a substitute for religion, or to supplement it, an emergent nationalism, excluded from the government of the state, may find its outlet in the arts (especially music and literature) and in higher education. Thus nationalistic Poles have sung their folk-songs and played—and played up—Chopin. The Czech renaissance was aesthetically expressed by Smetana and Dvorak. The "blood and iron" of Bismarck's Reich was rendered into appropriate music by the pompous Wagner, who was understandably a favorite of Hitler. The significance to nationalism of the arts lies in their appeal to the intelligentsia, who have been the prime movers in modern national uprisings. This further explains the interest of nationalists in the field of education, in fostering their own language and in organizing institutions of higher learning. Hence the importance of Charles University in Prague to the Czechs; of the Hebrew University to the Zionists; of the University of Cairo to the Egyptians. Hence the well-known phenomenon of an ardent nationalism and political activity on its behalf, among the university students of so many lands. Hence the insistence of nation-builders on reviving their ancestral tongue—as Hebrew became again a living language in Palestine, and as the government of Eire officially adopted Erse while brilliant Irish literati like Shaw, Joyce, O'Faolain, and Yeats were writing in matchless English! [28]

The interaction that has so often occurred between national feeling and cultural achievement is an important and significant fact. The foundations of the state may be embedded in the material needs of safety and prosperity. But while it is essential that these needs be satisfied, they do not alone complete the development of man or fulfill his every aspiration. Political organization, which serves our creature comforts and is the guardian of life itself, can also minister to the spirit. When a governmental system imbues a people collectively with self-respect and happiness and strength, the most gifted individuals in the group may be stimulated by the surrounding élan to creative production in literature, philosophy, the sciences, and the arts. Thus it is that great luminaries have often shone with intellectual and aesthetic brilliance in the very century when a people

---

[28] Shaw himself was the first to admit that his own work was as good as Shakespeare's.

attained politically "their finest hour." It was hardly an accident
that the most glorious period of Athenian culture was contempo-
raneous with the rise of Athenian power to its zenith after the heroic
combat against the Persians; that the golden age in Roman literature coincided with the establishment of the Augustan peace; that
the thirteenth century, which witnessed so fine a flowering of medieval genius, saw the Papacy at the height of its ascendancy under
Innocent III and his successors; and that the reigns of Elizabeth I
and Victoria, which represent the high-watermarks of Britain's
political influence, presided over some of the most notable of her
achievements of the mind. With each unit of government, therefore
—with city-state, empire-state, and nation-state—examples can be
found of a correlation between political success and cultural greatness.[29]

   That the love of one's country has often provided an inspirational
focus for rare creative work is evidence of the capacity of the
nation-state to serve humanity well. Countless are the poets, writers,
musicians, painters, scientists, and scholars who have been stirred
by national pride to activity of intellectual or imaginative eminence.
Such an emotion has offered to many a sensitive spirit an attraction
that is not to be equated with the crudities of jingoism. On that note
of appreciation, before the analysis turns to consider the pathology
of nationalism and the decline of nation-states, let this chapter end.

   [29] The two are not always correlated, however, for example, the Italian
Renaissance, despite Machiavelli's pleadings, did not produce a political record
that matched the artistic output.

CHAPTER 14

FIFTH ISSUE:

(2) NATION-STATES AND INTERNATIONAL ORDER

The Crisis of the Nation-State. There is no unit of government that has conformed with consistency to its own ideal. The system of classical Greece, with its principle of autonomy for each urban-rural cluster, negated the possibility of wider union either through a free combination of states or through imperial subjection to one. Efforts of the former kind were not long enduring; and efforts of the latter description, though repeatedly made, provoked opposition and war. Rome, which commenced its political history as a city-state like the rest, was the one which did succeed in the policy of imperial conquest, thereby eliminating the city-state as an independent unit and substituting for it the new unit of a widespread empire. But even Rome could not command the world,[1] and the unity and peace that were her ideals arrived at their bounds to the north and east. A similar story was repeated in the Middle Ages, when the dream of a universal order was pursued by Papacy and Holy Roman Empire alike. In practice, however, neither in the secular sphere nor the spiritual was universality achieved. Each of these three experiments was an endeavour to provide a structure within which men could build their welfare in safety. Each lasted for as long as it was able to fulfill that need, and collapsed when it could no longer do so.

In this respect, the history of the nation-state is identical with that of its predecessors. The nation-state emerged at a time when

---

[1] The concept of expansion from a city to the world (*ab urbe ad orbem*) was a rhetorical flourish, never a political reality.

it was more capable than the medieval system of supplying humanity with security and well-being. But this unit of government, like the rest, has failed to apply its own ideal, with the result that it is now decaying or even dying. Our contemporary world is in the throes of a major transition from the out-moded nation-state to some new unit. Thus, seen in historical perspective, the age in which we live is comparable to the readjustment that occurred between the break-down of the *Polis* and the rise of the Roman Empire, or between the fall of Rome and the emergence of the medieval order, or be-tween the collapse of the latter and the founding of the nation-state. Once again, a fresh attempt is being made to discover the territorial unit best adapted under twentieth-century conditions to furnish men with their basic political needs. Since modern internationalism, however, is a reaction to the declining adequacy of nationalism, the threads of the discussion must be picked up at the point where the last chapter left off. What failings has the nation-state revealed? Is there a superior alternative in sight?

Despite the strivings of states to build nations and of nations to organize states, a perfect correspondence has not been everywhere achieved between nationality and statehood. The world still abounds with instances of people united by a common culture, language, and religion, who are striving toward a national consciousness and seek-ing to formalize it in a state of their own. Such aspirations are es-pecially noticeable nowadays in the colonial dependencies of impe-rial powers. Conversely, there are cases aplenty of states that have continued to include in their jurisdiction a subject people who are unincorporated in the national body politics. In some countries those subjects are a minority; in others, South Africa, for example, they are the majority. These are facts that require an explanation. If the nation-state was in vogue and set the fashion for over four centuries, why has there been so imperfect a correlation between statehood and nationality?

Imperialism and Sea Power. The answer—which is a product partly of historical timing and partly of economic and military fac-tors combining in a political result—is most revealing. It must not be forgotten that, when the nation-state was born, there came simul-taneously into the world its twin—sea-powered imperialism. How inseparably these were connected is plainly written in the annals of Spain, Portugal, England, France, and the Netherlands. Of course, the practice of imperialism, which can be defined as the forcible subjection of a community to alien rule, was no novelty. Nor was the employment of sea-power, as the Athenians, Phoenicians, Norsemen, and Venetians, may bear witness. What was new, however, was the expansion of political power upon an oceanic scale. The discovery that the earth was round and could be circumnavigated was quickly put to a use that challenged comparison with Rome. The peoples of western Europe first mapped the world; then with gunpowder, galleons, and gumption, they partitioned it.

The result inevitably was a succession of struggles for maritime supremacy, for colonial acquisition, and for the wealth to be gained thereby. The first pair of competitors were Spain and Portugal. Between their claims Pope Alexander VI arbitrated in 1493, so that by his award and the Treaty of Tordesillas in 1494 the ownership of the non-European world was divided. To Spain was assigned the exclusive possession of all that lay more than 1110 miles to the west of Cape Verde; to Portugal, all that lay east. Such an award was no more acceptable to Catholic France than to Protestant England, both of which had ambitions of their own. When the might of Spain was humbled by the English victory over the Armada and the Dutch had successfully fought for independence, the Atlantic seaways were open to a new round of contestants. Neither France nor England could take full advantage of its opportunity until internal disunion was overcome. This was achieved in the seventeenth century by the triumph of Catholicism and absolute monarchy in one country, of Protestantism and Parliament in the other. The two powers were then ready to inaugurate their second Hundred Years' War over wider battlefields on sea and land. The epoch that opened with England's resistance under Marlborough [2] to the aims of Louis XIV closed with Napoleon's downfall at Waterloo. In between, there occurred the colonial rivalry, extending long and far, wherein France during the Seven Years' War (1756-1763) bowed to the British in India and North America, but secured a partial revenge by aiding the United States in the War of Independence. To the latter setback Britain resiliently responded, both by speeding up the technological revolution of her industries in the struggle against Napoleon and by reorganizing her empire on the principle of self-

[2] John Churchill, first Duke of Marlborough, victor of the battles of Blenheim (1704) and Ramillies (1706) was the ancestor of Winston Churchill.

government for the component parts as they matured.[3] Thus, with her nearest military rivals worsted or enfeebled, Britain pre-empted the nineteenth century.

Secure in the assets of a factory system whose productivity then led the world and of a navy and merchant marine predominant in every ocean, the peoples of a small island off the coast of Europe constructed and commanded an empire that by 1914 covered one-fourth of the land surface of the globe and one-fourth of its population. In this climatic episode, sea-power, the progenitor of the nation-state, had reached the ultimate. To make it all possible, the varied talents of an ebullient age contributed their quotas—Victoria, the queenly symbol; Palmerston, the swashbuckling spirit; Disraeli, his imagination and brains; the City of London, the financial sinews; Kipling, the ballads; and Gladstone, the outraged liberal conscience in self-rebuke for the sins it did not prevent.

Contradictions of Sovereignty. The success of imperialism, however, and its duration for four centuries, involved the nation-state in a fundamental inconsistency. Depending on the angle from which it is viewed, this unit of government can be considered the opposite of either localism or internationalism. Both of the latter principles were characteristic of the medieval period, one receiving theoretical [4] lip-service and the other reflecting more accurately the realities of social organization. Since the nation-state marked a rejection of the system immediately preceding, neither local nor international influence was tolerable to its architects. The centralizing tendency of the nation-state, drawing powers and functions from the localities to the capital, was described in a previous chapter.[5] Now is the place to discuss the international relations of nationalism.

As in other respects, the doctrine that was the maid-of-all-work for the nation-state—the theory of sovereignty—here, too, was enlisted into service. Sovereignty was construed to mean that the government of the nation-state, supreme within its own jurisdiction over local bodies and churches, acknowledged no political or legal superior beyond its territorial boundaries. "My dogs," as Queen

---

[3] This principle was first officially recommended for Canada in Lord Durham's Report (1839) and applied in that country in 1846-1847.

[4] Except in the ecclesiastical sphere, where the international force of the church was more than theoretical.

[5] See Chapter 11, pp. 273-4.

Elizabeth I of England once phrased it, "shall wear no collars but mine own." Authority, allegiance, and law, were to be the exclusive monopoly of the nation-state, and, as such, were not articles for import across national frontiers. Were they, however, articles for export? There precisely lay the inconsistency. The nation-state, whatever its professions, acted upon a double standard. Both in external and internal affairs it claimed to be a law unto itself. Limitations upon its freedom of action diminished its sovereignty and consequently were inadmissible. But, though unwilling to submit to control from outside, it professed to see no wrong in subjecting others to its will. The practice of imperialism violated the principle of sovereignty by denying to others the very freedom on which the nationalist insisted. In effect, throughout the entire era of the nation-state, there never was a time when the political ordering of mankind conformed consistently to the idea of having a number of separate units of government, each self-contained. Imperialism meant a division of the human race into élite peoples who ruled, and whose nationality could find outlets for expression, and subject peoples whose national aspirations must be suppressed. Hence imperialism negated the first premise from which the nation-state proceeded. Therefore it is no accident that the twins, which were born together and have lived in perennial conflict, in this century are dying together.

This combination of nationalism with imperialism and the ensuing dilemma produced an economic counterpart. During the sixteenth, seventeenth, and eighteenth centuries—that is, before the philosophy of laissez faire became prevalent—prosperity was sought by methods that exactly applied political concepts to economics. The politics of nationalism were matched by the economics of nationalism, which was the essence of the mercantile system;[6] and, correspondingly, political imperialism was yoked to economic imperialism. Colonies, considered the "possessions" of the imperial power, were organized to supply it with raw materials and precious metals, as they were also to import its manufactures and carry on their commerce in its ships. This is not to deny that additional motives influenced the settlement or acquisition of colonies. The desire of dissident minorities to emigrate; the strategic quest for bases, ports of call, and defensible frontiers; the work of missionaries who preached the

[6] See Chapter 8, pp. 179-81.

Christian gospel—many a magnet, besides trade, attracted nations to plant their flag on distant shores. But that the single most important factor in empire-building was the economic, can hardly be denied. Through imperialism the nation-state could grow more prosperous—or so it was hoped.

From the standpoint of security an empire might be judged as much of a liability as an asset. It was true that the treasure which some colonies yielded could be used to build more warships and pay more troops that would then defend the mother-country and also keep subjects more surely in subjection. But, situated across the oceans, colonies were remote and exposed. They might prove hard to defend against an invading rival or to hold against a rebellion. Furthermore, when the imperial power was itself in danger of attack on its home terrain, less force could be spared for garrisons abroad. By spreading its resources thin, the imperialist nation-state held out many hostages to fortune. It was therefore vulnerable to either amputation at the extremities or attack at the heart. The latter alternative was, of course, the primary concern of nation-statesmen, since colonies were of no avail if the motherland were insecure. Hence in every case the organization of the nation-state passed through a phase of expansion and consolidation, wherein the purpose was to arrive, if possible, at a defensible frontier. Let us observe what happened and the consequences.

The United Kingdom, as Great Britain is officially called, was created in a series of absorptions and additions. England, itself a fusion of smaller and previously separate kingdoms, provided the nucleus for a larger union. Amalgamation with Wales was achieved in 1284. Scotland and Ireland, being larger than Wales and less easily accessible, presented more formidable problems. But their independence posed a threat to England since a continental enemy like France could form an alliance with the Scots or Irish and threaten England from the flank or rear. An island has an obvious frontier in its coastline. The union of England and Scotland, facilitated by the triumph of Protestantism both north and south of the border, was formally effected in 1707. "John Bull's other island," [7] whose proximity made it strategically vital, could be conquered, but largely because of religious differences could not be absorbed. All that remained thereafter was for Britain to control the seas

[7] The title of a play set in Ireland by G. B. Shaw.

around her coasts and prevent any one power from dominating the European mainland. If this was done, her security was assured. The same problem confronted the continental nation-states, but with an important difference. They had a land- as well as a sea-frontier to defend. Besides navies, therefore, they had to maintain standing armies that affected their internal politics, tending to reinforce the authoritarian structure of their government. Armies, more easily than navies, could reach the heart of an enemy state, as Napoleon was able to cross the Pyrenees but not the Channel, and as Frenchmen and Germans have been moving in and out of each other's territories for centuries.

The military conditions that geography imposes go a long way toward explaining why it was Britain and not any of her rivals that in the nineteenth century emerged as the highest-ranking power. But in that century new factors intervened which in the short run enhanced the might of Britain, yet in the long run have contributed both to her decline and to that of the nation-state system. The intruding element was the technology of industrialism and the economic potentialities thus unleashed. Its immediate effect was to create a productive capacity that exceeded the needs and the resources of the nation-state. Britain had always had a foreign trade. But now in volume and extent this trade grew to unprecedented proportions. The terrain that the nation occupied did not yield all the raw materials that manufacturers required. Nor did its population offer a market sufficient to consume their output. More than before, the prosperity of peoples became interdependent.[8] If somewhere in the world there occurred a curtailment of production or a decline of purchasing power, a fall in the prevailing price of a commodity or its replacement by a substitute, other economies thousands of miles away were intimately affected.

Anarchy Among Nations. The nation-state was now hopelessly caught in a tangle of contradictions. As if it were not already difficult enough to make the boundaries of state and nation co-extensive, it now became abundantly plain that the territorial unit chosen for military purposes was completely at variance with the area appropriate to economics. Protection was organized to run along national

---

[8] The British adoption of free trade in the 1840's was a frank recognition of this fact.

lines; prosperity, to run across them. The task of organizing a unit wherein the needs of nationality, security, and prosperity would harmoniously coincide was well-nigh impossible, and the situation was rendered more chaotic by the competition between states for the same objectives. An area that a state considered strategically necessary for its own protection might be inhabited by people whom its neighbor regarded as belonging to its own nationality. Valuable economic resources that lay in the borderland between two states would be sought by both. Thus Alsace-Lorraine, the Low Countries, the Brenner Pass and the Trentino, Bohemia, the Polish Corridor, Suez and Panama, all these and others became foci for international rivalries and scenes of conflict.

Under such circumstances, it is not surprising that the nation-state became less and less capable of providing for the minimal needs of protection and order. Even at its best, though it maintained order within its own territory and minimized, without eliminating, the possibility of civil war, it could not guarantee that international relations would be peacefully conducted. The very doctrine of sovereignty meant juxtaposing internal stability with external anarchy. In all essentials, therefore, the history of the nation-state merely repeated (with a change of scale, because the unit was larger) the earlier experience of the city-state. International relations were like inter-*polis* relations, and the old drama was re-enacted in modern dress. Nation-states, like city-states before them, were small, medium-sized, or big. If small, their only chances of survival was to accept protection from the biggest power nearby, or, if they lay between rival powers, to announce their neutrality and trust it would be respected. Medium-sized states could also serve as buffers to keep their larger neighbors from one other's throats. They might, however, be induced to enter into systems of alliances since their support or opposition could have some effect on the balance of power. Their riskiest policy, of course, was to be afflicted with delusions of grandeur and dress in big power costume without having the chest to fill it, as has been true of Italy.

The major states themselves took up the script where Athens, Corinth, Sparta, and Thebes left off. Each in turn strove for leadership. Each was destined to strut and fret its hour upon the stage—Spain, Austria, France, Britain, and Germany. All had their periods of ascendancy. None could perpetuate its domination, because new challengers arose against every champion. The net result was that throughout a period of more than four centuries the nation-state system was incapable of securing a lasting peace. Major convulsions recurred with frightening regularity—the Thirty Years' War (1618-1648), the War of the League of Augsburg (1688-1697), the War of the Spanish Succession (1701-1713), the Wars of the French Revolution (1793-1815), World War I (1914-1918), and World War II (1939-1945). These were interspersed with more limited conflicts, so that scarcely a decade went by without an outbreak of hostilities somewhere. Indeed, the history of any important country contains testimony to prove that the establishment of a nation-state gives no assurance that its citizens will escape the horrors of war. For example, during the one and three-quarter centuries that have elapsed since 1776, the United States has engaged in four major wars (1776-1783, 1861-1865, 1917-1918, 1941-1945) and four minor ones [9] (1812-1815, 1846-1848, 1898, 1950-1953), so that its peace has been broken on an average every twenty-two years.

The Consolidation of Land-Masses. The perennial anarchy of the nation-state system, and the discordance between national politics and international economics were not the only reasons for the ending of an era. Another significant factor was the declining effectiveness of seapower. By the end of the nineteenth century the peoples on the Atlantic seaboard of Europe were losing the monopoly of advantages that had so long been theirs. It was to the east of them and to the west that fresh opportunities for expansion were being discovered. The new goal was to consolidate the continental land masses under the jurisdiction of a single state. Three attempts of this kind were made. The first was launched by Germany. The marriage of the Prussian army with the industries of the Ruhr and Rhineland created a formidable power in the north-center of Europe. From this base, with a strategy formulated in terms of land-domination, the efficient and ruthless German *Reich* set out to unify the continent. Twice its leaders tried to do this in wars they welcomed and instigated. Twice their efforts were beaten, but at a dreadful cost. France was plunged into a decline from which she has never recovered.

---

[9] This distinction means that victory in a major war requires the mobilization of a people's entire resources in order to survive, while a minor war will take only a limited effort to win and does not involve a danger to survival.

Britain survived, though gravely weakened because she was forced to expend much of the reserve wealth accumulated during the nineteenth century. Since Germany with its central position enjoyed the advantage of interior lines, she could be defeated only by encirclement. Thus the Atlantic nations perforce were allied with the autocracy of the Czar in World War I and with that of Stalin in World War II. Even the western front could not be maintained by Britain and France alone, who in both wars relied on American participation to push back the common foe. Europe's loss of power in contemporary world affairs is the price paid by an entire continent for the necessity of curbing the Germans.

The other two attempts have had different results. From its birthplace on the Atlantic seaboard the United States expanded westward to the Pacific, spreading the Constitution and applying the principles of representative government over an area three million miles square. Simultaneously, Czarist Russia fanned out eastward along the northern part of Asia, incorporating Siberia in its dominion and even crossing the Bering Strait into Alaska. The phenomenon of states like these that filled a continent was noted by de Tocqueville, who in 1835 made this prophetic comment:

> There are, at the present time, two great nations in the world which seem to tend toward the same end, although they started from different points: I allude to the Russians and the Americans. Both of them have grown up unnoticed; and while the attention of mankind was directed elsewhere, they have suddenly assumed a most prominent place among the nations; and the world learned their existence and their greatness at almost the same time. All other nations seem to have nearly reached their natural limits, and only to be charged with the maintenance of their power; but these are still in the act of growth; all the others are stopped, or continue to advance with extreme difficulty; these are proceeding with ease and with celerity along a path to which the human eye can assign no term. The American struggles against the natural obstacles which oppose him; the adversaries of the Russian are men; the former combats the wilderness and savage life; the latter, civilization with all its weapons and its arts: the conquests of the one are therefore gained by the plowshare; those of the other by the sword. The Anglo-American relies upon personal interest to accomplish his ends, and gives free scope to the unguided exertions and common sense of the citizens; the Russian centers all the authority of society in a single arm: the principal instrument of the former is freedom; of the latter servitude.

Their starting point is different, and their courses are not the same; yet each of them seems to be marked out by the will of Heaven to sway the destinies of half the globe.[10]

By the time that the United States and Russia had attained a size that dwarfed the nation-states of western Europe, the same technology that had already outmoded the economics of nationalism shattered its military defenses. If the nation-state floated into history on the wave of sea-power, it sank under assault from the air. Blériot flew across the English Channel in 1909. Alcock and Brown made the first trans-Atlantic flight in 1919. Applied on only a limited scale in World War I, air-power was a decisive factor in the strategy of World War II. When the Nazis in 1941 defied the British control of the sea and captured the island of Crete from the air, they ran down the curtain on an epoch. Four years later when the Japanese surrendered their islands after the dropping of two atomic bombs, they acknowledged realistically that the old politics must conform to the new physics. The foundations of the state are being resited and rebuilt—up above in the stratosphere.

Collective Insecurity. There is abundant evidence to confirm the fact that the nation-state is no longer able to provide protection and prosperity within its own borders. In the first half of the twentieth century two wars occurred whose world-wide scale of operations was without precedent in history. Together they demonstrated that the anarchy of the nation-state system breeds an insecurity that is contagious and allows few to isolate themselves from its effects. The fears, suspicions, and distrust of nation for nation cause each to maintain what armaments it can afford, and their costliness is a drain upon economies that otherwise could make more progress in the arts of peace. For other than military reasons, these same economies have become interdependent, which renders them vulnerable to world-wide movements over which no single nation has control. To this truth the depression of the early 1930's bore witness. As a plague that sweeps across political frontiers, the same malady struck at one country after another producing the same symptoms: falling prices, lowered purchasing power, rising unemployment, reduced revenues from taxation, unbalanced budgets, bankruptcies, bank failures, and default on debts. Prosperity, as well as peace, had become indivisible.

---

[10] Alexis de Tocqueville, *Democracy in America*, Part I, trans. Henry Reeve (New York: J. & H. G. Langley, 1841), chap. 18, pp. 470-71.

This world-wide succession of events in a thirty-year period—war, depression, and war again—offered the clearest proof that an international society was emerging for which the nation-state was an unsuitable unit of government. Not only in trade and commerce, but in cultural contacts and the movement of ideas, communication between peoples had become easier and more rapid. Just as in the fifteenth and sixteenth centuries, therefore, a national order could not predominate unless the localism of the medieval system was abandoned, so in the twentieth century an international order could not prevail if politics were conducted through national channels. For, in paradoxical fashion, the determination to build security within the borders of the nation-state contributed to insecurity all around. States were severally behaving like individuals who place their reliance on self-protection and carry weapons on their person instead of resorting to public agencies such as police and courts. That system, as imagined by Hobbes or as practiced under frontier conditions, can be productive only of general disorder, which is precisely what happened in the world of nation-states. The efforts of each to build its own protection one-nationwide ultimately brought little protection to anybody. What is more, the particularism of nation-states defeated any possibility of a political development from the protection of each to an order embracing all. International politics had thus reached an impasse that illustrates the general problem of human associations discussed in Chapter 2. Instead of achieving a satisfactory balance between cooperation and competition, the relations between states were characterized by too much of the latter and too little of the former. All states were suffering from the harmful effects of an excess of competition pursued in self-centered isolation. They were insufficiently aware of the fact that the objectives which all had sought separately could be better achieved if all cooperated collectively. Somehow a method had to be devised of securing protection through order and of infusing the latter with a concept of justice. In short, the need to reorder the relations between states was similar in principle to the problem of harmonizing associations within the state. The jurisdiction of government had to become more nearly co-extensive with the ambit of society.

The Remedies of International Law. What steps have been taken in this direction? Among the constructive efforts to mitigate the imperialism of the strong and to remedy the general anarchy of interstate relations, the developments in international law, international arbitration and adjudication, and international organization, have become cumulatively significant. While each of these, it is true, has received its most vigorous extension during the present century, their roots can be traced back in one form or another to earlier periods. For instance, the attempt to formulate and systematize the rules of international law was begun only a short while after the establishment of the nation-state. Thus it was in 1625 that Grotius published his treatise *De Jure Belli ac Pacis* ("On the Law of War and Peace") which is ordinarily considered the foundation of the modern writings in this field. Moreover, the need that prompted some outstanding minds to turn their attention to this subject is indicated by the type of country of which they were nationals. Grotius [11] himself was Dutch; as was one of his eminent successors Van Bynkershoek. Pufendorf worked in the service of Sweden, of Brandenburg, and of German universities at a time when there was not a formidable German *Reich* and the term Germany was merely a cultural expression; and Vattel came from the brave little state of Switzerland, which, situated between big and belligerent powers, had already adopted its non-aggressive policy of permanent neutrality. Thus the classic early contributions to international law were penned, appropriately enough, by representatives of small, weak states that wanted the protection of law because they were inadequately supplied with the protection of force. How deep was their concern to retrieve a modicum of security from the anarchy of the nation-state system is further revealed by the emphasis of the leading seventeenth- and eighteenth-century treatises, much of whose content is devoted to outlining principles that might regulate the conduct of war and mitigate its ferocity and might insulate neutrals from some of its effects.

The formulation of international law—that is, of rules of conduct for states to observe in their dealings with one another—has now been proceeding for over three and a quarter centuries. There has, of course, been much disagreement concerning the substance of these rules, because the governments of different states have had different views of their respective interests and advantages and, if a law of nations is drafted, it must somehow reconcile the competing, private,

---

[11] This was his Latinized pen-name for his Dutch name, de Groot.

national interests into a cooperative, public, international order. The task is rendered yet more complex by the diversity of sources from which the content of international law derives. Included in these sources are the customary practices, which states have habitually followed in their external relations; the substance of treaties, both bilateral and multilateral, to which the constituted authorities have put their signatures; principles of justice, as expressed in ethical philosophy; the opinions of courts, whether national or supra-national, when they pass judgment on international matters; and the systematic treatises of learned jurists, who have followed the trail that Grotius blazed.

Despite these manifold complications, it is well within the scope of human ingenuity to devise a satisfactory body of rules that could ensure a place in the sun for all peoples of the world and eliminate the excesses of competitive hostility. But law, when framed, requires a framework of institutions in which to operate. For rules will some-times be violated; and, if so, they must receive enforcement—or they will be disregarded with impunity and will then cease to have any utility as rules. Hence the same problem that existed originally in the foundation of the state is repeated—identically in principle, al-though differently in scale—in the construction of order among states. Merely to rest content with the writing of law is insufficient because, as Hobbes observed long ago: "Covenants being but words, and breath, have no force to oblige, contain, constrain, or protect any man, but what it has from the publique Sword." [12] The same truth is understood in every city which places signs on the highway warning the motorist: "Traffic Laws Enforced." A committee of competent international jurists could codify an equitable set of rules of international conduct. But how are such rules to acquire official recognition, public acceptance, and authoritative enforcement? Without international government, international law is left hanging, as it were, in the air.

The Growth of International Institutions. Hitherto no inter-national government has been created to supersede or bridle the nation-states. But what may be its embryo is growing. Already be-fore World War I some specialized agencies had been set up by agreement between governments to administer particular services.

[12] *Leviathan,* chap. 18.

Examples of this are the Universal Postal Union and the International Red Cross. Such bodies have suggested the possibility that, just as the growth of the nation-state promoted and was aided by the centralized administration of services (for example, highways, courts, and defense), so might a superstate develop from the internationalization of governmental functions. Moreover, since mankind's greatest man-made scourge—warfare—is due in part to a failure to settle disputes by peaceful means, and since the settlement of disputes is aided by the existence of institutions and procedures, a number of experiments of this kind have been initiated. In the attempts of states to devise methods of resolving controversies without resort to war, a long and significant progression leads from direct diplomacy between the parties concerned through the intermediate steps of good offices, mediation, conciliation, and arbitration, to the goal of adjudication by an independent tribunal. What takes place in such a process, if and when it is completed, is that the disputants finally invoke a third party to render a decision, and it is that third party's interest to see both that justice is done and that the general framework of order is undisturbed by violence. In other words, to refer again to the Herodotean story about the kingdom of Media,[13] the modern problem has been to produce an international Deioces at whose tribunal just rules would be impartially applied. Prior to 1914 this need was acutely felt. Some states were already employing the system of arbitration to settle disputes that arose between themselves. This happened especially in the relations of the United States and Great Britain, which between the end of the American Civil War and the outbreak of World War I reached agreement in five disputes through a series of notable arbitrations. In fact, the demonstrable usefulness of this technique prompted the signing of an international convention at the Second Hague Peace Conference of 1907, whereby the procedures of arbitration and a panel of arbitrators were made available to states that wanted to use them.

The outbreak of World War I, the German government's guilt in violating its treaty obligations, the long grimness of the conflict and its bloody slaughter so shocked the conscience of civilized humanity as to bring about a climate of opinion in which Woodrow Wilson, and other men similarly inspired, could work. The result was the establishment in the years 1919-1921 of a trio of institutions dedi-

[13] See Chapter 3, pp. 48-9.

cated to noble conceptions. The International Labor Organization, representing governments, employers, and labor, set out to raise progressively the minimum level of working conditions throughout the world, so that states which improved the lot of their workers and thereby raised their own costs of production would be less at a disadvantage in competition with sweatshop-countries. The Permanent Court of International Justice, with a bench of judges drawn from the principal legal systems of the world, was established as a judicial body to give advisory opinions on points of international law and to try any case that disputing states would submit to its jurisdiction. Most comprehensive in scope, however, and most ambitious in aim was the League of Nations whose avowed objective was to prevent future wars and provide a regular international forum where states would debate, and supposedly settle, their differences.

Such institutions did not create an international government or super-state. But they constituted a remarkable forward step in both principle and practice. The International Labor Organization was novel because from every member-state it included representatives not only of the government but also of employers' groups and of trade unions, which signified some recognition of the emerging international society in its economic aspect. The Court, as its name implied, was meant to be more than a tribunal for arbitration. Its authority to render decisions, however, was limited by the willingness of states to accept its jurisdiction; and in fact many of the states that ratified the Court's Statute (or constitution) reserved certain classes of disputes concerning which they would give no general prior undertaking to "go to court." And in any case, if a decision were rendered, who would enforce it upon the losing state? For, as has been noted earlier in this book, while power seeks translation into authority, authority, to be effective, must be backed by power. Where then did power lie under the Peace of Versailles?

The League of Nations. In an ultimate sense this was the gap in the system that the League of Nations was supposed to fill. The League was the product of some eminently sound reasoning. Before 1914, it was pointed out, the methods employed for restraining the excesses of competition among states relied on direct diplomacy, the formulation of rules of international law, and the development of arbitration. Each of these was useful in itself. But even added together, they were inadequate. By direct diplomacy the negotiating states might reach agreement. But it might be an agreement to sacrifice or victimize a third state (as when Poland disappeared under partition). Law and arbitration were necessary. But not all controversies that lead to war are justiciable, that is, appropriate for settlement in a court according to rules of law. Many disputes involve conflicts of interest, where choices must be taken between alternative policies and the values or ideals they embody. Consider, for instance, the heavy cost of armaments and the militarization of youth that occur when the governments of states are mutually hostile or suspicious. No rules of law, no panel of arbitrators, no bench of judges, could decide on the wisdom of disarmament or the appropriateness of various levels of armament. Thus there were issues— vital issues, in the sense that they related to the lives of men and states—which call for determination by political means. What Wilson and the other architects of the League were hoping was that regular, public discussion in the continuous conferences of the League would lead to an atmosphere of trust and good will and make cooperation possible for an international order.

At its best, therefore, the League was a convenient instrument for cooperation, available to those who felt a need to cooperate. It offered admirable facilities for discussion, negotiation, and compromise. It could proceed to a vote and make recommendations to the governments of member-states. There, however, its effectiveness ceased. Power within the League still remained with the parts; it was not transferred to the whole. The League lacked authority to take decisions because it did not possess its own means of enforcement. As was proven in the critical cases of Japan's aggression against China and Italy's aggression against Ethiopia, a resolution of the League could not be put into practice unless national governments placed their forces at the League's disposal; and this meant, when the aggressor was itself a major power, that other major powers must take up the cudgels on the League's behalf and their own. The big nations, however, did not yet feel a sufficient community of interest to intervene jointly in restraining one of their number that ran amuck. The League was paralyzed by the coolness between Britain and France, by the nationalistic violence of Italy and Japan, by the renewal of German aggressiveness, by the disorganization of China, by the mutual antipathy between the Soviet Union and the non-Communist world, and by the non-membership of the United States. What is more, the meetings of the League were attended only by the delegates of governments who functioned as a conference of ambassadors. The opposition parties, within those nation-states where they existed, had no mouthpiece at Geneva, and the deliberations of the League were therefore not broadly representative of peoples. Of course, for this weakness in the League's structure the peoples of mankind had only themselves to blame, since their loyalties and allegiances were still overwhelmingly national. Until they could acquire a sense of international kinship, the looseness of international machinery accurately corresponded to the political divisions of the human race.

This continuation of old attitudes that no longer chimed with newer realities found its confusing way into the Versailles Treaty. President Wilson had correctly diagnosed the military and political needs of his age when he called for an association of states to make security collective. There spoke the internationalist. But at the same time he inconsistently espoused the doctrine of national self-determination, approving the dismemberment of the Austro-Hungarian Empire and the multiplication of states in central and eastern Europe. There acted the nationalist. International organization was then supposed somehow to unite a larger number of smaller nation-states than had existed before. That faith was wrecked by two miscalculations, one political and one economic. The political error was the unawareness that a nationalism, which is highly sensitive because it is new, is generally reluctant to accept any external restraints, including even those that emanate from an international source. The economic fault lay in the opportunities thus provided for economic nationalism. More miles of political frontiers meant so many extra miles of customs barriers—a truth that was clearly evidenced in the early 1930's when states the world over reacted against the depression and the shrinkage of international trade with foolish attempts to insulate and isolate their economies.

The United Nations. At the end of World War II mankind was offered its second chance within the span of a generation. The problem that confronted the victors in 1945 was even more urgent than that which existed in 1918 because prosperity and security were far more seriously jeopardized. Not only were the economies of so many countries disorganized and damaged, but the long-range bomber loaded with an atomic cargo and flying at jet-propelled speeds now constituted a greater menace to life than any destructive weapon previously used by man. To organize a general economic recovery and to police the world against future acts of aggression would require global solutions. So during the years 1944-1946, a number of new international bodies were established. All but one of these are specialized agencies in the sense that their work in each case is limited to a particular function or service whose program and problems are often highly technical in content.[14] The exception is the United Nations, which, as the successor to the League, has taken over the general responsibility of promoting cooperation between states and keeping them at peace.

Any judgment about an institution of this character that has, at the time of writing, been only in existence for approximately a decade is plainly premature. But some observations may be attempted. A comparison of the League Covenant with the United Nations Charter shows clearly that the latter was intended not to repeat its predecessor but to improve upon its defects. Though it embraces a wide range of international problems from declarations of human rights to control of atomic weapons, the United Nations Organization has been influenced from the start by more realism and fewer illusions than was the case with its predecessor. The League did not measure up to its great ordeals in the 1930's because it had no bullets to secure obedience to its ballots. Consequently, when the Charter was drafted, great attention was paid to provisions for enforcement, and the Security Council thus became the hard core of the new organization.

Its strength was quickly put to the test. Almost from birth, and before the bone structure had hardened, the United Nations were forced to take arms against a sea of troubles. A number of major assumptions that had run current in 1945 were then found wanting. In the first place the British economy was discovered to have suffered a more severe strain than most people had imagined. Hence the full recovery of the nation that in 1938 accounted for one-fifth of the world's trade has been delayed, and Britain has been too impoverished to shoulder all the commitments that she formerly undertook.

[14] Examples are the International Monetary Fund; the International Bank for Reconstruction and Development; the Food and Agriculture Organization; the World Health Organization; and the United Nations Educational, Scientific, and Cultural Organization.

Second, the expectation that Chiang Kai-Shek and the Kuomintang would retain their position in China and guide its postwar reorganization has not been fulfilled. Their replacement by a Communist regime brought at one stroke nearly one-quarter of the human race under their control, with profound consequences for relations between East and West. Third, the belief that western states, after defeating Japan, would be able to maintain their former empires in Asia has been falsified. India secured complete self-government from Britain, but because of religious antipathies betwen Hindus and Moslems split into two states. Both of these chose to remain within the British Commonwealth of Nations, unlike Burma which preferred the road of complete independence. The Dutch empire of the East Indies has been converted into the new self-governing state of Indonesia, which continues to be loosely associated with the Crown of the Netherlands. In Indo-China the constitution of the French Union has not hitherto provided a structure that could pacify the colony in the face of Communist and nationalist opposition.[15]

Elsewhere, too, the sometime dominance of occidental powers has evoked a reaction of angry outburst and violent challenge. The temper of middle eastern peoples has exploded in the unilateral acquisition by Iran of the properties of the Anglo-Iranian Oil Company and in the strident demands of Egyptian governments to secure exclusive control of the Suez Canal. While the former Italian colony of Libya has been reconstituted an independent state, the French have encountered increasing resistance to their sway in Tunisia. Moreover, in east-central Africa the Mau Mau movement of Kenya has advertised to the world in savage terms the resentment of Negroes at the possession of African land by whites. Assuredly, in these middle decades of the twentieth century, uneasy lies the head that rules an empire.

The East-West Split. Politically, however, the most important of all problems since 1945 has been the changed relationship of the Soviet Union with the West. The effectiveness of the United Nations was based upon the expectation that the coalition of states which were allies from 1941 to 1945 would continue to act with a

[15] The independence of the Philippines was promised, by an Act of the United States Congress passed in 1936, at the end of a ten-year period. In 1946 the promise was fulfilled.

substantial degree of harmony. Indeed in no other way could the veto right of the five principal powers on the Security Council be justified, since, if they failed to cooperate, the United Nations were doomed to permanent deadlock. But ever since 1947 that is exactly what has happened. The Soviet government's policy of sealing off its nationals from free communication with other peoples; its decision, though invited to participate in the Marshall Plan for European economic aid, to obstruct its working in every possible way; the parrot-like repetition of the same line by Communist parties in all countries save Yugoslavia; the *coup d'état* of the Communist party in Czechoslovakia—such actions seemed to the vast majority of persons in the western world impressive evidence that trusty cooperation with Communist regimes is impossible. When finally in 1950, in plain violation of the United Nations' Charter, the North Korean Communists launched out of the blue an unprovoked military assault on South Korea, no one could any longer have reasonable doubts of the Cominform's expansionist aims. The resolutions of the Security Council that condemned the South Korean invasion and authorized collective military aid to South Korea under the United Nations' auspices were rendered possible only by the self-imposed absence of the Soviet delegate from the Council table.[16] Otherwise his veto would assuredly have prevented such action. But the precedent thus set has incalculable importance, since for the first time in modern history land, sea, and air forces contributed by as many as twenty-seven states have served together under the flag of an international agency and under a single commander.

With the exception of the aggression in Korea and the approval of partition for Palestine, the United Nations have on all major issues been so split by internal hostilities that they lack the capacity for decision and enforcement. Throughout the political acrimony of the cold war, the Security Council and the Assembly could serve little more than as a debating forum where speakers talk mainly to their home audiences and have scant prospect of convincing their principal antagonists. Nevertheless, even in this restricted role, the institution performs an invaluable function. It remains the one asso-

---

[16] In January, 1950, the Soviet delegate walked out of the Council because of that body's unwillingness to admit a Communist representative to China's seat. He walked back in August 1950, when it was his turn, under the system of rotation, to occupy the chair.

ciation that houses the divided fragments of humanity. Its freedom of debate impels all governments to reply in public to the worst criticisms, whether merited or false, that foes can hurl. Its existence and its survival in each passing year represent an advance toward the ultimate goal of "the Parliament of Man, the Federation of the world." [17] From the realization of that ideal, however, humanity today is still far, far removed, and the rate at which we travel toward it does not appear at the moment to be breaking any political speed records.

International Relations in a Double Standard World. There are more reasons than one for the present tensions between the group of countries associated with the United States and the group that is dominated by the Communist party of the Soviet Union. Directly relevant to politics is the contrast in the opposing practices of two governmental systems, one of which makes the state officials and a single political party supreme over individual citizens whereas the other offers a choice of parties that, together with the civil service, are subordinate to the people. The consequence in one case is a glorification of the state and idolatry of its leaders; in the other, a respect for the common man and a utilitarian attitude that the state is there to serve him. In addition to the military control of the Red Army in eastern Europe there are social and economic factors that explain, in part, why Communism acquired sway in that region and why its propaganda has attracted followers elsewhere in the world. A fundamental cause of much of the unrest that hitherto has plagued this century is the inequality of conditions which divide vast sections of the human race. Most of mankind—throughout eastern Europe, Asia, Africa, and South and Central America—are chronically undernourished and suffer periodic starvation. They are illiterate, miserably housed, and poorly clad. Victims of endemic disease, they die before they are middle-aged; and sunk in poverty, they lack any possessions except the simplest and most rudimentary.

Probably the great majority of people have always fared this way—or at least have so fared throughout the few millennia over which historical records extend. It is impossible for a double standard world to be a contented one, and inequality, as Aristotle noted, has ever been a fertile source of revolution. But, though social up-

---

[17] The words are Tennyson's, from the poem *Locksley Hall*.

heavals have not been wanting in the past, their effects when they occurred were less widespread and less interconnected than those that characterize our epoch. Until a few centuries ago, large segments of humanity and entire civilizations endured in comparative isolation from one another. A change of dynasty in China stirred not a ripple in Europe. The death of a Russian autocrat caused little concern to any beyond the borders of Muscovy. Discussions and decisions on the banks of the Potomac or the Thames did not make the whole welkin ring. The supply and control of iron ore, oil, and uranium were not matters of global life or death. We have succeeded in changing all that. For our woe or weal, we have made of all the world a single stage where the drama of man's fate is enacted in scenes that shift rapidly from place to place, but form part of one plot.

What distinguishes our age from those that have gone before, and complicates the solution of its problems, is the extension of the community of interests to an area as wide as the world, the greater spread of information, and the deeper awareness by millions of their common lot. The huddled masses of humanity are not only yearning to breathe free; they are also craving a share in things they have never enjoyed. Such circumstances become a spawning ground for political movements of many kinds. People who have become resentful of their underprivileged status, but who are politically unsophisticated, will readily listen to promises and follow a prophet. They may be fortunate in receiving wise counsel and discovering a government which has their interests at heart. Or they may fall dupes to false propaganda and power-seeking politicians. Or again, they may be checked by the stubborn opposition of those who do not accept as legitimate the claims of the masses to more equal treatment. Out of this milieu spring personality types as diverse as Gandhi, Nehru, Lenin, Stalin, Tito, Chiang, Rhee, Mao, Kemal, Mossadegh, Naguib, Malan, Cardenas, Vargas, and Perón. Out of it come regimes that may be fascist, communist, nationalist, militarist, racist, theocratic, or democratic. When the lid is off and the genie is out of the bottle, there is no telling what shape it will assume.

At the time when the Charter of the United Nations was being written, many statesmen recognized that colonial aspirations for independence and the general desire of people in underdeveloped areas for higher living standards are a constant source of friction and hence a possible cause of war. For this reason the structure included among its principal organs a Trusteeship Council and an Economic and Social Council. The function of the former has been to safeguard the interests of weaker peoples, whose government is entrusted by the United Nations to another state. The latter's objective is to diminish the gap that separated the technologically advanced communities from backward ones. Despite inadequate budgets that have severely limited the programs, much significant aid has been rendered to underdeveloped countries by the Technical Assistance Administration of the United Nations and by the special agencies that operate in the fields of health (WHO), education (UNESCO), labor (ILO), food and agriculture (FAO), and investment and economic development (International Monetary Fund and International Bank for Reconstruction and Development). Besides the granting of loans, this help consists in gathering and publishing information on each of these subjects, in disseminating scientific knowledge, and in recruiting teams of experts and individual technicians who are sent to cooperate with countries that request assistance. The details of such programs, like the work of any national government, are for the most part concrete, practical, and specialized; for instance, the authorization of a loan to construct a steel mill, the launching of reforestation schemes, development of fisheries, eradication of malaria, control of narcotics, reduction of illiteracy, safety for civil aviation, reorganization of a revenue system, and so on.

Problems of International Cooperation. Though self-evidently constructive, activities of this character do not lack their quota of difficulties. Most international agencies have inadequate budgets. The poorer countries, which need help, have little to give. Richer ones, which in any case contribute a high proportion of the total, may feel that they are already paying enough. They may then oppose a budgetary increase since they are the donors, not the recipients, of aid. Competent personnel are hard to recruit, because many individuals can see better career opportunities in their own national civil service or because governments are sometimes disinclined to make their best men available to an international agency. Agreement about programs may not be so difficult to elicit when the subject matter, as in the case of food or health, is of universal interest and has a direct connection with life. But in an agency like the ILO, which treads the thorny path of employer-employee relations, or one such as UNESCO, which seeks to combat ignorance and enrich humanity with the treasures of the mind, the conflict between competitive interests or opposed philosophies is a hindrance to positive action.

What accentuates these problems is the touchiness of national governments whenever an issue is raised which they deem vital. Where a great power is involved, experience has shown that other states are reluctant to outvote, and do not dare to coerce it. But even small states produce governments and leaders who can be violently stubborn and self-willed in what seems to them their national interest. Witness such phenomena as Malan, Mossadegh, or Rhee. In particular, the rulers of countries that have recently emerged from a dependent or colonial status are torn two ways in their external policies. Without aid from outside—loans, investment, goods, and technicians—they cannot develop their economies and raise their living standards to the level they desire. But aid will normally be accompanied by some list of conditions, some attachment of strings, which then is interpreted in the guise of "foreign control." Those who a short time ago were subject to another power will chafe at new restraints, even when their source is an international agency. Furthermore, men who can consistently espouse idealism when they are in opposition, find themselves making concessions to expediency when in office. How else could Nehru's position in the Kashmir dispute be explained?

The crux of the problem can be simply stated. All over the world there are people who in economics and technology are dependent, but in politics feel strongly about independence. That paradox is perhaps explicable in terms of the time-lag that has occurred in the spread of the nation-state. This unit of government, as we have seen, originated in the fifteenth and sixteenth centuries in western Europe. Its force was not fully felt in eastern Europe until some time later. Among colonial peoples the first effective blow for national independence was struck in 1776 in North America, and Latin America followed suit almost five decades afterwards. Not until the closing decades of the nineteenth century did the force of nationalism begin to explode in Asia, with results that have been manifest of recent decades. Latest of all, and last on the list, is

Africa—a continent where some writing is already on the wall and grimmer histories have yet to be written.

It is a truly formidable task, therefore, to construct an international order out of such discordant elements. The mansion of peace and prosperity has to be built out of bricks of different materials and different size and shape. The edifice must include states that once were leading powers and continue to be profoundly important but now have suffered a relative loss of strength, like Britain and France; states that today stand in the front rank, like the United States and the Soviet Union; states that are the homes of proud and ancient civilizations and could once again be mighty if their potentialities are unleashed, like India and China; states that give few thanks to the past, but consider themselves, as does Brazil, "lands of the future"; states that have made their bid for hegemony and failed, like Germany and Japan; decadent states of the type of Spain or Greece; medium-sized states, some of them peaceably expansive like Canada, others as aggressive as the Argentine, and still others of which little need be said except that they exist; and finally the small fry—buffer states, like Belgium, Austria, or Uruguay; honest neutrals of the Swiss model; client-states like Albania, Paraguay, Transjordan, and Tibet; courageous new creations like Israel; and oddities like Iceland, Panama, and Luxembourg. If statesmanship is an art, as is sometimes said, what artist ever worked in so refractory a medium?

There exist then certain basic conditions, some of which serve to encourage, others to delay, the formation of an international community. First is the fact that no nation-state today is adequate to provide within its own boundaries all that is required to be safe and prosperous. Second is the inequality of living standards, provoking the resentment and envy of the underprivileged. Third is the survival of strongly-held nationalist sentiments, not the least among those to whom nationhood arrived late. Fourth is the mutual antagonism of two political systems, each headed by a mighty state, deriving from different historical traditions and representing contrasted forms of social, economic, and governmental organization.

The addition of this fourth element to the other three has injected into international affairs an incalculable and disturbing force. Instead of an era of peaceful reconstruction, we have found ourselves in an atmosphere of hostility, rearmament, and renewed warfare.

Each of the parties to the cold war has felt the need to mobilize support, organize alliances, build coalitions, and court the neutrals. On our side we have felt ourselves at a disadvantage because of the methods of conspiracy, subversion, and distorted propaganda which the Communists so expertly employ. They, conversely, feel their disadvantage in the face of the superior resources and more advanced technology of the West. The pressure generated by this rivalry has had the two important effects of splitting open the international organizations [18] and of groping for substitutes to take their place.

Region-States in the Making. The realization that the world politically is not yet one in heart and spirit has persuaded many persons, however reluctantly, that prosperity and security may perhaps be organized in some third manner intermediate between the nation-state, which is outmoded, and a global state, which mankind is still too divided to accept. Indeed there are signs that plainly show that a new, and possibly workable, unit of government is already evolving. The peoples who live around the coasts of the Atlantic are now experimenting with a variety of novel and imaginative unions. These include on the mainland of western Europe such projects as the Council of Strasbourg, the Iron and Steel Authority, and the European Army. Linking the two sides of the Atlantic are the Economic Cooperation Administration and the North Atlantic Treaty Organization. All of these schemes envisage, if they are to succeed, the enlargement of the area of military, political, and economic cooperation and the patient building of the appropriate machinery by people sufficiently like-minded to trust each other. In eastern Europe something of the same kind is being attempted, though with vastly different political methods, by the Soviet Union and the Communist governments adjacent to its borders. There, too, intensive bonds are being formed that make more extensive the size of territory and population covered by a single jurisdiction. What all this amounts to is the nascent development of a governmental unit that might be called the region-state—to distinguish it from either a nation-state or world-state. Here in the emerging region-state some portions of mankind may perhaps construct their

[18] On this point it is worth noting that the Soviet Union is not at present a member of the ILO, FAO, UNESCO, the International Bank and the Monetary Fund, or the International Civil Aviation Organization; and it has announced its intention to withdraw from WHO.

temporary political defense against economic blizzard and aero-atomic war.

Yet a word of caution is necessary, lest hopes again be raised too high and be dashed more cruelly to the ground. A region-state will present problems of organization fully as complex as its predecessor. If it was difficult to delimit the boundaries of the nation, it will be no less hard to define those of the region. An example is the fact that the North Atlantic Treaty Organization already reaches as far afield as Greece and Turkey. Some states, moreover, have in-terests—geographically and economically—in more than one region. Britain, for instance, is located in the Atlantic but is united with the member-countries of a Commonwealth whose scattering is the very antithesis of regionalism. The United States belongs to the North Atlantic Treaty Organization as well as the Pan-American Union, and has a major stake in the affairs of the Pacific where it has con-tractual commitments with Australia, New Zealand, the Philippines, and Japan. Nor should anyone assume that wars between region-states are impossible. The region-state can justify itself for the time being only if it provides a broader framework for enhancing the economic well-being of all its members, and if each region-state presents such a formidable picture of strength to a possible antago-nist that nobody will run the risk of initiating a third general war from which none can conceivably come out unscathed.

Nor should it be forgotten that some of the same factors that impede the task of international organization can also be obstacles to the formation of region-states. To create the latter, a union is required between a nuclear power and the countries associated with it. But nationalism and differences of living standards may provoke a rift in that relationship. At present, for example, the United States supplies the leadership to a large and loose coalition of peoples in which are included virtually all of the world's most advanced com-munities and many of the most backward. Out of their rich re-sources, financial strength, and great productivity capacity, the American people have rendered economic and military assistance to numerous governments in the hope that such aid would increase their means of resistance to armed aggression from without and political subversion from within.

The results of this program have been as varied as the characters of the recipients. In a country like Britain, where the government is honestly organized and the people in general are hard-working and self-disciplined, the joint Anglo-American contribution to the restoration of Britain's economy has been notably successful. There are other countries, however, in which corrupt cliques and incompetent governments have misused or squandered much of the aid that was granted. In those cases it is only natural that the donors should feel disposed to attach conditions which the recipients must fulfill. But when that is done, the nationalistic pride of the latter is likely to be outraged and they will voice angry protests that their "sovereignty" is being invaded. The American public sees a portion of its tax-dollar appropriated to finance the foreign aid programs that, while they help other countries, simultaneously promote the interests of the United States. That such efforts sometimes provoke resentment rather than thanks is often a matter of surprise to those who provide the money. But it is not a normal human trait—in the relations between groups, any more than in the relations of individuals —for the stronger, wealthier, and luckier to meet with gratitude and affection, or for the dependent to like their position. Furthermore, differences of opinion may arise even among friendly nations concerning the best way to distribute aid in order to combat a versatile and aggressive rival. If the primary emphasis is placed upon the danger of Russian military might, the counter-measures will take the form of rearmament. If, however, the main strength of the Communists is the appeal of their ideology to the underprivileged, the remedy is to offer a better ideal and to remove the social and economic conditions that draw some persons to Marxism.

In the Communist solar system a number of satellite bodies revolve around the central Russian sun. Almost without exception,[19] the countries under Communist rule are socially, economically, and politically underdeveloped. During Stalin's lifetime, the relations of the Soviet Union with other "dictatorships of the proletariat" were far from harmonious. The fanatical imposition of Moscow-directed programs, the requirements of a rigid orthodoxy in word and deed, and the doctrinaire application of uniform principles to diverse situations, generated much discontent even within parties as strongly disciplined as the Communists are wont to construct.

---

[19] From the standpoint of living standards and general development, the most advanced area under Communist rule was, at the time when it was sucked into the Soviet orbit, the Bohemian portion of Czechoslovakia.

Between 1947 and 1952 a spectacle frequently witnessed in one eastern European country after another was the "discovery" of treasonable plots within the party hierarchy, and the vilification, imprisonment, or execution of men until recently idolized as Communist heroes. There seems little doubt that much of this was due to the subordination of other peoples' interests to that of the Russians and to the understandable reaction of various Communist leaders in satellite states who had to espouse and represent the feelings of their fellow-nationals. In the most explosive instance of all, namely Yugoslavia, a tough-minded political boss, master of his own domestic situation, dared to flout the Kremlin by giving first priority to what he considered the interests of his own country.

It is evident, therefore, that though the area encompassed by the nation-state no longer accords with some basic needs of contemporary government, the accompanying sentiments die hard. Region-states may be in the making. But the gestation period and the delivery will be long and painful. As for a world-state, while the consummation is devoutly to be wished, the possibility of "civil war" erupting within the world society cannot be totally eliminated. Anyhow, the question of what will happen after a world state is constituted is, for the moment, a piece of idle speculation. It is fantasy for anyone now living to expect to see in his or her lifetime a politically unified world.

CHAPTER 15

THE DYNAMICS OF
POLITICAL CHANGE

The Unity of the Political Process. When a surgeon operates upon the human body, he must sew his patient together again and see that the severed tissue reunites. When a psychiatrist unravels the tangled complexes of the unconscious mind, he must reknit the threads of personality to a changed design. The same obligation befalls a political scientist who subjects the social order to his analysis. Dissection of a whole into its parts contributes to clarity of understanding. But unless the parts are reassembled, what is thus obtained is an understanding only of isolated fragments, not of the related pieces of a unity. The purpose of this concluding chapter, therefore, is to stitch up the seams and observe the pattern that results.

The discussion of the ten preceding chapters may be summarized in a few sentences. Politics is the process by which a human community confronts a series of great issues and makes its decision about each. Nowadays the institution under whose auspices this is done is almost universally the state, though there have been occasions when the same role was performed by religious, kinship, or economic groups. Government is the name for the machinery and methods used by the state in carrying out its functions. In every political situation, in each kind of state, and under all forms of government, the same basic issues are perennially present and all must receive a solution. Since every issue admits of more than one choice, states and their governments differ from one another in the various choices they embody and in the manner of combining them.

This way of looking at politics offers some insights into certain of its fundamental characteristics whose significance would otherwise be missed. Too many political analyses have suffered from the fault of reducing their subject-matter to terms and categories that are primarily static. That is an unfortunate by-product of an attempt which is laudable in itself—the effort at logical exposition. Logic aims at concepts and propositions that are, as far as possible, clear-cut, unambiguous, firm in outline, and mutually exclusive. But the actual content of politics—as distinct from theories about it—is fluid and mobile. It is therefore difficult, and can even be inaccurate, rigidly to impose a logical framework upon a shifting material. A political philosophy that satisfies conceptually the tests of a logical system often fails before the no less rigorous task of explaining political phenomena as they have been, as they now are, and as they may yet be. A political analysis that is to be successful must meet two criteria. It should designate the underlying problems that are the invariable constants and indicate the variable ways of resolving them.

The reasons for these requirements, and for the two being jointly necessary, are implicit in the treatment attempted throughout this book. To argue that the political process is composed of certain constant factors is to recognize the similarity between situations greatly separated in time and place. If it is meaningful to speak of the existence of politics, state, and government in Greece of the fifth century B.C., in Rome of the first century A.D., in the age of Thomas Aquinas, in the revolutionary century from 1688 to 1789, or in the world of Roosevelt, Churchill, Stalin, and Hitler, then there should be some unifying threads that, despite the manifold differences, persist unbroken. Presumably the problems that confronted Pericles or Augustus, Louis IX or Louis XIV, or any of their modern successors, bore some resemblance to one another and may be appropriately grouped as aspects of man's incessant striving to control and reorder his environment. It was a stroke of fancy to conceive of the Connecticut Yankee at the Court of King Arthur. But a Pericles in the White House would have found himself as much in his element as a Roosevelt in the Athenian Assembly. The issues that both statesmen faced and the skills they practiced were sufficiently alike for their abilities to be transferable. Likewise a Clodius with his gang-fights in the streets of Rome could have changed places readily with a Capone and his Chicago gang. As there is a stream of history that flows uninterruptedly from pre-historic times to the present without regard for our divisions into periods, so there is a stream of politics that rises at a source concealed in the forests of man's primeval past and follows its single course down to the rapids and whirlpools of our own troubled age.

Permanent Problems, Changing Solutions. Though its flow be continuous, a stream will change direction. Its main channel of movement can shift. Its current for a while may be fast or sluggish. Precisely similar is the action of politics. For the continuity of politics represents the unity of energy, not of mass. It is a unity of flux and movement. It extends over time, not over space. Throughout its process runs a rhythm that is ceaselessly changing because it is patterned from issues whose solutions are ever changing. In the opportunity of choice that each issue confers lie the springs of political dynamics.

How do such changes manifest themselves? Many examples have already been noted in this work of the human tendency to tack and turn, like yachtsmen taking advantage of the wind. The history of politics reveals an expanse of creative activity that allows wide room for inventiveness and resource. After making what progress they can in one direction, men veer around and strain their efforts towards another point. Thus the monistic city-state of Greece and Rome was replaced by the Christian experiment in church-state dualism. This in turn gave way to the monism of nation-state sovereignty, which was later followed by the attempt to separate the economic order from politics. The unit of government has likewise passed through a succession of forms. City-state, empire-state, and nation-state have all been tried and tested. Each yielded what benefits it could and then succumbed to conditions for which it had ceased to be appropriate. So too with the other great issues. Mankind perennially explore new ways of meeting old problems, as the United States in 1787 pioneered with the structure of federalism; or they revive under different circumstances a system used centuries before, as the American Republic designed its institutions with the separation of powers that the Roman Republic once employed.

Interaction between the Great Issues. There is, however, another aspect of the process of political change whose operation is more intricate than what has so far been described. If it is correct to suppose that politics forms a single compound, even though it can be analyzed into five basic elements, it would seem to follow that when one of the components undergoes a major alteration, the remainder are likely to feel its effects. This probability raises a fundamental question. When people turn to a different solution of one of the great issues, are there any consequent changes which that decision tends to produce among the rest? Does the evidence of history, subjected to this kind of analysis, suggest that specific solutions of the respective issues ordinarily accompany each other in pairs or groups? If so, one could indicate which alternatives are mutually compatible, and which are not—and that would constitute a valuable guide for interpretation of the past and prediction of the future. Or again, it may be found that no relation—positive or negative—can be traced between some pairs of issues, in which case a choice among one set of alternatives would be unconnected with, and thus irrelevant to, a choice among another set. There is only one way of finding out whether this is the case. Every issue must be discussed in its relation to each of the other four, so that any pattern in which their solutions tend to combine will be detected.

(*1*) *The Relations of Privilege or Equality to Other Choices.* Consider first the choice between a regime of privilege and one of equality. What correlation is there between either of these and the manner in which other issues are solved? Does a swing from privilege to equality, or vice versa, lead to any corresponding reversals in the treatment of other issues? Wherever a few privileged persons are in a position of superiority over a much larger number, the dominant oligarchy will use all means that enable them to stay on the top of the heap. Necessarily, the favored few must possess political power and therewith must control the state—or they would eventually be ousted from influence by those who do. Does this mean, however, that when an elite monopolizes the government the entire society is subordinated to the state in monistic fashion? Or is it possible for privilege to be associated with pluralism, in which case, though politics would be reserved for the few, the functions of the state vis-à-vis other associations would somewhere be limited?

The historical answer is that the principle of oligarchy, as such, does not necessitate either a pluralist or monistic policy by the state toward society. Oligarchies have in fact been indifferently associated with one or the other. Thus in the medieval period when the state was controlled by an oligarchy of nobles and the church by an oligarchy of priests, the prevalent theory of the state was steadfastly opposed to monism. Where a conquering people have taken over the government of the conquered, the victors have sometimes been content to restrict their authority to a few bare essentials (for example, finance, police, and military affairs), leaving their subjects free from state intervention in other matters. Such, in general, was the character of British rule in India. By contrast the Czarist autocracy in Russia during the eighteenth and nineteenth centuries contrived a complete subordination of society to the state. Similar in spirit have been the modern one-party dictatorships—whether Fascist, Nazi, or Communist—whose efforts to make the functions of the state co-extensive with the whole range of social activity have become a by-word.

What happens when a regime of privilege is replaced by one of equalitarianism? Does the latter have a closer affinity with monism or pluralism? The evidence indicates that a sizable extension of the citizen-body is likely to be accompanied by an extension of the functions of the state, though there may be a time-lag before the latter takes full effect. The period that can throw most light on this problem is, of course, the century from 1840 to 1940. During that time the spread of democracy culminated in many states with the achievement of universal suffrage, and with this was associated a tremendous increase in the functions of their governments. Was this combination of events a mere coincidence or a case of cause and effect? Without much doubt it was the latter. Generally, the impetus behind the movement to extend the franchise came from a desire to remedy specific ills by political action. Some of these ills were due to differentiations of humanity into classes that determined the breadth of opportunity available to their members. Other ills, however, were of economic origin and stemmed from the union of industrialism with urbanism. Political equality, signalized by the ballot, was desired as a means to social and economic betterment, and the state was employed as the instrument of equalization. Hence as new voters were enrolled, political parties formulated programs to represent their interests and these were eventually translated into legislative and administrative form. Being composed of people who were poorer and underprivileged, the recently enfranchised electorate were disposed to invoke the powers of the state since other institutions of society relegated them to an inferior position.

An apparent exception to this generalization is provided by the United States in the period from 1820 to 1860. What impressed de Tocqueville most about the America he saw was the equality of social conditions, contrasting so vividly with the aristocratically-dominated countries of Europe. Along with this social equality went a system of popular participation in politics, which, though not yet perfected, had already been extended to a degree without parallel in any European state save Switzerland. But simultaneously the America of pre-Civil War days paid obeisance to the economic doctrine of laissez faire and the Jeffersonian maxim that the least governed are the best governed. Here then was the phenomenon of equalitarianism associated with a government whose functions were cut to the bone. How is that to be explained?

The most plausible single explanation is the existence of the frontier. In nineteenth-century Britain social and economic inequalities could not be removed unless political equality was achieved first. But in the United States the undeveloped territories of the West, providing an open field for people who were ready to take a chance, placed social and economic equality within the grasp of millions, and political equality followed next as a consequence. Had there not been, however, a huge expanse of land rich with exploitable resources, it is dubious whether equalitarianism could have been achieved by any other means than positive state action. Moreover, it should be remembered that after the Civil War, when industrial expansion was superimposed upon the agrarian economy, the distribution of wealth and influence rapidly became so unequal that governmental measures (for example, graduated taxation, public regulation, and social services) were politically achieved to restore a semblance of equality. It was therefore the special, and temporary, circumstance of settling the frontier that accounted for the otherwise unusual combination of more equalitarianism and fewer state functions.

The choice between privilege and equality can be far more precisely correlated with the next pair of alternatives, namely irresponsible or controllable government. A system dedicated to the exaltation of a privileged few dares not submit itself to any genuine procedure of control by the governed. The texture of privilege is shot through with the dye of authoritarianism, for in no other way can a minority obtain and enforce the submission of the majority. No less true is the converse. Wherever equalitarianism is substituted for privilege, the governed develop institutional means of keeping the power of their officials within bounds. Equalitarianism is no more compatible with authoritarianism than is privilege with accountability.

When one turns, however, to the choice between the unity or dispersion of power, no definite correlation can be noted with either oligarchical or majority government. A few examples will make this plain. In the Middle Ages, when politics were certainly reserved for the few, the structure of authority was loose-knit and powers were highly dispersed. The church struggled with the state. The localities resisted the center. The nobility defied the king. On the other hand, various modern oligarchies, especially those of Nazi Germany and Fascist Italy, have been centralized and integrated to the nth degree. The same contrasts may be observed among equalitarian systems. Whereas government in the United States was constructed according to the principles of federal decentralization and the separation of branches, the British system has evolved into the predominance of central over local authority and of the cabinet over the other institutions at the center.

The same can be said concerning the size of the state and its possible effect upon the enlargement or contraction of citizenship. A comparison of ancient city-states with modern nations confirms the view that either oligarchy or its opposite can flourish indifferently in states of Lilliputian or mammoth size. This conclusion is further reinforced if the opinion expressed in the previous chapter is correct, namely that a new governmental unit—the region-state—is nowadays being founded. Here again, within units of comparable scale, the same contrast may be observed of a privileged Communist Party hierarchy in the eastern bloc and a significant approximation to political equalitarianism in the Atlantic [1] community. The size of the political unit, therefore, has no direct bearing on the internal distribution of rights and influence.

(2) *The Accompaniments to Monism and Pluralism.* The same method of analysis must be applied to the second of the great issues.

---

[1] Spain and Portugal are the principal exceptions to this statement.

The preference for a state of limited or comprehensive functions has already been discussed in relation to the alternatives of privilege or equality. How are the other choices affected by the adoption of either pluralism or monism? The answer will readily appear after a look at some contrasted examples. Medieval society was emphatically pluralist in principle and practice alike. The same society both in church and state exhibited a government that was not responsible to the governed. Pluralism by itself, therefore, is no certain guarantor of freedom. On the other hand, as the case of nineteenth-century America will demonstrate, pluralism and freedom can readily be mixed in one compound. The same story can be told of experiments in monism. There are classic instances of a monistic state combined with a controllable government. Such was the Athenian *Polis* in the heyday of its glory. Such is contemporary Britain where a parliamentary majority may legally do anything. Such, too, is contemporary New Zealand where the state is all-powerful within society and the government is definitely subject to popular control. Yet it is true that monism can also be a harmonious bedfellow with dictatorship. Indeed, the most notorious dictatorships of this century are pre-eminently noted for their determination to make state and society indistinguishable. One could hazard the hypothesis that, because the modern dictatorship arises for military or economic reasons or from a desire to accomplish rapidly some cultural revolution (for example, Kemalist Turkey), it is now less likely than in the past that an authoritarian regime can be safely pluralist. For beyond the line where the boundaries of state action are drawn, opposition may develop against those in power.

The other aspect of power, its unity or dispersion, has a more obvious connection with monism and pluralism respectively. There is an understandable tendency for a monistic state to construct authority according to a centralized and integrated plan. Where a state assumes the responsibility for the over-all co-ordination of other associations and their activities, it is less practicable to have a governmental structure in which the branches are too independent and the localities too autonomous. A monistic state like Britain, therefore, has its powers both centralized and integrated. In a pluralist state, on the other hand, both separation of branches and devolution from the center are suited to the prevailing character of a government whose functions are of limited scope. Where the activities to be conducted are fewer, the chances of overlap, duplication, or conflict between agencies and their programs are fewer. Hence there is less demand for a unified focus of power. Moreover, as American experience in the twentieth century abundantly testifies, a government of restricted scope that is impelled by economic and military necessity to expand its activities must simultaneously modify its previously accepted canons of separate branches and federal-state dualism. Today in the United States there is much more evidence than fifty years ago of unification among branches and levels of government, precisely because there is more to be done by every branch of government at every level and these additional activities would collide with one another unless centrally co-ordinated.

Whether the size of the state has any influence upon the functions it undertakes is more difficult to determine. History suggests on this point some tentative hypotheses, but no conclusive verdict, as a review of the evidence will show. The classic case of a state whose expansion covered a huge area and contained a large population is the Roman Empire. Rome was successful in organizing an administrative apparatus, a legal code, and a military machine, to unify its diverse and scattered provinces. It was much less successful in uniting the peoples of its empire with a common emotional bond. By deliberate policy efforts were made to employ religion for this purpose. But when little headway was made with the official ritual of the Olympian deities, or with the worship of Mithra, or with the deification of Emperors, Constantine turned to the Christian faith to inspire a unity of sentiment that was otherwise lacking. The effect of his action, however, was to substitute dualism for monism, and thereby to reduce the scope of state activity. Hence the problem of extending the size of the state outwards was solved only by diminishing the sphere where the state could operate inwards.

Similar in a sense was the experience of the United States. The process of peopling a continent from the Atlantic to the Pacific, from the forty-ninth parallel to the Rio Grande, was accompanied by the organization of society along pluralist lines. The circumstances under which the state expanded its territory and population in North America were ill-suited to a monistic view of the role of government in society. Elsewhere, however, there have been instances to the contrary. The growth of European Russia was associated with the establishment of a powerful state that embraced and absorbed the entire social order. Later, when Czarist power spread across central Asia to the Pacific, the same all-pervasive state controlled and directed the expansion. The mere change in scale never resulted in modifying the monism of the Russian *vlast*.[2] However, in drawing this contrast between the United States and Russia, one should recall the pertinent fact that the expansion of the United States, though it encountered opposition, did not face a hostile neighbor of equal force on the same continent. The consolidation of the Muscovite state, on the other hand, was achieved in the teeth of prolonged and repeated warfare against nearby powers (Poland, Sweden, Prussia, Turkey, and so forth) and the military stamp left an ineradicable imprint on Russian government in the form of complete state domination of society, which the Communists have continued with their more thorough-going methods.

If large states then can be either monistic or pluralist, what about small ones? There is some evidence to justify our supposing that, as the size of the unit of government progressively decreases, the number of functions performed by the state in society progressively increases. At any rate, the smallest of all territorial units in the recorded history of the West, the Greek *Polis*, was characterized by comprehensive state control. So little was that control questioned that Plato and Aristotle do not even include in their political theory a discussion of the possible or desirable limits of state activity. Nor is it hard to understand why monism should bring certain advantages to the smaller units. Where a state is composed of a small population in a small area, it is simple, effective, and inexpensive to organize the activities of society under one institution only. In such a community many, if not most, of the inhabitants can have direct, face-to-face contact with each other. If separate institutions are created for governmental, religious, economic, and other purposes, their members are likely to be the same persons reassembled in different guises. In a little state pluralism would seem superfluous; only in larger units can it be defended.

(3) *How the Remaining Issues Combine*. The third great issue, in which men must choose between dictatorial or responsible government, was considered above in its relation to the extensiveness of

---

[2] A word, not precisely translatable into English, meaning governmental power viewed in its totality. It corresponds fairly closely to the Roman concept of the *imperium*.

citizenship and of governmental functions. But how do the rival conceptions of the source that validates authority affect the problem of whether powers are better unified or dispersed? Between these pairs of alternatives there seems no positive correlation. The United States and Britain are countries in whose political systems the authority of officials is derived from the will of the governed. Yet the structure of power is highly dispersed on the American side of the Atlantic and highly unified on the British side. Apparently, therefore, it is not directly relevant to the politics of freedom to inquire whether the mechanics of government conform to the one design or the other. The same alternatives may be found in regimes of authoritarianism. In the medieval period the mass of the populace was expected to obey the established authorities and not to question them. Nevertheless those authorities were subdivided into numerous fragments. In the modern dictatorship—Fascist or Communist—to give the same unswerving obedience to officialdom is the duty of the masses. But authority in this case is solidly compacted together, and the colossus that doth bestride the state reveals on its surface no seams or fissures.

Whether the size of the state has any connection with authoritarianism or its opposite is the next question. At first glance, size appears immaterial since the governments of both small, medium, and huge states have belonged to either variety, some being controllable and others irresponsible. Sparta, Spain, Germany, and the Soviet Union are examples of one kind. Athens, Switzerland, Britain, and the United States illustrate the opposite. Mere size, however, is not the only factor to be considered here. In a world that contains many states, size is relative. A state may be weak or powerful, safe or insecure, according to the kind of neighbors it has and their friendliness or hostility. Irrespective of size, any state that feels itself threatened or that harbors aggressive intentions will emphasize the need for military organization, and the tendency of the latter is generally to influence the character of the government in an authoritarian direction. The so-called "garrison state," [3] applying to government the discipline of a barracks, can often [4] be

[3] A phrase of Harold D. Lasswell.
[4] Not always, of course. Some garrison states are such because a conquering elite is holding down a larger subject population, for example, Sparta.

explained in terms of relations between states and not as the phenomenon of a single state that stands in isolation.

Finally, to complete the circle of correlations, there remain two
issues whose effects upon each other must be discussed. Can any
connection be traced between the size of the state and a preference
for a dispersed or unified structure of power? To answer such a
question one must recall, as was suggested earlier,[5] that relations
between levels of government are not the same as relations between
the branches that function at the same level. The problem of centralization is not identical with that of integration, and the size of the
state bears more immediately upon the former than on the latter.
It needs little elaboration to show that, the smaller the state, the
less the likelihood of decentralization.[6] Indeed, in the city-state
virtually all government is conducted at one center. Conversely, as
population and territory increase, the sheer growth in size creates
complexities and adds to the difficulty of communications. Regional
diversities are likely to become pronounced. Differences of soil,
climate, and resources will lead to divergent economic interests.
Expansion may be accompanied by the absorption of mixed cultures
with hankerings for autonomy. Separatist tendencies will be a by-
product of bigness; as witness the attitudes of the Old South to the
United States, of the Ukraine to Russia, of Western Australia to the
Australian Commonwealth, of Manchuria to China. No matter what
the internal character of its government may be in other respects,
any large state must permit a measure of decentralization. Neither
Washington nor Moscow,[7] neither Rio de Janeiro nor Ottawa, can
undertake the entire government of the sprawling territories under
its general jurisdiction. Understandably, therefore, federalism is
found in some of the world's largest states.

As contrasted with the problem of centralization, the choice between integrating or dispersing the structure of governmental
power is not so obviously linked with the factor of size. States with

[5] See Chapter 11, pp. 269-70.
[6] The exceptional case of Switzerland is due to the mountainous geography
and cultural dissimilarities.
[7] The genuineness of federalism in the Soviet Union is vitiated by the
power monopoly of the Communist Party, which achieves the maximum of
political centralism. Some administrative decentralization, however, is necessitated by the physical extensiveness of the U.S.S.R.

tightly integrated institutions have run the gamut of size, from diminutive to huge. It is questionable, however, whether the same can be said about the separation of branches and its application to states of different magnitude. The two most famous instances of governments deliberately embodying the principle of separation are the republics of Rome and the United States. But it was the tragedy of the Roman Republic, and also a fundamental reason why the century from 133 B.C. to 31 B.C. suffered from prolonged constitutional crisis and spasmodic civil war, that the checks and balances between the branches of the Roman government were utterly unsuited to the enormous territorial expansion of Rome's imperial power. When the Senate clashed with the consuls, and the home authorities conflicted with a mighty proconsul in an outlying province, civil turmoil and military weakness were the result. Hence, in order that an empire might be governed, the emperorship arose to integrate the powers that lay at the center.

How does this apply to the United States? Has the expansion of the American republic imposed any strain on the traditional separation of government into three branches? Undoubtedly it has. The adjustments that were required by the economic depression of the early 1930's certainly evoked the need for closer cooperation between Presidency, Congress, and Supreme Court. Still more acute have been the tensions arising in the aftermath of World War II. The acceptance by the United States of the responsibilities for leading a world-wide group of nations made it necessary to pursue long-range policies and shoulder long-term commitments on which foreign states could depend. For this purpose not only harmony between the President and the Congress, but also agreement between the major parties, was required. The results were substantially good until the bipartisan foreign policy foundered in 1949 and 1950 on the issues of China and Korea. Simultaneously a new problem was precipitated to the forefront of American politics. The dissension between President Truman and General MacArthur, climaxed by the latter's dismissal, involved more than the supremacy of civil over military authority. For the first time the American republic faced the same question that Rome confronted in the case of Sulla or Caesar, and Britain in the case of Clive or Hastings in India: How does the home government control a strong and imperious commander in a distant theater? To solve this problem, the Republic of

Rome gave way to an Empire; the balance between royal prerogative and parliamentary power in Britain was superseded by the rise
of an all-powerful Cabinet. Whether the necessities of leadership in
the non-Communist world will evoke some comparable change in
the structure of American government remains to be seen.

The Nature of Revolution. The foregoing analysis of the relations
between the several issues suggests some further reflections about
the dynamics of political change. The role of government in guiding the evolution of society is profoundly affected by the timing of
the changes that occur as well as by their content. Few social orders
are ever completely static for any length of time. Most societies generally undergo continuous change that is imperceptibly absorbed. But
there are occasions in the history of a community when the rate of
change is for a while accelerated, and adjustments are attempted or accomplished with rapidity and a sense of urgency. Any kind of change,
of course, imposes a strain, since it involves humanity in a departure
from settled practices and a dislocation of established institutions.
Excessive speed may make the strain intolerable and lead a society to
breaking-point.

Changes can differ in depth, as well as in speed. Some modifications
of an existing order may be only surface deep. Others may reach
far down and upset the foundations of society. When a party defeats
its rival at a free and peacefully conducted election, and a new
administration and legislative majority replace their predecessors,
the top personnel and some of the programs of government will
alter. But the civil service, the judiciary, and most of the policies
already in force, continue to operate without change. This method
of assimilating innovations gradually, and on the whole harmoniously, has become the standard practice in states that are democratically organized. A deeper change is one that alters not merely
the government, but also the constitutional system under which it
is organized. The Philadelphia Convention of 1787, for instance,
had to reach decisions on more fundamental matters than are ordinarily settled in periodic elections. But the most profound changes
of all, inducing the greatest disturbance and most intense controversy, are those that refashion the main structural pillars on which
society reposes. The substitution of one form of property for another and basic modifications in ownership and distribution, a major
religious upheaval, or any sharp challenge to long-cherished cultural

values—such movements impinge on entrenched interests and arouse strong emotions. It is impossible to consummate changes of this sort without producing political repercussions.

The most extreme changes are known as revolutions. In the light of the preceding discussion, what does this term mean? When one group of persons takes over power from another within the framework of the same constitutional system and by a procedure constitutionally defined and mutually accepted, that is no revolution. But when the constitution as well as the government is reconstructed, then a revolution occurs. If, besides constitutional renovation, society is transformed root and branch, the character of the revolution becomes still more thorough-going and the most turbulent disorders usually ensue. When finally changes of government, constitution, and social order are simultaneously achieved at break-neck speed, state and society suffer agony and convulsion under the momentum of the driving force. In this way it is possible to distinguish between some of the major revolutions that have taken place in the last three hundred years. The American Revolution from 1776 to 1789 involved a change of government and constitution, but otherwise conserved the social fabric—its economic system included—in much the same shape as before. The English Revolution between 1640 and 1688 altered both constitution and government, settled the issues of Protestant-Catholic and church-state relations, and confirmed the prominence of a new urban commercial class. The French Revolution that began in 1789 went much further than the English in the ferment—economic, philosophic, and cultural—that it evoked throughout society as a whole.[8] The Communist Revolution, inaugurated in Russia in 1917, probed the deepest of the four and has been responsible for one of the most penetrating and intensive overhauls of a social order of which history has record.

All four revolutions, it may be noted, were accompanied by warfare, which in the English case took the form of civil war only, and in the other three cases involved conflict with foreign powers as well. While the constitutions that emerged from the English and American Revolutions successfully provided a peaceful method of governmental change for the future, it should be remembered that

---

[8] This explains why Edmund Burke, who approved the principles, methods, and results of England's seventeenth-century revolution, was aghast at the French Revolution, and reacted to it conservatively.

violence was initially required to lay that groundwork of constitutionalism. The three revolutions whose effects were not confined to the state but spread to society, namely the English, French, and Russian, produced the phenomenon of dictatorship with extraordinary powers concentrated in the hands of one man or a tiny clique. Significantly, the American Revolution, which was content to limit itself to a political change without transforming the social order, did not succumb to dictatorship; and while other countries had resort to Cromwell, to Robespierre and Napoleon, to Lenin, Trotsky, and Stalin, the needs of the United States were adequately served by Washington and Jefferson.

Dictatorship in a Time of Change. Besides the cases just cited, there are many recent instances of peoples that spawn a dictatorship while undergoing drastic change. Witness the power acquired by Hitler or Mussolini, by Kemal or Naguib, by Trujillo or Perón, by Gottwald or Tito. The frequency of this occurrence suggests some further reflections on the subject of change. Undeniably a community in convulsions is prone to yield to a Directory, a Politburo, a military *junta*, or to the dynamism of a "strong man" whose personality thrusts itself above the leading clique. The reason is to be found in the practical demands and the psychology of crisis conditions. A society that must decide major issues faces momentous, and perhaps irrevocable, choices. Collectively its members share the *élan*, the heightened tension, the sense of adventurousness, and with these the latent fears and anxieties concerning the outcome, that any period of rapid flux calls forth. It is always more difficult politically to chart a course for change than one for conservatism. The former opens up many avenues of choice. The latter prescribes one route—continuation, as far as possible, of the status quo.

To minimize the risks and uncertainties of change, and to offset the weakness that division produces, a society in crisis will be urged to submit to a pattern of discipline and thus reassert its unity and solidarity. Authoritarianism will be represented as a source of strength, because it is supposedly efficient, single-minded, and fast-moving. In the century in which we live, many circumstances have appeared to set a premium on such factors. People who seek in warfare an outlet for their aggressions, or who smart under the humiliations of a defeat, have often acquiesced in dictatorship. A long-lasting and widespread economic depression brings loss of savings, unemployment, or bankruptcy to many individuals who then lend a willing ear to the advocates of desperate political remedies. Or again, a technologically backward community, proud of its ancient memories, faces the challenge of a different culture equipped with superior machines and scientific knowledge. Forced to adapt themselves to alien novelties, yet wishing to preserve enough of their traditional ways so that their identity may not be lost, millions of people will attempt to combine the seemingly contradictory policies of heavy borrowing from abroad and a positive reaffirmation of their own cultural distinctiveness. The psychological result in this last case is a state of ambivalence. The dependent group admires and respects those whose techniques it copies, but is also fearful of them and resentful. The political result, not infrequently, is like a state of siege.

This helps to throw some light on one of the most interesting political problems of our century: the common association of dictatorship with nationalism. The building of a nation-state does not, in and by itself, necessitate either dictatorship or democracy. There are, however, two sides to nationalism and they face in different directions. So far as its internal aspect is concerned, nationalism is a feeling that unites people with a common loyalty to their political association. It imparts a sense not only of belonging together, but of belonging together as equals because nationality does not admit of degrees. In this way nationalism and democracy are fully compatible, and it is therefore understandable that many political leaders with perfect consistency have been nationalists and democrats, for example, Lincoln, Mazzini, Masaryk. Viewed externally, however, nationalism asserts the individuality of the group and its separateness from other groups. When this emphasis upon uniqueness happens to be linked with the uncertainties of a time of troubles—due to military or economic reasons or cultural readjustment or a combination of these—the aggressions and frustrations that exist within the group are siphoned into the channels of dictatorship. That has occurred not only in European states that yielded to the embrace of fascism or communism, but also in Latin American and Asiatic countries that wanted to catch up with western technology and at the same time rid themselves of colonialism.

Of the five great issues there are three that act as prime movers in relation to the processes of change. Analyze the revolutionary crises of history and you will find that one or more of the following fundamentals have always been in dispute: the extensiveness of citizenship, of state functions, and of the size of the state. A major increase or contraction in any of these is likely to start off a chain reaction of consequent changes. The two issues that deal with the subject of authority—the question of its source and its unity or dispersion—are not themselves the independent originators of political change. They resemble rather what statisticians call "dependent variables." A change from dictatorial to responsible government, from unity of power to dispersion of powers—or vice versa—is likely to follow, and not precede, a shift of preference between equality and privilege, pluralism or monism, and a big or small area. Those directing the transition from any [9] one of these alternatives to its opposite have often employed authoritarian means, plus a concentration of power, to obtain their results. Especially does this happen when those who were influential under the older regime offer fierce resistance to change or when speed seems to the innovators a condition of their success. Contrariwise, the acid test of a mature and basically united people is their ability to absorb major changes without resort to dictatorship or loss of liberty.

The Classification of States. This analysis of politics into five great issues and of the shifts from one solution to another is applicable to a further question over which students of government have long speculated. When states of different character are examined and compared, they can be better understood if they are grouped according to their resemblances or distinguished by their contrasts. This involves the problem of classification. Is it possible for the political scientist to classify states in the way that the zoologist or botanist or geologist arranges animals, vegetables, and minerals by genus and species? Some system of classification is implicit, as a matter of fact, in the vocabulary that is ordinarily used to describe the various forms of government. If we speak of the United States, Britain, France, and Switzerland as democracies, we must have in mind some overriding similarities in their politics and institutions that warrant a common definition. Correspondingly, when states

---

[9] Including even the transition from privilege to equalitarianism. The overthrow of an oligarchy has at times been achieved by a dictator with a broader popular following whose rule has later been replaced by majority control.

are referred to as fascist or communist, within each group there must be resemblances to justify using the same label. There must also be distinctions between the two groups and between them and the democratic group.

Irrespective of what one classifies, the technique of classification requires that certain features be selected for making comparisons and contrasts. If an anthropologist, for example, divides humanity into segments according to skin color alone, he may designate the races as black, brown, white, or yellow. The question is then raised whether pigmentation offers a significant index for differentiating between human beings; and, if so, whether this is the only factor of significance. Variations in hair, size of skull, length and breadth of noses, the shape of eyes and eyelids may also be meaningful. Consequently, the anthropologist may decide to combine many characteristics in some single-word description like Caucasian, Mongolian, Negro, or Polynesian. He will then make generalizations that are true of the group on the average and that also include any feature for which the group is unique.

The political scientist faces the same kind of question. He too must make his selection from the various features that can serve as criteria for classification. He must decide whether only one criterion is meaningful or whether there are more than one. If the latter, he must further determine whether the states that are placed in their respective classes under one criterion fall again into the same groupings or are reassorted when judged by another criterion. In other words, does the use of different criteria produce a cross-classification?

The problem is well illustrated by the famous classification of states that a succession of Greek historians and philosophers devised. Originally this was based upon a simple division in terms of the number of people holding supreme authority. Experience, as well as logic, seemed to show that there were three possibilities. Power could be lodged in the hands of one person, of a few, or of many. The advantages and abuses of each system were described by Herodotus, "the Father of History," in a passage [10] that gives him some claim to be considered a grandfather of political science. Since all three types could be productive of good or evil, the philosophers next introduced a second criterion which had an ethical flavor. In

[10] *Histories*, bk. III, chaps. 80-83.

whose interest, they asked, was government conducted? For the benefit of the rulers only, or of the whole community? If the former, power was being perverted; if the latter, the state was true to its purpose.[11] The final step was to superimpose this pair of alternatives upon the threefold distinction between the authority of one, few, or many. The result was the traditional classification that Aristotle presented in the following form: [12]

	IN THE INTERESTS OF ALL	IN THE RULERS' INTEREST
GOVERNMENT BY ONE	MONARCHY	TYRANNY
GOVERNMENT BY A FEW	ARISTOCRACY	OLIGARCHY
GOVERNMENT BY MANY	POLITY	DEMOCRACY

Not being the author of this way of classifying states, Aristotle felt free to criticize it. The difference between oligarchy and democracy, he pointed out, does not depend principally on a numerical division between a few persons and many, but on a division of wealth.[13] It is because the wealthy are few that they form an oligarchical government to protect their wealth. It is because the poor are numerous that they constitute a democracy in order to redistribute the wealth. Both systems in his judgment involve plunder—of the poor by the rich in an oligarchy, and of the rich by the poor in a democracy. That is why he characterizes both kinds of government as "perversions," not as "true forms" where the rulers govern in the interest of all.

A recent attempt to solve the same problem has been made by Robert M. MacIver, who proposes the following scheme of classification: [14]

[11] This point is made by Plato in his dialogue, *The Statesman.* Probably it had been advanced earlier by his master, Socrates.

[12] *Politics*, bk. III, chaps. 6-7.

[13] *Ibid.*, chap. 8. "The real ground of the difference between oligarchy and democracy is poverty and riches." (Barker trans.)

[14] *The Web of Government* (New York: Macmillan, 1951), p. 151. By permission of the publisher.

A	B	C	D
Constitutional Basis	*Economic Basis*	*Communal Basis*	*Sovereignty Structure*
1. Oligarchy	b1. Folk economy, primitive government	c1. Tribal government	d1. Unitary government
a1. Monarchy		c2. *Polis* government	d2. Empire colony dependency
a2. Dictatorship			
a3. Theocracy	b2. Feudal government	c3. Country government	
a4. Plural headship	b3. Capitalist government	c4. National government	d3. Federal government
2. Democracy	b4. Socialist government	c5. Multi-national government	
a5. Limited monarchy			
a6. Republic		c6. (World government)	

This modern version is necessarily more elaborate than the Greek one because the history of the intervening twenty-three centuries has exhibited fresh forms of government for which a classification must allow. It therefore embraces a wider experience and its categories are more complex. Nevertheless, despite the broader coverage, some essential issues that define the character of the state are omitted. For example, the problem of the functions of government, comprising the relation of the state to society and the choice between monism and pluralism which is the central theme of *The Web of Government,* is not included in the table, save to the partial extent that the "economic basis" may imply the practice of state intervention or abstention where economic matters are concerned. The medieval experiment, however, in church-state dualism involved other questions than economic and cannot be fitted into the chart. Furthermore no reference is made to the choice between the separation or fusion of the branches of government, which is all-important to the operation of the state. Nor are the facts of modern totalitarianism,[15] a concept considerably wider than dictatorship, adequately explained by MacIver's headings.

The analysis of political problems presented in this book contains a plan of classification in itself, since forms of government can be distinguished by the way in which they settle each of the great

[15] For a discussion of this, see below, pp. 401-2.

issues. A summary of the various solutions discussed in previous chapters is contained in the table on this page. It should be used with the following caution in mind: No chart can possibly express the constant flow and movement from choice to choice, or the countless subtle gradations that a single heading embraces. The United States, for instance, has been a federal union ever since 1789. But the relation of the federal government to the states was far from identical in 1800, 1850, 1900, and 1950. Nuances and transitions cannot be revealed in a classification, whose categories necessarily look more clear-cut than they are in real political life.

1st ISSUE	CITIZENSHIP	FOR A PRIVILEGED FEW (elitism) (oligarchy)	FOR THE MAJORITY		FOR ALL (equalitarianism)	
2nd ISSUE	FUNCTIONS OF THE STATE	REDUCED TO BARE MINIMUM (pluralism) (laissez faire) (individualism)	CONSIDERABLE EXTENSION (includes welfare, regulation)		TOTAL CONTROL OF SOCIETY (monism) (collectivism)	
3rd ISSUE	SOURCE OF AUTHORITY	RESIDES IN THE GOVERNMENT (authoritarianism) (dictatorship)	RESIDES IN THE GOVERNED (freedom, responsible government)			
4th ISSUE	UNITY OR DISPERSION OF POWER	UNITARY STATE (centralization) FUSION OF BRANCHES (cabinet system)	FEDERALISM (decentralization) SEPARATION OF POWERS			
5th ISSUE	SIZE OF STATE	CITY-STATE (Polis)	NATION-STATE	EMPIRE-STATE	? (REGION-STATE)	? (WORLD-STATE)

The Great Issues Applied to Democracy, Totalitarianism, Fascism, and Communism. How does this table apply to such concepts as democracy, totalitarianism, fascism, or communism? How are these systems to be defined in terms of the great issues? There are clearly two issues for which only one kind of solution is permissible if a state is to be democratic. On the subject of citizenship, such a state must adopt equalitarian principles and allow to all a fair opportunity to participate in the conduct or control of their government. To the extent that any are denied this right, the state has fallen short of democracy's ideal. Likewise, in a democratic state the source of governmental authority must lie in the governed who need effective means for bringing their representatives or officials to account. This is another way of saying that the essentials of democracy are equality and liberty. Fused together, these form the bedrock on which the foundations of democracy must always rest. With regards to the remaining issues, democracy is neutral. It has been associated with either pluralism or monism, with a concentration or dispersion of power, and with any size of territory or population.

Totalitarianism is indifferent to the size of the state. But on each of the other four issues its requirements are specific. It is the result of an alliance between privilege, monism, authoritarianism, and unity of power. When these are added together, the sum represents the most complete (that is, total) domination of society by the state and of the state itself by a few.

Fascism and communism are not easy to define or compare. For one thing, fascism did not take precisely the same form in Italy under Mussolini as in Germany under Hitler or in Spain under Franco. For another, the realities of communism deviate in so many respects from the principles of Marxism that one must be careful to state whether it is the theory or the practice that is being discussed. On the issue of citizenship, a fascist state is dedicated unequivocally to the idea that, because of human inequalities, participation in government is reserved for the few.[16] Marxian theory is strongly equalitarian, but communist practice, as initiated by Lenin and developed by Stalin, has been profoundly oligarchical and has re-established a society with sharp differentiations of rank and reward. The functions of the state know no limits in fascist theory, since it is the state that to Mussolini embodied the supremacy of the nation and to Hitler the supremacy of the "Aryan race." In practice, however, both regimes encountered opposition from the religious quarter and had to live with a church they could not crush. Monism is more complete in the communist state, where private ownership of the means of production is virtually eliminated, which is not the case under fascism, and where the church is subservient. Paradoxically, however, it was Marxism, from whose doctrines has emerged the most powerful state of all, that proclaimed that the state would wither away when socialism was achieved! Both communist and fascist systems, when they come to the problem of the source of power, are similarly authoritarian in theory as in practice. Each has aped the other in establishing the dictatorship of a single disciplined party ruling the masses by a mixture of propaganda and coercion. Likewise, the concentration of power has been pushed to the same extreme point by all these regimes. As to

---

[16] Hitler went much further than Mussolini in his racial doctrines and his exclusion of women from public life.

the size of the state, however, fascism and communism exhibit some differences. The former is fiercely and inherently nationalist. Communism in principle and by preference is international, since its fundamental concept of the proletariat leaps across all national boundaries. Yet, as Tito's Yugoslavia has demonstrated, communism too can be as thoroughly permeated with nationalism as any other political system.

Historical Perspective on the Great Issues. The classification of states in terms of the five great issues may serve another purpose. It can be applied chronologically to the successive broad periods in the political history of the West: the Graeco-Roman city-state, the Roman Empire, the Middle Ages, the nation-state, the twentieth century. Which solutions of the great issues were prevalent in the different periods?

(1) *The Graeco-Roman City-State.* Citizenship at that time was severely restricted in the oligarchies, but was considerably extended in democracies like Athens. Nowhere, however, was it perfectly equalitarian, since slaves and women were relegated to an inferior status. The functions of the state were everywhere considered to be co-extensive with society. Examples occurred of authoritarian and of responsible government, of the unity and the dispersion of power. Typically and ideally, the size of the state was the simple *Polis;* but the largest cities departed from type and tried to found empires.

(2) *The Roman Empire.* This state moved steadily from privilege toward political equality, though the latter was never granted to women or slaves. At the outset, the functions of the state were unlimited; but limits were accepted when Christianity was adopted. An unsuccessful attempt was made under the Republic to locate authority in the governed. Later, power was placed in the Emperor through his command of the army. Powers were centralized when the state was small; decentralized, when it expanded. At the center, powers were dispersed under the Republic, but integrated in the Empire. In size, Rome was the giant of antiquity, forming an antithesis to the *Polis.*

(3) *The Middle Ages.* In the eyes of God, all men were considered equal. In earthly practice great inequalities prevailed and

politics was an arena for the privileged. The functions of the state were drastically curtailed by its co-partnership with the church. Government was authoritarian in fact, though theories to the contrary persisted. Power was decentralized and dispersed to the maximum degree. The unit of government was as large as Christendom in the ecclesiastical sphere, but was overwhelmingly localized on the temporal side.

(4) *The Nation-State.* This period commenced everywhere with the rule of privilege, but in many states has since broadened out into equalitarianism. The early nation-state was allied with monism in the guise of the theory of sovereignty. In the nineteenth century, however, the challenge of economics led to doctrines of dualism and pluralism. Nation-states have had either authoritarian or responsible governments. Their power-structures have been either unified or dispersed. They have varied in size because of the difficulty of making nation and state co-terminous, and several of them have been builders of empires.

The Uniqueness of Twentieth-Century Politics. World depression, two World Wars, and the spread of revolutionary ferment are evidence that this century is one of crisis. When the nature of the crisis is clarified in terms of the great issues, it becomes apparent that our age possesses a unique character unparalleled in any earlier period. Modern society is now undergoing three major transformations simultaneously—in the relations of person to person, of state to society, and of state to state. What is happening in each of these fields is a drastic change of scale. The drive toward equalitarianism is bringing more people into the circle of political participation. Pluralism is steadily being abandoned in favor of increased state activity. Meanwhile, under the stress of military and economic urgency, new and larger units of government are being superimposed upon the nation-state. It is this threefold expansion—the phenomenon of the larger-sized state taking on more functions for a larger mass of citizens—that makes contemporary politics distinctive and gives our problems a quality without precedent. What the outcome of each issue will be, it is still too early to say. Today's political division between a group of peoples whose nuclear force is generated by the United States, a second cluster whose nucleus is in Russia, and a third group who are unallied, accurately reflects the truth that alternative solutions are possible. Any prediction of future trends, therefore, is hazardous. Nevertheless, the alternatives can be reviewed and their implications spelled out.

The age-old choice between privilege and equality has assumed a new form in the twentieth century. The social consequences of industrialism, which brought more people into closer contact in crowded cities and required literacy and further education; the invention of improved and speedier communications; the spread of the printed word by the cheap press and weekly magazines; the extended range of eye and ear through radio, motion pictures, and television; these and like innovations have ushered in an era of mass politics in which the power that drives the wheels of government depends on what beliefs millions accept and what facts they have been told. The masses of mankind are ceasing to be the passive subjects of politics, as was generally the case in the past. Instead, they are becoming active participants. Their participation, however, can be organized in alternate ways. The change of scale, tremendous though it be, has not removed the choice between privilege and equalitarianism. What it has done is to increase the complexity of achieving either kind of solution. The competition between democracy and communism is a struggle between rival systems for the same objective—the allegiance of the masses.

The promise of communism is to pulverize the existing order and eliminate whatever social and economic inequalities it contains. But the result, because of the monopoly of power by one party, is to re-establish a new type of privilege to which political power provides the *entrée*. The chief concession that communism makes to equalitarianism, and a major difference between the Russia of today and the Russia of the Czars, is that communism recruits its privileged oligarchy from a much wider segment of society. The promise of democracy, on the other hand, is to cut the ties between political power and privilege by offering the masses alternative leaders and programs through two or more parties and thus preventing the formation of any one permanent caste. The impact of the numerical increase in participants produces a different response in the two systems. The one-party state attempts the organization of millions by demanding uniformity and suppressing dissent. Outwardly this method gives an appearance of power by its display of solidarity. Inwardly, however, the canker of fear, spread by the presence of a secret police, saps the social fiber and weakens morale. The democratic state organizes its inhabitants by tolerating multiformity and leaving a wide arena for political competition. This is a source of strength, because divergences can then be freely expressed and discontents will receive an airing. But there are also the attendant risks that the conflict between groups may delay and even prevent decision or that private interests, uncontrolled, may capture public power.

If millions are to be organized for political action in a manner that keeps their loyalty, it is the performance of the system that means more than the promise. A major difficulty for communism is the glaring discrepancy between what it professes—a genuine equalitarianism—and what it practices—inequality.[17] The rigidities of the one-party system with its power monopoly make it difficult for the underprivileged to challenge their new masters. The latter, in order to explain away the contrast between their sayings and their doings, and justify perpetuation of their dictatorship, instil their subjects with the idea that they face an aggressively hostile world that seeks to destroy them. A communist-controlled state is, therefore, under the political necessity of prolonging tension within and crisis without, in which respect it exemplifies the dictum that "Politics as a practice, whatever its professions, had always been the systematic organization of hatreds."[18]

Democracies, too, will depart at times from their own professed principles and permit substantial discrimination against racial, religious, ethnic, or economic groups within their midst. Serious difficulties arise when a democracy omits to apply in other sectors of society the equalitarianism that it considers cardinal to politics. Thus, in Britain during the nineteenth century the equalitarian tendencies expressed in the broadening franchise ran counter to the privileged status of the aristocracy and the general stratification of people into upper, middle, and lower classes. Similar were the consequences that industrialism, allied with laissez-faire notions, produced in the United States and Britain. By the time World War I broke out, gross inequalities prevailed in the distribution of property and income. Indeed, the contrast then existing between the political

[17] George Orwell in *Animal Farm* satirizes this inconsistency in the slogan: "All animals are equal. But some animals are more equal than others."
[18] Henry Adams, in *The Education of Henry Adams,* chap. 1.

power of the many and the economic power of the few supplied a vivid and disquieting repetition of the Aristotelian view that democracy is a struggle of the poor against the rich. During the last three decades, therefore, democracy has tackled and continues to confront a pair of associated problems: how to transfer the fundamentals of equalitarianism from politics to the rest of the social order, and, while levelling up, to avoid an excessing levelling down that would destroy incentive and deny recognition to talent. Suffice it to say that the democratic state has made much progress on the former problem but has not yet come fully to grips with all the implications of the latter.[19]

The Twilight of Pluralism. It is, thus, no accident that the modern emergence of the masses has been accompanied everywhere by an expansion of the functions of government, and that surely and steadily the politics of equality have provided an impetus toward monism. In the nineteenth century the nations that were foremost practitioners of laissez faire in the relation of politics to economics, and of pluralism in the relation of the state to society were of two kinds. A country like Britain led the field in industrialization; while in the United States, there was a vast territory to people and develop, and such was the distribution of property that private associations could finance an economic transformation with substantial independence of the state. In this century, however, circumstances have fundamentally altered. Intensified competition for foreign trade among industrialized states; the vanishing of the frontier in the once-new world; domestic political pressures for social and economic aid to the underprivileged; the need for regulation of overmighty private groups; and finally the mobilization of entire peoples for victory in war and their impoverishment afterwards; these inescapable facts have aggrandized the state and made the twentieth a century of monism.

Because a society in rapid flux requires a central focus for organization, the latter-day advocates of pluralism have been placed on the defensive and forced into retreat. Some, like G. D. H. Cole, who was a pluralist in the days when he argued for guild-socialism, or Harold J. Laski, who wrote from a pluralist standpoint until the depression of the 1930's, reversed their positions and accepted the

[19] As may be seen in countries like Australia and New Zealand.

logic of monism. Others have maintained their original view, but with increasing difficulty. Robert M. MacIver, for instance, admits the need for society to be unified, but refuses to acquiesce in the state as its unifier. Instead—as a Greek playwright whose plot had become too tangled used to bring in a deity to extricate his characters in the last scene, or as Adam Smith relied on unseen hands to bring harmony out of competition [20]—he introduces his ideal of "community." This is a sense of belonging together that people are supposed to feel in sufficient force to prevent a plurality of associations from flying asunder. But how "community" is realized and made articulate never becomes clear, especially since MacIver will not concede that it be organized and expressed through any association with power to override the rest—which would be tantamount to monism.

Other pluralists do modify their basic theory and make such concessions to the state that, after denying admission to monism at the front door, they let it creep in at the back. Thus, Friedrich A. Hayek, who pleads eloquently against socialism and planned intervention by the state in economic matters, writes in favor of planning *for* freedom and insists that powerful private monopolies and combines must not be allowed to stifle genuine competition.[21] Inevitably, however, this ideal, to be enforced, requires a stronger state and far more governmental regulation of the economy than fit his premises. Still other pluralists endeavor to distinguish between the internal structure and external activities of private associations. They agree that the state should have the power to intervene in external conflicts (for example, a strike or lockout in a major industry) because these may disturb the peace and prosperity of the whole society. Then they perceive that the policies pursued externally by such an organization as a big business firm or a big union may be closely connected with the character of its internal structure. Oligarchical tendencies, whether in corporation management or in trade union control, may sometimes lead a business executive or union boss on the path of aggression so that he may maintain his dominance within this organization by the victories he wins against opponents outside. Consequently the pluralist may admit that there is a case for the state to prescribe the conditions that the

---

[20] See Chapter 2, p. 18.
[21] *The Road to Serfdom* (Chicago: University of Chicago Press, 1944).

government of a private association must satisfy. But all these varied expedients lead to the same conclusion. Any pluralist who holds that society is or should be a unity, or who recognizes the need to mitigate public clashes between private groups, must eventually admit the fundamental point of monism that society requires a co-ordinator, and must face the political corollary that the state best qualifies for that task. The only genuine pluralist now left would be the anarchist, who wants to be rid of government altogether. But his philosophy has never found a workable formula for its ideal of spontaneous, voluntary, cooperation.

Problems of the Monistic State. A state that embraces monism avoids the weaknesses by which pluralism is beset, but confronts problems of its own. Monism may assume one of several guises. In its extreme form, as envisaged by Plato, the state settles the difficulty of rival associations by eliminating them and absorbing their functions. But the notion that a single institution could serve all the social needs of twentieth-century men, though a logical possibility, is no more practicable, in view of the scale and complexity of the requisite organization, than the opposite extreme of anarchism. Of workable monism there are two alternatives. One method is for the state to enforce its control over other groups by permitting no more than one association to serve each of the major needs and interests of man. Thus organized, society would possess a single system of public education permeated by only one philosophy, a single state-established church intolerant of heterodoxy, a single state-directed economic structure professedly abolishing struggles between occupations and classes, and so on. Monism of this sort, unlike the Platonic variety, is not confined to the realm of specula-tion. It is the goal to which all totalitarian regimes aspire. The closest approximation to it ever achieved is to be found in the contem-porary Soviet Union.

The third kind of monism is one that tolerates a variety of asso-ciations for each of man's needs. Thus, if people are left free to worship in the way that their individual consciences dictate, society will contain numerous religious faiths preaching different creeds. If opportunities exist for a person to learn various skills and move from job to job, or to own property and invest in a choice of enterprises, divergent economic interests will arise that reinforce themselves by establishing rival associations—corporations, trade unions, and the like. Under such circumstances, the principle of toleration or, in its wider sense, freedom, has the result of dividing society into competitive groups. Men who are pulled apart, however, by economic institutions, or organized religion, or cultural traditions, can be reunited through citizenship. In that case, as the monist sees its functions, the state serves as the binder of society. It then becomes irrelevant whether one is agnostic or Catholic, Jew or Protestant, male or female, manufacturer or employee, farmer or teacher, provided that all alike are citizens who share the same basic rights and duties, and owe the same allegiance. Thus on the political plane, through sharing the same citizenship, the same human rights, and the same governmental services, mankind can acquire a sense of belonging together and achieve the unifying focus they otherwise lack.

Attainment of this goal through the politics of monism depends on successful avoidance of certain pitfalls. For one thing, the possibility of unifying society by means of the state is qualified by the size of area and population to which the jurisdiction of a single government extends. When continents and people are parcelled out among nation-states, the solidarity that each state achieves within its borders stops abruptly at international frontiers. The nation-state system unites the nationals of a state, but sharply separates them from nationals of other states. Pluralists point out, however, and with truth, that social relationships, though most numerous among persons of the same state, do reach further afield. Religion is a bond that links the citizens of many countries. Trade relations create a common interest between the producers of one nation and the consumers of another. Scientific, professional, and cultural bodies draw their membership from the practitioners of different lands. The present boundaries of society are far wider, therefore, than the boundaries of politics.

Some states respond to this problem with an extreme reaction. By coercive methods, Iron Curtains and the like, they demand that their nationals desist from social relations with nationals from another state. In this way they seek to cut society down to the size of the state. The alternative is not to shrink society to the confines of the state, but to stretch the state so as to correspond more adequately with the extension of society. A move in this direction is the contemporary trend to lay the foundations of a new unit of government such as the region-state, which, though not perfect, would certainly be better adapted to the regulation of social relationships than are our existing states. Whatever the future may hold, this at any rate may be said with certainty about the present, that nationalism now operates as a repellent, dividing mankind into mutually exclusive groups. Politics cannot satisfactorily perform its role as the unifier or binder of society until the state has ceased to be a nation-state.

Any institution that aspires to unify society must raise its sights and enlarge its conceptions to fit its broader responsibilities. It was noticed in an earlier chapter [22] that several associations—religious, economic, and familial—have essayed experiments in monism. However, a church, corporation, or family was always handicapped by its inability to unify society in any other fashion than by assimilating every association to its own primary characteristics with the result that society then wears the guise of a congregation, business, or clan, writ large. Monism confronts the same difficulty when it is the state that takes the role of integration. Is there the possibility of the state suffering from a similar handicap? Is there anything in the origins of government that can mar its efforts to co-ordinate society?

From Protection to Welfare. The risks involved are revealed by a glance at the functions of the state. Government originates, as was discussed earlier, in humanity's need for protection, which requires the organization of force. The state amasses forces initially, and monopolizes it finally, in order to repel any threats, internal or external, to life and limb. But the history of the functions of the state consists in an advance from protection and order to justice and welfare. This does not mean that the state abandons or surrenders its duty of protecting its members. Far from it. The state that ceases to give protection ceases to be a state. But, after ensuring the conditions that make life possible, the state must proceed toward the goal of the good life. It is precisely this change-over that presents a supreme challenge to the architects of government. For how does force or power fit in with welfare? The concept of welfare is a broad one. It embraces economic prosperity, moral well-being, and the whole system of values that compose what we call a civilization. Such considerations transfer the issues of politics from the

[22] See Chapter 7, pp. 150 ff.

starting point of physical safety to the terminus of an ethical ideal. The creation of the state resembles the construction of a dwelling to shelter the life of society. A house has foundations to stand on, just as a state is built upon man's fundamental need for protection. But people do not lead their daily lives in the basement of their homes. The living room is raised some feet above ground level, and it is here that the members of the household develop the relations that give to life its quality of humdrum or stimulating, mean or gracious, petty or noble. And it is, or can be, the same with politics. No state can be suspended in mid-air without foundations. The latter are always indispensable. But their function is to support the upper framework that houses the political life of man and makes him civilized.

That actual states do not always reach the ideal, and at times depart from it by deliberate decision, is true and obvious enough. There have been, and continue to be, many governments that build no higher than the basement and force their subjects to stay there. Also, when the warlike politics of an anarchic world compel all states, even those concerned with welfare, to re-emphasize the priority of physical protection, humanity looks to the refuge of the bomb shelter and scurries back from living room to basement. The state may fail, then, to subordinate the force it must employ to the ethical ideal for which men grope. What was the servant may emerge the master. The power that founded a government can become the means whereby the will of the governing group is forcibly imposed throughout society. In that case, their regime is a tyranny, and, when linked with monism, the product is totalitarian. Hence, the crucial test of the would-be monistic state is to keep its stock of power within bounds and sublimate power in the service of welfare. Unless this is done, there is no superior merit in monism as against the pluralist alternative. For why should one flee from anarchy into the embrace of despotism?

The first problem, then, is to organize power, yet keep it under control and legitimize it as authority; to unify society through the state, but avoid the authoritarian means and the regimented end. That is the third of the great issues, which offers the choice between freedom and dictatorship. There is no certain way of guaranteeing freedom. It is possible, though difficult, to establish and operate a politically free society. It is not too difficult to suppress freedom

entirely by a perversion of power. All that can be prescribed is a
set of conditions that, if adhered to, tend to encourage the attainment of freedom and discourage its opposite. These conditions
depend upon the planning of a constitutional system that builds
the right of criticism and opposition into the central structure of
government. Applied in detail, this principle spells itself out into
universal suffrage, periodic elections, the co-existence of two or
more parties, and opportunities to form new political combinations.
Where such requirements are met, liberty is better guaranteed than
by the pluralist reliance on mutual conflict between private associations and their general rivalry with the state.

Politics and the Good Life. But institutional checks just mentioned, while basic to the politics of freedom, do not ensure the
politics of welfare. Though liberty may be secured through procedural arrangements, the purpose of the latter, after all, is to
reach decisions about policies. The substance of such decisions, as
well as the way of reaching them, must be included in the philosophy
of the state, since the ends accomplished can scarcely be deemed
less significant than the means employed. Hence, it is incumbent on
the monistic state to embody an ethical ideal in terms of which it
integrates society. Otherwise, instead of welfare taking priority
over power, power will steal the priority from welfare—in which
case no reply can be given to Augustine's question: what else is
the state but a great robber band if it is lacking in justice? But as
it happens, two of the great issues, the first and the second, have a
direct bearing on the contents of policy. Whenever the state administers a program, a service is being supplied to some or all of its
citizens. This fact evokes controversies over the appropriateness of
the service and the designation or selection of recipients. Should
the state, for instance, pay and provide for large-scale schemes of
low-cost housing? If so, to whom should houses be assigned?
Should the state embark on programs of social security, covering
all major hazards, economic and physical, that flesh is heir to between
birth and death? If so, who should be eligible for benefits, and how
should the financing be apportioned?

Questions like these have other implications for society than that
of freedom. They suggest that the state accept some responsibility
for influencing the distribution of material goods; that it provide at
least a minimum below which no person be allowed to sink, while

encouraging everyone to raise his status above the minimum by his own efforts. To say this is to recognize that social and economic privilege—when expressed in a grossly unequal distribution of property, income, security, and living standards—is no more desirable than the political privilege of a limited class or caste. That, in other words, is an affirmation of the principle of equality. How can the state that assumes the direction of society organize the race of life so as to mix equality with liberty? It is possible to do this if the state ensures equality for all at the starting-tape; if it offers prizes for the more talented; and if it guarantees to each contestant a minimum reward in token of his participation. These criteria would seem to satisfy the test of welfare. More than that, by blending the rights and duties of the individual with those of society, they point the way to a conception of social justice. It is only when this is achieved that power, besides being rendered safe by the politics of freedom, also acquires a moral legitimacy. The degree of approximation to this standard faithfully measures the level of civilization that a people have attained. Conversely, a subordination of welfare to power and the disregard of social justice is an index of immaturity and inhumanism.

Finally, it is through this concept that the difficulty stated in the beginning of this book may be resolved. Human beings, as was observed, are driven to associate in groups under the contrary impulses of cooperation and competition. But to reconcile the two and dovetail them within the same structure has always been a problem. Perhaps, however, the answer is found when liberty and equality are synthesized under the master-concept of welfare. It is in the attainment of equality through the mechanics of the state that men express their altruism, cooperativeness, and sense of solidarity. It is in voicing opposition and responding to incentives of personal advancement that they display their egoism, competitiveness, and individuality. To maintain both principles in equilibrium and guide the two constructively toward the solution of the great issues is the wisdom of statesmanship. When the power of government is directed in the service of that ideal, the good life emerges into the realm of the possible and the art of politics becomes a voyage of ethical discovery.

BIBLIOGRAPHY

As soft, doughy bread is bad for the teeth, so soft, doughy books are bad for the mind. Indispensable for understanding politics are the classic works of eminent thinkers which have stood the test of time. All these are easily accessible, in their original English or in translation, in a variety of editions—such as those of Everyman's Library (published by E. P. Dutton and Company, New York, and J. M. Dent and Sons, London) or the Modern Library (publishers, Random House, New York). This bibliography will cite a particular edition of a classic only if it possesses some special advantage over others. In the western tradition, political science is born in the *Histories* of Herodotus and Thucydides, and subsequently grows to maturity in the care of philosophers. The fundamentals of the subject are probed in four Platonic dialogues: *Crito, Statesman, Republic,* and *Laws.* Of these the *Republic* is the most famous because of its logical systematism, artistic and literary excellence, and analytical rigor. His uncompromising argument for absolutism in metaphysics and politics and his elitist assumptions have brought Plato equally strong admirers and critics. The *Republic* can be most conveniently studied in A. D. Lindsay's translation, published with his introduction in the Everyman's Library. A more moderate philosophy of the state is expressed in the *Politics* of Aristotle, which also introduces, and employs in a masterly fashion, the method of a comparative analysis of actual governments. The translation by Ernest Barker, together with his notes and explanatory essays, is excellent (New York: Oxford, 1946).

The Romans, whose abilities lay in action rather than in thought, produced the raw materials for a study of government, but not the study itself. Many valuable insights, however, into the politics of an authoritarian regime are revealed in the *Annals* of the trenchant historian, Tacitus. The Christian impact on political thought can best be observed in the treatises of Augustine and Thomas Aquinas. The former's *City of God,* written during the collapse of the western half of the Roman Empire, outlines the double standard of values which was basic to the philosophy of the Church. Aquinas' *Summa Theologica,* the architectonic achievement of medieval philosophy, affirms the subordination of politics to ethics and to a hierarchy of law whose highest manifestations have to be taken on faith.

415

The sixteenth, seventeenth, and eighteenth centuries—a period of political ferment—were productive of fundamental political thinking in an altered vein. Machiavelli's *Prince* and *Discourses* (printed together in the Modern Library) are the distilled observations of a scholar and diplomat who truthfully mirrored his times, possessing loftier ideals than most of his contemporaries and fewer illusions than most of his predecessors. The *Leviathan* of Thomas Hobbes is an intellectual *tour de force* that combines psychology and ethics with a drastic political philosophy, but terminates in theological polemics. The political section includes assertions and assumptions about the basic issues on which each has to make up his own mind. Separated from the *Leviathan* by only four decades, John Locke's *Second Treatise of Civil Government* is worlds apart in temper and objectives. While his discussion of property has earned Locke a place in the ranks of conservative thinkers, his emphasis on individual rights—including the right to rebel against autocracy—and his justification of legislative rather than monarchical supremacy make him a founding father of liberal democracy.

The growing chorus of French protest against the absolute monarchy produced in the eighteenth century two books that have remained classics. Montesquieu's *Spirit of the Laws* is notable for its use of the comparative method and for its elaboration of the principle of the separation of powers. It should be consulted in the Hafner Classics (New York: 1949) along with the introductory essay by Franz L. Neumann. Rousseau's tempestuous writings reached their climax politically in the *Social Contract*, a work for the most part closely reasoned, yet containing illogical lapses and elusive concepts which have yielded equal inspiration to mutually incompatible successors.

The era that opened with the American, French, and Industrial Revolutions has been prolific with political speculation. Certain works stand out from the rest for their intrinsic quality or because they have had wide influence. A conservative attitude towards the process of change is eloquently expounded by Burke in his later speeches and in such booklets as the *Reflections on the French Revolution*, where many gems of political wisdom are enshrined in the incidental remarks. A philosophy of reaction, as distinct from conservatism, is contained in Hegel's *Philosophy of Right*, which is in essentials a philosophy of the far right. The *Federalist* papers, composed by Hamilton, Madison, and Jay to persuade New Yorkers to ratify the Constitution of the United States, are an incomparable blend of clear analysis, historical scholarship, and keen practical judgment. The noblest aspects of liberalism are nowhere better portrayed than in J. S. Mill's *Essay on Liberty*, a brief masterpiece whose universal tolerance and even the internal contradictions testify to its author's open-mindedness and humanity. His *Considerations on Representative Government* bespeak the problems of giving institutional concreteness to general principles in an age of reform when the extension of the suffrage and of governmental functions imposed new stresses on legislative, administrative, and party organization. These two works of Mill, along with his philosophy of *Utilitarianism*, are printed together in Everyman's Library.

The attacks on liberal democratic ideals and institutions that emanate from the extremes of left and right are in general too patently hate-inspired to attain a high level of sophistication. The *Communist Manifesto* of Karl Marx belabors the single theme that economic relationships are fundamental to politics and intermingles historical generalizations with the distortion of the propagandist. Among his successors, Lenin's *State and Revolution* and Trotsky's *History of the Russian Revolution* explain, prospectively and retrospectively, the technique of violent overthrow of government as understood by two who proved themselves adept at the practice.

Fascism, repudiating thought in favor of action and reason in favor of emotion, produced little coherent philosophy—and that little grandsired by Hegel. Two statements have a certain significance because of the names attached to them rather than for their intellectual content. Mussolini's *Social and Political Doctrine of Fascism* concisely summarizes the ethos of the movement he led; while Hitler's *Mein Kampf* (New York: Reynal and Hitchcock, 1939), published several years before he came to power, is a lasting record to racial prejudice and to the dangers of underestimating an egomaniac with ability.

For a general review of the main currents of political thought, seen in relation to the ebb and flow of historical tides, a superb treatment in a single volume is George H. Sabine's *History of Political Theory* (New York: Holt, 1950).

Modern attempts to analyze the nature of politics begin with scholars who were not political scientists. The *Introduction to Political Science* by J. A. R. Seeley (London: Macmillan, 1919) is the work of an experienced historian, just as the *History of the Science of Politics* by F. Pollock (rev. ed., London: Macmillan, 1911) comes from the pen of an eminent jurist. Harold J. Laski wrote *The Grammar of Politics* (London: Allen and Unwin, 1925) in the period when he was still a pluralist. Also composed from a pluralist standpoint are two notable volumes by the sociologist Robert M. MacIver; *The Modern State* (London: Oxford, 1926) and *The Web of Government* (New York: Macmillan, 1951). Harold D. Lasswell's *Politics: Who Gets What, When, How* (New York, London: McGraw-Hill, Whittlesey House, 1936) illustrates the use of Freudian psycho-analysis and the power approach to the study of politics. Charles A. Beard's *Economic Basis of Politics* (New York: Knopf, 1945) is an illuminating and thoroughly sensible treatment of a problem which the Marxists have made controversial.

Comparisons of the governments of a number of countries have been tried in alternative ways. One is to analyze the entire government of a country, then to do the same successively for others, and finally to compare them and draw conclusions. The supreme example of this method is James Bryce's *Modern Democracies* (New York: Macmillan, 1921). The second way is to analyze the subject into topics and discuss under each heading the experiences of various countries. Instances of this approach, employed by contemporary scholars, are Herman Finer's *Theory and Practice of Modern Government* (rev. ed., New York: Holt, 1949) and Carl J. Friedrich's *Constitutional Government and Democracy* (rev. ed., Boston: Ginn, 1950).

Finally, a few books require mentioning which are important to political scientists, either as brilliant treatments of a special topic or as offering the insight of a neighboring field. De Tocqueville's *Democracy in America* is a profound evaluation by a gifted Frenchman of the American form of government—novel in Old World eyes—as it existed in Jackson's time. The English translation, done by Henry Reeve in 1835-40, sadly needs revising, but is still reprinted in the recent editions. Walter Bagehot's *The English Constitution,* a pioneer of realism when first printed, contains many observations that are still challenging. Because he wrote at the time of the American Civil War, he tended to be more impressed with the weakness than the strength of the American system. Yet, through Woodrow Wilson and others he exercised no little influence on thinking in the United States. The World's Classics edition (New York: Oxford, 1942) includes the preface that Bagehot wrote to the second edition of 1872, and an essay by Lord Balfour. Howard L. McBain's *The Living Constitution* (New York: Macmillan, 1937) is a short, outstanding analysis by a twentieth century scholar continuing in the same tradition and probing for the actualities that lie behind the forms.

Among the writings of modern philosophers, whose interests embraced the field of action as well as the realms of thought, both John Dewey and A. D. Lindsay have left behind them books which possess enduring qualities; for instance, the former's *The Public and its Problems* (New York: Holt, 1927) and the latter's *Modern Democratic State* (New York: Oxford, 1947). The issues that arise in the relations of politics to economics are masterfully handled in Joseph Schumpeter's *Capitalism, Socialism, and Democracy.* Nor has the Muse of History been wanting. Two remarkable and provocative works by historians, one Swiss and the other British, are "musts" on any list. These are Jacob Burckhardt's essays and lectures, republished in English under the title *Force and Freedom* (New York; Pantheon Books, 1943) and Arnold J. Toynbee's *Study of History* (one-volume abridgement by D. C. Somerwell, New York: Oxford, 1947).

INDEX